THREE-RING CIRCUS

THREE-RING CIRCUS

KOBE, SHAQ, PHIL,

and the

CRAZY YEARS

of the

LAKERS DYNASTY

JEFF PEARLMAN

Houghton Mifflin Harcourt
Boston   New York
2020

To Gary Miller
Whose selfish need to be Gene Simmons *and* Paul Stanley
nearly ruined a friendship

(Some 40 years ago)

For information about permission to reproduce selections from this book,
write to trade.permissions@hmhco.com or to Permissions, Houghton Mifflin Harcourt
Publishing Company, 3 Park Avenue, 19th Floor, New York, New York 10016.

hmhbooks.com

Library of Congress Cataloging-in-Publication Data
Names: Pearlman, Jeff, author.
Title: Three-ring circus : Kobe, Shaq, Phil, and the crazy years
of the Lakers dynasty / Jeff Pearlman.
Description: Boston : Houghton Mifflin Harcourt, 2020. |
Includes bibliographical references and index.
Identifiers: LCCN 2019057830 (print) | LCCN 2019057831 (ebook) |
ISBN 9781328530004 (hardcover) | ISBN 9781328530660 (ebook)
Subjects: LCSH: Los Angeles Lakers (Basketball team) — History. |
Basketball teams — California — Los Angeles — History. |
Basketball players — United States — Biography.
Classification: LCC GV885.52.L67 Pff 2020 (print) |
LCC GV885.52.L67 (ebook) | DDC 796.323/640979494 — dc23
LC record available at https://lccn.loc.gov/2019057830
LC ebook record available at https://lccn.loc.gov/2019057831

Printed in the United States of America
DOC 10 9 8 7 6 5 4 3 2 1

To men and women who want to do things, there is nothing quite so driving as the force of an imprisoned ego. All genius comes from this class.

— MARY ROBERTS RINEHART

Contents

Author's Note

On the morning of January 26, 2020, I was sitting inside the Corner Bakery in Irvine, California. My laptop was open. A hot bowl of oatmeal rested before me, alongside one of those sugary crisp biscuits and a cup of coffee.

At exactly 11:37 a.m., my iPhone made a noise. *Ping.* I lifted the device from the table. The text was from my friend Amy Bass . . .

News reports that Kobe Bryant is dead

Wait.

Wait.

Wait.

What?

Kobe Bryant couldn't be dead. There are things in this world that are possible, and things that are impossible. *This* was impossible.

Kobe Bryant was just 41 years old. He was a husband, a father of four, an entrepreneur, a youth coach, a regular church parishioner, an active and involved Orange County resident. His videos were all over social media. Kobe shooting hoops with Gigi, his 13-year-old daughter. Kobe snuggling with his wife, Vanessa, and their newborn. More than 15 million followers hung on @kobebryant's latest tweets, and with good reason. His was a simultaneously comforting and electrifying presence.

Kobe Bryant couldn't be dead.

He just couldn't.

• • •

Over the previous two years, I had worked nonstop on this book, *Three-Ring Circus*. And while this is a chronicling of the 1996 to 2004 Los Angeles Lakers, it is also — in a sense — the story of Kobe Bryant's development as both a professional basketball player and a fully functioning human being.

Upon joining the franchise at age 17 in 1996, Bryant was a typically overconfident, largely insufferable teenager. Like most of us emerging from high school, he believed all the answers resided inside his head, and that his elders were both misguided and out of touch. He thought he could average 30 ppg as a rookie. He thought Shaquille O'Neal was lazy and Eddie Jones underwhelming and Nick Van Exel overrated. He thought he should be starting from Day One, and that Del Harris — the veteran head coach — knew not whereof he spoke.

Through the eight years that followed, Bryant was as beloved as he was disliked. He could do magical things on the court while behaving as a selfish child off of it. He treated many fans like his closest friends while treating many teammates (especially undrafted rookies) like empty soda cans resting alongside a gutter. He had little use for some coaches and overwhelming respect for others. He was dour and peppy; intense and playful; cruel and loving. He was accused of raping a woman, proclaiming his innocence even as he came *very* close to serving time.

Jerry Buss, the Lakers' owner, viewed him as a son, in the way he also viewed an earlier Lakers star, Magic Johnson, as a son. Jeanie Buss, Jerry's daughter, considered Kobe a brother. Shaquille O'Neal eyed him skeptically, wearily. Other teammates didn't know Bryant beyond the court. *Hi, Bye.* Little more.

"You never knew where you stood with Kobe," I was told.

"You always knew where you stood with Kobe," I was also told.

When the reality of Kobe Bryant's death finally hit — when we learned that a fiery helicopter crash had not only taken his life, but that of Gigi and seven others — I found myself thinking long and hard about the fragility of existence, about the end of an icon's being.

About a person's legacy.

I am fortunate to count several tremendous sportswriters as friends, and this concept — *legacy* — is something we've broached at length. It's actually (in a way) one of the flaws of the medium. When one writes the story of an era, he is charged not with dishing out hagiography, but an honest, sincere, detailed recollection of a period. In doing so, however, an author asks the reader to understand that a sliver of time is not an eternity.

Or, put differently: A book freezes people.

This is my clumsy way of saying that the Kobe Bryant of 1996 to 2004 is not the Kobe Bryant of 2005 to January 26, 2020. He was not then the contemplative adult who raved of having four daughters. He was not then the doting husband. He was not then the Academy Award winner.

He was not yet comfortable in his skin.

What I hope to supply here — for good or bad — are not merely the highs and lows of a dynastic basketball team, but the early steps and missteps of a player who arrived in professional sports as a child and, tragically, died days ago as a fully formed human. Just as you cannot explain Albert Einstein's brilliance without first examining his days as a youthful Bern patent clerk, and just as you cannot know Amelia Earhart without grasping her time as a homeschooled child in Des Moines, it is hard, if not impossible, to love the richness of Kobe Bryant's life without observing his days of stubbornness and social experimentation and development.

When a legend dies, we feel lost.

Sometimes, I hope, it eases that grief to know how he began.

To celebrate it.

Jeff Pearlman
February 10, 2020

Prologue

It's February 21, 2002. We are in Cleveland. Only this is pre-LeBron Cleveland, a ceaselessly pewter-skyed city that provides the razzle of an armpit. There is nothing of particular note to do here, so when NBA players come to town, they do — largely — nothing. Sit in the hotel room. Flick around the remote control. Eat. Sleep.

That's why Samaki Walker, Lakers power forward and a man who stands 6-foot-9 and weighs 240 pounds, is in his room at the Ritz-Carlton. Sitting. Flicking. Eating. Sleeping.

Then something catches his eye. It's the red blinking light atop the phone on his night table.

Blink.

Blink.

Blink.

Walker assumes it's rote road-trip insignificance. Housekeeping, maybe. A left-behind message for a departed guest. But then, out of curiosity, he presses the VOICEMAIL button and holds the receiver to his ear.

Yo [sob] *Samaki* . . .

Is that . . . ?

Maki [sob], *look, you're* [sob] *my boy* [sob] . . .

Could that be . . . ?

I [sob] *just . . . I just* [sob] . . .

That sounds like . . .

Man [sob] . . . *I'm so* [sob] *sorry* . . .

Kobe Bryant?

Maki [sob], *really, I'm* [sob] . . .

And is he crying?

Walker is in his sixth NBA season, and while the onetime Louisville star has never quite lived up to the potential that made him the ninth overall pick of the 1996 draft, he has seen *a lot*. In no particular order: Walker's father spent 13 years in prison for aggravated robbery. His mother battled severe alcoholism. He skipped his senior year of basketball at Whitehall-Yearling (Ohio) High because he hated the coach. He left Louisville early after being accused of using a Honda Accord given to his father by a booster. He was once arrested for driving a motorcycle more than 100 miles per hour through the streets of Columbus, Ohio. All those nuggets in time and space were jarring.

But this . . . *this* is something Samaki Walker can't wrap his head around.

He continues to listen.

Yo, Samaki . . . [sob] *I don't know what* [sob] *I was* [sob] *thinking. You're a friend, man* [sob]. *A good* [sob] *friend. I'm so* [sob] *sorry. I'm so* [sob], *so sorry. Really, just* . . .

Click.

As he marinates within the silence of his room, Walker replays the events of the past 24 hours — a string of happenings that, weirdness-wise, rivals anything he has experienced through his first 26 years of existence.

It's the previous day, and the Lakers are holding a morning shootaround at Gund Arena in Cleveland. Toward the end of the session, as ritual dictates, the members of the team line up to launch half-court shots, with the winner collecting $100 from each participant.

As befits an organization coming off two straight NBA championships, the enlistees form a Who's Who of modern basketball achievement. There's Robert Horry, the dead-eye three-point gunner whose penchant for late-game heroics is legend. There's Rick Fox, the savvy small forward whose cinematic appearances and marriage to Vanessa Williams make him Tinseltown royalty. There's Brian Shaw, the cerebral point guard and locker room sage. There's Derek Fisher, the fast-talking spark plug from tiny Arkansas–Little Rock. There's Shaquille O'Neal, the larger-than-life's-largest-life 7-foot-1, 325-pound center. There's Kobe Bryant, the sixth-year straight-out-of-high-school superstar many consider to be the second coming of Michael Jordan.

The men line up to shoot. And miss. And shoot. And miss. And shoot. And miss. Familiar trash talk serves as the soundtrack. Slang barbs. Surface insults. Finally Bryant — 6-foot-6, 212 pounds of long, sinewy muscle — picks up a ball, takes a bunch of steps behind the half-court line, trots four long paces forward, elongates his arms, pushes forward, and . . . and . . . and . . .

Swish.

Fuuuuck.

"Gimme my money!" Bryant barks toward his teammates.

"Gimme my fucking money!"

The Lakers are paying Bryant $12.3 million for the season, and he'll land an additional $20 million in endorsements with such companies as McDonald's and Sprite. The $1,200 in half-court-shot winnings is chump change. But that's not the point. It's pride. Status. Strike or be struck — that's been Bryant's modus operandi since entering the league. Nobody was going to make Kobe Bryant his bitch. To some, these contests are mere game. O'Neal participates, sideways grin glued to his face, knowing he can't possibly win. The same goes for Mark Madsen, the lumbering 6-foot-9 forward out of Stanford. But in Kobe Bryant's world, nothing is a game. Ever. Not checkers, not chess, not Connect Four, certainly not a half-court shot with $1,200 on the line. That's why, when the practice ends, he marches from teammate to teammate, palm extended. He takes the $100 from O'Neal, the $100 from Fox, the $100 from Shaw, the $100 from Horry.

Bryant looks Walker over. "My money?" he commands.

"I gotta get it to you later," Walker replies. "I don't have it on me."

Bryant flashes an agitated look but walks off. Within the Lakers organization, there's an understood 48-hour window for debts to be paid. Bryant is young and rich and averaging 25.2 points per game for a team expected to win yet another NBA crown. What's a delayed $100 in the grand scheme?

Now, however, it's the following morning — around 10 a.m. on February 21. The Laker players file onto the chartered team bus to make their way back to the facility for a brief practice run before the night's matchup against the lowly Cavaliers. Befitting their status as two of the team's key veterans, O'Neal and Fox head toward the vehicle's rear, which they lovingly refer to as "the Ghetto." They plop down into seats behind Jelani McCoy, a reserve center. Walker follows, settling into his regular spot. They are all listening to individual CD players, nodding their heads to the beats.

Then Bryant boards the bus.

He marches toward Walker, glares downward. "Yo Maki," he says, "you gonna give me my fucking money?"

Walker pretends not to hear, so Bryant gets louder. "Maki, where the fuck is my fucking money?"

This time Walker doesn't merely ignore him.

This time, Walker doesn't merely laugh at him.

No, this time Walker waves him off like an errant gnat. "I'll give you your money," he says, "when I have it."

To Walker, it's all a joke. He and Bryant entered the league together, and the majority of players on the roster view Kobe's latest efforts not unlike MC Hammer's forever lampooned 1994 attempt at gangsta rap.* Bryant is a "Thank you" and "You're very welcome" type of guy — polite, suburban, cultured, well-heeled. Truth be told, he's always been a clumsy fit for this league of superstars with well-earned street cred — the Allen Iversons and Stephon Marburys. The cursing is the latest addition to Bryant's paint-by-numbers approach to sounding hardened, and it's as authentic as $5 mink.

"It was his Beanie Sigel phase," says McCoy. "Really fake."

Now, if one looks closely enough, he can see the steam rising from Bry-

---

* *Vibe*'s Charles Aaron called *The Funky Headhunter* "one of the most stunning curios of pop marketing hubris ever perpetrated."

ant's ears. The four-time All-Star leans past Fox, draws back his right fist, lunges across Walker's head, and — *pop!* — punches him in the right eye.

For a moment, everyone on the bus freezes. Just for a moment.

Walker, 28 pounds heavier than Bryant, gazes toward McCoy, his closest friend on the roster. "Did this fucker just hit me?" he says. "Did *he* just hit *me*?"

McCoy nods.

Walker rises, clenches a fist, and — *whoosh!* Jerome Crawford, O'Neal's King Kong Bundy-esque bodyguard and constant companion, charges from five rows up. He wraps Walker in a bear hug, but not before Walker launches his Discman at Bryant's head. Not surprisingly, the career 63 percent free throw shooter misses. The device hits the floor and cracks apart. Walker is screaming at Bryant. "Fuck you, bitch!" Bryant is screaming at Walker. "No, fuck you!" O'Neal, whose relationship with the young guard is both well chronicled and chronically awful, looks Walker in the face. "You've gotta fuck him up!" he says in his deep baritone. "Fuck. Him. Up."

Walker nods, then gazes toward Phil Jackson, the veteran head coach, whose ability to grasp (and manipulate) the psyches of his players is a longtime calling card. "Phil," Walker says, "can you please stop the bus?"

In his two and a half seasons with Los Angeles, Jackson has endured some absolutely crazy moments. He's watched awful Shaq movies and heard Bryant's ear-melting attempts at hip-hop. He's had a player turn up with a PLEASE EXCUSE HIS ABSENCE FROM PRACTICE note from a hotel clerk and wondered whether certain men were performing under the influence.

Now, the Lakers are somewhere in downtown Cleveland. Jackson has no great desire to have his two-time defending champions pull to the side of a road in downtown Cleveland. However, he sees what his players also see in Kobe Bryant — a selfish, entitled, me-first human whose social skills lag far behind his athletic gifts. "Hey," he says to the driver, "pull over when you can."

The bus stops. Walker, his voice emotionless, looks at Bryant, who gazes toward the floor.

"Well?" he says. "You wanna step off and take care of this?"

Bryant ignores his teammate. The silence is palpable.

"That's what I thought," Walker says.

A pause.

"You little bitch."

With that, NBA life seems to continue as normal. The bus arrives at the arena, the Lakers practice (without Walker, who is told by Jackson to remain in a side room and calm down), the men return to the hotel to rest before the night's game. In his mind, Walker imagines a scenario in which he yanks Bryant aside and beats the snot out of him. He pictures ramming his fist through his face. He pictures elbowing him in the gut. He doesn't merely want to hit Kobe Bryant. He wants to hurt him. Walker is a product of the inner city, a man whose time in Columbus taught him how to handle business. "I'm gonna fuck that boy up," he tells O'Neal at one point. "There's gonna be nothing left of him."

This is what Walker is pondering when he notices the light blinking on his hotel room phone; when he listens to a sobbing Kobe Bryant; when he realizes his teammate isn't exactly a model of emotional stability.

Later in the evening, shortly before tipoff against the Cavs, Walker is on the treadmill at Gund Arena. He is still angry, though the rage has subsided. This is what it is to be a professional athlete. You set distractions aside. You move on. You march forward. You focus on the task at hand. You . . .

"Hey, Samaki."

It's Crawford, O'Neal's bodyguard.

"I've got this fucker outside," he says. "He wants to talk to you."

Moments later, Bryant approaches. His voice is unusually soft. His shoulders are hunched. He looks wounded, as if he's about to once again weep.

"Maki," he says, "I'm really sorry. That's on me."

The forward stops jogging and steps from the treadmill. He actually feels surprising pangs of sympathy for the kid. Walker — 100-mile-an-hour motorcycle roadster — knows what it is to mess up.

"Listen," he says, "we're good. Seriously, we're good. But you can't go around hitting another man. There are some issues you've gotta work out. You can't live life this way."

That night, the Lakers take down the Cavs, 104–97. Kobe Bryant scores a team-high 32 points on 13-of-24 shooting. He plays like a man possessed.

"Kobe," Walker would say, "was a great basketball player. No doubt. But sometimes you had to wonder whether he was comfortable being himself. Whether he knew who he really was."

THREE-RING CIRCUS

1

Magic

The comeback was destined to be remarkable.

How could it not be, if you think about it? On November 7, 1991, four and a half years earlier, Earvin "Magic" Johnson, transcendent guard for the Los Angeles Lakers, had announced his retirement from basketball after contracting the HIV virus. It was one of those where-were-you-when stoppages in time, not on the *Is the world coming to an end?* level of the John F. Kennedy and Martin Luther King assassinations, but certainly right there with the *Challenger* explosion for modern *holy shit is this really happening?* blunt-force trauma.

All these decades later, it's hard to sit with a millennial and explain the impact of Johnson — the face of the NBA, the face of athletic joy, the face of goodwill, the face of vigor — standing before the media inside the Great Western Forum, leaning into a microphone, and saying, "Because of the HIV virus that I have attained, I will have to retire from the Lakers."

Gasp.

Yes, many other celebrities had died before our eyes from AIDS, but this was different. Freddie Mercury, Liberace, Anthony Perkins, Gia Carangi — they were people who shared our dimensions and gravitational limitations. Plus, we had our own built-in excuses. They were gay. They were drug addicts. They screwed around. They lived lives of ill repute. They *asked for it*.

The idea of bearing witness to a superhero like Magic Johnson developing lesions, losing most of his weight, needing a walker, fading to dust before our eyes . . . well, it was too much to handle. Wrote Gary Nuhn of the *Dayton Daily News*, "I guess we're going to watch Magic Johnson die just as my father's generation watched Lou Gehrig and Babe Ruth die. Slowly. Painfully. Irreversibly."

So when Magic Johnson didn't develop lesions and lose most of his weight, when he didn't need a walker or fade to dust before our eyes — it felt almost biblical. And as the years passed and Johnson opened movie theaters and coffee shops and shook 10 million hands and hugged 10 million babies and smiled that 10-million-megawatt smile, there was this growing idea that if anyone could accomplish the unaccomplishable, it was Magic.

Especially on the basketball court.

Not that the Los Angeles Lakers were uniquely unsalvageable. It's just that, in the years following Johnson's departure from the National Basketball Association, the franchise had morphed from a tulip glass of perfectly chilled Cristal to a Dixie cup half filled with some flat, lukewarm 7-Up. Gone were the days of Magic tossing a no-look pass to Michael Cooper on the break. Gone were the days of Kareem Abdul-Jabbar skyhooks over Jack Sikma. Between Johnson's rookie year of 1979 and his retirement, the Showtime Lakers not only hung five championship banners inside the Forum, but they did so with style and panache and unbridled zest.

But with Johnson's absence, that changed. The 1990–91 Lakers went 58-24 and reached the NBA Finals under Magic's leadership, but one year later, minus their retired star, they fell to 43-39 before exiting the season with a listless first-round playoff defeat to Portland. The next year was even worse (a punchless 39-43 mark), and the one after that (33-49) all the more limp and pathetic. These were the listless Lakers of Sedale Threatt. Of marginal placeholders who felt like purple-and-gold basketball impostors.

When the highly regarded Del Harris was hired as coach before the 1994–95 season, and his team went a surprising 48-34, some optimism returned to Los Angeles. There was talk of a youth movement, what with the emergence of a feisty point guard, Nick Van Exel, out of Cincinnati, and a sleek shooting guard, Eddie Jones, from Temple. The 1995–96 campaign got off to an okay start — through mid-January the team was hanging around .500, seeking that spark; that jolt; that energy; that . . .

Return.

To be honest, Magic Johnson was bored. *Really* bored. If there is nothing more exciting than running the point of a well-oiled NBA juggernaut, there are few things more dispiriting than *having* run the point of a well-oiled NBA juggernaut. Especially when, deep down, you know you're better than the people out there. And that was how Johnson felt in the winter of 1996, kissing babies and opening theaters but watching the mediocre Lakers — *his* mediocre Lakers — and whispering, "I'm better."

So while Van Exel piloted the show aboveground, Johnson found himself in the shadows, lifting weights, running sprints, popping jumpers, thinking that maybe, just maybe, it was time for a comeback. He had toured Asia, Australia, and New Zealand with a Globetrotters-like squad made up of former college and NBA players, and his skills remained sharp. Plus, attitudes about HIV and AIDS changed, hadn't they? Back before the 1992–93 season, Magic's first planned return to the league had been stopped dead in its tracks when several players — including Utah Jazz star Karl Malone — expressed trepidation over competing against a man infected with the HIV virus. In the time that had passed, though, much had been learned. Namely, that on-court basketball-player-to-basketball-player transmission was as likely as human-to-rock transmission.

On January 17, 1996, *USA Today* ran a piece headlined MAGIC: NO PLANS TO RETURN TO LAKERS, in which a writer named Jerry Langdon reported that Johnson was working out with the team, but only to stay in shape. Nine days later, the Associated Press's Ken Peters caught up with Johnson to ask about reports that he was "all but guaranteed" to return.

"Let's just say," Johnson told Peters, "I haven't decided."

He had decided.

"Jerry West called me in one day and said, 'So, Magic wants to come back,'" recalled Del Harris of the team's executive vice president of basketball operations. "Jerry told me that Magic thinks he can play, that he's in really good shape, that he wants to help. But he said it was completely up to me. That it was my decision."

Harris asked to speak to Johnson. They met inside the Lakers' offices, and the veteran coach told the veteran player that he could not (a) be the point guard (Van Exel was terrific and emotionally fragile), (b) be the shooting guard (Jones was terrific and emotionally fragile), or (c) expect to start. Harris liked the idea of having Magic Johnson on the roster, because, well, who wouldn't like the idea of Magic Johnson on the roster? But it was important for the coach to stress that times had changed and Pat Riley was no longer running things. Johnson would need to adhere and adjust and, perhaps, accommodate. If that was possible, Harris was all in.

On January 29, 1996, Magic Johnson made it official, signing a one-year, $2.5 million contract, surrendering his 4.5 percent ownership share in the franchise, and rejoining a team that genuinely wanted him. Harris, the headman, said, "We're adding a wonderful piece, a wonderful element." Jones, the second-year star shooting guard, said, "We need him. He'll make us a better team." Point guard Van Exel said, "With Magic back, I think we're a true contender."

Johnson commenced his heroic second act as a Los Angeles Laker on January 30, 1996, with the visiting Golden State Warriors in town and tickets being scalped outside the Forum for All-Star Game prices. John Black, the team's media relations director, distributed three hundred press credentials for the game. At 7:20 p.m., with Randy Newman's "I Love L.A." blaring from the speakers, Johnson jogged back onto the court in his purple-and-gold warm-ups. Some things were different: at 36, he looked older; with 27 extra pounds, he looked heavier; with Van Exel at the point, he was now a power forward. The mojo, though, was familiar. "It was electric," said John Nadel, who covered the Lakers for the Associated Press. "He was the hero, coming in to save the day."

In an effort to show his players that — *really, truly, I mean it* — not much would change in their lives, Harris had Johnson begin the evening on the bench, a scrub situated alongside George Lynch and Derek Strong.

Yet 2:21 into the first quarter, after Elden Campbell picked up his second foul, Harris motioned toward the returnee and said, "Let's go." Johnson walked to the scorer's table to check in. The capacity crowd of 17,505 rose, and shortly thereafter Johnson scored his first basket, a vintage drive toward the hoop and past an overmatched forward named Joe Smith. The entire night was, truly, a magical buffet of snazzy passes and high fives and standing ovations, and when it ended the Lakers' new-old-new star had scored 19 points with 10 assists and 8 rebounds in a 128–118 victory.

"It's amazing," Vlade Divac, the Los Angeles center, said afterwards. "Having him back is great. I can't even describe it. Everybody is a better player with him on the team. How can you detract from the chemistry when you make everybody better?"

And, for a spell, everything seemed peachy. The Lakers went on an eight-game winning streak as packed crowds greeted the team at home and on the road. Showtime had returned, with Magic Johnson once again leading the way.

Only ... well ... um ... eh ... it's sort of unclear whether the other members of the Lakers actually wanted Magic Johnson leading the way. Oh, on the surface they certainly did. You don't add a 12-time All-Star, with his enlarged jersey literally hanging above you, and not embrace the guidance. But *these* Lakers weren't *those* Lakers, and while Kareem Abdul-Jabbar and James Worthy were always willing to overlook/accept Johnson's propensity for the spotlight, now Magic seemed to be more obnoxious uncle than peer. Just two days after his comeback, Johnson explained to the Associated Press's Wendy E. Lane that he deserved to be considered for the upcoming United States Olympic team ("I know I can get out there and do my thing"). Then he informed the media that — should the comeback somehow not work out in Southern California — he would love to play the following season for the New York Knicks or the Miami Heat. There was always a microphone, a TV camera, a notepad, and Johnson never bypassed an opportunity to tell his story, share his beliefs, propose his ideas. He also showed little to no interest in his teammates, whom he seemed to deem fortunate to live in his presence. They were props. Nice props. Productive props. But, ultimately, just props, perfectly situated in the locker room when Johnson felt compelled to break out the tired ol' "I got these five rings on my fingers and I don't know what to do — my hands are getting heavy" line. If he spent time with anyone, it was Jerry Buss, the franchise owner, who considered Johnson a son. When he first rejoined the team, Johnson went directly to his old locker — now filled with the belongings of George Lynch, the third-year forward out of North Carolina — and reclaimed it. He didn't ask, or offer money. He just took it.

By his fourth game back, Johnson was insisting that he needed to be on the court come crunch time. By his fifth game, opposing players were starting to whisper again about whether it was safe to be competing against a man with HIV. When Johnson spoke, it was 99 percent "I," 1 percent "we." Worst of all, his presence was beginning to adversely impact his teammates. Los Angeles dropped a 98–97 crusher to Orlando on March 17 when the normally cocksure Van Exel bypassed a potential game-winning shot — one he certainly would have taken had Magic not been on the floor. That was unfortunate, but the player who reacted most negatively to Johnson's presence was Cedric Ceballos, the starting small forward and a man whose minutes were impacted by the roster change.

A sixth-year veteran out of Cal State Fullerton, Ceballos had been a cancerous presence on the team since his arrival via trade from Phoenix in September 1994. He was your classic egomaniacal professional athlete, told far too many times how great, amazing, and awesome he was when, in fact, he was neither great nor amazing nor awesome. Ceballos's defensive intensity was nonexistent. He passed once or twice a month. What he possessed in droves, however, was chutzpah. Having averaged 21.7 points for the 1994–95 Lakers, he nicknamed himself "Chise" — short for "Franchise," as in "franchise player." Perhaps the case could have been made were Ceballos a member of, oh, the hapless (and new) Minnesota Timberwolves. But on the Lakers, whose all-time roster included George Mikan, Jerry West, Wilt Chamberlain, Elgin Baylor, Gail Goodrich, Jamaal Wilkes, Kareem Abdul-Jabbar, James Worthy, and (ahem) Magic Johnson, it rang preposterous.

"We laughed at him," said Eddie Jones. "You can't pick your own nickname. Ever."

"He gave himself a nickname," said Corie Blount, a Laker forward. "Think about the arrogance of that. *Franchise?* Really? *You're* our franchise player? Okay, buddy. You ride that one out . . ."

Mark Heisler, the *Los Angeles Times*'s tremendous basketball writer, referred to Ceballos as a "preening peacock," and this was correct. Ceballos won the 1992 NBA Slam Dunk Contest and also made the 1995 All-Star Game. He cut a rap record. All combined, he deemed himself legend. And legends take a back seat to no man.

On March 20, one day after playing a season-low 12 minutes in a home win against the Sonics, then hearing Magic say he believed he should be starting at small forward, Ceballos went AWOL, skipping a team flight to Seattle and failing to show up for the 104–93 loss. Fred Slaughter, Ceballos's agent, had no new information. Neither did Mitch Kupchak, the Lakers' general manager. Ceballos was losing $27,378 per game, and because no one on the Lakers cared much for him, no one knew where he happened to be. The only peep in regard to his whereabouts came from Dean Messmer, owner of the Boat Brokers, in Lake Havasu City, Arizona. "He's out water skiing, having a great time," Messmer told a reporter. "I just saw him. He rented a SeaDoo and is waiting on repairs on his boat, which we have."*

Finally, five days after he vanished, Ceballos returned, armed with a nonsense excuse ("I had some very personal and family problems to deal with") that failed to conceal his frustration with life beneath/alongside Magic Johnson. One teammate after another took a turn berating their missing cohort, and someone even placed a milk carton in his locker stall, with the words WHERE IN THE WORLD IS CEBALLOS? pasted on one side. "He was just an all-time phony," said Scott Howard-Cooper of the *Los Angeles Times*. "You'd talk to him and he could call you every name in

---

* Mike Penner of the *Los Angeles Times* wisecracked that Ceballos's absence against Seattle would be marked "DNP. Skipper's decision."

the book. Then a TV camera turns on and he's all smiles. No teammates trusted him." The most unlikely and unqualified captain in modern sports history, Ceballos was stripped of his title and given the silent treatment on a four-and-a-half-hour flight from Los Angeles to Orlando. Yet it was only when Johnson ultimately spoke his piece that the tone and texture of the scandal changed. Unlike the other Lakers, who bemoaned what Ceballos had done to the team, Johnson expressed anger over how the affair had impacted *him*. This was ruining his comeback season. This was taking away from *his* moment in the spotlight. "This is the worst time for all this to happen," he said. "I'm really sick and tired of it. Maybe I won't throw myself back into next season. I don't know. It's hard for me to do with all this. I'm too old."

What one month earlier had seemed the happiest revival story in professional sports was turning into mud. Powered by a four-game winning streak, the Lakers clinched a playoff berth on March 28, then two weeks later lost Van Exel when he shoved a referee in Denver and was suspended for seven games. Johnson, being Johnson, wasted no time berating his teammate for failing to keep his cool — then bumped a referee and was suspended three games himself during a win over Phoenix. Ira Berkow, the *New York Times*'s star columnist, took the NBA to task for letting Johnson off with but a wrist slap, and he was right. The whole thing was preposterous.

"It became a circus," Harris said years later. "You had Magic criticizing Nick, then doing the same thing on the court that Nick did. You had Ced giving himself his own crazy nickname, leaving, returning, pouting. We had really good players. But it all fell apart at the absolute wrong time."

From behind the scenes, Jerry West was aghast. The legendary Laker could (generally) handle losing if he felt the Lakers were headed in the right direction. One season earlier, for example, he viewed the growth and maturation of Van Exel and Jones as signs that the organization's future was increasingly bright. Now, though, he concluded that Johnson's return — while momentarily glorious — had been a mistake. He was the wrong guy in the wrong time period; a clumsy marriage between a pulled-from-the-mothballs 1980s superstar and a bunch of hotheads with 1990s attitudes (and a guy who nicknamed himself "Chise"). When, on April 18, 1996, the Lakers blew a 21-point third-quarter lead and lost at San Antonio, 103–100, it became obvious that this had no shot of working. Two weeks later, the 1995–96 Los Angeles Lakers were put out of their misery with a forgettable three-games-to-one first-round playoff setback to Houston.

Afterwards, Johnson — front and center, as always — was asked about the problems of a lost season. "So much has been going on, we never could get on the same page, we never could be as one," he said. "I was spending most of [my energy] fighting battles within the team. It seemed like every game we had something else going on, every shootaround, every practice. That's what was going on here. You guys don't know the half of it. We couldn't get it done. The ship had too many holes."

The next day, three players — Van Exel, Threatt, and forward Anthony Miller — skipped their season-ending exit meetings with Harris. Van Exel and Miller didn't even fly back from Houston with the team.

"Is it my last game?" Johnson said to the assembled media, sitting before a locker stall inside the Houston Summit. "I want to come back. I want to win. We have to get this thing solved in L.A."

On May 14, less than two weeks after the final loss to Houston, Johnson issued a brief statement announcing his this-time-it's-for-good retirement from professional basketball. "I was satisfied with my return to the NBA, although I would have hoped we would have gone further into the playoffs," he wrote. "But now I am ready to give it up. It's time to move on. I am going out on my terms, something I couldn't say when I aborted a comeback in 1992."

Somewhere in the suburbs of Philadelphia, a high school senior with plans of NBA dominance was wondering what the news meant to him.

Somewhere in the city of Orlando, Florida, a 7-foot-1, 320-pound giant was wondering what the news meant to him.

And somewhere in Los Angeles, pacing back and forth around his office, Jerry West was busy hatching a plan that would alter professional basketball.

Without Magic Johnson.

2

The Chosen One

Following the disappointing conclusion to the 1995–96 NBA season, Jerry West knew things needed to change. The executive vice president of the Los Angeles Lakers liked his coach, the steady if unspectacular Del Harris, and believed the front office personnel (GM Mitch Kupchak, consultant Bill Sharman, scouts Gene Tormohlen and Ronnie Lester) were skilled, wise basketball men capable of rebuilding a dynastic brand. But when he looked at the roster and scanned the names, West saw problems. His favorite player, point guard Nick Van Exel, was gutsy, talented, rugged — and incapable of controlling his hair-trigger temper. You could win *with* Nick Van Exel. But you wouldn't win *led by* Nick Van Exel, because at some point he'd slug a referee or tell your coach to fuck off. Similar shortcomings applied to Eddie Jones, the silky off guard and the team's first-round pick in the 1994 draft. A product of the mean streets of Pompano Beach, Florida, then Temple University, Jones was a legitimate third offensive option for any competitive NBA club. He averaged 12.8 points in 1995–96. But, like Van Exel, he wasn't a front-of-the-pack guy. Not even close.

With Magic Johnson gone, the Lakers' neon name was Cedric Ceballos, the self-anointed franchise player. There was nothing about Ceballos's game or approach that appealed to West. In fact, the Lakers' vice president considered him to be everything that was wrong with the modern basketball player rolled into one figure: selfish, self-absorbed, incapable of passing, unwilling to play defense, who measured the game not by team benchmarks but by his numbers at the conclusion of 48 minutes. The majority of Ceballos's points were achieved off of junk baskets and roaming the baseline seeking out scraps. "Ced was weird," said Kurt Rambis, the 1980s Lakers' stalwart power forward who had just retired to become an assistant coach. "At some point in his career his ego replaced his sanity."

The remainder of the roster? Meh. Vlade Divac was one of the NBA's better passing centers. Elden Campbell was a limited yet sound power forward. Forward George Lynch and guard Anthony Peeler were okay contributing pieces. But Fred Roberts, Sedale Threatt, Derek Strong, Anthony Miller . . .

It wasn't ideal.

West was a realist. Mediocre sports executives are known for seeing the best sides of their players, even when a roster is overloaded with misfits and discards. West, on the other hand, was consumed by flaws, shortcomings, warts, potholes. It was his method of survival during an unparalleled 14-year playing career with the Lakers that saw him average 27 points and make 14 All-Star Games, yet rarely (never?) take personal satisfaction. If West shot 13 of 14 from the field, he dwelled on the single miss. If a teammate botched a last-second shot, West beat himself up for delivering a slightly-to-the-left pass. As an executive, he could barely watch his teams play, oftentimes pacing alone in a hallway. It wasn't that Jerry West was incapable of happiness. It was that he was incapable of creating happiness for himself. There was always something better that could have been done.

So, in reviewing the roster, West blamed himself. The Magic Johnson return, in particular, was something he could have (and should have) done without. It was more gimmick than substance, and the whole carnival set back the franchise's progress.

As soon as the 1995–96 season came to an end, West — who the columnist Jim Murray once wrote "could spot talent through the window of a moving train" — began looking ahead. By virtue of their 53-29 record, the Lakers held the 24th pick in the upcoming NBA draft — an unsatisfying slot for an organization that needed an infusion. Dating back to its 1947 inception, the draft had boasted its good years and its bad years. The 1984 edition gifted the world with four future Hall of Famers — Hakeem Olajuwon, Michael Jordan, Charles Barkley, and John Stockton. The 1986 edition was pocked by criminals, busts, and, in No. 2 selection Len Bias from Maryland, a tragic death from a cocaine overdose. For every Lew Alcindor going first overall (Milwaukee, 1969) you had a LaRue Martin (Portland, 1972) also going No. 1. For every draft that led off with Cazzie Russell and Dave Bing (1966), you had a draft leading off with Joe Barry Carroll and Darrell Griffith (1980). "You never truly know," West noted, "until the players enter the league."

That said, most scouts agreed that 1996 had the potential to be the deepest collection of new NBA talent in decades. Admittedly, there was no Kareem Abdul-Jabbar or Wilt Chamberlain who would, via sheer physical force, change a franchise's dynamic. But thanks to 18 players declaring early, as well as an influx of foreign stars, one was right to believe that the 10th pick wasn't decidedly less valuable than the first or second. Among the splashy neon names were a trio of guards — Allen Iverson of Georgetown, Stephon Marbury of Georgia Tech, and Ray Allen of Connecticut — who lit up their respective conferences and were generating most of the pre-draft headlines. The Lakers didn't so much as bother to work the three out. What was the point? Iverson, Marbury, and Allen would be long gone by the time the 24th slot came along.

However, that didn't mean West couldn't get creative.

On April 29, 1996, one day before the Lakers would lose Game 3 of their first-round playoff series against the Houston Rockets, a senior at Lower Merion High School, in suburban Philadelphia, called a preposterous press conference to make a preposterous announcement about an utterly preposterous idea. It was held in the high school gymnasium, only this felt like no ordinary assembly. A reporter for the school newspaper, the *Merionite*, fought for elbow space with scribes representing the *Washington Post* and *Sports Illustrated*. The four members of Boyz II Men, not far removed from releasing one of the biggest-selling albums in history, stood in the back, intrigued over the hometown buzz. The kid — lanky, broad-shouldered, shaved head — entered wearing an oversized suit and a pair of designer sunglasses perched atop his scalp. "God, it was so arrogant," said John Smallwood, who covered the event for the *Philadelphia Daily News.* "Just the look alone. Seriously, it was one of the worst things I'd ever seen."

With two dozen (or so) reporters crammed inside, the curiously named Kobe Bean Bryant — aged *seventeen* — walked to a table at the front of the room, unfolded into his seat, rubbed the scruff along his chin, leaned into a microphone, smiled somewhat apprehensively, and said, "Kobe Bryant has decided . . . to skip college and take his talents to the NBA."

Um . . .

"Kobe Bryant"?

The students in attendance went crazy, screaming, clapping, applauding.

The adults — not so much.

"Here was this high school kid, and he came out dressed as if he were a member of the Rat Pack," recalled ESPN's Jeremy Schaap, who was present. "What the heck was going on? He wore sunglasses. Sunglasses! And they may well have been drugstore shades, but they looked Armani on him. It was hard to accept the total lack of humility and the sort of Hollywood quality to it. I'd been around Michael Jordan, I'd been around Charles Barkley, but I'd never seen anything so show-offish."

At 6-foot-6, Bryant boasted the height of an NBA off guard, and his father — Joe (Jellybean) Bryant — had played eight seasons in the NBA before moving to Italy and putting in another eight in various European leagues. Hell, at age five Kobe was bouncing a basketball on a court with Magic Johnson. So there was size and there was pedigree.

Yet, truly, this was insane.

Bryant had averaged 30.8 points, 12 rebounds, 6.5 assists, 4 steals, and 3.8 blocked shots per game while leading Lower Merion to the Class AAAA state title, but he was playing alongside Robby Schwartz and Dave Rosenberg and a gaggle of Joe Schmo suburbanites with terrific futures in law or accounting. Plus, guards did not jump straight from prep hoops to the NBA. It just wasn't something to be done. In the history of basketball, five other high schoolers had gone direct to the Association, and all five were forwards or centers. The last one to make the move, a Farragut Career Academy senior named Kevin Garnett, stood 6-foot-11 and was a rebounding and shot-blocking machine. Even with his size and strength, he joined the Minnesota Timberwolves in 1995 and averaged but 10.4 points per game. "It was," he later said, "really hard."

On the surface, nothing about Bryant's move felt logical. He was a B student with a 1080 SAT score. He was being recruited by everyone, with Duke considered the most probable landing spot. He had yet to work out for a single NBA scout, many of whom had never actually heard of him. "He's kidding himself," Marty Blake, the NBA's scouting director, told the *Los Angeles Times*. "Sure he'd like to come out. I'd like to be a movie star. He's not ready."

"You watch Kobe Bryant and you don't see special," said Rob Babcock, Minnesota's director of player personnel. "His game doesn't say, 'I'm a very special talent.'"

"I think it's a total mistake," said Jon Jennings, the Boston Celtics' director of basketball development. "Kevin Garnett was the best high school player I ever saw, and I wouldn't have advised him to jump. And Kobe is no Kevin Garnett."

What many failed to understand — *couldn't possibly understand* — was that the Kobe-Bryant-to-the-NBA train had left the station long before an announcement in a high school gymnasium. Beginning in the mid- to late 1980s, with the rise of Nike and assorted top-level sports academies and camps, highly skilled American athletes were discovered at infantile ages, developed, coddled, labeled, marked, tagged, stalked, and processed. It was no longer sufficient to let kids be kids, and have Junior progress gradually. No, today's adept six-year-old dribbler was — maybe, just maybe — tomorrow's Isiah Thomas, and that had to be developed ASAP. That, in many ways, explains Garnett's move from high school to the NBA. Enormous at an early age, he was a commodity before he knew the definition of the word.

Bryant, on the other hand, felt more hidden gem, buried somewhere off the radar.

Though Joe Bryant was a former NBA player and a 1975 first-round draft pick of the Golden State Warriors, he was one of those dime-a-dozen guys who comes, plays, then slinks from the spotlight. Over his eight seasons with three organizations, he averaged a pedestrian 8.7 points and 4 rebounds. He appeared in 30 playoff games, never starting one. His greatest professional claim to fame came on May 5, 1976, when Philadelphia police attempted to pull him over for a busted taillight. Bryant fled the scene before crashing into three parked cars. He was arrested, and officers found several bags of cocaine in his vehicle. "He should have been much better than he was," said Dick Weiss, the longtime Philadelphia basketball scribe. "Joe had tremendous athleticism, he had a lot of Kevin Durant skills well before Kevin Durant. But it never really came together."

His departure from the NBA was greeted with a collective shrug. Fred Hartman of the *Baytown* (Texas) *Sun* noted on August 7, 1983, that "Bryant completed his contract last year and is an unsigned free agent." And that was that.

Kobe was just under five years old at the time — the youngest of Joe and Pam Bryant's three children. (He has two sisters, Sharia and Shaya.) A couple of months earlier, his parents had signed him up for a karate class at a Houston dojo. He was on the fast route to advancing from white belt to yellow belt when one day the teacher had him battle a brown belt. The opponent was a big kid — taller, heavier, significantly more experienced. Kobe began to cry, to which the instructor responded, "You fight him!" Little Kobe stepped forward and swung away.

Resiliency was a thing with the Bryants. Around this period, Joe took a job selling cars at a dealership in Houston, but it was a terrible fit. He was a tall black man, just 28 years old and born to play basketball, pushing Fords on uncomfortable white customers who eyed him (tall, muscular, unhappy) warily. When he was initially presented with the idea of playing overseas, Joe expressed skepticism. Would the money be worth it? Would Pam — born and bred Philadelphian — be okay with yet another basketball-related relocation? Would the level of play be anything better than mediocre?

Within a few months, the Bryants found themselves in Rieti, a city of

40,000 located 48 miles north of Rome. Joe was the newest member of AMG Sebastiani Rieti, who would provide housing and an automobile and pay him big bucks to be their Dr. J. Amazingly, it worked. Joe Bryant averaged a team-best 30 points per game and along the way rediscovered his love for the sport. So what if he was dunking over gangly 18-year-old Italian boys named Francesco and Mattia? In the NBA he'd rot on the bench, moaning as less talented teammates took his minutes. In Italy he was free, flamboyant, jovial. As Roland Lazenby noted in his Kobe Bryant biography, *Showboat,* Italian basketball fans came to use a singular word to describe Joe's play: *"bella."*

Over the next eight years, the Bryant family called Italy home, and young Kobe's game took on a distinctively European flair and feel. He would tag along to practices with his father (who played with four different Italian League teams), shooting jumpers and playing light games of one-on-one with Joe's teammates. "From day one I was dribbling," Kobe Bryant said. "I just found basketball to be the most fun. It wasn't just watching my father play. It was the fact that you could dribble the ball around everywhere. You could play the game by yourself and envision certain situations." Kobe spoke fluent Italian, enrolled in ballet classes, excelled in organized soccer, developed a taste for bruschetta and panzanella. Basketball existed as a thing in Italy, but not a big thing. So when the Bryants installed a hoop at the end of the driveway, it was unusual behavior. As his Italian peers were watching *Mio Mao* and *Quaq Quao*, Kobe was absorbing the VHS tapes sent to him by his grandfather — the ones showing Magic and Bird and a young Chicago Bulls star named Michael Jordan. "I loved the feel of [the basketball] in my hands," he once recalled. "I loved the sound of it, too. The tap, tap, tap of when a ball bounces on the hardwood. The crispness and clarity. The predictability."

As Kobe grew, Joe and Pam signed him up to play on Italian youth basketball teams. He was always the best player, and the least-liked player — so superior to his teammates that he rarely looked their way. Peers would scream, "Kobe, *passa la palla!*" ("Kobe, pass the ball!"), and he would respond simply, "No" ("No"). Not unlike a good number of children with famous parents and a shiny silver spoon, Kobe was known to be arrogant, curt, dismissive of other children. He wasn't hated so much as he was disdained. The only arrow in the other players' quill was something they repeatedly told Kobe — "*Sei bravo qui, ma non sarai molto in America!*" ("You're good here, but you won't be much in America").

Each summer, with the conclusion of Joe's seasons, the Bryants returned to Philadelphia. But it was a clumsy fit for Kobe, the African American kid with the European air and the slightest hint of an Italian accent.

In July 1991, shortly before his 13th birthday, Kobe Bryant was signed up by his father to compete in the summertime Sonny Hill Community Involvement League, where Philadelphia's best young basketball players went at it on courts in Temple's McGonigle Hall. Joe had starred in Sonny Hill games back in the day, and he thought the hardened stylings of the city's fiercest ballers would do his son good. So he filled out the application, then handed the sheet of paper to his son, who had to enter some personal information. When Kobe arrived for his first day of competition, a counselor read over his replies.

NAME: KOBE BEAN BRYANT
AGE: 12
HOMETOWN: PHILADELPHIA
FUTURE CAREER PLAN: NBA

"Are you being serious?" the counselor asked.

Bryant nodded. He was indeed — which led staffers to pay extra attention to the boy with the oddball name and the written swagger. What they found was laughable. In Italy, the kids wore volleyball kneepads in games. So Kobe, thinking this was the norm, brought the style (or lack thereof) to Philly. "I'm out there looking like the Cable Guy," he later recalled. In Italy, he was an unstoppable basketball force, driving in for layups with no worry. Back in America, he was a fish-out-of-water scrub with poor fashion sense and Osgood-Schlatter disease, which shot excruciating pain through his knees. In 25 games, Bryant tallied zero points. "I didn't score a basket, a free throw, nothing," he recalled. "At the end I sobbed my eyes out."

While Kobe Bryant stunk, though, he didn't plan on stinking for long. He was back at Sonny Hill the following summer, played passably well, scored a few baskets, performed admirably on defense.

The Bryants left Italy for good after the 1991–92 season, and Kobe's return to full-time American life commenced as an eighth grader, when he enrolled at Bala Cynwyd Junior High, in the leafy western suburbs of Philadelphia. The school was 70 percent Caucasian, and Kobe struggled to fit in with anyone. He wasn't white. His "blackness" felt forced. He spoke Italian, and *nobody* spoke Italian. All the faces were unfamiliar. He was far more poised than your average student, and this made him come across as aloof and arrogant. Thanks to his athletic gifts and his status as an American outsider, Kobe had spent most of his early years standing out. Now, back in the fold of the United States, he still felt as if he stood out. As if he were, somehow, better.

Which he was.

The rich talent that congregated at Sonny Hill every summer couldn't be found at Bala Cynwyd, and Kobe — armed with increased skills, legitimate experience, dreamy genetics (not only was his father a former NBA player, but Pam's brother, Chubby Cox, spent part of the 1983 season with the Washington Bullets), and unyielding confidence — dominated. Now standing 6-foot-2, he played for the school's eighth-grade team and owned the court, averaging 30 points per game. It was a laughable sight: the sleek, smooth Bryant having his way with the overmatched children surrounding him. Gregg Downer, the varsity coach at Lower Merion High, heard of the youth's exploits and invited him to participate in one of the Aces' varsity practices. Kobe entered the gymnasium accompanied by his 6-foot-9 father. "Holy shit, that's Joe Bryant," Downer whispered to an assistant. "*Jellybean* Bryant."

A former player at Division III Lynchburg (Virginia) College, Downer was 27 and immediately recognized that the boy was no ordinary basketball player. Bryant showed no fear. He threw elbows at the varsity players, set crushing picks. Five minutes into practice, Downer turned to someone and said, "This kid is a pro."

"I knew right away I had something very special on my hands," Downer said. "He was so fundamentally good at the age of 13, and I thought to myself that he was going to get nothing but taller and stronger."

As a freshman at Lower Merion, Bryant made Downer's varsity squad, starting and averaging 18 points for a team that went 4-20. What stood out was his ferocious intensity. Bryant didn't merely dislike losing—he abhorred it. He didn't merely fret over missed free throws — he burdened himself with their existence. Other players laughed off a poor showing, a sloppy pass, a lazy turnover. Not Bryant. He believed in perfection, and nothing short of that ever seemed to satisfy him. Once, during a practice, Downer barked at his freshman for failing to play defense the Lower Merion way. "Well," Bryant replied, "that's not what I'm going to do in the NBA!"

On a school trip to Hersheypark, a student named Susan Freedland asked his assistance in helping her win a stuffed animal at a free throw shooting stall. Classmates gathered around, laughing, giggling. But Kobe stoically grabbed a ball, lined up, stared down the rim, and shot — *swish*.

Shot again — *swish*.

Shot again — *swish*.

Susan was handed a blue elephant with green tusks, and thanked Kobe for his assistance. But he wasn't done. He returned to the game, plunked down another $3.

Shot again — *swish*.

Shot again — *swish*.

The man running the booth — agitated, defeated — surrendered another elephant and told Bryant to bug off.

This wasn't fun for Kobe. None of it was. It *meant* something. Being the best. Finding greatness. Refusing to surrender. Over the next two decades, people questioned the desire's origin, wondered what had made Kobe Bryant a Jordanesque basketball killer. The answers, truly, can be found at Lower Merion, where in his relative isolation and solitude he committed himself to his closest friend: the game of basketball.

Kobe Bryant was an awkward kid. Handsome and intelligent, yet equally cumbersome and uncertain. He didn't fully grasp the rhythms of casual conversation, was clumsy and clammy-handed around the opposite sex, wasn't fully caught up on pop culture or music. It's a tricky thing, being one of the few African American kids in a predominantly white school. Certain behaviors are (unfairly) expected. So are certain language choices. *Street. Hood.* Kobe Bryant wasn't that guy. His efforts to fake his way through the long high school hallways were — in one regard — admirable, but largely unsuccessful. Even later, when he began to grace magazine covers, friends and teammates found his efforts laughable. Here was Kobe Bryant, peering from a *Sports Illustrated* or *Slam* front, the model of masculine cool, and he was actually a dork. The by-product of such discomfort was a commitment to singular excellence in the endeavor of shooting, passing, rebounding, stealing, blocking shots. Young Kobe ran the streets of his neighborhood until he vomited, lifted weights until his muscles burned, monitored every calorie and drop of water. He pursued greatness, not merely because his father was great but because that pursuit was — outside of a close-knit family — all he had.

The buzz over Bryant built during his sophomore year at Lower Merion, when he led the Aces with 22 points and 10 rebounds per game and guided a once miserable program to a 16-6 record. "He played with this giant chip on his shoulder," recalled Shaheen Holloway, a point guard at St. Patrick High, in Elizabeth, New Jersey. "He always acted like he had something to prove. Part of that might be because he lived in the suburbs, went to high school in the suburbs. So people thought he was soft. Well, the boy was a cold-stone killer." Thanks to neon statistics and some highlight-reel dunks, Bryant's name was landing in an increasing number of *Philadelphia Inquirer* stories, but few outside of the area took him seriously. There was a general belief that he was yet another above-average-but-nothing-special basketball player feeding on the carcasses of suburban math buffs.

That's why what happened next was so important. Back in the summer of 1972, Joe Bryant, 17 years old and a year away from enrolling at La

Salle, was named MVP of the Dapper Dan high school all-star tournament, held in Pittsburgh. The man who ran the event was Sonny Vaccaro.

Now, 22 years later, Joe Bryant was reintroduced to Vaccaro by a mutual acquaintance, the noted AAU coach Gary Charles. Bryant reminded Vaccaro of their past history; reminded him of the way Dapper Dan had changed his life. He told him that he had left the NBA for Italy, then returned to the States. Joe had recently been hired as an assistant coach at La Salle, and he was doing great, and his wife was doing great, and everything was great, and . . .

"I have a favor to ask," he said.

"What," Vaccaro replied, "might that be?"

Best known as the man who, as an executive with Nike, signed Michael Jordan to his first sneaker deal and changed the face of athlete marketing, Vaccaro now worked for Adidas and ran the company's ABCD All America Camp, an elite showcase of the nation's 125 top high school basketball standouts. He had started it in 1984 as a way of endearing himself (and whoever he worked for) to the next generation of hoop royalty. And, whatever his motivations may have been, before long ABCD emerged as the place where the best of the best of the best had to be.

"Sonny," Joe said, "I have this son — Kobe. And he's really good. I want to see if you can give him an ABCD spot."

Vaccaro was initially hesitant. How many times had he endured this one? *My son is amazing, he'll dominate your camp, he just needs a shot* . . . And how many times did the kid wind up stinking up the court? "I'd never heard of Kobe Bryant," he said years later. "No one knew who he was, what he could do. But I felt like Joe and I had a history, and maybe he was telling the truth. So I told him, 'Okay, I'll let him in.'"

On July 7, 1994, Kobe Bryant reported to the campus of Fairleigh Dickinson University, in Teaneck, New Jersey, for a week of high-level basketball most presumed he would not be ready for. He was one of four high school juniors in attendance, and the majority of the buzz was directed toward a pair of New York City guards — Stephon Marbury, of Lincoln High, and Shammgod Wells, from New York City's La Salle Academy. To be a lesser-known player at ABCD is to shuffle with one's head down, with eyes glued to one's sneakers. It's intimidating, it's jarring — "You're there with guys who can do amazing things," said Holloway. "You're the best where you're from. But going there is an eye-opener."

From day one, Bryant walked as if he belonged. He played hard, played fast, refused to kneel before Marbury or Wells or the fantastic Tim Thomas of Paterson, New Jersey. He wore three chips on his shoulders — the kid from Italy nobody worried about, the kid from suburbia nobody worried about, the son of an NBA alum. The star of the camp was Marbury, who at one point shook Holloway, rose from the free throw line, and carried his 6-foot-1 body toward a 6-foot-9, 240-pound shot blocker named Patrick Ngongba. With an audible grunt, Marbury dunked in the giant's face, landed, screamed "*Wooooooo!*," grinned from cheek to cheek, walked the full length of the court, out the gym, and onto the bus that ferried participants to and from the facility.

The other players hooted and hollered with glee.

Bryant joined the audible circus, but inside, jealousy consumed the teen. That should have been him. That *would* be him. When the camp concluded and Marbury and Thomas were named most valuable players, Bryant approached Vaccaro and tapped him on the shoulder.

"Mr. Vaccaro," he said, "I want to apologize to you."

"What do you mean?" Vaccaro said.

"I'm just telling you, next year I'll be the MVP here. I'm sorry I let you down."

Vaccaro was speechless. Kobe Bryant owed him no apology. But the integrity and intensity were unlike anything he'd seen in ABCD history. "I've never forgotten that," he said years later. "His mindset was not 'Hey, thanks for having me. I've enjoyed the opportunity and I look forward to returning.' It was 'Fuck that. I'm gonna be MVP.' Call it what it is — confidence, arrogance, self-assurance. He knew he'd be great, and at that moment I knew he'd be great. And at that moment — that very moment — I also knew Adidas would be in the market for Kobe Bryant."

Over the next two years, Kobe Bryant went from *here* to HERE. As a junior at Lower Merion, he averaged 31.1 points, 10.4 rebounds, and

5.2 assists and was named Pennsylvania's Player of the Year. Everything about Bryant was ferocious. He would arrive at the school gymnasium at 5 a.m. to shoot on his own, then stay two hours after practices in the evening. What he lacked in social skills he made up for with doggedness. Lots and lots *and lots* of doggedness. "People think his athleticism was the most impressive thing — and they're wrong," recalled Emory Dabney, the Lower Merion point guard. "It was the drive. He wasn't psychotic, but he bordered on psychotic." In particular, Dabney recalled one 95-degree summer day when he and his star teammate worked out on the track at nearby Saint Joseph's University, then went across the street to Episcopal Academy to play pickup. "Kobe would get in the car after running and turn the heat up to 90 degrees because he didn't want his muscles to cool down," said Dabney. "You'd be like 'Wow, this is nuts.' But it separated him from everyone. He didn't just want it. He *wanted* it."

Bryant returned to ABCD for another summer and, as promised, was named the camp's MVP after averaging 21 points and 7 rebounds. This was perhaps the greatest collection of talent in ABCD history — not merely Bryant but also Thomas, Jermaine O'Neal of Eau Claire High (South Carolina), and Lester Earl of Glen Oaks (Louisiana). In a moment that, two decades later, Vaccaro still found uproarious, in one game Kobe soared toward the basket and slammed powerfully over an overwhelmed opponent. As the ball rattled through the rim, Bryant fell to his feet, smiled, and yelled at Vaccaro, "Was that better than Stephon's?"

"No," Vaccaro replied, "but it was damn good."

If Bryant's confidence was high off of his ABCD showing, a couple of closer-to-home experiences took it to another level. Even though he was but a high schooler, Bryant spent plenty of time playing pickup inside Temple University's Pearson Hall gymnasium. These weren't run-of-the-mill battles against Joe Frat Boy. No, his opponents included many of the Owls stars, including future NBA players Rick Brunson, Aaron McKie, and Eddie Jones. "God, he was so polished for a high school kid," recalled Jones. "Flat-out talented. Most impressive, he wasn't scared. We were All-Americans, big names in college basketball. And Kobe just brought it right at us. You knew this kid was NBA-bound. There was zero question."

Around this time, the Philadelphia 76ers were holding off-season workouts on the campus of Saint Joseph's. Because he was a big local name and bodies were needed (and because Tarvia Lucas, the daughter of 76ers coach John Lucas, attended Lower Merion), Bryant, along with Dabney, was allowed to play. These were the 18-64 Sixers of Shawn Bradley and Sean Higgins; of Elmer Bennett and Greg Graham. But they were still an NBA team, and Kobe Bryant was still a soon-to-be high school senior.

What transpired is the stuff of myth. In large part because much of it *is* myth. According to the eternally repeated story of 10 million witnesses (there were no more than 30 people in the gym), Bryant lit up Jerry Stackhouse, Philadelphia's fantastic young shooting guard. He took Stackhouse left, he took Stackhouse right, he dunked over Stackhouse while eating a ham sandwich and humming Peter Cetera's entire musical catalog.*

Truth be told, Bryant played extremely well against Stackhouse, as well as solid NBAers like Vernon Maxwell, Richard Dumas, and Sharone Wright. He wasn't the most polished player on the court, or even the 10th most polished on the court. He was undisciplined, sloppy, erratic. He took shots one shouldn't take and committed turnovers that, were this a regular game, would land him on the bench. But he was absolutely fearless — and that stuck. Plus, while he didn't destroy Stackhouse, he did get under his skin. "Stack had a very short fuse," said Dabney. "He didn't take well to a 17-year-old bringing it to him." John Nash, general manager of the Washington Bullets, caught up with Lucas.

"How's Stack doing in your workouts?" Nash asked.

"Fine," Lucas said, "but he's the second-best two guard in the gym."

Nash made a mental list of the Sixers' shooting guards. It wasn't a par-

---

* I reached out to Stackhouse, a nice man I once profiled for the *Wall Street Journal*. He DM'd back: "What's up brother. Hope all is well. Probably not the one to talk much about Kobe, to expand on all the myth of him beating me as a high schooler but to his credit I've never heard him say it but he hasn't denied it either. So basically, fuck him."

ticularly impressive collection. "John," he finally said, "who's the best two guard?"

"Kobe," Lucas replied.

Whoa.

Shaun Powell, a *Newsday* reporter who covered a lot of NBA, was walking through the New Jersey Nets' locker room one day when he was stopped by Rick Mahorn, journeyman power forward. "You know who you need to write about?" Mahorn said. "Jellybean's kid."

"Jellybean's kid?" Powell replied.

"Yeah," said Mahorn. "His name is Kobe. And in the summer when we all played pickup ball, he ran with us. And he *wasn't the last one picked . . .*"

Around this time, Bryant began working daily with Joe Carbone, a personal trainer and retired professional weight lifter hired by the family to transform the kid from sapling to oak. The goal was to build someone described as "wiry" into a machine capable of enduring an 82-game season against large men. Before long, Bryant was a weight room regular, benching, squatting, curling. "We put about 20 pounds on him," Carbone said. "He's not a heavy gainer, so the weight came on as he got stronger."

By the time he returned to Lower Merion for his senior year of high school, Bryant — bolstered by the ABCD experience, by the games at Temple, by his play with the Sixers, by the fitness regimen — knew he would not be attending college. "He told me that summer," said Dabney. "Bluntly — 'I'm going to the NBA next year.'"

If Bryant knew, it was something of a secret to those hoping otherwise. The college recruiting letters arrived by the boatload — from Duke and North Carolina, from UCLA and USC, from Delaware and Drexel and Villanova and Temple. This was the fall of 1995, and at the time Joe Bryant was in his second year as an assistant at nearby La Salle University, his alma mater. He had been hired in 1993 by Speedy Morris, the head coach, and while the official reasoning was that the program needed a replacement for the recently departed Randy Monroe, the reality was different. "Did I think it'd help us get Kobe?" Morris said decades later. "Yes. Of course. Joe was not a good assistant coach. He didn't work hard, he didn't actually know that much. Nice guy. But he was there so we'd get his son."

Kobe Bryant basked in the attention, took a handful of campus visits, pretended he was genuinely torn over what to do next. He liked to show off all the recruiting letters he received, and proudly stiffed Kentucky coach Rick Pitino, failing to show up for a scheduled visit to campus. He acted as if college were a legitimate option. Only it really wasn't. Because he had never signed with an agent, or accepted so much as a dime from a sneaker company, he remained eligible should he change his mind. But he wasn't changing his mind. The recruiting letters ultimately found themselves at rest alongside half-eaten burgers and empty yogurt containers in the Bryant family trash bins. That June he had competed in the War in the Woods, an outdoor tournament held in Penns Grove, New Jersey. As Kobe lit up the court, his father watched alongside Gary Charles, veteran AAU coach and Sonny Vaccaro's confidant. With each Kobe three-pointer, Joe turned to Charles to say, "See that?" With each dunk, "Amazing, right?" When the game ended, Joe went serious. "Gary," he said, "I think my kid wants to come right out from high school. But we, as a family, would be worried because there are no guarantees."

Charles grinned. "What if I can help you get a guarantee?" he said.

Joe Bryant was confused.

"What," Charles said, "if I can help Kobe get a shoe deal?"

"Wait, you can do that?" Bryant replied.

"You know," Charles said, "I believe I can."

That evening, Charles placed a call to Vaccaro.

"Sonny," he said, "Kobe Bryant can be *the kid*."

By *the kid*, he meant The One. Ever since joining Adidas in the early 1990s, Vaccaro had been seeking out the next Michael Jordan, jock marketing goliath. At the time, the shoe company was known for being dull and unimaginative and a pimple on Nike's back. Bryant's ABCD showings had opened Vaccaro's eyes, and there was a lot to like. Bryant was mature, Bryant was savvy, Bryant was handsome, Bryant could flat-out play, Bryant had NBA blood. "And the name —'Kobe Bryant,'" Vaccaro said. "There's something about it. 'Kobe Bryant from Italy'— it's intriguing, it's a little mysterious."

Vaccaro loved what he was hearing. He reached out to Joe Bryant to make sure there was legitimate interest. Then he kicked back and watched Kobe piece together one of the best seasons in local high school basketball history, leading Lower Merion to its first state championship since 1943. He concluded his high school career as southeastern Pennsylvania's all-time leading scorer, with 2,883 points, and was named the Naismith High School Player of the Year, Gatorade Men's National Basketball Player of the Year, and a McDonald's All-American. "The most amazing thing was he never lost a drill," said Jeremy Treatman, an assistant coach with the Aces. "Four years, and Kobe never lost a game of one-on-one, a scrimmage, a sprint. He just didn't allow losing." By early in the season, word had gotten out that Bryant was thinking NBA, and the league's scouts (the ones who took him seriously — many did not) began to dot the Lower Merion bleachers during home games. Pete Babcock, general manager of the Atlanta Hawks, flew in and saw a kid "[d]o whatever he wanted to without anyone knowing how to stop him." Larry Harris, a Milwaukee Bucks scout, came three times, often wondering if what he was witnessing was, in fact, real. "He wore number 33, and that immediately made me think of Scottie Pippen," Harris said. "He had this Pippen-like length, and also this comfort with his own athleticism. Once the game started, there was no messing around, no settling for jumpers. It was business. That jumped out to me."

Vaccaro was now more determined than ever to make Bryant the face of Adidas. Midway through the high school season, he convinced the company to spend $75,000 to move him from Southern California to New York City in order to be closer to the high school supernova. He never attended Lower Merion games, for fear that Nike or another rival apparel company would learn of his plans, but had Charles show up as his go-between. The two sides talked about fame and glory and talent. But mostly they talked about sneakers. The Bryant family wanted a financial guarantee, and Vaccaro and Adidas were willing to offer one. They would pay Kobe Bryant $48 million, provide another $150,000 to Joe Bryant, and make Kobe the face of Adidas. The sell, in a sense, was Michael Jordan. Bryant was told he would be the new Jordan — beginning with a signature shoe and a glitzy marketing campaign based around the concept "Feet You Wear." It played to both his ego and his love of basketball history.

College? Who needed college.

Kobe Bryant had decided to take his talents to the NBA.

When one is aligned with a sneaker company, and when said sneaker company is paying one millions of dollars to promote the brand, things can get complicated.

Especially when one is a high school kid.

Especially when one would happily play for any NBA team.

Especially when one's sneaker company has designs on certain geographic markets.

In the aftermath of Kobe Bryant's going-to-the-NBA announcement, a slew of franchises asked him to come to their facilities for workouts. This is how things work in professional basketball, and a young player would have to be either dumb, uninformed, or supremely confident (nay, arrogant) to turn down an invitation. Especially a young player with no Division I college experience.

Kobe Bryant turned down plenty of invitations.

For the not-yet-18-year-old guard, this was never about preferring the sun over the ski, or Pacific time over Eastern time. Nope, this was about selling sneakers. As soon as Vaccaro convinced Adidas to spend millions on the kid, it brought forth an immediate two-way loyalty. When Bryant (and his parents) went about finding an agent, he selected Arn Tellem, the Los Angeles–based power broker whose closest friends included Vaccaro and Lakers vice president Jerry West. Tellem, like Vaccaro, knew the importance of a big city for Kobe the basketball player and Kobe the apparel salesman.

The Toronto Raptors, talentless, anonymous, and gifted with the second overall pick in the 1996 draft, asked Bryant to come for a visit. No. The Vancouver Grizzlies, talentless, anonymous, and gifted with the third overall pick in the 1996 draft, asked Bryant to come for a visit. No. The Milwaukee Bucks, talentless, anonymous, and gifted with the fourth overall pick in the 1996 draft, asked Bryant to come for a visit. No. One after another, Bryant offered a sincere thanks-but-no-thanks to the majority of organizations that wanted to see him in a controlled setting. On June 24, he was scheduled to fly to Charlotte and perform for the Hornets, owners of the 13th overall selection. That morning, without warning, he canceled. A day later, he did the same to the Sacramento Kings. No heads-up. No advance notice.

Bryant worried about his reputation, and whether organizations would hold it against him come draft day. Tellem, whose client roster included baseball players such as Nomar Garciaparra and Mike Mussina and basketball star Reggie Miller, promised all would work itself out. "We have to be selective," he told him. Indeed, the teams that had seen Bryant in person were blown away. Barry Hecker, the Los Angeles Clippers' assistant coach, wanted nothing to do with a high school kid when his bosses said Bryant would be arriving for a workout. "I was very skeptical," Hecker said. "I didn't think our organization would be a good spot for someone that young, and I also assumed he wouldn't be ready for a man's game. Well, that was misguided." Standing alongside Bill Fitch, the head coach, and assistant Jim Brewer, Hecker steeled himself to see the worst. Then — WHOOSH! Bryant was instructed to do the old Mikan Drill, which involves a rapid-fire series of close-to-the-basket hook shots. But instead of hooks, Bryant dunked. Bam! Bam! Bam! Bam! "Ten times in a row — left, right, left, right," said Hecker. "Jesus Christ."

Hecker was impressed. As were the New Jersey Nets, owners of the eighth overall pick. Officially, they had Bryant come to the team facility for three different workouts. Unofficially, that number was actually four. Or, ahem, maybe five. "Which is probably against NBA rules," said Bobby Marks, the Nets' basketball operations assistant. "But that's okay." Marks was in charge of scheduling Bryant's arrival via train or plane. He would pick him up from the station or airport, drive him to the facility, arrange for a series of challenges. At the time, the Nets were simultaneously awful and young, and it wasn't hard to rope in a green player or two to square off against a prospect. So one day Marks requested that guard Khalid Reeves and forward Ed O'Bannon come in early and rough up the high schooler. Both men boasted sterling basketball pedigrees. Reeves had been a first-round pick of the Miami Heat after an All-American career at Arizona. O'Bannon had been a first-round pick of the Nets after an All-American career at UCLA.

Kobe Bryant waxed them.

"It was always some sort of two-on-two or three-on-three, and Kobe had his way," recalled Marks. "He was the best player on the court every single time, and it was against established NBA players."

Word quickly spread that New Jersey was a likely destination for Bryant. That's why Jerry West considered Bryant worth little thought. The Lakers were picking 24th overall. The kid would be long gone. Plus, he was a high schooler, and Los Angeles was looking for help-now talent. "I didn't know much about him," West later said. "We weren't focused on getting Kobe Bryant."

Tellem, though, loved the idea of Los Angeles — the big market, the historic franchise. He called West and asked that the Lakers bring his client in for a workout. So they did. Bryant was in town for a commercial shoot, and he arrived at the Inglewood YMCA at the same time as Dontae' Jones, the Mississippi State forward who had recently led the Bulldogs to the Final Four.* Over the next 45 minutes, Bryant reduced the 6-foot-8 Jones to a bowl of melted ice cream. With Larry Drew, a Lakers assistant coach, monitoring the workout, Bryant and Jones played a series of one-on-one games that left the college senior gasping for breath. "You don't realize," Jones said later, "a 17-year-old could do all the things he was even attempting to do."

In his three and a half decades in professional basketball, West had seen everything. Elgin Baylor, Kareem, Magic, Bird, Jordan, Yinka Dare. This, though, was different. "Oh my God," West recalled. "You have to be kidding me. No disrespect to anyone, but as soon as I saw him it was clear

---

* An interesting side note: Bryant came to Los Angeles immediately after having worked out for the Nets. Bobby Marks booked his flight, and he had Bryant placed in a middle seat in coach. Tellem was livid, and Marks forever wondered whether that did New Jersey in. "Or at least contributed to it," Marks later said.

this was a complete no-brainer. I swear to God, I would have taken him with the No. 1 pick in the draft over Allen Iverson. He was *that* good."

A couple of days later, the Lakers asked Bryant to attend one final workout. This time at Inglewood High School, he was to play one-on-one against Michael Cooper, the former Laker star now working as an assistant coach with the club. Though five years retired, the 40-year-old Cooper looked a lot like the 30-year-old Cooper. He was sinewy, muscled, very much in shape. West asked his former player to give Kobe Bryant a beating. "Make him work," West said.

Cooper nodded. "No problem."

For 30 minutes, Bryant plowed through Cooper just as he had plowed through Jones. Slicing left, twirling right, dunking, gliding. West cut the one-on-one session short and turned to John Black and Raymond Ridder, two of the team's media relations heads. "Okay, I've seen enough," he said. "Let's go. He's better than anyone we have on our team right now."

He concluded: "Best workout I've ever seen."

Later that day, West reached out to Tellem. "Kobe Bryant," he told him, "just played like I'd never seen a kid play before. Obviously we'd love to have him as a Laker. Not sure how that happens, but . . ."

The 1996 NBA draft was held on June 26, inside the Continental Airlines Arena, the East Rutherford, New Jersey–based home to the Nets. At approximately 8 p.m., Commissioner David Stern announced that, with the first pick, the Philadelphia 76ers would take Iverson, the superlative Georgetown guard. The team had worked out Bryant — "and we loved him," said Brad Greenberg, the general manager. "But we didn't need a two guard. So he wasn't really considered." That was followed by Toronto going with UMass center Marcus Camby and Vancouver selecting Cal's Shareef Abdur-Rahim. As one player after another came off the board, John Nash, New Jersey's newly hired general manager, grew excited. One day earlier, West had called Nash, offering Laker center Vlade Divac for the pick. It took the Nets three seconds to reject the offer, and another three seconds for Nash to turn to the team's new head coach, John Calipari, and say, "If Jerry West thinks Kobe Bryant is a star — *he's a star*." A few hours later, Nash and Calipari dined with Joe and Pam Bryant. At one point, Nash silenced the table with his hands and bluntly declared, "If Kobe is there at number 8, we're going to take him." Then: "How do you feel about that?"

How did they feel about that? The Bryants were elated. Their son would be playing less than 100 miles from home, in a major market, for an organization that coveted him. "That," Joe replied, "would be wonderful."

On the afternoon of the draft, Nash and Calipari had lunch with Joe Taub, one of the franchise's owners, and told him the plan was to take Kobe Bryant and build the Nets around his genius.

Taub frowned. "The high school kid?" he asked.

"Yeah," Nash replied. "Kobe Bryant's going to be a star in this league."

"But he's so young," Taub replied. "What if we put all this energy into developing him and by the time he's good he leaves as a free agent? That would be a disaster."

Nash looked at Calipari, hoping for support. There was none. "Joe," Nash said, "you don't get a chance at talent like this very often. Trust me."

The lunch ended and Nash retreated to his office, still believing the plan was in place. What followed was all sorts of crazy. Calipari received a phone call from Kobe Bryant, who told him he wanted to get away from his parents, that New Jersey was too close to Philadelphia and he needed space. Nash received a call from Tellem, who created — in Nash's words — "some cockamamie story about Kobe having a disagreement with his parents and wanting to head west." Calipari then received a call from Tellem, who was actually sitting alongside one of his clients, Nets forward Kendall Gill. "I heard it all," Gill recalled. "Cal told Arn Tellem the Nets were taking Kobe. And Arn said to him — and this is exactly what he said — 'John, I swear to God, if you take him we'll hold out. I have a deal already worked out between the Hornets and Lakers, and you better not mess it up. You'll pay.'"

An ashen Calipari and an exhausted Nash met in the office hallway, and the 37-year-old coach asked the 48-year-old executive what he thought of it all. "Give me an hour," Nash said. "Something isn't kosher here." He proceeded to call Bob Bass, general manager of the Hornets, holders of the draft's 13th pick. Even before Calipari informed him of the Tellem conversation, Nash had heard the rumors of Charlotte and Los Angeles plotting something big. "Bob," Nash asked, "do you have a deal pending with the Lakers?"

Bass hemmed and hawed. Hawed and hemmed. Said a lot, while saying nothing.

"It was pretty clear at that moment," Nash said, "that we were being played."

As all this was transpiring, Calipari took a call from David Falk, the agent representing Villanova's All-American guard, Kerry Kittles. Having spent his college career playing a stone's throw away, Kittles very much wanted to land in New Jersey. That's why Falk, noted bulldog, told Calipari that unless the Nets picked his client, no one he represented would ever consider playing for the franchise.

"So John runs into my office and tells me this," Nash recalled. "I said, 'John, come on. You don't believe this bullshit, do you? It's all bluster. The family. The agents. It's total bullshit. Trust me.'"

Calipari didn't trust Nash. He was still green to the professional game. Really, still green to the game, period. His one head coaching position had come at UMass, and before that he was an assistant at Kansas and Pittsburgh. The man had yet to coach a professional contest and barely knew the names of the players on New Jersey's roster. The Falk threat was terrifying enough. But Calipari was never 100 percent sold on drafting Bryant. He was taking over a team that had finished 30-52 the previous season, and the pressure was real for a young coach with a reputation for making quick fixes. The Nets were paying Calipari a league-high $3 million a year, and that came with final say on all basketball decisions. "We're not winning with a high school kid," Calipari said to Nash. "You know that, right?"

"John," Nash said. "You have a five-year guaranteed contract. Everyone knows this is a building process."

Two hours before the draft was to begin, Nash agreed to see if the Nets could trade down a few slots. That way the team might gain another pick and, perhaps, take Bryant a bit later. Win-win. He called a handful of franchises, but there were no takers. At 6:30, Nash and Calipari met with the team's full ownership group at the restaurant inside the arena.

Everyone sat down. Steak was served. Bottles of wine were opened. There had been so much back-and-forth, but finally Nash was content. He was quite certain how the opening seven picks would go, and that New Jersey was set to grab Kobe Bryant without much drama. There would, of course, be the oohs and aahs of the Nets selecting their first-ever straight-from-high-school player. But the media would love the kid at his introductory press conference. He was poised and wise and savvy beyond his years. There was the whole dad-played-in-the-NBA angle. It was terrific. No, better than terrific. It was . . .

"I have an announcement to make!"

Fuck.

Calipari stood up at the table. Everyone ceased speaking. "If Kerry Kittles is on the board," he said, "we're drafting him. And if he's not there, we're taking Kobe Bryant."

Nash felt his heart sink. Kittles was a very solid player who would go on to average 14.1 points over eight NBA seasons. He was good without ever being great, steady without ever being spectacular. In fact, Kittles and Bryant had played pickup a couple of times at Saint Joseph's University, and the Villanova star was impressed. "Kobe was amazing," Kittles later said. "If I'm making the decision, I'm probably drafting him over me."

In hindsight, Nash felt that 100 forces of NBA evil were conspiring against him. Calipari was a young, dumb, easily intimidated coach who knew not whereof he spoke. Falk wanted his client happy. The New Jersey owners didn't aspire to babysit a child. Kobe Bryant wanted to sell sneakers, and Arm Tellem (via Sonny Vaccaro) thought the best place to sell sneakers was Los Angeles. The Charlotte Hornets sought to acquire an in-his-prime NBA center, and the Lakers wanted to acquire the best young prospect their talent evaluators had ever seen. "I still can't believe Cal let a high school kid bully him," Jayson Williams, the Nets' power forward, later said. "I mean, Cal was a bit of a bully himself. So to give up one of the five best players in NBA history because he threatened you? That's pretty weak, man. That's pretty damn weak."

Not long after Kittles went to New Jersey ("I was thrilled!" Kittles said years later), West was on the phone with Bass, the Hornets' general manager. If all went as planned, and the Mavs, Pacers, Warriors, and Cavaliers didn't grab the high school phenom with their picks, the Hornets would take Bryant at 13, then swap him to Los Angeles for Vlade Divac, who had averaged 12.9 points and 8.6 rebounds in 1995–96. At just 28, he remained one of the NBA's best centers. ("We offered Elden Campbell," said Harris. "But it had to be Vlade.")

West waited.

And waited.

And waited.

"I couldn't have been any more nervous," he said later. "We had a lot riding on this."

When, with the 12th slot, Cleveland grabbed Wright State center Vitaly Potapenko, West shouted gleefully. He dialed Bass's number.

"Bob, we have a deal?" he said.

"Yup," Bass replied. "We sure do."

West immediately called Jerry Buss. "Believe it or not," he crowed, "I think you've got the best player in the draft."

That night, when the final selection was made, Nash was approached by Rod Thorn, the NBA's executive vice president of basketball operations. "I really thought you were taking Kobe Bryant," he said. "So did Jerry West."

Nash could barely conceal the pain.

"So did I," he said, shuffling toward the exit doors. "Fuck. So did I."

3

Kazaam!

O n February 11, 1995, Paul Michael Glaser met Shaquille O'Neal.
Cinema would never be the same.

Best known for his portrayal of Detective Dave Starsky in the 1970s
hit TV show *Starsky and Hutch*, Glaser was in Phoenix for the following day's NBA All-Star Game, which he would be attending with his son,
Jake. The meetup between actor and athlete took place at a restaurant
near America West Arena — arranged by a mutual friend who knew of
O'Neal's desire to enhance his Hollywood cred and Glaser's desire to show
his son a good time.

After shaking hands and exchanging pleasantries, the 5-foot-10 actor,
who was transitioning his career toward directing, glanced upward at
O'Neal's eyes and said, bluntly, "You look like a genie to me."

And that's how this whole Los Angeles Lakers 1990s dynasty thing began.

Sort of.

One year earlier, O'Neal had made his cinematic debut, playing Neon
in the Nick Nolte–led basketball film *Blue Chips*. The movie was neither
particularly good nor particularly bad, and O'Neal's performance (stretching his chops to play a highly recruited basketball player) was no more
or less interesting than an office manager's desk lamp. Glaser, however,
saw something sparkly in the large man with the physical presence and
blinding smile. In fact, he had been on a desperate search for something

sparkly for the past few months, ever since his wife, Elizabeth, entered the final throes of her 13-year battle with AIDS. Glaser's life had been one tragic moment after another — Elizabeth contracted HIV in 1981 via a contaminated blood transfusion while giving birth. The virus was passed on to their infant daughter Ariel, who died seven years later. Jake was born in 1984, and he, too, contracted HIV from Elizabeth in utero.

"Paul had so much darkness," said screenwriter Roger Soffer. "He was seeking something bright."

Shaquille O'Neal was bright. And bold. And powerful. And perfect. Despite his enormousness and intimidating on-court scowl, you wanted to hug the man, just as one wants to hug an oversized FAO Schwarz teddy bear. While his wife was in her last days (she died in December 1994), Glaser found himself absorbed by this idea that kept circulating inside his mind — a story involving an imaginary 3,000-year-old hip-hop genie and a little boy. The saga became an obsession — an ode to youthful joy and larger-than-life bliss and the power of goodness, of love, of compassion, of eternal happiness. Glaser didn't merely aspire to create the film. He *needed* it to be created.

Hence, before long, O'Neal found himself cast in the title role of *Kazaam* — a well-intentioned, beautifully motivated cinematic think piece . . . that makes *Ishtar* seem downright *Casablanca*-esque.

Everything about *Kazaam* is a dumpster fire. The film's two writers, Soffer and Christian Ford, were handed a start-immediately shooting schedule before a single word had been applied to the page. (Ford recalled, "I woke up one Saturday morning at six o'clock, and friggin' Starsky is outside my window screaming, 'Wake up! Time to get to work!'") Glaser was a walking stick of TNT who spent his days on the Los Angeles–based set either screaming, laughing, or sobbing. At one point he was fired by the studio, then rehired, then fired again, then rehired. "It was a time in my life when . . . I wasn't entirely there, you know?" Glaser said years later. "I mean I was getting the job done, doing the best I could. But my son had just lost a mother. I had just lost a wife. And so I was just doing the best I could to stay afloat."

Francis Capra, the 12-year-old who played opposite O'Neal as Max, turned down an offer to co-star with Robin Williams in *Jack* so he could take the gig, then, one morning on set, accidentally caught on fire before shooting. O'Neal was asked to rap lyrics such as: "My name is Kazaam / I've got the whole plan / So listen to the man / 'Cause I'm the Sultan of Slam." On one particularly dark day, James Acheson, the thespian enlisted to play Nick, announced, "To hell with this fucking bullshit!," stormed off the set, and walked the nine miles to Los Angeles International Airport. "It all got very weird," recalled Ally Walker, who played Capra's mother. "V-e-r-y weird."

If the project was doomed, someone forgot to tell Shaquille O'Neal. Through the bumps and bruises, screaming and shouting, the film's star had the time of his life. Interscope paid him $7 million to be a pajamas-wearing genie, and agreed to enough scheduling flexibility so he could come and go as off-season basketball workouts demanded. On set, O'Neal was a bundle of joy. He gifted the cast and crew with sneakers, T-shirts, and CDs and would often wrap shoots by heading to Capra's house for Kentucky Fried Chicken and marathon *Tekken* battles on the PlayStation 1. Soffer's wife, Martha, was pregnant at the time, and one day O'Neal grabbed a marker and drew a to-scale basketball hoop across her belly. "It was like having a little brother with you on a job," said Walker. "He was sweet and enthusiastic, even as we were making this pretty bad movie."

Kazaam hit theaters in the summer of 1996, and the result was not wonderful. It grossed $18.9 million, and *Empire Magazine*'s Barry McIlheney spoke for the masses when he wrote that the movie was "mind numbingly bad. It has no redeeming features unless you like big men dressed in camp genie costumes."

And yet . . . O'Neal didn't care. He dug the buzz, the excitement, the getups, the special effects. He dug walking the red carpet at the movie's Hollywood premiere. Seeing himself on billboards was a little boy's biggest dream bursting to life. "It was great — all of it," O'Neal recalled years later. "I loved Los Angeles. I actually lived there when I first left college. During the off-season, L.A. was the place to be for marketing, for commercials. And you'd see everybody. I saw Eddie Murphy walk into a restaurant in all leather. All fucking leather. Being in Los Angeles taught you how to be a superstar. I saw the stars in L.A. and thought, *This is what I want!*"

In short, the spotlight loved Shaquille O'Neal as much as Shaquille O'Neal loved the spotlight.

And the spotlight was in Southern California.

That's how Leonard Armato, O'Neal's Hollywood-based agent, thought of these things, and it was hard to argue with. The whole make-my-client-a-global-phenomenon-to-rival-all-global-phenomena concept first hit him back in the spring of 1992, not long after O'Neal wrapped his junior season at Louisiana State and decided to enter the upcoming NBA draft. At the time, O'Neal was being hailed as the most dominant college center since Kareem Abdul-Jabbar, a quick, powerful, unstoppable force who averaged 24.1 points and 14 rebounds for the Tigers. O'Neal's dunks were nightly ESPN highlights. "He was the most unique player I ever had," said Dale Brown, LSU's coach. "So many surprising things he could do."

Despite the siren call of dozens of agents promising all sorts of riches, O'Neal had chosen Armato based on his integrity and stand-up reputation. Throughout O'Neal's college career, Armato would come to occasional games, but only to show his face and make clear his future interest. There were no underhanded payments, no blathering compliments, no false sincerity. "I told his parents they could always ask my advice," Armato said, "but they couldn't give me anything of value in return." O'Neal's decision was actually made on the morning of November 30, 1991, shortly before LSU and UNLV were scheduled to battle in Las Vegas. Armato was in town to watch his hoped-to-be future client play, and as he sat on his bed inside the Mandalay Bay, a note was slipped beneath the door. "I opened it up," Armato recalled, "and smiled." It read: "Hi. Please don't tell anyone I'm writing you this letter, but I'm going to come out after my junior year and I want you to be my agent. Really, don't tell anyone."

Armato was giddy. As the draft approached, he decided to develop a hyper-specific plan for his newest client. To most people, the all-time greatest athletic-product pitchman was Michael Jordan, the Chicago

Bulls guard who earned millions upon millions per year in endorsements, from companies ranging from Nike to McDonald's. Armato admired what David Falk, Jordan's agent, had done for his client. But he also recognized a slight flaw. "Jordan was the king, and he made a load of money," Armato said. "But he never owned anything. None of it was his. So I said to Shaq, 'Let's turn you into a brand and have intellectual property so that you can own what you do and spread across entertainment, sports, technology.'"

On June 24, 1992, the Orlando Magic used the first overall selection to pick O'Neal, and over his initial four seasons he surpassed expectations. He was a four-time All-Star who averaged 27.2 points, 12.5 rebounds, and 2.8 blocks. In a league filled with dominant big men (Patrick Ewing, David Robinson, Hakeem Olajuwon, Alonzo Mourning, Dikembe Mutombo), O'Neal emerged as king. "When he'd go up and dunk, it reminded me of a Christmas tree, with defenders hanging off of him like ornaments," said Greg Kite, Orlando's backup center. "Or they were the bowling pins, and he was an enormous 300-pound ball. I'd never seen anything like it." The Magic organization was only three years old when O'Neal arrived and had never posted a winning season. That changed immediately — with him at center, the team won 41, 50, 57, and 60 games and reached the 1995 NBA Finals. Best of all, he was a PR executive's dream. The Magic placed O'Neal front and center in every marketing campaign, had him make an endless string of appearances and talks. His nickname — Shaq — was worth millions, but the outsized jolliness that accompanied the word was priceless. In 1991–92, Orlando's ugly black-and-white pinstriped jerseys ranked near the middle of overall NBA sales. With Shaq's arrival, they turned beautiful and trailed only the black-and-red Bulls' duds made famous by Jordan. "Traveling with our team became like traveling with the Beatles," said Alex Martins, the Magic's media relations director. "Regardless of the time of day, you'd have hundreds waiting outside the hotels when we played on the road. They always use the term 'larger than life' to describe people, but he was genuinely larger than life."

O'Neal loved it. He and Dennis Tracey, his pal and college teammate, lived in a 35,000-square-foot lakefront mansion in Isleworth, and when he wasn't playing basketball or hanging with his neighbors (including Tiger Woods and Ken Griffey Jr.) he could be found swimming in his pool, jet-skiing, hitting the clubs, or recording his debut hip-hop album, *Shaq Diesel*, which was released by Jive Records in 1993. "I remember getting calls from his neighbors, asking me to ask him to turn down the volume on his music," said Selena Roberts, a writer for the *Orlando Sentinel*. "I'd ask if they were going to file a complaint. It was always 'No, because he's so beloved by everyone in the neighborhood.'"

Meanwhile, Armato's marketing plan was coming to fruition. O'Neal signed a $20 million sneaker deal with Reebok, as well as a multimillion-dollar deal to promote Pepsi. All the while, O'Neal retained ownership of what he called the "Dunkman logo" — a silhouette of Shaq hanging from a bent rim. "Whenever Shaq was used in an ad, the company had to use one of the trademarks we created," Armato said. "It made him a very wealthy man."

As the years passed, however, the appeal of Orlando — a charmless, in-the-middle-of-nowhere city that was home to Disney World and 12,471 strip malls — began to wane. "There was nothing to do there," said Susan Slusser, an *Orlando Sentinel* beat writer. "Just nothing." One season after O'Neal's arrival, the Magic added rookie point guard Anfernee "Penny" Hardaway from Memphis State, and while he and Shaq formed one of the league's great duos, there was an ever-increasing level of friction over who ran the show. Such was the by-product of big-fish-small-pond-itis, where a limited media pool sought any daytime drama it could find. "Shaq couldn't handle a guy as good or better than he was getting a lot of the attention," said Brian Schmitz, a *Sentinel* writer. "Even though Penny was a quiet guy, he was very talented, and Shaq couldn't deal."

As O'Neal's New Jersey–based family spent more time in Orlando, the Magic star seemed to like the city less. The spotlight was dim. The chance for media exposure was limited. The quick flight from New Jersey meant an ever-flowing stream of relatives, which meant an ever-flowing stream of people asking for favors and attention. There were aunts, uncles, first cousins, second cousins, third cousins, fourth cousins, non-cousins pretending to be cousins. "Everyone wanted in," Tracey said. "I'm not saying Shaq always wanted to leave for Los Angeles, but moving away became appealing. There comes a point, after yet another person expects to be on your payroll, when you start thinking, *Enough*."

This was music to the ears of Armato, who — from the day O'Neal declared for the NBA draft — wanted his star client closer to Disneyland than Disney World. "It was constant brainwashing from Leonard Armato to Shaq," said Tracey. "Every year — 'L.A., L.A., L.A.' It's like when you're the kid and your mother spends all the time telling you how bad your dad is, and how you want to be with her. You start to believe it all. It was always 'Shaq, come to L.A.'"

Back in the days leading up to the 1992 draft, O'Neal and Tracey were at the agent's Brentwood, California, home when the selection order was determined. It came down to three teams — Orlando, Minnesota, and Charlotte — and when the Timberwolves were slotted third, O'Neal and Tracey let out a cheer. "Yes!" Tracey screamed. "We're not gonna freeze our balls off!" O'Neal noted that he would be happy with either Charlotte or Orlando, to which Armato replied, "Don't worry — eventually we're going to get you to L.A."

What?

"Shaq," he said, "you need to be in Hollywood. You're a star."

Now, in the wake of the *Kazaam* experience, O'Neal was beginning to consider Armato's thinking. But it was more than just the lure of the bright lights, of Armato saying "Hollywood" in between (*Hollywood*) every few words (*Hollywood*) when they (*Hollywood*) spoke to (*Hollywood*) one another. In the summer of 1996, there was no maximum salary provision in the league's collective bargaining agreement — meaning that, while there was a salary cap of $24.3 million, a team could spend whatever it needed in order to retain a player. As a free agent who just happened to be the NBA's most dominant physical presence, O'Neal (logically) assumed Orlando would do everything within its power to bring him back into the fold. The team, after all, was young, exciting, built for a sustained run as an Eastern Conference power. Along with O'Neal and Hardaway, the roster boasted one of the game's elite three-point gunners (Dennis Scott), a dangerous shooting guard (Nick Anderson), a power forward with three championship rings from his Chicago days (Horace Grant), and a deep, well-stocked bench. Sure, the Magic had been swept by the Bulls in the 1996 Eastern Conference Finals. But this was the dynastic run of Jordan, Scottie Pippen, and Dennis Rodman. There was no shame in such a setback, and Orlando was well positioned to be an elite franchise for the next decade. "We were on the verge of something amazing," said Scott, O'Neal's closest friend on the team. "If you look at the talent, the age, the finances, the Orlando Magic should have owned the NBA for the next decade."

All the team had to do was pay Shaquille O'Neal what he deserved.

This wasn't a complicated proposition. Though one can debate the merits of surrendering boatloads of cash to, say, a 6-foot-4 shooting guard who averages 18 points per game, or a burly center with shot-blocking gifts but limited low-post moves, there was only one Shaq, and he was worth a ton of dough.

That's why, when Orlando made an initial offer of $54 million over four years, O'Neal and Co. simultaneously laughed and cried. "The ownership was so naive, it was painful," said Schmitz. "They couldn't wrap their heads around giving $100 million to a 24-year-old kid." The bid was comical. First because, in 1996, it just wasn't all that much money for a superstar entering his prime. But second because both Alonzo Mourning of the Miami Heat and Juwan Howard of the Washington Bullets were about to receive seven-year, $105 million offers from their respective franchises. Those men were excellent players — Mourning a future Hall of Famer and one of the league's top five centers, Howard a consistent low-post scorer with a bevy of moves and a recent All-Star Game appearance. But neither was in O'Neal's class. "I listened in on the first calls when we were negotiating with the Magic, and they were treating Shaq like a run-of-the-mill free agent, not a generational talent," said Joel Corry, Armato's assistant. "I remember thinking to myself, *Do they not get this? Do they not understand the magnitude of the player?*" During one of those conversations, John Gabriel, Orlando's general manager, repeatedly insulted O'Neal's defense and rebounding skills. "It was just weird," said Corry. "Do you not know what you have? Do you not understand how good Shaquille O'Neal is? They were acting as if he were a football team's second wide receiver."

As soon as he hung up, Corry turned to a colleague and asked, "Do they even want to sign Shaq?"

It was a fair question.

Orlando was a peculiarly run operation — it stressed adherence to family values and community but often had a funny way of showing it. "I'll put it this way," said Tracey. "The Orlando Magic didn't know their assholes from a hole in the wall." The team's owner, Rich DeVos, was the multibillionaire co-founder of Amway, a company that espoused fundamentalist Christian ideals while being accused of running a pyramid-scheme-type system. DeVos was a huge believer in loyalty. He felt that, without question, employees needed to be loyal to a company, that players needed to be loyal to a team.

Practicing such ideals, however, was complicated. Earlier that April, O'Neal had left the Magic for a few days after his grandmother, Odessa Chambliss, died from cancer. It was a terrible shock. Chambliss was a Jesus-loving woman who had helped raise a young Shaquille. After signing his first professional contract, O'Neal built her a mansion in Newark, New Jersey. When he learned of her passing, "I went downstairs and cried by myself for three hours," O'Neal recalled. "I had never lost anyone close to me. I cried and cried."

The funeral was held on a Thursday, and the Magic were slated to play next on the following Sunday. When O'Neal failed to call the team with a precise schedule of his return, management unloaded, blasting him as juvenile and unreliable. After that, "I had no desire to play for the Magic," he recalled. "None whatsoever."

He was able to move on, but the slight stuck. So did the feeling among Magic players that the organization was a bit, well, racist. Or, if not racist per se, racially tone deaf. The front office was all white. The coaching staff was all white (save for Tree Rollins, a player-coach in 1994–95). The fan base was 99 percent white. Though famous for the glitz and pizzazz of the Magic Kingdom, Orlando is a fairly right-wing corner of America, where the N-word (at least in the mid-1990s) was thrown around far too regularly. Members of the Magic didn't overtly accuse DeVos and family of being outright bigots, but it was discussed more than once in the locker room. There was an air of *up here vs. down there,* as if these large black men with physical talents should consider themselves lucky to have been chosen by the DeVos gang.

O'Neal *felt* it.

So when the Magic offered a paltry $54 million, he didn't just view it as an opening salvo in contract negotiations. No, to O'Neal and Armato and Tracey and the entire Shaq crew, it was an effort to put a superstar in his place. Even worse, the team backed its hesitancy at offering O'Neal enormous dollars by explaining how, in another year, Hardaway would be a free agent, and the Magic *needed* him to stay in the fold. According to O'Neal, Gabriel literally told him, "We can't give you more than Penny. We don't want to upset Penny."

"When he said that, I was out," O'Neal recalled. "Inside I was fuming. I said to myself, *I'm not messing with these guys. They're worried about Penny's feelings being hurt?*" (Years later, Gabriel said he always thought O'Neal had used the Hardaway talk as rationale to leave. "We had to cut up the business between two superstars who were both going to make $100 million," Gabriel said. "Shaquille didn't want to hear that. But it's far more complicated than he led people to believe.")

Though Armato was all about California, he had O'Neal list the franchises he would consider playing for. There were five: Lakers, Knicks, Pistons, Heat, and Hawks.* The one that appealed most was Los Angeles. On May 30, 1996, O'Neal was spotted having lunch with Lakers guard Nick Van Exel on the Sunset Strip, and two weeks later he took a visit to Rodeo Drive, where spectators were shocked to see a 7-foot shopper in their midst. The *Orlando Sentinel* caught wind of the superstar's Califor-

---

* Atlanta, strangely, was appealing because of the presence of guard Mookie Blaylock and forward Christian Laettner — both of whom O'Neal (wrongly) considered to be foundational players.

nia excursions and led with the headline SAY IT AIN'T SO! SHAQ CHIL-LIN' ON RODEO DRIVE, O-RIOTS, O-SORROW. During this time, O'Neal also started house hunting — the first definitive nod to the Lakers that they might get their man. It went unreported in the media, but Jeanie Buss, daughter of team owner Jerry Buss, was in the process of selling her Manhattan Beach property. "Shaq came to look," Jeanie recalled. "I don't even think he knew it was my house — I wasn't there when he looked. But I thought, *Oh my God, this must be a sign!*"

Inside Orlando's offices, executives began to panic. The idea of O'Neal actually leaving had never truly crossed their minds. The Magic drafted Shaq, nurtured Shaq, built a quality product around Shaq. The team owed Shaq nothing. *He* owed *the team* everything. That's the way the thinking went in Orlando — a franchise that, pre-O'Neal, never possessed a marquee star to coddle and nurture and placate.* DeVos owned the team, but it seemed as if he also felt he owned the players. "He didn't get it," Dennis Scott said. "Someone needed to say to him, 'You made your money selling soap and dish products, but this is professional basketball and this is a beef and we have him in his pre-prime years. *Pay him.*'" From the vantage point of the Orlando Magic, perhaps the initial contract offer was underwhelming, but that was how these things went. *Offer, counter, another offer, another counter.* Brian Hill, the Magic head coach, had warned ownership that Armato was pressuring his client to go for the big-market, multimedia splendor of Hollywood, yet his cries fell upon deaf ears.

When asked, O'Neal maintained that he was open to staying in Orlando. But he was not, unless the team was going to pay him astronomical amounts of money. The official NBA free agency period opened on July 9, 1996, and the Lakers wasted no time. The franchise presented O'Neal with a seven-year, $95.5 million package with an out clause after the third season.

The Magic — threatened, bewildered, panicked, caught off guard —

---

* Apologies to Mark Acres and Morlon Wiley.

fired back with a $100 million deal, a pathetic offer that infuriated the star. When that backfired, DeVos tried to right the ship by putting forth a contract that would pay $115 million over seven years. Jerry West, the Lakers' executive vice president, immediately grew despondent over his organization's suddenly diminished chances. When Los Angeles agreed to send Vlade Divac to Charlotte in the Kobe Bryant trade, the thinking was that O'Neal would replace the departed Serbian in the middle of the Lakers' attack. Yes, it was probably overly optimistic. But West aimed high and believed in the power of the purple and gold. And now, with the Magic joining in the ritualistic throwing of ludicrous dollars toward a tall man, Los Angeles seemed less inevitable.

And then, *it* happened.

On the morning of July 16, 1996, readers of the *Orlando Sentinel*, the city's daily newspaper of record, were greeted by a front-page poll question: IS SHAQUILLE O'NEAL WORTH $115 MILLION OVER 7 SEASONS? The ineloquently phrased inquiry ("Sophomoric," said Brian Schmitz, the writer; "*that's* the right word") was the brainchild of Lynn Hoppes, an editor at the paper who wanted to engage readers in what was an increasingly heated debate throughout central Florida. In the pre-Internet world of polling, consumers were asked to call 420-5022 to vote yes, 420-5044 to vote no.

When polling closed, 91.3 percent of 5,111 participants voted no — Shaquille O'Neal was not deserving of $115 million for seven years. The whole enterprise was preposterous, misleading, and grade D journalism. There was no context. Was Shaquille O'Neal worth $115 million over seven years? Of course not — because no one on the planet is worth $115 million over seven years. Not Pamela Anderson, not Bill Clinton, not Stanley Herz, America's finest executive search recruiter. The money was silly, and even O'Neal and Armato (in private) would admit as much.

But in the context of the National Basketball Association, where Alonzo Mourning and Juwan Howard were making $105 million, was Shaquille O'Neal worth $115 million? Yes, he was.

Later that day, Rex Hoggard, a 27-year-old *Sentinel* staff writer who had been with the newspaper for only a couple of months, was told by Hoppes to write a piece about the poll results. "It wasn't until after lunch that I first actually glanced at the question and thought, *Oh, this won't go well*," Hoggard recalled. "It was just *so* negative." In particular, Hoggard recalled a good number of the respondents leaving racist voice messages. It was gross stuff— *How dare the entitled Negro not be grateful for all we've given him*. On July 17, Hoggard's piece, headlined SHAQ ATTACK: CALL-ERS JUST SAY NO, ran in the paper. The writer knew there would be some backlash. But not *this* level of backlash. Readers who wanted O'Neal to stay with the Magic were livid. Executives with the Magic were also livid. (Gabriel called the newspaper to chew out the sports staff.) Worst of all —O'Neal was incensed.

"It stung a lot," he said years later. "A *lot*. I wouldn't say it hurt me, but I don't like being underappreciated."

That summer, O'Neal was a member of the United States men's Olympic basketball team. The Games, being held in Atlanta, were set to begin on July 19, and in the lead-up the squad was training in Orlando. When Hoggard's piece on the poll came out, O'Neal's Olympic teammates —NBA veterans who knew the importance of getting paid—teed off. In particular Charles Barkley, the Phoenix Suns forward and resident trash talker, refused to hold back. "Are you fucking kidding me?" he told O'Neal. "You bring glory to this redneck, one-horse town, and this is what they think of you? Get out as soon as you can. Fuck these people."

It was harsh. But it was also correct.

"I picked up the phone at one point and called John Gabriel," said Dennis Scott. "I screamed, 'What the hell are you doing? What the hell are you people doing?' It was crazy. But as poorly as the Magic handled it, that poll was the straw that broke the camel's back. Shaq can deal with a lot. He can. But when the whole city is saying he's not worth it . . . nope. He was gone. And I didn't blame him."

The Magic still believed they could appease O'Neal. So, for that matter, did Jerry West, who really didn't want to go with the team's second choices at center, an eccentric Clipper named Brian Williams and Dale Davis of

the Indiana Pacers. Right around the time the *Sentinel* poll was being conducted, West reached out to Stu Jackson, general manager of Vancouver,
to make an offer he believed could not be refused. In exchange for two Diet
Pepsis, a $25 Tim Hortons gift card, and two future second-round draft
picks,* the Lakers would surrender forward George Lynch and shooting
guard Anthony Peeler.

Both men were talented, committed, and in their mid-twenties. Both
men would serve as automatic upgrades to a franchise that finished a
league-worst 15-67 the prior year. And, from West's vantage point, the
departure of both men would clear up another $3.63 million in salary
cap space to add to the O'Neal offer. "Those guys were good players," West
said. "They weren't super players, but they were good players. They were
NBA players. But we needed to get Shaquille, and that was the only way.
Finding creative methods to have more available money."

The Grizzlies were hesitant to pull the trigger. Then Del Harris called
Larry Riley, his former assistant coach in Milwaukee who was now Vancouver's director of player personnel. The men went back — Riley had
coached two of Harris's children; Harris had delivered a eulogy at the
funeral for Riley's son. "I was at a pay phone in Long Beach," Harris recalled. "I said, 'Larry, this is a no-brainer. You're trying to develop a team
and we're about to hand you the sixth and eighth men off a team that won
53 games. Don't be stubborn.'"

The trade was consummated on the morning of July 16. One of the first
to learn it might have gone down was Gabriel, who called Jackson's office
in Vancouver, hoping the rumors were incorrect. The executive assistant
to the general manager answered.

GABRIEL: This is John Gabriel, down in Orlando. Is Stu there?
ASSISTANT: I'm sorry. He's not available right now.
GABRIEL: Please don't tell me he's at a press conference. Please don't . . .
ASSISTANT: I'm sorry, John.

---

* Actually, no soda or gift cards were involved. Just two second-round picks.

The blowback was fierce. Jackson, trying to create a winning organization from liquid sludge, was hammered for taking two salaries off the Los Angeles payroll and allowing the Lakers to now offer (gulp) $120 million. "But what was I supposed to do?" he said years later. "I had so little talent. We weren't going to be challenging for a championship. We just needed to improve." Lynch, a third-year pro who averaged 3.8 points and 2.8 rebounds coming off the bench, was driving down the 405 to host a basketball camp in Palos Verdes. His girlfriend called and said, "Did you know you were just traded?"

"To where?" he asked.

"Vancouver," she replied.

Lynch was livid. "Jerry should have told me in person," Lynch said. "It was upsetting."

Yet of all the anger the trade created, nothing matched the reactions of people inside the offices of the Orlando Magic, who understood the intent behind Lynch-and-Peeler-to-Vancouver. Shortly after the deal was completed, the Magic sent Alex Martins, the media relations director and a man who maintained a solid relationship with O'Neal, to the Disney Institute, where the Olympic squad was wrapping up before departing for Atlanta. DeVos had written a letter to O'Neal and placed it inside an envelope with the organization's final offer — $115 million over seven years. Martins was instructed to hand the note to Shaq. So he did. "I begged him to read it," Martins recalled. "He took it and walked out to get on the plane to Georgia. I honestly don't know if he looked at it."

Gabriel wasn't willing to go down without a last fight. He reached DeVos and said, "We need to get a G4 in the air as soon as possible!" Armato was already in Atlanta with his girlfriend, the Olympic beach volleyball star Holly McPeak. DeVos hedged a bit at the request. Earlier that day he'd told an *Orlando Sentinel* reporter, "If they are trying to squeeze another million or two out of this, then the Lakers can pay it." He was sick and tired of the whole back-and-forth. But, with DeVos's grudging blessing, Gabriel and Bob Vander Weide, the team president, made the 1-hour, 25-minute flight to the Peach State and found Armato in the sand by a lake, decked out in T-shirt and sweatpants and collecting the errant balls his love hammered over a net.

Gabriel was wearing a suit and tie. He walked across the beachy surface and told Armato the Magic would pay Shaquille O'Neal $115 million.

The agent listened, but didn't really listen.

It was too late.

"Thanks for nothing," Gabriel said as he walked off.

"Why do you say that?" Armato replied.

"Because," Gabriel said, "I know it's over."

On July 17, 1996, at precisely 2:15 a.m., O'Neal agreed to play with Los Angeles for $120 million over seven years, the biggest contract in the history of professional basketball. The news was a bombshell across the sports landscape. There were big signings and bigger signings. This was right there with Reggie Jackson joining the New York Yankees, Nolan Ryan becoming a Houston Astro. The Associated Press distributed a story headlined FROM KAREEM TO KAZAAM: LAKERS STAND TALL AGAIN. Because the agreement coincided with the first full day of the Olympics, O'Neal chose to say nothing. His Summer Games teammates, on the other hand, couldn't stop talking. Penny Hardaway learned the news and buried his head in his chest. "It's kind of devastating," he admitted, then came a pained pause — probably to consider the Magic with Jon Koncak at center. "You have to wish him the best."

The following afternoon, West and O'Neal convened a press conference in Atlanta at the Reebok corporate tent near Centennial Olympic Park. The newest Laker would switch numbers from 32 (which belonged to Magic Johnson) to 34. Ticket prices at the Forum would bump up a bit. He was excited to play with Nick Van Exel and Eddie Jones. He liked purple and gold. He smiled a lot. He waved.

He . . . lied.

"It was a very, very tough decision," O'Neal said with a straight face. "I said all along that Orlando was my first option, and this was one of the hardest decisions of my life. It was very hard, but I think I made the right decision." He added that the move had nothing to do with the newspaper poll (wrong). Or money (wrong). Or celebrity (wrong). Or the dullness of Orlando (wrong). That he thought the Lakers' high-flying, fast-moving system was more befitting of his talents than the Magic's, um, high-flying, fast-moving system that perfectly befitted his talents.

"It was all nonsense in my opinion," said George Diaz, the *Orlando Sentinel* columnist. "He left because California offered something Orlando couldn't.

"He left for the glory."

4

Formation

T he mythology began here.

On the day.

At the moment.

Only nobody knew it.

As the years passed and the legend grew, it became an increasingly daunting challenge to separate fact from fiction; giant from gnat. That's what happens when we anoint our heroes with nicknames and expectations and an unusual largeness generally reserved for skyscrapers and grand canyons.

But here, inside this peculiarly shaped building in Long Beach, California, we knew far too little to understand what would ultimately unfold. It was July 18, 1996, 22 days after the Los Angeles Lakers drafted a high school kid named Kobe Bryant and a week after the team formally introduced him to the world with a splashy, pastry-filled press conference. (En route to the event, Bryant was asked on the plane whether he was an athlete. "Well, I play for Lower Merion High School," he responded, then quickly corrected himself. "You know, I'm a Los Angeles Laker.") The NBA's annual Fila Summer Pro League was under way at the Pyramid, on the campus of Long Beach State, and through his first three games the early take was that the Lakers' star rookie had played well, though hardly magically. He scored 27 in his debut vs. the Pistons, then 22 more in an exhibition against the Chinese national team. In a weird battle with a Warriors/Pacers hybrid squad, he added 15. It was all plenty good but — when it came to discipline and court sense — left much to be desired.

"Right before Kobe arrived, Jerry West called me into his office," recalled forward Corie Blount, new to the Lakers after two seasons in Chicago. "He told me, 'Look, the young fella is coming to town. Help him get acclimated and make him feel comfortable.' But I don't think he needed much. Kobe knew what he was doing."

This time the Lakers would be hosting a Phoenix Suns squad featuring the immortal likes of Russ Millard, Paul Lusk, and John Coker. This exemplified, for the most part, the NBA's off-season offerings: borderline pros from schools like Bucknell and Delaware fighting for a look, a glance, enough statistical juice to leave here, fly 14 hours to Kiev, and sign a sweet deal with SK Mykolaiv. Sure, hope was real, but it was also illusory. Players the likes of Lusk (slow Southern Illinois guard) and Millard (slow Iowa power forward) would not spend years battling Scottie Pippen and Clyde Drexler as members of the Suns. They were basketball tackling dummies, and the summer league was a chance to get tackled.

Within those confines, however, the summer league also served as an unofficial coming-out party. Or, to be more precise, a formal, post-press-conference announcement to the professional world. Seventeen years earlier, a 6-foot-9 Michigan State guard named Earvin "Magic" Johnson had been drafted first overall by the Lakers. He was as famous as a college basketball player could be — a coast-to-coast superstar, a *Sports Illustrated* cover subject, a do-it-all hoops wizard who led the Spartans to an unforgettable NCAA title over Larry Bird and Indiana State. As with Kobe Bryant, there was the press conference, the interviews, the expectations. Yet even Johnson — toothy smile, George McGinnis size — wasn't a real Laker until July 27, 1980, when he trotted onto the court inside the Cal State Los Angeles gymnasium for a summer league game and scored 24 points, with 9 assists and 4 steals. The moment screamed, "I am here, and I mean business!"

Just as Kobe Bryant wasn't a real Laker until he trotted onto the court to face Phoenix — and screamed, "I am here, and I mean business!"

For the most part, the Los Angeles roster was a collection of misfit toys. There was David Booth, the long-ago DePaul forward in his fifth fruitless year of chasing the NBA dream. There was Blount, the anonymous forward recently sold by Chicago to the Lakers for a small wad of cash. There was Juaquin Hawkins, a defensive specialist out of Long Beach State who shared a name with former St. Louis Cardinals pitcher Joaquín Andújar (as well as the same odds of making the opening-day roster). There was Derek Fisher, the little-known Arkansas–Little Rock point guard selected by Los Angeles with the 24th pick in the first round.

So as the afternoon began and the anticipation built, and roughly 4,200 fans filed into the dimly lit 5,000-seat arena, there was a question that — even three games into summer league — continued to hang over the building. What could the high school kid *really* do?

"Seriously, no one had any idea," said Booth. "It was all brand-new."

The starting lineups were announced, beginning with Booth, then former Temple forward Derrick Battie. Neither man elicited so much as an inspired clap. Blount, owner of 19 lifetime NBA starts, was introduced next as "the man in the middle!" — and his name was familiar enough that three or four attendees sounded somewhat happy. Fisher, donning No. 9 and sporting a perfectly executed flattop, received a strong level of applause.

Then . . .

"And at the other guard, from Lower Merion High in Pennsylvania, six-five, number 32, Kooooobeeee Bryyyyant!"

He was wearing a blue T-shirt over his jersey and an enormous white wristband on his left forearm, and the likelihood is he was wearing the blue T-shirt over his jersey and sporting the enormous white wristband on his left forearm because none of the others were wearing blue T-shirts over *their* jerseys or sporting enormous white wristbands on *their* left forearms. It was, past and future teammates insist, the way of Kobe Bryant. Standing out. Making deliberate statements, but wanting them to appear undeliberate. He slapped the hands of the other four Lakers starters, huddled briefly, exchanged words with head coach Larry Drew (Del

Harris's top assistant during the regular season), licked his lips, tugged on his baggy gold shorts, removed his blue T-shirt, and sauntered onto the court, where the Suns players awaited.

Being a professional basketball player means looking like a professional basketball player, so the Phoenix starters greeted Bryant nonchalantly, as they did Booth and Battie and the rest — *hey, hey, slap, slap.* But it was not real. Darryl Wilson, the Suns' point guard, was three and a half months removed from leading Mississippi State to the Final Four. He was the Bulldogs' top scorer for three straight seasons and made many of America's best collegiate guards look foolish. "I'll be 100 percent honest — I was thinking, *This kid is straight out of high school and I'm straight out of the Final Four — there is no way he comes out here and dominates,*" Wilson recalled years later. "At least not on me."

Brian Green, a Suns shooting guard who started for two seasons at Nevada, knew the crowd was there for Bryant, as was the TV crew setting up equipment to grab footage for Kobe's upcoming Sprite TV commercial. It was irksome. "I'm 22, which is a big jump from 18," Green said. "You feel like you deserve some of the respect the kid is getting. So did I want to show him what was what? Yeah, I did."

None of the Suns knew what to expect, and as Blount won the opening tip by slapping it toward Bryant, there was an overwhelming air of anticipation. The ball found its way into the hands of Fisher. He dribbled eight times before passing down low to Bryant, who posted up Green. The recent high school grad caught the ball with his left hand, dipped his shoulder, dribbled, dribbled, dribbled, pushed backward with his torso, threw a slight elbow, leaned into Green — and was fouled. During the possession, Booth was wide open at the top of the key. Blount was wide open to his left. Battie stood all alone in the corner. Bryant did not notice, or attempt to notice.

On the Lakers' next possession, Bryant dribbled the entirety of the court, ignored an uncovered Fisher dashing to the right. He stood before Green, who had scored seconds earlier, dribbled, dribbled, dribbled, dribbled. Dribbled, dribbled, dribbled some more. Teammates were waiting, slicing, cutting, writing long letters to family members, and eating seven-course meals. Nothing. Finally, Bryant used Hawkins's pick to slice through the lane and miss a layup. He was fouled by Mario Bennett, the Suns center, and proceeded to hit both free throws — placing him officially on the day's books.

On the Phoenix side, mouths were agape. Wilson couldn't believe the quickness. Green, a self-anointed defensive stopper, saw a gold blur doing whatever he chose. "I've played against very few people who made me think, *Damn, that guy's just better*," Green recalled. "But that's how I felt. He was 18, and he had positioning, footwork, body control. He was a kid and I was a man, but he was better. Simply better. I couldn't stop him, and I hated it."

Bryant was flashy and breathtaking, and more confident than he'd been in the first three games. It made no logical sense. A high school kid playing against adults *should* be tentative and deferential. There has to be a level of uncertainty, right? Yet with Bryant, such tentativeness failed to exist. He didn't merely believe he belonged. No, he believed he was the absolute best player on the court, in the league, on the planet. He knew he was good for 30 points per night — *on an off day*. "You could see the swagger about his walk," Drew recalled. "He was a confident kid who didn't shy away, who had no fears about going against pro players." Against the Suns, there were zero pauses or delays. He seemed to have made a decisive decision that, on this day, he would shoot first, shoot second, shoot third — and pass only if a brick wall fell onto the court.

Brian Tolbert, a feisty Suns guard out of Eastern Michigan, split time with Wilson, his summer league roommate. He began the third quarter concentrating on Bryant, and thought maybe — just maybe — he could slow the Laker down by using some of the hand-checking techniques he'd learned in college under Ben Braun, the longtime Eagles head coach. Tolbert looked at Bryant the same way the others did — a boy in an adult's world. There was an audacity to it all. Who did this child think he was, stepping onto a professional court? So Tolbert lined up across from Bryant, set in his best defensive posture, and . . .

It was ugly.

"The ball swung Kobe's way," Tolbert recalled. "He caught it at the top of the key, maybe a step behind the three-point line. I was waiting for him to make his move and before I knew it — *whoosh!* — he was gone. He cut hard left, dribbled twice, and dunked on Mario Bennett *sooooo* hard."

Bennett, the Suns' first-round pick a season earlier, glared toward Tolbert and screamed, "Whose fucking man was that?"

Tolbert bowed his head. "It was embarrassing," he said. "We didn't know that Kobe Bryant would become *the* Kobe Bryant. He was a kid making us all look stupid."

The NBA's summer league has now been in existence for 50 years, and never before — or since — has there been a single game so dominated by one player. Bryant cleared big men out of the paint so he could shoot. Bryant ignored wide-open teammates so he could create. He shot from all angles, all slants, all gravitational locations. Underhand. Sidearm. Though the slam over Bennett was glorious, his most spectacular play came in the third quarter, when he knifed past Tolbert, took two steps into the paint, rose, and dunked — tomahawk-style — over the hapless Coker, a 7-foot center out of Boise State who had spent 11 glorious minutes on the court with the 1995–96 Suns. Coker waved listlessly as the ball slid through net, and even though the basket was nullified by a foul on Tolbert, the crowd exploded. This was no ordinary athlete. This was Michael Jordan circa 1985. He scored 36 points on 9-of-22 shooting (17 of 21 from the line), along with 5 assists and 7 turnovers.

For all of the kinetic energy surging through the Pyramid, however, to be a Laker summer league player not named Kobe Bean Bryant was to live on a basketball island, isolated, alone, uninvolved, and exasperated. Bryant struck his teammates as aloof and arrogant. He kept to himself, ate with his parents (Joe and Pam Bryant had relocated to California to live with their son, who purchased a $2.5 million six-bedroom home in Pacific Palisades), received a weekly spending allowance from Mommy and Daddy, spent his time either at the gymnasium practicing jump shots or in the weight room getting stronger. He enjoyed Shirley Temples and hip-hop. Otherwise, nothing. "He was mentally prepared to avoid all distractions," said Booth. "It was extreme. You could tell his father had said to him, 'Look, you're going to the NBA. Focus.'"

But it was his refusal to engage teammates *on the court* that was infuriating. Bryant was quick to wave other Lakers out of the post, as well as to cast harsh glares in their direction when he disapproved of a shot selection. He would bark and snarl, moan and overemote. "And he *never* passed the ball," recalled Blount. "That's not an exaggeration. When the ball came to him, he wasn't giving it up." Kurt Rambis, the recently retired power forward who was a new assistant coach with the franchise, heard the gripes from players sick of the selfishness. They were trying to make the team, and Bryant wasn't giving them opportunities to shine. Rambis had none of it. "You guys are the ones passing him the ball," he replied. "Don't pass him the ball, you won't have a problem."

Throughout Bryant's four summer league games, Harris — the stoic Lakers' head coach — sat in the stands, notepad in hand, taking in the action and wondering what exactly one does with a nuclear bomb lacking an instruction manual. Yes, he was curious about Fisher and hopeful that maybe a forward or two might earn a training camp invite, but mainly it was an education on Kobe. Harris was about to begin his 12th season as an NBA head coach, and he had never before added a straight-from-preps phenom. His early conclusion: The kid was supremely talented and not even remotely ready.

"It was obvious the skill was there," Harris said. "But he wasn't prepared for the league. He didn't fit into the NBA game at that time.

"Kobe needed a lot of work."

The Los Angeles Lakers would officially open training camp on October 4, 1996, and if the plan was to have some sort of grand rollout — what with a new larger-than-life starting center, a new electrifying rookie, a new hope of returning to the Showtime glory of the 1980s — this wasn't quite the way to show it.

Beginning in 1988, Dr. Jerry Buss, the franchise owner for nine years at the time, insisted that camp be held in Hawaii.* It was both a method of getting away from distractions and a way to showcase the glory and pres-

---

* There was a one-year gap, in 1991, when the Lakers held camp in Palm Springs.

tige of the NBA's marquee franchise. Let the Pistons train in Michigan, let the Bucks train in Wisconsin. The Lakers would be hanging with the hula girls and palm trees.

Now, however, as the players readied to arrive at the Sheraton Waikiki, a time of renewal felt complicated and unclear. First, there was the issue of Shaquille O'Neal, the NBA's $121 million man. When one signs a contract *that* large, it comes with expectations. You show up early, you behave professionally, you embrace your status with class, dignity, even a bit of humility.

Instead O'Neal spent part of the summer on the down-low, unresponsive to Laker phone calls, blissfully unaware of the responsibilities that accompany stardom. When he finally was reached, he told the team he expected three members of his personal entourage (including his longtime bodyguard, Jerome Crawford) to be added to the Laker payroll. Wrote Larry Guest of the *Orlando Sentinel*, "Welcome to Shaq's World, Lakers. Orlando Magic officials have knowing smiles these days." O'Neal then mentioned that, um, training camp might have to begin a few days later than usual — unless the team was willing to hire a helicopter and send it to the latest movie set, chopper him over to the airport, then fly him daily via private jet (paid for by the team) to Hawaii.

Why?

Because hoops needed to wait while he filmed *Steel*.

Yes, *Steel*.

It had been nearly three months since *Kazaam* hit theaters, and the responses gravitated between "This is the worst movie ever" and "Please kidnap Shaquille O'Neal so he never acts again." Following an opening weekend gross of $5 million, the film vanished into the abyss. He later admitted it wasn't the best career decision, telling *GQ* that "I was a medium-level juvenile delinquent from Newark who always dreamed about doing a movie. Someone said, 'Hey, here's $7 million, come and do this genie movie.' What am I going to say, no?"

Now, though, Shaq was back and creating the type of motion picture his people believed would propel him into the Stallone/Schwarzenegger stratosphere of action heroes; the type of motion picture Leonard Armato, his agent, dreamed of when he urged his client to bolt central Florida for Hollywood.

He was creating *Steel*.

(Glub.)

The script revolved around John Henry Irons, an oversized soldier who dons a suit of iron and becomes the enormous superhero. This was just seven years after Michael Keaton made *Batman* into a worldwide cinematic phenomenon, and Kenny Johnson — the director and writer — saw a grand opportunity to piggyback off that success. Quincy Jones, the producer, signed Johnson on to the project, then told him what he had in mind.

"A black superhero," Jones said. "That's what I want. A black superhero."

Johnson was enamored.

"Who do you see playing the lead?" Johnson asked — envisioning the likes of Denzel Washington, of Blair Underwood, of Wesley Snipes . . .

"Shaq!" Jones replied.

Shaq?

"I heard he's a nice guy," Johnson said. "But he's not a star, Quincy. He can't open this film."

Jones disagreed, and O'Neal signed on.* Shooting commenced shortly after Shaq inked his Lakers deal, and over the next month the *Steel* cast and crew traveled across Los Angeles, creating a cinematic masterpiece that would gross (and you are not about to misread this) $870,068 on a $16 million budget. O'Neal's co-star, Annabeth Gish (best known from her work in *Mystic Pizza* and *Wyatt Earp*), recalled a "gentle giant" who made up for cinematic woodenness with charm and warmth. "This fell a little short of an Academy Award," Gish deadpanned. "But he tried."

One day Venita Ozols-Graham, an assistant director, brought Brigitte,

---

* Until one week before shooting began, Warner Bros. was strongly considering pulling Shaq and replacing him with Snipes. When Johnson later asked why they stuck with the basketball player, he was told, "Marketing thought they could sell more toys with Shaq than Wesley Snipes."

her five-year-old daughter, to the set. The girl was attached to a silk gecko that she kept in a box, and between takes O'Neal approached, leaned down, and said, softly, "What's in the box?"

"It's my gecko," she whispered.

"Is it real?" O'Neal replied.

"No," Brigitte said.

She opened the box, and O'Neal — hands the size of bread baskets — petted the little animal.

"Brigitte," he said, "would you like a real one?"

The next day, Ozols-Graham was working when her daughter came running. "Mommy! Mommy!" she yelped. "Come with me!" Brigitte grabbed her hand and pulled her inside O'Neal's trailer, where she was greeted by an enormous terrarium, overflowing with rocks and plants and starring a pair of fat-tailed geckos. "It's all yours," O'Neal said. "The only condition is you have to name one of them Shaq."

Brigitte did.

"My daughter later came to the set with the box and the gecko doll," Ozols-Graham recalled. "She opened it and gave the doll to Shaquille. It was a really beautiful moment."

O'Neal's one demand of Warner Bros. was that he be provided an on-set mobile workout facility complete with a gym and a basketball hoop. He lifted weights and shot baskets between filming sessions, but come October 4 — when he showed up on time in Honolulu, thanks to an accelerated shooting schedule — O'Neal was hardly in tip-top shape.

That, however, was nothing compared with the other major Laker headache.

In the aftermath of his sizzling four-game summer league run, Bryant expected to join the team and immediately emerge as a superstar. Only, well, he did something extraordinarily stupid. Because Bryant was young and dumb and a 24/7 hoops junkie, on the afternoon of September 2 he visited the famed pickup courts of Venice Beach to get in a few runs. After leaping at the hoop to tip-dunk the ball, he fell toward the pavement and tried to catch himself with his left wrist. His 200-pound body landed atop his arms, and moments later he saw three knots bulging below his hand.

The wrist was broken — and Jerry West was dumbfounded. He greeted the news of the malady with stunned silence, responding to Gary Vitti, the team's trainer, with a blank stare.

"He was doing what?" West asked.

"Playing basketball at Venice," Vitti explained.

"Wait," West said. "Wait, wait. Wait. What?"

It would be one of the last times the Lakers didn't include a NO PICKUP BASKETBALL clause in the contract of a rookie signee.

Though the wrist required no surgery, Bryant had to sit out the entirety of training camp and miss a total of a month and a half. All he had wanted to do was come to Hawaii and prove his worth. Instead, he came to Hawaii and watched.

"I can't begin to tell you how damaging that is to a young player," Harris said years later. "Especially a kid going from high school to the NBA."

On the night before the first practice at the University of Hawaii's gymnasium, Harris called the team together for a meeting inside the conference room at the Sheraton Waikiki, the Lakers' training camp headquarters. He looked around at the 16 players in attendance — a strange brew of iffy leftovers, highly touted newcomers, and a few warm bodies. Then he began to talk.

And talk.

And talk.

And talk.

And talk.

Harris talked about commitment.

Harris talked about shot selection.

Harris talked about his boyhood in Indiana.

Harris talked about coaching the 1981 Houston Rockets to the NBA Finals.

Harris talked about his wife and kids, his friends and colleagues. He talked about Honolulu's marvelous beaches and which restaurants one might avoid. He talked about Nick Van Exel's shot selection, Eddie Jones's toughness, power forward Elden Campbell's rebounding.

He talked.

"He was nicknamed 'Dull Harris' for a reason," said Scott Howard-Cooper, the *Los Angeles Times* beat writer.

And talked.

"You could get trapped quite easily," said Brad Turner, the *Riverside Press-Enterprise* beat writer. "The monologues went long."

And talked.

"Such a nice man," said Mark Heisler, the *Los Angeles Times* basketball scribe. "So much to say."

And talked.

"I really like Del," said Van Exel. "But the meetings — they weren't short."

And talked.

"It was like hearing your grandfather talk sometimes," recalled O'Neal.

And talked.

"Chuck Daly had a saying when he coached the Pistons," said Brendan Suhr, the longtime NBA assistant coach. "He'd say, 'You have to learn to speak to the players in sound bites.' Del would speak for 45 minutes on a press defense. Chuck would do it in 30 seconds."

And . . .

There are *maybe* a dozen people in NBA history who know more about the intricacies of basketball than Harris, a silver-haired man who looks more like a Princeton economics professor than a head coach. He was 59 in the summer of 1996 but seemed older — a by-product of the hair, the air of gravitas, the slow, somewhat mumbling approach to dialogue. Having been born and raised in Plainfield, Indiana (pop. 2,585), Harris oozed small-town simplicity. He was a 4-H fair, a pony ride, a picnic on the church lawn, a calm breeze, and a cool glass of lemonade. Harris was ordained as a minister at the Christian Church at Plainfield, and after graduating from Milligan (Tennessee) College in 1959 with a bachelor's degree in religious studies, he coached junior high hoops in Johnson County, Tennessee, then returned home to head the boys' team at Roachdale High, 28 miles from his birthplace. Harris spent five years at three different Indiana high schools. His big break came in 1965, when he was hired to be the head basketball and baseball coach at Earlham College, an NAIA school known as one of Indiana's finest Quaker institutions.

In its 69-year pre–Del Harris history of fielding a basketball team, Earlham had but 24 winning seasons, and posted a putrid all-time record of 445-536. Harris — who also taught theory of coaching, physical education, and athletic training at the school — guided the Quakers to a 175-70 mark over nine years, and used his spare time to write a pair of bestselling books on basketball theory for Prentice Hall while also coaching seven seasons in the Puerto Rico summer pro league. (He guided Federico to three straight titles.) He was an interesting man to play for — calm but demanding. A glare that could kill, coupled with a genius aptitude for strategy. "He was always a very respected coach," said Howard Beck, the longtime basketball writer. "I don't think I've ever heard anyone question his ability to teach the game."

During his days in Puerto Rico, he met Tom Nissalke, head coach of the Utah Stars of the American Basketball Association. One day, somewhat randomly, Nissalke turned to Harris and said, "Why don't you come to Utah and be my assistant?"

It sure beat another year at Earlham.

"You never know when your break is going to come, or from where it will come," Harris said. "You're coaching small-college basketball, sort of unknown. And then you land in the pros. Just like that."

He spent one year at Nissalke's side, and when the ABA folded, the two men jumped to the NBA's Houston Rockets. Harris took over the head coaching gig in 1979 and guided the team to three playoff appearances and an NBA Finals loss to the Boston Celtics in 1981. The Rockets, however, willingly self-imploded in 1982–83, when ownership traded its star, center Moses Malone, to the 76ers, then tanked in an effort to land the top selection in the 1984 draft. "They wanted us to finish last," Harris recalled. "It was awful. Do you know what it's like coaching when ownership wants you to lose?"

With a skeletal roster of has-beens and never-weres, Harris's 1982–83

Rockets went 14-68. He was fired at season's end, then waited four years before Milwaukee called with another head coaching opportunity. Harris's four full seasons with the Bucks resulted in a 183-145 record, but when the squad started 8-9 in 1991, he was again kicked to the curb. The knock on Del Harris was a familiar one — great guy, smart guy, well-intentioned guy. But no pizzazz, no imagination, and just too much jabbering.

"There are long-winded people in this world," said Corie Blount, the longtime NBA forward. "But Del takes it to a different level. Nobody dislikes him. But basketball players want to play. And Del wanted to discuss every way to get open. Then reexamine the discussion."

Another man prone to extended dialogues was Jerry West, the Lakers' executive vice president of operations, who, while serving as general manager in 1994, found himself exasperated by his beloved franchise's lack of productivity. In the six years since Pat Riley left the sidelines, the Lakers had gone from NBA elite to sad sideshow. Mike Dunleavy Sr. coached the team for two winning seasons, then Randy Pfund followed with badness, then Magic Johnson — retired and fidgety — with even more badness (a 5-11 mark in 16 sad 1994 contests).

West and Harris had a friendship that dated back to the 1970s, when the two would spend a week together working at Auburn University's basketball camp as a favor to the head coach, Sonny Smith. "We'd play golf, we'd fish, we'd talk basketball," said Harris. "It was a real connection."

In the summer of 1994, Harris was *this* close to accepting the general manager position with the Sacramento Kings. He was actually in California's capital city, negotiating a contract, but had gotten stuck on one point: Jim Thomas, the franchise's owner, insisted that Harris's first task on the job would be to fire Garry St. Jean, the Kings' coach.

"Jim," Harris said, "I can't do that to him. I *won't* do that to him."

As this was transpiring, West called to ask whether Harris had signed anything with Sacramento.

"No," Harris replied.

"Well, don't," West said. "We want you to coach the Lakers."

Del Harris didn't have to think twice.

And now, two years later, Harris was in Hawaii, talking. And talking. And talking. And talking.

The assembled talent before him was breathtaking. Finally, after finishing his 17-and-a-half-year monologue, Harris asked each man to stand and introduce himself. O'Neal, jolly and giggly, stood first, nodded, said, "What's up? I'm Shaq. Let's do this."

One by one, the other men followed.

"Hey, I'm Derek Fisher. Rookie. From little ol' Arkansas. Ready to get to work."

Next.

"Nick Van Exel. Fourth year here."

Next.

"Eddie Jones. I'm from Florida. Went to Temple . . ."

Next.

"My name's Trev. Trevor Wilson. Don't wanna brag, but I played in Sioux Falls last year. Won a CBA championship."

Next.

"I'm Jerome Kersey. This will be my — what? — 13th year in the league. Crazy."

Next.

"I'm Ced."

Next.

"Yo, I'm Kobe. Kobe Bryant. I'm from PA — went to Lower Merion High School, dominated everything." (*Pause.*) "I just want y'all to know, nobody's gonna punk me. I'm not gonna let anyone in the NBA punk me. So be warned."

Awwwwkward.

"It was like 'Yo, Kobe, relax,'" recalled David Booth, who landed a camp invite off of a strong summer league showing. "He was trying to establish himself, which I understand. But it didn't play very well."

"Not the best way to start things," said Blount. "But you have to remember, he was a child."

In a strange way, Bryant's injury proved beneficial, both to the youngster and the team. Although NBA rookie hazing has rarely reached the level of Major League Baseball rookie hazing or National Football League rookie hazing, it certainly existed with the Lakers. Along with Bryant, the team had two other newbies in camp: Fisher, out of Arkansas–Little Rock, and a gangly 7-foot, 235-pound center from UConn named Travis Knight. The recent first-round draft pick of Chicago, Knight had become a free agent when the Bulls — set with a loaded roster and uninterested in providing Knight with the requisite three-year minimum guaranteed contract — renounced his rights. "I got to pick my team, which was pretty amazing," Knight recalled. "I grew up in San Diego, I played AAU ball in L.A. I was a Southern California guy."

When he came to Hawaii the day before camp opened, Knight hit up a shopping mall to grab a sandwich. While sitting in the food court, he heard a loud noise coming from down a hallway. "I looked up from my lunch," he said. "It was Shaq. A bunch of people were following him, naturally. I just sat there looking at him, same as everybody else. I didn't want to bother him."

Less than 24 hours later, Knight was O'Neal's rookie — meaning he was charged with carrying his shoes to practice, dropping them at his locker after practice, taking smacks to the back of the skull should he lay a ball in instead of dunking. "He was very cool," Knight said. "Nothing with Shaq was ever very serious." Fisher, soft-spoken and appreciative, was handed similar tasks by Van Exel and Jones — grab food, make sure the drinks were cold. Light fare.

Unlike his two peers, Bryant was an enticing target. His first-day introduction was received like spoiled milk, and as camp progressed, the veteran Lakers were taken aback by his perceived smugness. When Van Exel joined the Lakers out of Cincinnati in 1993, he had arrived humble and quiet. When Jones came a year later, he had arrived humble and quiet. Knight was humble and quiet. Fisher was humble and quiet.

Bryant was neither humble nor quiet. But he sat, unavailable, with a bum wrist. So he was deemed largely off-limits. "We did not get to haze him quite as much," recalled Cedric Ceballos. "Getting doughnuts and carrying bags and that sort of thing. Shaq did have him do some goofy things, like bust a freestyle rap for all of us.

"[Kobe] was different. Most rookies want the approval of veterans. He never really was that way."

Had Bryant been participating, he would have — most veterans later agreed — ruined camp. Or, if not ruined, *severely damaged*. Van Exel, Jones, and Ceballos, the three returnees with the greatest offensive responsibilities, needed to adjust to O'Neal's dominant low post presence, and the addition of a can't-touch-this, better-than-the-best ball-hogging teenager was not a requisite ingredient. On the sidelines, and in limited drills, Bryant took pleasure in showing off twisting layups and off-balance jumpers. He wanted people to notice, desperately wanted teammates to see what all the hype was about. O'Neal began referring to him as "Showboat," and if the nickname wasn't direct ridicule per se, it was anything but a compliment.

What struck some of the Lakers as most odd was the kid's mimicking of Michael Jordan, the legendary Bull whose VHS tapes Bryant watched growing up in Italy. It wasn't just a basketball thing. It was an *everything*. Bryant licked his lips like Jordan, shrugged his shoulders like Jordan, patterned his speech like Jordan. Homage was one thing. But this was not so much homage as stalker. "He clearly wanted to be Michael Jordan at the beginning," said Knight. "In every way imaginable."

With Bryant sidelined, the team jelled at a rapid pace. The Lakers opened the preseason on October 10 with an evening game against the Denver Nuggets inside Honolulu's Special Events Arena, and anyone expecting gradual growing pains was terribly mistaken. Wearing his new No. 34 purple-and-gold uniform and slimmed down from a week of sweaty gym work, O'Neal played 26 minutes, scoring 25 points on 11-of-13 shooting, with 12 rebounds and, in the words of Mike Fitzgerald of the *Honolulu Star-Bulletin*, "several thunder dunks that could have caused tsunami warnings." During one thrilling second-quarter sequence, he scored 6 points in less than 60 seconds, with a blocked shot and a rebound tossed in. Los Angeles won 111–101, a meaningless victory that was anything but meaningless. With 10,225 spectators on hand, Van Exel and Jones seemed at ease dumping the ball down low, spreading out, letting O'Neal dictate the pace. Even Ceballos, selfish as the sun is bright, stayed free of the paint, granting the big man his space. Afterwards, O'Neal stood in the joyous locker room and bragged of his greatness.

"No one can out-surf me!" he said. "I am the Big Kahuna!"

Six days later, after the Nuggets and the Lakers squared off one more time before returning to the mainland, Bryant finally became an active NBA player — at 18 years and 55 days of age the youngest man in league history. The Lakers traveled to lovely Fresno, California, to battle the Dallas Mavericks in an exhibition, and in the leadup Bryant was like a puppy seeking table scraps. He paced the locker room, paced the hallways. Shortly before training camp commenced, the Lakers had signed Byron Scott to a one-year free agent contract for a meager $247,500. Now 35 and coming off a 10.2-points-per-game season of misery with the ghastly Vancouver Grizzlies, Scott was a key piece of franchise history. In 10 seasons as Magic Johnson's sidekick, he had averaged 15.9 points per game while helping the team win three titles. No longer particularly quick or physical, Scott had now reappeared as a Laker to (a) provide some shooting spark off the bench and (b) babysit and mentor Kobe Bryant.

Not in that order.

He was the perfect man for the job. A product of the tough streets of Inglewood, Scott grew up in the shadows of the Forum — able to smell the buzz but not afford the tickets. After starring at Arizona State for three seasons, he was selected fourth overall by the San Diego Clippers in the 1983 NBA draft. When he hesitated at the idea of joining the league's saddest franchise, Scott was dealt to the Lakers in exchange for Norm Nixon, the club's talented point guard. The transaction was hardly greeted warmly in Los Angeles. *Byron Scott? Who the hell is Byron Scott?* The boos followed, as did the recurring doubts swirling through the rookie's head. It was hard enough jumping to the NBA. But doing so with extra spotlight? Nearly impossible.

Before long, however, Scott established himself as a cornerstone of the

Showtime dynasty. The day of his 1993 release by the Lakers was a heart-breaking one in Los Angeles.

And now he was back — here to nurture, educate, explain via firsthand experience to the youngest Laker what it was to be the youngest Laker. During warm-ups before tipoff, Scott stood by Bryant's side, advising him to take it easy, relax, enjoy the moment. Scott loved the kid's passion and drive, but he recognized a familiar eagerness to run before walking. "Your time will come" was a familiar mantra. "Your time will come."

Harris viewed Bryant as a deep reserve whose minutes would be limited. He allowed him to enter the game with 7:49 remaining in the second quarter, and the 10,274 fans at Fresno's Selland Arena chanted, "Ko-Be! Ko-Be!" The first time he touched the basketball, Bryant — nervous, a bit clumsy — mishandled it. He recovered, then passed to center Sean Rooks under the basket for a quick score. Moments later, his sneaker (the Adidas EQT Elevation he was paid millions to wear) fell off, and he fumbled to return it to his right foot as action resumed. Late in the game, after scoring his first-ever bucket on a three-pointer, followed by a turnaround jumper, a breakaway dunk, and a 16-foot jumper, Bryant dribbled and dribbled and dribbled some more, until the mild-mannered Harris screamed, "Hey, pass the ball! This isn't high school anymore!"

It was, overall, a strong debut — 10 points on 4-for-4 shooting. In the Lakers' locker room, teammates were largely complimentary. They understood that a high school guard making his NBA debut was the story that needed to be told, so Van Exel said that Bryant had "shot the ball pretty well. He's real active." Harris added that he'd "made some mistakes and he did some good things."

When O'Neal emerged, he was asked to add his assessment. He began to sing — tune by Whitney Houston, lyrics by Shaquille O'Neal.

"I believe that Showboat is the fuuuture . . ."

It was going to be an interesting season.

5

Nick the Quick

When Nick Van Exel was a boy of five, growing up in the projects of Kenosha, Wisconsin, his father took him on drives.

The two would head to various events — basketball games, tournaments of different sorts — where people parked their cars for predictable periods of time. If a Kenosha High hoops game was scheduled to start at 7 p.m., for example, dad and son pulled up at 7:15.

Then, without fail, Nick Sr. would open his door, lean in toward his son, say, "Wait here" — and go about the business of breaking into the vacant vehicles. "He snatched out their stereos and things like that," Nick recalled. "I was riding in the car with him. I was scared for me at a young age."

Two years later, Nick Van Exel Sr. was arrested and sent to prison. With that, he vanished from his son's life. He never wrote. He never called. There were no visits, no optimistic discussions of "When I get out . . ." or "I can't wait to . . ."

Nope.

Nick Van Exel Sr. was gone.

And, like that, his son was largely alone, living in a breadbox-sized apartment with a single mother, Joyce, who worked two jobs, including the 3 p.m.–1 a.m. shift on the assembly line at the nearby Chrysler plant, the Kenosha Engine factory. Nick would come home from school to either 30 minutes of mother time or, more commonly, the quiet grimness of an empty space and a 13-inch television. "It turned me into a loner," he said. "Not having anyone there."

In the late 1980s, Nick Sr. was finally released from prison, and his son was excited by the idea of his father's return. Only, instead of coming back to Kenosha, Nick Sr. divorced Joyce and moved to Georgia.

"I really didn't have a father figure in my life, a person who can sit there and tell me, 'No, you're not going to do this' or 'Yes, you're going to do that,'" Nick Jr. later said. "I never had that. I never had a guy who I had to take command from."

The product of isolation swirled with abandonment was ferociousness. Van Exel — whose full name is Nickey Maxwell Van Exel and who went by "Nickey" until college — was a small, skinny runt of a kid who simply refused to back down or take shit. At school and at home, he seemed quiet, almost shy. But on the basketball court — pure rage. No father? Crippling loneliness? Sadness? Heartbreak? To hell with all of it. "The thing about Nick — he carried that edge," said Wagner Lester, a youth basketball rival. "He was quiet, but it wasn't a placid quiet. It was more 'I think messing with this kid would be a very bad idea.'"

Life was one kick in the teeth after another. One day, out of the blue, his father called, offering a plane ticket to come visit Georgia. The kid was euphoric — finally, he would have the relationship he'd long craved. Nick Sr. told him to head to General Mitchell International Airport, in Milwaukee, that there would be a ticket to Atlanta with his name on it waiting for him at the Delta counter. "When I got there," Nick recalled, "there was nothing."

Thanks to his athletic gifts and financial neediness, Nick received a scholarship to St. Joseph Catholic Academy Kenosha, a private school where nearly all the students were white, nattily dressed, and drivers of either a BMW or a Mercedes. "You're thinking everyone is looking at you," he said. "You're thinking everyone is going to make fun of you."

Van Exel was a guarded yet warm kid who camouflaged his insecurities with bling. He was one of the first boys in his school to sport a gold earring, and he accompanied the metal with a thick layer of gold chains lassoed around his neck. He shaved two diagonal marks into his eyebrows. On the court, he was a basketball giant. As a senior shooting guard, Van Exel propelled St. Joseph to the WISAA Class A championship game while leading the state in scoring with 29.8 points per game. His 42-point outburst against Marquette High is still discussed. Yet, because he failed to post a 2.0 grade point average, Van Exel was ignored by the state's two basketball powers, Marquette and Wisconsin. So, with nowhere to go, he took his game to Trinity Valley, a junior college in middle-of-the-tumbleweeds Athens, Texas. He was advised to do so by Jerry Tarkanian, the corrupt UNLV coach who told Van Exel he would ultimately have a spot with the Runnin' Rebels — then ignored the kid throughout his juco experience. Athens was a place where no right-minded human aspired to be, but a place where future standouts with academic issues tended to land. (On his visit, Van Exel was hosted by Shawn Kemp, the future six-time NBA All-Star.) On endless occasions, Nick called Joyce, begging her to let him return, to get him out of a spot he called "the worst place ever," to remove him from hell. "He wanted to drop out and come home," Joyce recalled. "I said, 'You see how I'm working hard? If you come home, you're going to do this, too.' I talked to him. I mean, I really talked to him. I said, 'This doesn't happen for everybody. This is your chance.'"

In a pair of juco seasons, a miserable Van Exel averaged 19.2 points and 6 assists per game, enough to keep Division I schools from focusing on his troubles (he allegedly kicked an unconscious teammate during a fight) and draw scholarship offers from DePaul, Oklahoma, Nebraska, South Alabama, New Mexico State, and Cincinnati. He chose the Bearcats, whose up-and-coming program was led by Bob Huggins, a coach surrounding himself with castoffs and rejects. Van Exel was his type of kid — "You had to earn his trust," Huggins recalled. "He didn't give it to you for free. You worked to get it." During practices, Huggins used to ask his players, "If I had a piece of pie, just one piece left, who do you think would get it?"

The answer was always the famished Van Exel.

In his first year as a Bearcat, Van Exel majored in sociology and averaged 12.3 points. "Bob Huggins told me some really sad stories about

Nick," said Tony Dutt, his agent. "He said he'd go home on a weekend from Cincinnati and the family would lock him out of the house. So he'd just come back to campus." Van Exel was sitting in his dorm room one evening during the season, watching a television show about abandoned children and — specifically — a son meeting up with his long-lost father. He was bawling uncontrollably, snotty tissues in hand, when the phone rang.

"Nick?" the unfamiliar voice said.

Yeah — who's this?

"It's your dad."

What?

"It's your dad."

Indeed, Nick Sr. was on the other end of the line, requesting a reconciliation. The young man and the older man spoke at length. Nick learned that he had two half sisters and that his father had been living cleanly. Toward the end of the discussion, Nick Jr. invited Nick Sr. to an upcoming game in which the Bearcats were facing Alabama-Birmingham down south. But even when his dad arrived at courtside, Nick Jr. never felt entirely comfortable about it. "It seemed like he had a certain motive at that point," he recalled years later. "You know, knowing maybe I have a chance to play in the NBA, knowing you have a chance to get yourself a nice house, to get yourself a nice car. It just didn't sit right with me."

It all served to fuel Van Exel's drive. Huggins was a notoriously ornery coach who ran his players to exhaustion — and Nick embraced it. He cherished the pain, the anger, the frustration. He wanted you to punch him in the jaw, so he could fire back twice as hard. In his first year as a Bearcat, he took over the starting point guard job and guided the school to its first Final Four appearance in 29 years. The following campaign, he led the team in scoring (18.3 points per game), assists (4.5), and steals (1.8), was named a third-team All-American, and carried the Bearcats into the Elite Eight. "He was the best big-shot guy I ever had," said Huggins. "If you need one guy to take the last shot — one guy out of anyone who has ever shot a basketball — it's Nick Van Exel."

NBA scouts near and far came to watch him play, and the reviews were . . . mixed. Though listed at 6-foot-1, Van Exel was closer to 5-foot-11, with more bone than muscle. And while he was unafraid to take the last shot, would he be able to get it off against big professional guards? Plus, he was moody and volatile, unpredictable and off-putting, and a tiny bit self-sabotaging. When the season ended, Van Exel was invited to work out for a bevy of franchises. In Seattle, he was told to start at the baseline and sprint to the far free throw line six times. With Sonics coach George Karl watching, Van Exel jogged the first one.

"Nick," Karl growled, "I know you can do better than that."

Van Exel shrugged, chuckled, and said, "The next one is my cooldown." He knew the Sonics' roster was loaded at point guard and presumed the team wouldn't want him.

"We saw an individualist," Karl said.

The Sonics weren't the only team turned off by Van Exel's attitude. Twice, he skipped workouts in Charlotte. "I started to read the magazines, the publications, saying I'm one of the top guards in the country," Van Exel said. "It got to me."

"Nick is the only client I ever had who took himself out of the first round," said Dutt. "It relates to trust. He didn't trust anyone."

When the draft was held on June 30, 1993, he plummeted into the second round, where the giddy Lakers grabbed him 37th overall.*

Even though it was, in part, a fate of his own making, Van Exel took the drop slights personally. "You could feel the chip on his shoulder," said Erikk Aldridge, the Lakers' assistant public relations director. "'I should have been a first-rounder and now I'm gonna show it.' Nick had that urban hood edge to him. He had a cut on his mouth, a scowl. He could intimidate you because you didn't always know where he was coming from." Van Exel took over as Los Angeles's starting point guard as a rookie, averaging 13.6 points and 5.8 assists, then improved as a sophomore, upping his av-

---

* That year, the Orlando Magic brass reached out to Shaquille O'Neal during the draft. The team held the 26th overall pick, and asked their center whether he would enjoy playing with Van Exel. "I don't give a fuck," O'Neal replied — and the organization selected Geert Hammink, who played five total games with the team.

erage to 16.9 points and 8.3 assists. In the post-Showtime era, he became a reason to watch a team not otherwise worth watching. He played with heart and emotion. The Lakers became *his* Lakers, and as Nick Van Exel went, so went Los Angeles.

But now that had changed. Shaquille O'Neal was the new superstar in town, and before he even played a game, the Lakers were *his* team. O'Neal was featured on the cover of the 1996–97 media guide, alongside the jerseys of Kareem Abdul-Jabbar and Wilt Chamberlain, the two great Los Angeles centers of the past. Billboards with his visage popped up all over the city. Upon joining the franchise, he purchased a $350,000 Ferrari, and sightings of O'Neal in his luxury automobile driving down Rodeo Drive were accompanied by squeals and shouts.

Van Exel was a basketball player. An excellent basketball player, but a mere basketball player.

O'Neal was an enterprise.

The new, Shaq-fronted Lakers opened the season on November 1 inside the Forum, and a sellout crowd of 17,505 jammed the building for the dawning of a new era. Playing against a mediocre Phoenix Suns team, Los Angeles jumped out to a 15-point first-quarter lead. O'Neal's stat line (23 points, 14 rebounds) wasn't overwhelming, but his presence was. No one this physically dense had ever worn the purple and gold, and if his existence made the Lakers better, it also made his teammates appear smaller.

Less than three minutes into the game, after Van Exel picked up his second foul, Del Harris replaced him with Derek Fisher, the rookie point guard, and hardly a beat was skipped. The Lakers won 96–82, with the name Nick Van Exel appearing in few to none of the "Shaq Makes Debut" stories that ran all across the nation. Two days later, Los Angeles won again with a 91–85 triumph over Minnesota, and another O'Neal demolition (35 points, 19 rebounds, 3 blocked shots) carried the narrative. The second story of the day was the regular season debut of Kobe Bryant, who at 18 years, two months, and 11 days supplanted Philadelphia's Stanley Brown (who was 18 years, four months in 1947) as the youngest player in NBA history. Bryant entered the game with 2:58 left in the first quarter, received a standing ovation, wiped dust from the bottoms of his Adidas

— then promptly dribbled into a crowd, found himself trapped, and traveled. Moments later, center Cherokee Parks blocked his shot and the ball fluttered to the court. In six minutes of action, Bryant shot 0 for 1, with a rebound, a foul, a turnover, and a block. "It was one of those things," Harris said — coachspeak for "He's a child who's not quite ready for this stuff."

Though it was early in the campaign, a pattern was forming. O'Neal was the story — always the story. Then there would be a side note, a secondary tale: Bryant's debut. Harris yelling more than usual. Eddie Jones breaking out. Elden Campbell stepping up as a rebounder. Fisher, the obscure rookie, surprising everyone. In this realm, Van Exel had his place. When he played well, the media wrote about it. But he was no longer the featured player. Why, on November 5, 1996, alone, the *New York Times* ran a piece headlined CAN O'NEAL CHARM WAY TO TITLE? *USA Today* ran a piece headlined LAKERS FANS NOT GAGA OVER SHAQ JUST YET, and *Newsday* ran a piece headlined A GRUDGE MATCH: SHAQ'S IN LA TAKING A LITTLE EDGE OFF. Van Exel wasn't one to openly express his frustrations — but he was frustrated. His career had been growing, with the understanding that the offense was his to run. With Eddie Jones streaking down the wing and the cocky Van Exel firing away from all depths and angles, the Lakers were high-octane and explosive. Now, though, there was a fireplug in the middle, and the first directive was to get the ball down low.

"I love Shaq," Van Exel said years later. "But it was an adjustment."

Through the season's first three and a half weeks, the Lakers were erratic. Bryant rarely played, Ceballos was out with a partially torn patella tendon, slugs like Travis Knight and Corie Blount were getting surprising minutes, Harris kept talking and talking. Late into a November 12 double-overtime win at Houston, O'Neal — frustrated by his team and furious at fouling out — entered the locker room and ripped a bathroom stall door off its hinges, then tore a mirror from the wall. (Said one team official: "The way it sounded, you thought the whole room was going to be destroyed.") Five days later at Phoenix, Bryant played 14 minutes, scoring a career-high 16 points on 5-for-8 shooting. During a time-out, O'Neal complained to the NBA newcomer that he wasn't getting him the ball.

"Fuck that," Bryant replied. "Get it off the rebound if I miss, bro." O'Neal seethed. In the aftermath of a 100–88 win at Philadelphia on November 26 that raised the team's record to 10-5, Van Exel could not contain his anger. He had spent all but 93 seconds of the fourth quarter on the bench, watching Fisher run the offense, and the frustration was too much. When Scott Howard-Cooper of the *Los Angeles Times* inquired as to whether he was surprised by having just 21 minutes of court time, Van Exel snapped. "Nothing surprises me with the coach we got," he said. "Nothing."

"What do you mean?" Howard-Cooper asked.

"He expects me to be the leader on the court, the quarterback, and then he takes me out of the game," Van Exel replied. "I'm over there guessing, like, 'What can I do?' But he's the coach. You've got to stand by his rules."

The Lakers were too talented to be bad. And they weren't bad. They were just meh. Goodish. On November 28, a day after his calling-out of Harris, Van Exel organized a players-only meeting in the rear of the plane on the flight from Boston to Detroit. As the men gathered by the restroom, Van Exel — just 25 but the second-longest-tenured member of the team — insisted that things needed to improve. Communication among the players was crap. Harris's rotation was erratic. The minutes made no sense. There was talk of making Jerome Kersey, a 13-year veteran with dead legs, the starting small forward, which confused everyone involved. "A lot of the guys were getting frustrated," said Byron Scott. "A lot of people had some things they felt they wanted to get off their chest."

Because clear-the-air meetings are always (without fail) deemed successes in professional sports, the clear-the-air meeting was deemed a success. (Van Exel: "We were energized.") The Lakers beat Detroit the following afternoon, then won seven of their next eight. Still, nothing felt quite right. In a private conversation with a friend from his Orlando days, O'Neal admitted that he was fed up with Van Exel and longed for the companionship of Penny Hardaway, the Magic point guard extraordinaire. "Now I know what everyone was talking about," he said of Van Exel's shortcomings.

The one thing the players agreed on was that Harris was the wrong coach at the wrong time. Nobody hated the man, in large part because

Del Harris is eminently unhateable. But from 1 through 15, the Lakers found him to be rigid, unimaginative, dry. The team practiced no longer or shorter than the NBA's 28 other franchises, but the coach's winding lectures made the sessions feel eternal.

The Harris–Van Exel marriage was particularly off. The hostility had some history. Following his senior year at Cincinnati, Van Exel had participated in a pre-draft camp at Phoenix. Harris worked the event as a coach, and during games he went with Kansas's Rex Walters as his primary point guard. Van Exel fumed on the bench. "Nick was far more talented, but he never listened," Harris said. "Even back then. It pissed him off. I know he never forgot it."

They were two men from different worlds, with different outlooks on basketball. "Del tried everything to be cool with Nick," Jones recalled. "But Nick had his mind made up already on Del, and they never got along. You'd never see Nick high-five Del, have a meeting with Del. Normally a coach and his floor leader work together. Not with us." During one practice, Harris felt that his point guard was going through the motions, throwing lazy passes, making halfhearted moves.

"Nick," Harris finally said, "what is wrong with you?"

Van Exel wasn't having it.

"Listen, I know what the fuck I'm doing," he replied. "Leave me alone."

Harris was an ordained minister with a degree in religious studies. He cursed as often as he painted his toenails.* "What the fuck did you just say?" the head coach of the Los Angeles Lakers barked toward his starting point guard — then pushed him in the shoulder.

"Don't you ever put your hands on me again," Van Exel replied. "*Bitch.*"

Did Nick Van Exel just call Del Harris a bitch?

"I'll beat your fucking punk ass!" Harris screamed. "Get your punk ass out of my practice!"

Van Exel marched toward the door, opened it, exited to a thunderous *slam!*

---

* Del Harris never painted his toenails.

Players were speechless.

"I guess Del had been watching a lot of TV and wanted to try to get in with the brothers," O'Neal recalled. "I have to admit, it was good entertainment."

Despite the turmoil, the Lakers reached the All-Star break with a 35-13 mark, good for a 2½-game lead over the Seattle SuperSonics in the Pacific Division and the league's third-best record. Although few people were happy inside the locker room, Mitch Kupchak, the general manager, and Jerry West, executive vice president of basketball operations, were thrilled with Harris's work. What impressed them most was his approach to Bryant, whose merging of impatience and arrogance made life quite miserable.

Because he was young, and just as socially clumsy ("He was born without an antenna," said Mark Heisler of the *Los Angeles Times*), Bryant was incapable of biding his time, waiting his turn, letting the game come to him. "He wasn't ready," Eddie Jones recalled. "It was mainly defensive things. He could go out there and score with the best of them, but the toughest part of the game for young players is the defensive side. Del didn't want him to lose confidence, and at the time in the league, teams would isolate anyone who couldn't guard. I thought Del did the perfect job with Kobe."

Few days passed without Bryant begging Harris or one of his assistant coaches for extra minutes. From the bench, he averaged a paltry 15½ minutes per game while watching opposing shooting guards and knowing he was superior. After practices, he nagged teammates into sticking around and playing him to 10. The games were electric odes to gravity-defying circus tricks. But Bryant still didn't understand that one-on-one tomahawk slams had nothing to do with five-on-five NBA success. Five years earlier, the Miami Heat had wasted a first-round pick on a USC guard named Harold Miner, whose portfolio of dunks made him, for a sliver of time, the talk of basketball. Then he arrived in the league, thought he could soar over the masses, developed no other skills, and flamed out after starting 47 games in four seasons. Harris did not want this fate to befall Bryant. "Kobe thought he should be starting over Eddie or Nick as a rookie," said Brad Turner, the *Riverside Press-Enterprise* beat writer. "He was *that* confident. But Del was steadfast."

Bryant begged, Harris ignored.

Bryant begged more, Harris ignored more.

"One time, as a rookie, he asked Del why he couldn't run some post-ups for him instead of Shaq," said Heisler. "Kobe didn't get it."

In early December, Bryant failed to appear in two of three games — a pair of DNPs that humiliated the youngster. Whenever he touched the ball, Bryant's first move was the same — put it on the floor, then attempt some sort of shake-and-bake. Which had worked wonders against Devon Prep's Julian Risco and New Hope–Solebury's Chad Hopenwasser. But here, in the NBA, it was dime-a-dozen trash. "I remember playing against Kobe for the first time that season, and he was coming down, dribbling like crazy between his legs," recalled Nets forward Kendall Gill. "Nick [Van Exel] looks at me and rolls his eyes. Like, 'Yeah, this is the shit we deal with.'" When Bryant received minutes, oftentimes toward the end of blowouts, the sight wasn't pretty. He dribbled into double teams as often as he made correct reads. As was the case in the summer league, he repeatedly ignored open teammates to find a shot for himself.

"Kobe never really liked me," Harris said. "He felt like I held him back, which I did, but for a good reason. He wanted to play all the time and he never wanted to come out of a game." During one particularly frustrating stretch, when Bryant was openly griping to teammates, the coach pulled the man-child aside. "Listen," he said, "you chose not to play with kids in college and instead to compete with men. That was your decision. And that's fine. But I need to treat you like a man. I can't teach you like a kid. Think of yourself as a contender in a heavyweight match. You can't get a draw and take the guy's belt. You have to knock someone out. And right now you're not there."

A reprieve from the misery of a splinter-inflicted season came with All-Star Weekend, held in Cleveland on February 8–9. Two Lakers (O'Neal and Eddie Jones, who was averaging 17.2 points) were selected for the game itself, but Bryant — lover of the spotlight — would walk away from Gund Arena as the talk of the gala.

On Saturday night, Bryant captured the Slam Dunk Contest with a breathtaking display of style mixed with athleticism. On his winning jam, he sprinted toward the hoop, soared through the air, passed the ball between his legs, and concluded with a right-handed windmill, à la Dominique Wilkins. Upon landing, he walked toward a bench where the following day's All-Star Game participants sat and flexed while puckering his lips. It was arrogant and preposterous — and everyone seemed to eat it up.

A couple of hours earlier, Bryant had been a member of the Western Conference squad in the Rookie Challenge game. In its fourth year of existence, the contest was an ode to the otherworldly gifts of the 1996 draft. Four participants (Bryant, Philadelphia's Allen Iverson, Milwaukee's Ray Allen, and Phoenix's Steve Nash) would wind up in the Basketball Hall of Fame, and altogether the 16 men would tally 51 All-Star Game appearances over the ensuing years. For fans of passing, defense, and smart, heads-up basketball, the game was a soiled diaper. Yet for Bryant, it was a chance to explode. All the pent-up anger and frustration accumulated over six months of inactivity was let loose, and he spent a game-high 26 minutes of court time dead-set on showing off. Bryant shot 8 for 17 from the field and 13 for 16 from the line, and while his 31 points led all scorers, the performance was everything Harris hated about the rookie's makeup. Though he was playing alongside a fantastic young forward, Vancouver's Shareef Abdur-Rahim, Bryant seemed to relish ignoring the Grizzly's repeated post-ups down low, instead hucking up ill-advised three-pointers. Teammates later agreed his behavior was awful. Calling the game for TNT, an exasperated Hubie Brown finally grew tired of the selfishness, lecturing, "Kobe Bryant is showing us an awful lot of energy, but I also think he should try and play with the other four guys that are on the floor." Bob Neal, his colleague in the booth, chuckled — but the veteran coach was dead serious.

"If you can't pass the ball," Brown later said, "you can't succeed at this level."

• • •

On the night of January 5, 1997, in the fourth quarter of his team's 109–102 loss to Boston, Phoenix Suns forward Robert Horry threw a towel in the face of his coach.

If that sounds quaint by modern standards of societal violence, head back in time two decades, when peace, love, and harmony ruled the day and professional athletes weren't quite as prone to go on the attack. This is nearly a year before Latrell Sprewell of the Golden State Warriors choked P.J. Carlesimo, nearly seven and a half years before Indiana's Ron Artest climbed into the stands at the Palace of Auburn Hills to maul some obnoxious Detroit Pistons fans.

So, yeah — throwing a rectangular slice of 100 percent cotton fabric at Danny Ainge was nothing to sneeze at.

Horry, though, felt there was reason. A two-time NBA champion with the Houston Rockets, he had been traded to Phoenix five months earlier — and hated everything about it. He didn't like the city, he didn't like playing for Ainge, he certainly didn't like going from one of the league's elite franchises to a team that started the year 0-13. Horry was known for clutch shooting, but what's clutch shooting when your team is never close to winning?

With 7:12 remaining in the final period and Boston up 89–84, Ainge replaced Horry (who had just thrown up a wild three-point shot that came nowhere close to the rim) with Rex Chapman. As the forward walked toward the bench, he barked at his coach, piecing together an impressive string of expletives. A handful of teammates pulled him away, but Horry continued to curse him out. A former Celtic guard with a fiery reputation, Ainge shot back, sans censor. Horry replied with, in the words of *Arizona Republic* columnist E.J. Montini, "a cursing jag at Ainge." Then, without warning, he grabbed the towel that dangled from his neck and tossed it in Ainge's face. Horry turned his back on his coach, who later noted, "I've been in the NBA for 15 years. I've seen a lot worse instances involving a lot better players with better reputations."

The next morning's *Arizona Republic* led with the headline HORRY ACCOSTS AINGE. Which, while a bit much, was technically true.

As soon as the game ended, Horry entered the Suns' locker room, where he was confronted by Joe Kleine, the veteran center who had spent several years in Boston receiving leadership lessons from Larry Bird and Kevin McHale. "I'll be honest — I didn't like Rob in Phoenix," Kleine recalled. "I don't think he's a bad guy, but he didn't want to be there and he was difficult." With the other Suns players watching, Kleine lit into Horry, telling him his "minor league bullshit" had no place in the NBA. At 6-foot-11 and 255 pounds, Kleine wasn't one to be trifled with. He looked at Horry, half expecting a punch to the head.

"Instead," Kleine recalled, "he apologized."

Indeed. Horry apologized to Kleine, to the rest of the team, to Ainge. "The coaches, the training staff, everybody," he told the media. But then, before being suspended for two games, he lied to reporters and said the Suns coach took some blame for the altercation. "No, I didn't," Ainge fired back. "I understand Robert is frustrated. But never did I say that, not do I believe for one second any of the blowup was my fault."

And that, pretty much, was that for Robert Horry in Phoenix. Jerry Colangelo, the team's general manager, immediately placed calls to the league's 28 other franchises, seeking a warm body or two in exchange for the 26-year-old malcontent. The response was radio silence. Even happy, Horry was viewed as little more than a solid role player. But who in the world wanted to add someone with this type of attitude? This type of anger? Why, four years earlier Horry had earned league-wide disdain for shoving Bob Kloppenburg, a 66-year-old Seattle SuperSonics assistant coach, to the ground during an altercation, then ridiculing him as "senile."

Enter Jerry West.

Never one to shy away from risks, the Lakers' executive vice president of basketball operations saw this as a potential win-win. At the same time Phoenix wanted Horry gone, Los Angeles was itching to move Ceballos, who was averaging just 10.8 points in eight games and whose reputation had never been repaired since he ditched the club a year earlier to go water-skiing. West valued positive role models for the team's three rookies (Bryant, Fisher, and center Travis Knight), and Ceballos was anything but. Plus, with O'Neal's presence, the Lakers no longer felt compelled to tolerate the veteran's me-first nonsense, which included his habit of gazing into space during Harris's huddles and sitting away from teammates on the bench. In a says-everything-about-the-man moment, Ceballos once demanded that Lawrence Tanter, the PA announcer at the Forum, always introduce the forward last. "When he made the All-Star team [in 1995], he changed," said Erikk Aldridge, the assistant public relations director. "Ced was all about Ced."

On January 10, Los Angeles and Phoenix swapped problems, as Ceballos and the rarely used Rumeal Robinson were sent to Phoenix for Horry and (of all people) Kleine, the one Sun willing to call his teammate out. "I was bringing my kids home from school when Danny Ainge called me," Kleine said. "I was happy in Phoenix. I did not want to go to L.A. I was just a throw-in player, and I knew it. Robert needed to start over again. I didn't."

Inside the Lakers' locker room, the reaction was subdued euphoria. Ceballos was an obnoxious brat who played no defense and went AWOL.

Horry, on the other hand, was a 6-foot-9 outside gunner (he was a lifetime 34 percent three-point shooter) and low-post defender joining an operation in need of long-range shooting and low-post defense.

It was a trade that, by NBA standards, generated little attention.

It was a trade that changed everything.

Suddenly, instead of being a towel-throwing pain on an 11-24 team going nowhere fast, Horry was a coveted piece of a first-place club that sat 17 games over .500. During his first four NBA seasons, all with the Rockets, Horry had learned how to play with Hakeem Olajuwon, the 7-foot, 255-pound Nigerian center. He knew his job was to feed off the big man, and that a box score where Olajuwon scored 30 and Horry scored 12 usually meant Houston won. Now, with the Lakers, he was more than happy to acknowledge O'Neal's place as the center of the basketball universe.

Horry made his Laker debut on January 14, scoring 11 points in 26 minutes off the bench in a 91–81 win over the sad-sack Grizzlies. Over the three months that followed, he was the perfect extra part to a franchise headed in the right direction. He averaged 9.2 points and 5.4 rebounds in his first 21 games with the squad, and anyone expecting a towel-throwing whiner was mistaken. At the same time Ceballos was in Phoenix irritating an already irritable locker room, Horry was setting picks, playing perfect help defense, offering quiet snippets of wisdom to Bryant, Knight, and Fisher. In reality, many of those who thought Horry to be difficult failed to understand that, behind the scenes, he was living a nightmare.

On April 2, 1994, his wife, Keva, had given birth to the couple's first child, Ashlyn, who entered the world with 1p36 deletion syndrome, caused when a child is born missing a part of chromosome No. 1. Ashlyn arrived with part of her throat, the epiglottis, not properly formed. As a result, the infant struggled to breathe and eat. She spent months living in Texas Children's Hospital, and Horry would oftentimes wrap practice with the Rockets and bolt straight to her bedside. After winning his first NBA title, in 1994, as the rest of Houston went off to party, Horry returned to the neonatal intensive care unit, where Ashlyn, then three months old, was hooked up to oxygen.

"As soon as one thing would go wrong, boom, we'd be there," Horry said. "Some days, you want to just sit back and cry about it. But other days you'll be like 'Well, God did this for a purpose,' and you deal with it."

The move from Houston to Phoenix was rough, both because it took Horry from an NBA gilded castle to an NBA porta-potty and because it transported him 1,176 miles from Keva and Ashlyn. The assumption that he was merely a coddled punk with an oversized ego burned, but what was he supposed to say? That he missed his daughter? That he didn't want to be here? That it wasn't as simple as shifting hospitals? As uprooting?

Unlike the Suns organization, the Lakers quickly felt like family. Horry was embraced by Harris, whose deep faith and adherence to a Christian ethos made him see Horry not as athlete, but as human being. From the day he first coached Horry, Ainge had found the player to be cantanker- ous and distant — but never inquired as to the origin. Harris knew the truth: that Horry was struggling.

"He was a really great person," Harris recalled. "You never know what you're going to get when you add a person to the mix. But Robert was professional, caring . . . just the type of man every team wants. The day he became a Laker, the franchise took a big step closer to a championship. He was *that* important."

After five games, Harris inserted his new player into the starting lineup, and the transition was blissfully smooth. Between Horry's arrival and mid-February, the Lakers went 10-4, and now held a 1½-game lead over Seattle in the Pacific Division.

Then, disaster. First, in a 100–84 win over the Timberwolves, O'Neal (averaging 26.1 points per game) suffered a hyperextension of his left knee and would be forced to miss eight to ten weeks. Less than a week later, in a defeat to Seattle, Horry sprained the medial collateral ligament in his left knee and was deemed lost for six weeks. The Lakers tried bolstering the roster, offering Golden State center Sean Rooks and a first-round pick in exchange for Chris Mullin, the All-Star forward. But the deal fell through, and the best Los Angeles could do was ship the disgruntled Kleine to New Jersey for small forward George McCloud — a seven-year veteran who arrived for his first practice and couldn't believe what was unfolding. "I always got taped and put on my knee braces," McCloud recalled. "So I'm putting on my braces and Eddie Jones says, 'No, we don't practice like that.'"

McCloud was befuddled. "What do you mean?" he said.

"We're game players," Jones said. "Not practice players. Practice is chill." *What?*

"It was a weird group," McCloud said. "Nick Van Exel was wild and out of control. Shaq was funny as hell, but hurt. Robert was hurt. Eddie was talented but raw. Del was a nice guy, but too nice. He was so laid-back, and with that group he needed to be hard and hold 'em accountable. He couldn't do that."

The Laker most intriguing to McCloud was Bryant, the only member of the team who regularly stayed after practices to get in extra work. "I called him 'Kid KO,'" McCloud recalled. "He wanted to kill you." When Horry went down, a resigned Harris inserted the 18-year-old into the starting lineup at shooting guard (Eddie Jones was shifted to small forward, and Knight was the new center), then watched — eyes half covered

— as the perils of youth went on full display. Bryant made his debut with the opening five in a February 19 home game against Cleveland, and spent the next 23 minutes scoring 10 points and looking largely lost in a 103–84 defeat. The Newark *Star-Ledger* crowned the setback with the headline SURVIVAL, NOT 60 VICTORIES, IS LAKERS' GOAL NOW.

Bryant's run as a starter lasted that one game. He wound up the Lakers' seventh-leading scorer (7.6 points per game) and was replaced by veteran Jerome Kersey. Los Angeles scratched and clawed to survive the remainder of a rocky regular season. By the time O'Neal returned, on April 11 (he scored 24 points and added 11 rebounds in 24 productive minutes), the Lakers were 52-25, but 7½ games behind Utah in the Western Conference playoff seedings. The Sonics, looking up at Los Angeles when O'Neal and Horry were healthy, now led the Pacific, and if the Lakers were to somehow challenge for their first NBA title in nine years, it would have to come as a fourth seed.

"I thought we had a chance," said Corie Blount, the backup forward. "Probably not the best chance. But a chance nonetheless. We just needed everything to go right. We needed to play smart."

How was he there?

That's the question, isn't it? How was Kobe Bryant there, on a basketball court in Salt Lake City, ball in hand, season on the line?

How was he there?

Early on, the playoffs had unfolded so beautifully, even the most cynical Laker diehard was considering the possibility of a deep run. In the first round, Los Angeles squared off against a fifth-seeded Portland team that had taken three of four regular season games from them, and whose players had openly pined for a showdown with O'Neal and Co.

Therefore, when the Lakers won in an uneventful three-games-to-one breeze, the normally reserved Harris turned toward the spectators inside Portland's Rose Garden Arena and yelled, "Goodbye, folks! Nice to see you!"

The Lakers moved on to face the top-seeded Utah Jazz, whose 64-18 record trailed 69-13 Chicago for the NBA's best mark. One season earlier, the Jazz had advanced to the Western Conference Finals, only to fall to Seattle in a crushing seventh game. Now that same team, powered by forward Karl Malone and point guard John Stockton, as well as the league's deepest bench, was expected to steamroll the Lakers (even with a healthy O'Neal and Horry) and challenge for the franchise's first-ever NBA crown.

The best-of-seven series opened as expected, with Utah taking the first game at home in a 93–77 blowout, then winning again two days later, though by a much smaller margin (103–101 after a painful no call on a foul by Malone on Van Exel). "We all knew that we were the better team," said Adam Keefe, a backup Jazz forward. "As long as we went in and executed, it was reasonable to expect a win." Jerry Sloan, the Jazz coach, had a somewhat simple yet impactful defensive approach to beating the Lakers: Give everyone some room to shoot, save for O'Neal, whose life needed to be made miserable. Jazz center Greg Ostertag was a stronger-than-steel 7-foot-2, 280-pound lumbering oaf who spared no elbow, knee, or fist to Shaq's body. When he wasn't on the court, backup Greg Foster went just as hard. "You had to run the floor and tire Shaq out," said Foster. "Our whole thing was to sprint the floor, and on defense jump in front and contest the passes to him. Just make him work harder than he wants to, until you start seeing the heavy breathing."

On offense, Sloan's plan was even simpler. In Stockton and Malone, Utah possessed the best pick-and-roll tandem in NBA history. In O'Neal, Los Angeles possessed one of the most inept pick-and-roll defenders in NBA history. So the Jazz would pick and roll and pick and roll and pick and roll until there were no more picks and no more rolls. "To play the pick-and-roll, you either had to trap it or switch on it," Jones said. "Shaq was so big, and he was coming off an injury. He just couldn't react, and the Jazz exploited it nonstop. We could have come up with a better game plan. We certainly should have."

The Lakers returned to the Forum for Game 3 and, before 17,505 fans, blew the Jazz out, 104–84, in a wildly entertaining ode to athleticism and up-and-down hoops. Wrote Kevin Modesti of the *Los Angeles Daily News*: "If you want to be entertained, watch Shaquille O'Neal, Nick Van Exel, Eddie Jones and Kobe Bryant. They're the Lakers with the anaconda drives, the volcanic dunks and the 3-point spaceballs." Harris was actually allotting Bryant solid minutes, believing his freakish athleticism might befuddle the station-to-station Utah rotation, and his 19 points on 3-of-7 shooting (he hit 13 of 14 free throws) led the team. "They had all the energy," Stockton said. "They had everything. We couldn't deal with it."

Throughout the season, Kupchak and West had been nudging Harris to give Bryant slivers of playing time. They were thrilled with the overall manner in which the head coach had handled the kid, but they also knew an 18-year-old on the bench would grow restless and, perhaps, depressed. "There was definitely some pressure to get him experience," Harris later said. "Which I understood. I don't think it was easy being Kobe as a rookie, sort of isolated, much younger than the other people on the team." Against the methodical Jazz, Bryant served as an Energizer Bunny on speed. He was quicker, faster, more dynamic.

Los Angeles dropped Game 4 at home, a dispiriting 110–95 setback that reminded NBA fans why these Lakers weren't yet of championship stock. First, with a little less than two minutes gone by in the opening quarter, Harris yanked Van Exel, then watched as his point guard kicked a chair and engaged his head coach in an arm-waving sideline argument. Harris later explained to the media that he'd inserted Bryant for Van Exel so he could deliver a message to Campbell — a preposterous excuse that caused Van Exel to ask, "You believe that?" to assembled reporters. "I was on the court, I heard a horn, and I came out. He's the coach. He makes all the good decisions."

Two days later, the Lakers and Jazz returned to Salt Lake City and the floor of the Delta Center for Game 5. In order to advance to the Western Conference Finals, Los Angeles would need to win three straight ("It's a challenge," O'Neal said, "and I love challenges"), which was somewhat less likely than a manned mission to Pluto. The Jazz were, simply, the superior team — more experienced, more cohesive, more skilled, better coached. (Jerry Sloan, in his ninth season as Utah head coach, seemed to have answers for everything Harris tried.)

The game commenced at 7:30 p.m., and after Utah jumped out to a 53–45 halftime lead, it was fair to assume that the fragile Lakers would meekly fade away. But they didn't. Van Exel, starting at point guard despite the drama, was ferocious, charging straight at Stockton en route to 26 points and 4 assists. O'Neal, frustrated by Ostertag's physicality, added 23 points and 13 rebounds. With Byron Scott out with a sprained wrist, Harris summoned Bryant as his first man off the bench, hoping the rookie could handle the largeness of the moment.

The results were mixed. On the strength of a 10-point fourth-quarter surge, Los Angeles returned from the dead, tying the score at 70 with 8:01 remaining. But when O'Neal — trying to block a Malone jumper in the paint — fouled out with 1:46 left in regulation, and with Horry long gone after being ejected for forearming Jeff Hornacek, Harris needed to devise a revamped scoring strategy on the quick. His offensive options were plentiful: Van Exel, lightning quick and a deadly three-point gunner; Eddie Jones, not playing particularly well but owner of one of the best first steps in the game; Jerome Kersey, a bit battered by age but a man who had averaged 24.8 points per game in his Portland heyday. "We were really, really talented," recalled Jones. "Not the best team yet. But we weren't lacking guys who could put the ball in the hole."

That's what makes what followed so bewildering.

With 40 seconds on the clock, Stockton found himself guarded by Bryant just outside the three-point line. A year earlier, the youngster in charge of keeping the NBA's greatest point guard in check had been attending prom. Hell, he wasn't even that great a defender at Lower Merion. Stockton licked his chops, took a mini-step, then burst left past the rookie for an uncontested layup and a tied game at 89. It wasn't merely poor crunch-time defense. It was nonexistent crunch-time defense.

Yet if Bryant wasn't ready for the stage, his coach didn't see it. Earlier in the year, Harris had sat down with the rookie to ask how things were progressing. He meant adjusting to Los Angeles, life with his older teammates, navigating the highways. Bryant wasn't that type of conversationalist. Small talk wasn't a go-to. Without pause he replied, "Coach, if you can get Shaq out of the paint and give me the ball, I'll beat anyone in the league one-on-one." The answer was preposterous, but also oddly inspiring in its confidence.

The Lakers regained possession with 11.3 seconds left and the score knotted at 89. During a time-out, Harris looked around the huddle and decided that the man to have the basketball in his hands would be the untested, undeserving, untrustworthy Kobe Bryant. He received the in-bounds pass from Campbell and methodically dribbled up the court. Three times with his right hand. Two times with his left. Right. Right. Right. The time was ticking away. With 6.5 seconds remaining, Bryant crossed half-court. Bryon Russell, Utah's small forward, stood before him, crouching in anticipation. Van Exel, to Bryant's left, clapped twice. Not enthusiastically. Casually.

With 4.2 seconds left, Bryant drove to his right, dribbling toward the paint, where Russell and a collapsing Hornacek awaited. Standing at the three-point line, Van Exel could not have been more wide open. Standing along the baseline, Campbell could not have been more wide open. Jones, just outside the three-point line by the Lakers' bench, was all alone. In fact, as the team prepared the possession, Harris had urged Bryant to get it to Jones. "The play was designed for me," Jones recalled years later. "There's this myth that none of us wanted the ball. Not true. I was ready to shoot, I wanted to shoot. Kobe had his own plan." Bryant charged toward the paint, then stopped, planted 14 feet from the hoop, and shot a jumper over Russell that rose . . . rose . . . rose . . .

And touched nothing but air.

Malone grabbed the rebound and the clock expired. There would be overtime.

"It was a very weird moment," said Stephen Howard, a Jazz forward. "You have this guy right out of high school and you're putting the entire faith of the team in him breaking down Bryon, our best defender. *That's* your play?"

The extra period began well. Without O'Neal, Campbell won the tip and got it into the hands of Bryant, who — following a brief, indecisive pause — flipped it to Van Exel. The point guard pump-faked, moved in past Stockton, failed to look toward an open Jones, started to shoot — then heard a wide-open Bryant calling for the ball behind the three-point line. Van Exel passed to Bryant, who bent his knees, lowered his shoulders, and — with no Utah player within five feet — let loose a shot that rose . . . rose . . . rose . . .

And touched nothing but air.

Again.

"My bad . . . my bad," Bryant mouthed aloud as the sellout crowd delighted in the chant of *"Aiirr balllll . . . Aiirr balllll."*

Harris, pacing the sideline, clapping reflexively, looked exasperated. As did the other Lakers. Once again, Jones believed he would be getting the ball. "I mean, it was supposed to be mine," he recalled. "I would have loved for it to be mine to make or miss. But . . . Kobe." This made no sense. Even the last man in the rotation, rookie center Travis Knight, had played in some big games during his four years at the University of Connecticut. Why, with the heat turned up to 500 degrees, was Kobe Bryant launching shots?

"What the fuck are you shooting for?" asked Laker reserve forward Corie Blount. "That's what it was for me. It had to be Eddie or Nick — not Kobe. Nobody expected Kobe to take that shot, because in the flow of the game you swing the ball, swing it some more. You expect it back. Then it's up in the air, and then it's 'Holy shit — he just shot an air ball.' We knew we couldn't control his need to force his will on the game, but . . . man. What the fuck?"

"Kobe had a lot of talent," said Knight. "But he was not a very good jump shooter at that point. He definitely wasn't the guy on our roster to take those shots."

Over the next 3:09, the Jazz opened up a 96–93 lead, and the clock read :45 when Van Exel passed yet again to Bryant, two feet behind the three-point line. "We were on the bench saying, 'Give it to Kobe again,'" recalled Howard. "'Please give it to Kobe again.'" Had he looked right, even for a second, Bryant would have observed a wide-open Van Exel. Instead, he jumped into the air, extended his right arm, and let loose a shot that rose . . . rose . . . rose . . .

And touched nothing but air.

Sean Rooks, the backup center, standing beneath the basket, turned to flash Bryant a death glare. Bryant, walking back on defense, licked his lips and gazed straight ahead. "Once you shoot one air ball, you crawl into a hole," said Howard. "He kept shooting."

Surely this time Bryant was done.

Surely this time Bryant had learned his lesson.

The Lakers got the ball back for one final chance. Down 96–93. Fifteen seconds remained. Van Exel dribbled up the court, where he was met by Stockton and Russell. He dribbled to his left before bounce-passing to Bryant. (Asked why he continued to pass to Bryant, Van Exel said, "He was my teammate and he was out there and he was open. What other choice is there?") Jones stood alone in the corner, waiting for the pass that failed to come. With seven seconds left and Hornacek closing in, Bryant let loose a shot that rose . . . rose . . . rose . . .

And touched nothing but air.

On the Utah bench, Howard flashed a look of stunned disbelief as Foster and Chris Morris high-fived. The Jazz were moving on, the Lakers were going home.

And Kobe Bryant was . . . *what?*

As the Los Angeles players walked off the court, Bryant felt a large arm drape his shoulders. It was O'Neal, who later called BS on Jones's claims of wanting the last shot. ("He'd freeze up in a tight situation, then act like it was no big deal," he once wrote.) Having been the centerpiece of an Orlando team that was swept by Houston in the 1995 NBA Finals, O'Neal understood public sports humiliation. "Look at all these people laughing at you," he told Bryant. "One day we're going to get them back. Don't worry. Someday everybody's going to be screaming your name. Take this and learn from it." The words, meant to comfort, were the soothing whispers of a franchise centerpiece trying to act the part of a leader. To the youngster, however, they mattered little. Bryant didn't require coddling.

That night the Lakers returned home to Los Angeles for a long off-season of repair and introspection.

The next morning, Kobe Bryant was in the gym.

Taking 14-foot jump shots.

6

Fox Catcher

C onsidering the Los Angeles Lakers were a team with an all-world center, a teenage guard with oodles of potential, a starting lineup featuring no one older than 28, and a first-round playoff triumph under its belt,
in the aftermath of the four-air-ball Utah debacle, things sure felt messy.

To begin with, because of the George McCloud trade, the Lakers surrendered their first-round pick to New Jersey, leaving the franchise with
a pair of second-round selections, to be used on two men, Gonzaga center
Paul Rogers and Louisville guard DeJuan Wheat, who would play a combined zero regular season games for the team.

Second, there was a lingering uncertainty about whether the Nick Van
Exel–Del Harris marriage could continue. The point guard thought the
coach old-fashioned and ineffective, long (like, *reeaallllly* long) on talk
and short on keeping up with the game. In the time it took Harris to
explain an offense, Van Exel could have made three phone calls, watched
the complete third season of *Beverly Hills 90210*, and eaten half a pecan
pie. One time, when Harris lost his voice, he pulled out a VCR and had the
team watch a 30-minute video of him lecturing on defense. "The nonstop
talking drove Nick crazy," said Corie Blount. Harris, for his part, desperately craved Van Exel's approval. "I really wanted him to like me," he said
years later. "But I don't think he ever did." In this, Harris was correct. Van
Exel could not stomach the man.

Third, there was the departure of Byron Scott, the veteran guard who accepted a two-year contract from Panathinaikos Athletic Club to play in Greece. Though he averaged only 6.7 points per game in 1996–97, Scott had been the ideal mentor for Los Angeles's bevy of youngsters. Jerome Kersey, the other bench guru, also took off, signing a free agent deal with Seattle.

Fourth — *there was Bryant.*

In the history of professional basketball, one would be hard-pressed to find a player — *ever* — who shot four air balls in a single game, let alone at crunch time in a playoff decider. Back in 1976, the Rancho Cotate (California) High School varsity basketball team was skewered by the local newspaper for shooting four *total* air balls in the second half of a loss to Casa Grande. On December 3, 1982, the New York Knicks launched four air balls in a 105–98 loss to Washington. Bernard King had two, Truck Robinson one, and Ernie Grunfeld the other.

But four by one player? Implausible.

What confounded members of the Lakers about Bryant was that, instead of appearing remorseful or a bit gun-shy, there was only arrogance and resilience. He never apologized to teammates, never accepted blame, never really acknowledged that maybe (just maybe) he could have passed to Eddie Jones or Van Exel for open looks. The closest he came was during a chat with Kevin Modesti of the *Los Angeles Daily News* when he said, "My team trusted me and I didn't come through."

Because of his youth and inexperience, Bryant returned for another season in the Fila Summer Pro League, where his Laker teammates included Wheat and Rogers, as well as a rookie guard out of Tulsa named Shea Seals, former Georgia Tech star James Forrest, onetime Texas Tech standout Jason Sasser, and, perhaps most noteworthy, Jimmy King, who five years earlier had gained fame as part of the University of Michigan's Fab Five freshmen.

Never quite the caliber of Chris Webber, Juwan Howard, and Jalen Rose, the Wolverines' three marquee stars, King spent a productive four years in Ann Arbor, averaging a team-best 14.7 points as a senior before being selected by Toronto in the second round of the 1995 draft. His NBA career didn't amount to much — in 64 total games with the Raptors and the Denver Nuggets, King averaged 4.5 points and 1.8 rebounds. Most of the 6-foot-5 guard's 1996–97 season was spent in Moline, Illinois, with the Quad City Thunder of the Continental Basketball Association.

Yet even with the passage of time and King's basketball shortcomings, Bryant viewed him — first and foremost — as a Fab Fiver, forever decked out in the baggy maize-and-blue jersey and baggier maize-and-blue shorts, the shaved head, the cultlike fan following, the glow of 1,000 flashes.

When summer league team practices began on July 12, 1997, Bryant looked at King and saw not a 24-year-old trying to earn an invite to training camp, but a gilded rival attempting to steal what wasn't his. "Kobe," recalled Forrest, "was an animal."

It was ugly. Bryant took pleasure in talking all sorts of trash to King — about his game, his manhood, his history, his career. He was a bitch, a pussy, a cunt. "You can't shoot for shit!" Bryant yelled during a workout — and while this was true (King shot 43 percent from the field in his one NBA season), it felt unnecessary. "Everything with Jimmy was a battle to Kobe," said Ace Custis, a former Virginia Tech star and part of the summer league squad. "Kobe went at Jimmy, and it was lopsided. It became this trash-talking event, Kobe daring him to shoot jumpers, Jimmy missing, Kobe daring him to shoot more jumpers. It wasn't pretty, but if you wanted someone with a competitive edge, there he was."

"He'd say to him, 'I've got my own shoe!'" recalled Forrest. "I'll never forget that."

One of the summer squad's more popular players, King refused to direct scorn at Bryant, or mutter a derisive off-the-court word. Having played with the notoriously thin-skinned Webber in college, King knew insecurity when he saw it. He was actually dumbfounded when he arrived to the first few Laker practices and noticed two things — "one," King recalled, "no one acknowledged Kobe when he would enter the locker room. And two, no one talked to him. Ever. It was confusing. Was he socially awkward? Yeah. So I talked to him, just to help him get along with others. He needed that."

One year earlier, Bryant's summer league coach was Larry Drew, the

Laker assistant. This time, in an effort to work one-on-one with the kid in game situations, Del Harris took over. It was an opportunity to spend extensive time with Bryant, and Harris liked/disliked what he saw. Bryant was arrogant, Bryant was endearing. Bryant was a ball hog, Bryant was polite ("Yes sir, no sir," recalled Harris. "A good kid"). Bryant desperately wanted to be the next Michael Jordan, yet Bryant lacked Michael Jordan's self-awareness and willingness to, ahem, pass. "He was the worst teammate you could have if you were trying to make a team," said Wheat. "I was the point guard. My job, literally, was to be a point guard. But as soon as I'd start dribbling, Kobe would scream, 'Give me the ball! Give me the ball!' What was the point? He dominates the ball, so it's impossible to make an impression."

Unlike his players, Harris loved Bryant's seeming indifference to the four air balls in Salt Lake City. From Sidney Moncrief and Moses Malone to Jack Sikma and Terry Cummings, he had coached his fair share of NBA stars. One thing they all possessed was a short memory. In eight summer league games, Bryant averaged 20.9 points and 5.6 rebounds. But while he remained an irksome ball hog, his swagger was accompanied by genuine belief. In 1996, teammates felt that Bryant faked swagger to hide apprehension. Now, with a season under his belt, the apprehension was gone. "I'd never seen someone that age that self-assured," recalled Seals. "When he shot, he had no doubt the ball was going in. No doubt."

For the first time in nine years, the Lakers would skip Hawaii and hold training camp at College of the Desert, 130 miles away in Palm Desert. When the 20 invitees reported on October 3, they were again greeted by a meandering talk from Harris, who wanted to tell everyone about this and that and that and this and . . .

"I actually blew two stomach muscles out for Del," Shaquille O'Neal recalled. "I was on this sit-up kick, and I got about 1,000 sit-ups in and he was *still* talking." O'Neal laughed. "I think most athletes have ADD, like me," he said. "We need to be in and out — boom, boom, boom, boom, done. That wasn't Del."

When Harris wasn't talking, he could look around and appreciate the squad that Jerry West and Mitch Kupchak had assembled. O'Neal was healthy, Bryant was less green, Van Exel seemed to be in a shockingly upbeat mood, and Elden Campbell was in the best shape of his career. Horry, fully recovered from a sprained left knee, was perhaps the top outside shooter in the league, and Jon Barry, a five-year veteran guard, had averaged 4.9 points off the bench in Atlanta. He was a perfect free agent signee to back up Jones.

During an early practice, O'Neal was goofing around, dribbling the ball up the court, when Bryant reached in for a steal. The two stars collided, their bodies slamming into each other, then flying in opposite directions. "No foul?" O'Neal yelled.

"Pass the fucking ball," Bryant replied. "You ain't no guard."

Teammates loved it. The intensity was palpable.

"There were championship expectations, and nothing less," recalled Barry. "I hadn't been on a team with that level of buzz. I felt like the pieces were in place."

Especially with the most unlikely addition of all.

He wasn't supposed to be a Los Angeles Laker.

A Knick? Sure . . .

A Pacer? Why not . . .

A Piston, a Sonic, a King, a Warrior, a Buck? All seemed feasible.

But Ulrich Alexander "Rick" Fox, a Los Angeles Laker?

No way in hell.

Ever since he was selected out of North Carolina by Boston with the 24th overall pick in the 1991 NBA draft, Fox — scrappy, edgy, never afraid to throw an elbow to the chin — seemed perfectly fitted for the Celtics' green-and-white uniforms. When he arrived, it was the franchise of Larry Bird, of Kevin McHale, and Fox soaked up the tradition and lore. "Larry was the most amazing cat ever," Fox recalled. "It physically didn't matter what his body was like. He pushed through it. Just mentally blocked it out. I *wanted* that, too." Fox thought himself the next in line, the protector of a dynasty that made five NBA championship series appearances in the 1980s.

Yet as the superstars faded into the abyss (Bird retired after Fox's rookie season, McHale a year later), Fox's dreams of Celtic glory faded, too. Departing stars mixed with awful draft picks (Where have you gone, Gerald Paddio?), mixed with inept coaching, resulted in a precipitous slide, and the 1996–97 team finished 15-67, the worst mark in the 51-year history of the organization. On the bright side, Fox was the team captain, starting 75 games at small forward while averaging a career-high 15.4 points. On the down side, it was misery.

"God, we sucked," Fox said. "I was basically the captain of the *Titanic,* and the boat was sinking. All year, our coach and general manager [M.L. Carr] was running us really hard in practice, which confused me, because we were an exhausted team. Well, he was trying to wear us out so we'd suck and get the No. 1 pick in the next draft. He'd play the best guys three-quarters of a game, then take us out late when it was close. I'd be completely baffled. 'Why are we doing this?' Then it hit me — that was the year Tim Duncan was coming out of Wake Forest. It was all about getting Tim."

Regardless, Fox was a Celtic. That's why, when Boston replaced Carr with former University of Kentucky coach Rick Pitino, he was thrilled to hear the new leader say, "Rick, you're a Boston Celtic, and I want to build this team around you."

That was on a Monday. Two days later, Pitino (who was also serving as the general manager) and Fox agreed to a six-year, $33 million contract. For a kid who grew up in the Bahamas, itching for the American Dream, it was more than he could imagine. Rick Fox would spend his time as a lavishly paid Boston Celtic, under arguably basketball's hottest coach.

Or not.

Though Boston wrapped the 1996–97 season with the NBA's worst record, the draft lottery handed San Antonio the first overall pick. So instead of landing Duncan, one of the best low-post prospects of the past three decades, the Celtics used the No. 3 overall slot on Colorado's Chauncey Billups — a 6-foot-3 point guard in need of work. Pitino believed the franchise required, more than anything, a low-post presence, so right after telling Fox the $33 million would be his, he flew out to California to meet with Travis Knight, the Laker rookie, who'd averaged 4.8 points and 4.5

rebounds as O'Neal's backup. Boston offered Knight a seven-year, $22 million contract, and he couldn't turn it down. "I loved being a Laker, but they were way over the cap with Shaq there," Knight recalled. "I had to take the security."

Hardly an ethical model, Pitino asked Knight to keep the contract quiet for another few days, until he could sign Fox and finagle the salary cap numbers. Word leaked, however (KNIGHT GOES TO CELTICS, read the *Los Angeles Daily News* headline on July 8), and Pitino received a call from David Stern, the NBA commissioner, who said Boston had to pick either Fox or Knight and stop trying to circumvent league rules.

Oblivious to the financial issues, the following Monday morning Fox woke, went to the nearby barbershop for a trim, then expected to head to Boston Garden for a press conference announcing his return. He received a call from Bill Strickland, his agent.

"Rick, it's Bill."

"Hey, Bill. I'm excited for today. How are you?"

"Not the best."

"Why?"

Silence.

"Rick," Strickland said, "you've been renounced."

"What?"

"You've been renounced by Rick Pitino, and you lost your Bird Rights."

"My what?"

The Bird Rights, named for Larry Bird and also known as the Qualifying Veterans Free Agent Exception, allowed a team to spend beyond the $26.9 million salary cap to retain a player who had been with the franchise for at least three years. However, in order to sign other free agents (aka Travis Knight), a team would have to renounce its own players' Bird Rights.

So that's what the Boston Celtics did — without taking the time to tell its own player.

"I was furious," said Fox. "This was really late in the game, and teams didn't have any money left for free agents. So instead of making $33 million, I was pretty much available for $1 million. Which made me the hottest remaining free agent on the market."

Before long, Fox—who received inquiries from 15 organizations—went on a whirlwind tour, visiting the Knicks, the Hawks, the Rockets, and the Lakers. Like O'Neal, he had already dipped his toe into acting, landing a recurring role as a prisoner on the HBO dramatic series *Oz* as well as playing a basketball standout in the Whoopi Goldberg film *Eddie*. He was Hollywood handsome and red carpet charismatic. The idea of relocating to Los Angeles was appealing.

"I called my agent and told him I'd picked the Lakers," Fox recalled. "I'd only make $1 million, but it was an up-and-coming team in a terrific city."

Strickland asked his client to hang tight. The Cleveland Cavaliers had called at the last minute. They were in need of a starting small forward and could offer $20 million over four years.

"But Cleveland sucks," Fox said—referring to both the team (which went 42-40 in 1996–97) and the city (once ranked among America's most dangerous metropolises by CBS News).

"It's a lot of money," Strickland replied.

"Bill," Fox said, "tell them if they wanna pay me $42 million I'll go to Cleveland. Otherwise I'm joining the Lakers."

Rick Fox joined the Lakers.

There are good fits and there are great fits. From day one, Rick Fox was the *perfect* fit. He officially signed his contract on August 26 and reported to training camp a week later. The talent gap between the Celtics and the Lakers was the size of O'Neal's 35,000-square-foot Orlando mansion, and Fox was thrilled to be joining an organization that considered him, in the words of Jerry West, to be "the missing piece."

"I can't tell you how much we think the versatility of Rick will add to our team," West said. "I think we have the pieces in place."

From the very beginning, what Fox did best was make an effort—a sincere, dignified effort—to not merely understand Bryant, but help him. If 1996 in Hawaii was a tough time for the rookie, what with his hand injury, 1997 at College of the Desert was some variation of a revenge film come to life. *Kobe Bryant: The Empire Strikes Back.* His off-season was spent working out, and only working out. Prior to his debut season, he had hired Joe Carbone, a former professional power lifter, to move from Monsey, New York, to Los Angeles and serve as a full-time personal trainer. After the season ended, Bryant went at it — *hard.* No days off. No breaks for ice cream and cake. Strict diet, strict sleep pattern, strict everything. "I put him on a world-class weight-lifting program," Carbone recalled. "He would do the weight program, then shoot for a couple of hours, then do running and agility work, then come back the next day and do it again."

This was around the time Bryant began what would become known as his legendary midnight workouts — retreating to an empty gym to punish himself. "I always felt like if I started my day early, I could train more each day," he recalled. "If I started at 11, I'd get in a few hours, rest for four hours, and then get back to the gym around 5 to 7. But if I started at 5 a.m. and went until 7, I could do again from 11 until 2 and 6 until 8. By starting earlier I set myself up for an extra workout each day. Over the course of a summer, that's a lot of extra hours in the gym." When Bryant walked off the court after the Utah misses, he was 6-foot-6 and 200 pounds. He returned an inch taller and 10 pounds heavier. It was all muscle.

Fox liked the kid's approach. Loved it, actually. In Boston, far too many teammates had placed money and partying over basketball success. One Celtic, in particular, smoked marijuana on a daily basis — before games, after games. The casualness drove the hyper-competitive Fox to the brink of insanity. He could handle losses. But nonchalant indifference? Never.

Though Bryant and Eddie Jones shared Philadelphia ties, as well as something of a friendship (Jones tried encouraging the rookie — behavior many teammates could not claim), the now 19-year-old NBA sophomore saw the Lakers' starting small forward as a roadblock in his ascension to the starting lineup. Dating back to his days running pickup against Jones at Temple University, Bryant believed himself to be the superior player. But now, after Jones had seemed to disappear during crunch time in the Utah series, Bryant *knew it.* "Eddie spent most of his time looking over his shoulder at Kobe," O'Neal recalled. "He knew it, I knew it and Kobe knew it." Day after day during training camp, Bryant went after

Jones with a ferocity few had witnessed before. They played one-on-one, and Bryant attacked. They scrimmaged five-on-five, and Bryant attacked. Jimmy King failed to earn an invitation to camp, but he wasn't needed. Jones was Bryant's Jimmy King now, and it was ruthless. "Kobe wasn't even on my radar when I picked the Lakers, but — damn!" Fox said. "He was trying to bust a fucking door open. He made it clear from the very beginning that his intent was to push Eddie out the door and take his job. And I loved that."

Fox paused.

"Was Kobe actually ready to start?" he said. "No. Not at all. He could score, but he had a very narrow focus, and that doesn't work in the NBA."

The product of a Bahamian father and a Canadian mother of Italian and Scottish descent, Fox felt a bond with Bryant over language (both spoke Italian) and culture. Having been born in Toronto and raised in Nassau, and a high school star in Warsaw, Indiana, he grasped what it was like to not quite fit in. To feel like an outsider. "The immigrant story in me is that nothing's given to you," Fox said. "If you come to this country and you don't take advantage, you have no one to blame but yourself. Kobe came to practice every day and saw it as his land of opportunity. An opportunity for him to show that he deserved to play. And it wasn't just wanting to play. He wanted to be great."

Bryant viewed training camp as a way to convince Harris that he should be a part of the starting five. Harris didn't share the outlook. He moved the kid up the bench to sixth man but wasn't ready to commit to Bryant as his shooting guard.

Plus, there were bigger problems to address. In the early days of training camp, O'Neal took a pass on a three-on-two break, brought back his right arm, and prepared to let loose with a (in his words) "Vince Carter cuff dunk" on Campbell. He was too far from the hoop, however, overstretched, and suffered an abdominal strain that left him unavailable for the October 31 season opener against, of all the teams, the Utah Jazz at the Great Western Forum. It was dispiriting news for the Lakers, now forced to start Sean Rooks, the sixth-year backup.

None of this left O'Neal in a particularly warm mood. Though he didn't wear revenge in a public way, the center spent a good chunk of the off-season seething over the five-game loss to the Jazz and, specifically, the impression that Greg Ostertag, Utah's center, had gotten the better of him. Statistically speaking, the showdown was barely a showdown at all — O'Neal averaged 22 points and 11.6 rebounds, compared with his rival's 3 points and 6.2 rebounds. Yet with his size (7-foot-2, 280 pounds) and toughness, Ostertag played noteworthy defense.

Throughout the summer, O'Neal replayed the Utah games in his mind. More than that, he replayed Ostertag's mannerisms and boastfulness in his mind. When the Jazz won, the center — through O'Neal's prism — behaved like a conquering hero. He was the Shaq slayer. The man who derailed Shaq Diesel. "Nobody thinks I've done anything all year, especially Shaq," Ostertag said after the series triumph. "But I guess that's why he's playing golf right now and I'm in the Western Conference finals." Those seven words — *That's why he's playing golf right now* — were a punch to O'Neal's gut. Really, his pride. Plus, there were simply too many writers like Rick Bozich, the *Louisville Courier-Journal* columnist, who noted, "O'Neal has plugged soft drinks, fast food and sneakers. One thing he failed to plug was the Lakers' frontcourt. L.A. failed to make the NBA's Final Eight, and, yes, that was Greg Ostertag who blocked nine shots to Shaq's one."

Ouch.

Jazz-Lakers was scheduled for the night of October 31, and earlier that day the two teams held afternoon shootarounds at the Forum. Los Angeles went first, and Utah followed. There was a brief crossing of paths as players arrived and departed. Some pleasantries were exchanged. Some fists were pounded. O'Neal and Fox were standing in the tunnel near the court, Fox in T-shirt and shorts, and O'Neal in street clothing. "We were talking," Fox recalled. "Just talking."

Suddenly, O'Neal spotted Ostertag. The goon was by himself, walking toward the court.

"Rick," O'Neal said with a crooked grin, "watch this."

Three days earlier, O'Neal had been named team captain. Now, without warning, the Laker superstar approached the Jazz non-superstar.

"Listen," he told Ostertag, "stop talking shit about me. I have a son and he's reading what you say. People don't need to see that."

Ostertag looked at O'Neal and snapped, "Man, fuck you."

"Oh, fuck me?" he replied. "Okay."

O'Neal pulled back a cupped left hand and — *smack!* — nailed him flush in the cheek. The noise resonated throughout the building, the loud and fleshy sound of skin pounding skin.

"Holy shit," Fox said. "Holy shit."

Less than a month earlier, Lennox Lewis, the world heavyweight champion, had knocked out Andrew Golota 95 seconds into their bout in Atlantic City. This was far more dramatic. Ostertag dropped to the ground like a slab of raw meat, then cowered in a fetal position. Despite his size (the writer Michael C. Lewis said Ostertag reported to camp "looking as if he'd spent his summer in a deli") and reasonable skill, he wasn't someone who loved basketball or even needed basketball. Ostertag was here because the work paid good money and beat digging ditches. "It wasn't a passion for Greg," said Stephen Howard, the Jazz forward. "I remember many times when they'd have to send a trainer to find Greg when we were doing weights. He'd be hiding in the bathroom."

Now he wasn't hiding. He was crawling. "Where's my contact lens?" Ostertag cried out, crawling beneath O'Neal. "Has anyone seen my contact lens?"

Not one member of the Jazz stepped in. There were no punches thrown at O'Neal, no helping hands extended toward Ostertag. He was on the floor and then — sans assistance — he stood up, looked at a grinning O'Neal, saw some other Jazz players shuffling their feet, heard the guffawing Laker players, and walked off.

"Greg wasn't in any position to really defend himself," said Adam Keefe, the Jazz forward. "Shaq did what he felt he needed to do, and it was over. I'm not sure I ever thought of it again."

The same could not be said for Los Angeles, which was about to begin the season. That night, a less-than-capacity crowd of 16,234 entered the old building to see Harris's club exact revenge with a 104–87 drubbing of the Jazz. Was the head coach comfortable with O'Neal's antics? Hardly.

"I obviously prefer a calm sea," Harris said with a scowl before tipoff. "I will stand by Shaquille even though we're not happy about whatever happened." West was even more furious, positioning himself beneath his center's chin and screaming, "I won't tolerate that type of childish behavior! You embarrassed yourself, your team, your parents and this organization. If you do something like this again, I will trade you!"

Rooks played well in O'Neal's stead (12 points, 7 rebounds), and Van Exel was dynamic, hitting six of eight threes en route to 22 points. Fox fit in seamlessly, adding 8 points in 26 minutes and caring not whether he scored or rebounded, as long as the team won. The star, however, was Bryant, whose debut as a sixth man netted 23 points, 5 assists, 3 rebounds, and a steal.

"Kobe," Fox said, "was raw. But he could be dazzling."

Four nights later, Los Angeles improved to 2-0 by outlasting the Kings, 101–98. O'Neal had planned on participating, but decking an opposing player (even with an open hand) doesn't come cheap. He was suspended for one game (which cost him $156,794 in pay), fined $10,000, and asked (aka forced) by the organization to issue a comment of regret. "I apologize to Greg," he wrote. "I hope he accepts my apology and that he and I can put behind us any bad feelings."

It was laughable. O'Neal regretted nothing. He was informed that a physical statement needed to be made, so he (aka John Black, the team's PR head) made one. "Fuck that guy," he said years later. "He deserved it."

O'Neal finally made his 1997–98 debut on November 7, scoring 17 points and collecting 8 rebounds in his team's third-straight triumph, a 99–94 win against Patrick Ewing and the Knicks. If there was any concern over his health, it ceased in the fourth game, when O'Neal contributed 27 points and 19 rebounds in a 132–97 slaughtering of 0-5 Golden State. "He was the most unstoppable player in the league," recalled Olden Polynice, the journeyman center. "With that weight, with that size, with that strength, the great hands, the quickness — what were you really going to do?"

Before long, Los Angeles was the class of the NBA — winners of its first 11, leading the equally talented SuperSonics by two games in the Pacific.

O'Neal was his typical dominant self, Van Exel was running the offense like a maestro, Fox was embraced, and Horry was happy and content and sitting behind the three-point line, waiting for his shot. No, the Laker players weren't crazy about Harris, whose offense still felt boring and stiff and whose plodding speech patterns doubled as 600 tablets of Ambien. But winning cures most ills. And the Lakers were winning a ton.

There was just one issue.

As Kobe Bryant emerged as a key contributor (he scored 25 in 24 minutes against the Warriors, 11 in 16 minutes vs. Vancouver), Jones turned increasingly . . . what's the word? Lesser? Insignificant? Invisible? Dating back to his time as a prep star at Blanche Ely High, in Pompano Beach, Florida, it was easy to overlook Jones, whose slight frame and eyes-to-ward-the-ground body language suggested more wallflower than shark. "He had an edginess to him, but you had to look to see it," recalled Dean Demopoulos, an assistant coach who recruited Jones to Temple. "He was like Gumby, the way he could get through cracks and crevices. But it was subtle. You had to watch close to see how phenomenal he was." In college, Jones was part of an Owls squad that featured two other future NBA players (guard Rick Brunson and forward Aaron McKie), and while he was the most talented, the skill oftentimes got lost in coach John Chaney's team-first offense. Also, there was little to no bombast in Eddie Jones. He played, he played hard — then he went home. No smack talk. When Los Angeles used the 10th overall pick in the 1994 draft to add him to the team, the fan reaction was that of a 3 a.m. visit to the Mahopac Public Library reading room. Jones's game sizzled. His personality did not.

Regardless, the growing chorus of Laker fans who wanted more Kobe and less Eddie was confounding, because the third-year guard was playing the best ball of his lifetime. But Bryant was on the verge of legitimate greatness — a greatness that Jones (talent be damned) would never touch. And even as Jones torched the Raptors for 25 points and the Clippers for 32, he often felt forgotten. "Eddie was amazing," said Shea Seals, the rookie guard. "But Kobe was the most competitive human being on the planet. That, plus athleticism, took him to a different place."

The trade talks began in early November, when newspapers correctly reported that Jerry West was in discussions with Sacramento about an Eddie Jones–Mitch Richmond swap. "I know Kobe felt a bit constrained and wanted to show off more of his game," recalled Richmond, at the time an eight-year veteran and five-time All-Star. "I think there was a belief he and Eddie had too similar games."

Every day, there seemed to be a new rumor. Jones-for-Richmond persisted. As did Jones for Chicago's Scottie Pippen, Jones for Charlotte's Glen Rice, Jones for Seattle's Detlef Schrempf. Behind the scenes, O'Neal was openly rooting for a swap to take place. When he saw Jones, his mind immediately flashed to Nick Anderson, his former Orlando teammate who repeatedly wilted under the spotlight. Jones, O'Neal believed, was no different. He could score and defend for 82 games, but come playoffs — who knew?

Because he was quiet and reluctant to express himself to the media, Jones rarely commented. But the gossip gnawed at him. "I'm playing my ass off — *playing my ass off* — and you keep talking about trading me," he recalled. "How would *you* feel?" When Jones spoke to the media, he did so honestly. He wanted to stay in Los Angeles. He hated the uncertainty. It was hard to play with all the chatter. Chaney, his college coach, said the kid was incapable of lying, and recalled a radio interview conducted after a Temple loss back in 1991. "The host asked Eddie what I told the team in the locker room," Chaney said. "On air — on air! — Eddie said, 'Coach told us we were a bunch of pussies.' Boy, my wife was mad at me when I got home that night. But that was Eddie Jones. Honest and real."

On November 25, Pippen — in his 11th season with Chicago — told the *Daily Herald* of Arlington Heights, Illinois, that he wanted to be sent to either Phoenix or the Lakers. The seven-time All-Star was fed up with the Bulls' penny-pinching ways, and aspired to stand alongside O'Neal and Van Exel and create a new dynasty. The request blew up, and soon enough Jones-for-Pippen was a presumed inevitability.

Only the Lakers kept winning.

And winning.

And winning.

And winning.

Blockbuster trades are hard enough to pull off when your team stinks. But when you're on a roll, and everything is moving along at breakneck speed, who aspires to be the fool demolishing the bliss? The Bulls wanted to rid themselves of the headache that was Scottie Pippen. The Lakers wanted to rid themselves of Jones, a marginalized player O'Neal slammed for being "always mad."

Yet the Bulls were terrific, and the Lakers were terrific, and West decided against pulling the trigger.

"Looking back, I wish he did," Jones recalled. "Because the trade rumors never died."

The season was a weird one.

Not the weirdest. That comes later.

But weird.

Even as West insisted that Jones wouldn't be traded, the media refused to let the subject die. O'Neal, already out with the abdominal strain, suffered a hairline fracture in his right wrist while punching a heavy bag during a boxing workout (leading a befuddled Harris to wonder aloud why his oft-injured big man was punching *anything*). Mario Bennett, a backup center with Hakeem Olajuwon's physique, Spencer Dunkley's skill set, and a cucumber sponge's intellect, was unable to accompany the team to Vancouver because he lacked the proper documentation to enter Canada — despite Laker officials urging him on 743 (or so) separate occasions to acquire a passport. He was fined, and O'Neal greeted the news by laughing, then noting aloud, "Twenty-seven years old, and he still doesn't have a passport? Idiot. I-D-I-O-T." Then, three days later, O'Neal arrived at the Forum at 6:45 p.m. for a 7:30 p.m. start and blamed traffic. (He wasn't fined, and Bennett greeted the news by saying nothing.) On multiple occasions, the media speculated that Harris was about to be fired, and not without reason. West and Kupchak wondered throughout the year whether the coach had lost his players, especially as the Lakers endured a pair of three-game losing streaks.

Harris's efforts to connect with the team and stay relevant were both admirable ("How do I get Nick to like me?" was a common inquiry to the players) and sort of sad. At the behest of his wife, Ann, he hired a designer to create www.delharris.com, then charged visitors $20 for a one-year membership that included (as written on the home page) "these great benefits": an autographed photograph, an "official" Del's Club membership card, a quarterly newsletter, and a birthday card.

Fewer than 100 people subscribed.

On December 17, the Lakers — playing without an injured O'Neal — traveled to Chicago to face the Bulls in a battle of first-place teams with title ambitions. For Eddie Jones, it was an opportunity to show a potential employer what he was made of. (It turned out he was made of 1-for-11 shooting and 3 total points.) For Kobe Bryant, it was much more significant.

Dating back to his boyhood in Italy, Bryant had devoted much of his life to watching, studying, and mimicking the moves of Michael Jordan, Chicago's transcendent star, now in his 13th (and presumably last) season. As a rookie, Bryant got to face his idol on two occasions, but he received only 10 and 13 minutes of playing time. This time, however, Bryant was the Lakers' sixth man, and he couldn't wait.

It went badly.

Chicago destroyed Los Angeles, 104–83, and Jordan reminded everyone — beginning with Bryant — that there was an enormous difference between greatness and *aspirational* greatness. With the Lakers leading 5-0, the Bulls' megastar grabbed the basketball and stared toward his teammates. "You could just see it," Van Exel said. "He looked at everybody, told them to calm down and relax with his eyes and his motions." What followed was a 32–15 run that helped the hometown team build a 16-point halftime lead. The game was a blowout, and not a particularly engrossing blowout. Jordan scored 36 points on 12-of-22 shooting, lighting up Jones as if he were a stick trapped in mud. "Tonight," Van Exel said, "is just an example of what the Bulls can do."

The defeat was bad. Bryant's role in the defeat was worse. With increased minutes came increased confidence, and with increased confidence came increased arrogance. His Laker teammates knew Bryant was foaming at the mouth for the chance to show off to his hero. They *knew* it was coming. As Chicago's lead grew, Bryant seemed to view the night as an opportunity to audition for the Theater in Chicago production of *Like Mike*. He had waited his whole life to stand before Chicago's No. 23, and the moment was at hand. Wrote Roland Lazenby in his Bryant biography: "In the third quarter of the blowout, Bryant would find the moment he was looking for, with Jordan guarding him. He cut from the left wing to the deep right frontcourt, where he received the ball and promptly executed Jordan's own trademark move on the master himself. With his back to Jordan, Bryant twitched a fake to his left as if going baseline, then pivoted hard right and elevated to stick a twenty-foot jumper right in the face of His Airness. It was a moment to ignite both Bryant's confidence and the basketball public's perception that the game's next great player had arrived."

Indeed, the public's perception was ignited. But so was the agitation along the Los Angeles bench. When O'Neal defended Bryant after the four Utah air balls, it was the protective embracing of one teammate by another. When he jokingly nicknamed Bryant "Showboat," it was an acknowledgment of his propensity toward flair. Playful, not mean. But watching Bryant repeatedly charge at Jordan in a blowout loss was not received warmly. Yes, Bryant's moves were athletic genius. Yes, he was half Baryshnikov, half Terence Stansbury. But it was selfish, self-absorbed nonsense. Fox, his biggest defender among veteran teammates, wanted to applaud Bryant's heart. But *this* — this was too much. "Sometimes you had to wrangle the bull," Fox recalled. "I loved the kid. I did. But at different times — like when he went hard at Michael — I felt like I needed to get him to understand, 'Okay, Kobe, you want to take over. We get it. But that has to take a backseat to what we're trying to accomplish. There's a gracefulness to this all. You need to understand that.'" At one point late in the game, Bryant turned to Jordan and asked his advice on posting up. *Asked. His. Advice.* "It was kind of shocking," Jordan said — and not just for him. The legend had spent his evening pelting Jones with a blizzard of nonstop trash talk, and now Bryant (who finished with 33 points) was treating him like a long-lost uncle? It rubbed everyone wearing a Los Angeles uniform wrong.

The Lakers reached the February 6 All-Star break with a 34-11 record, two games behind Seattle in the Pacific. Based in large part on the eternally repeated *SportsCenter* highlights of his matchup with Jordan (*USA Today* took time to ask readers: *Who has the better smile? Michael? Or Kobe?*), Bryant (along with O'Neal) was voted a Western Conference starter by the fans. When Jones (averaging 18.4 points) and Van Exel (15.3 points) were named as reserves, Los Angeles could boast of having the league's greatest representation.

The All-Star Game, held at Madison Square Garden, in Manhattan, looked to be a bonanza for Bryant, who scored a team-high 18 points in the West's 135–114 setback. Behind the scenes, however, it was nightmarish. The teams stayed at the Grand Hyatt New York, and one day Bryant boarded an elevator occupied by (weird trio alert) Knicks forward Charles Oakley, Nets forward Jayson Williams, and a Manhattan businessman named Donald Trump, who happened to own the hotel. "Hey, Kobe," Williams said. "What's up?"

Bryant was listening to a Walkman, and while he heard the greeting, he merely shrugged and slurred, "Hey, big man," without looking up.

Williams, a 6-foot-9, 240-pound veteran with a quick fuse and an abundance of pride, never liked Bryant from afar, and he certainly didn't like the perceived disrespect. "Are you fucking kidding me?" he said. He then lunged at Bryant, landing a punch to his cheek. Trump, of all people, grabbed Williams and told Bryant, "Get out of here. Quickly." He exited the elevator.

"Kobe was cocky to everyone," said Williams. "Everyone. Michael Jordan was arrogant, but with a smile. Kobe was just a dick. I didn't appreciate it."

In many ways, the All-Star festivities were all a shiny distraction for an organization beginning to crumble from within. Van Exel had tuned Harris out long ago. O'Neal likewise had little use for the babbling coach. Worst of all, Harris seemed either unwilling or unable to communicate with Bryant. Part of it was age, part of it arrogance. Whenever Harris urged the kid to pass, he was greeted with a blank stare and an indifferent shrug. Nothing he said worked. Nothing he instructed mattered. Bryant wanted to score on every possession, only his head coach didn't share the sentiment. So, oftentimes, they spoke not at all. "Sometimes I'd say to Del, 'You've gotta go down there and talk to Kobe about why you took him out,'" said Kurt Rambis, the assistant coach. "You could tell, with that level of talent, he'd eventually be the star of the team, but Del didn't say much to him. I said to Del, literally, 'Kobe Bryant is going to be here a helluva lot longer than we're gonna be here. You have to engage him.' But it didn't work."

From afar, people presumed that O'Neal — large, gifted, wealthy — was the leader of the team. And he was. Kind of. When the center was in a good mood, happiness reigned, and the locker room would be filled with giggling and jokes. There was the time he tried outfitting his Ferrari with a fish tank, only the marine life couldn't withstand the high temperatures and died. The laughter and peppy ridicule that ensued ("Wait," Fox cackled, "you thought goldfish in a Ferrari was a good idea?") was pure behind-the-scenes bliss. On a flight to New York, O'Neal blasted "Macarena" from his boom box, stood, and — while singing an on-the-spot X-rated version of the tune — led a conga line up and down the aisle. He could be an amazing quote for reporters — witty, smart, full of quips and nicknames. There was a huge heart beating inside the huge man. When he first joined the organization, for example, O'Neal was upset to learn that Rudy Garciduenas, the longtime equipment manager, was not supplied with a team-funded vehicle. "He wanted to buy me a truck," Garciduenas recalled. "So we worked out a lease with a local dealership for a small pickup — paid by him." On numerous occasions, O'Neal would ask Garciduenas for a ride, then set up a beach chair in the bed of the truck. "It often turned into a parade, where cars would follow us, just to see Shaq," Garciduenas said. "He was different than anyone I ever met."

But O'Neal's frustration with Harris showed, too. ("Players couldn't take him," he recalled. And if you don't respect a man, you're not going to give your all for him.") "At some level I really love Shaq," said Michael Uhlenkamp, the assistant public relations director. "But, man, he could be surly." O'Neal was famous for his pranks. Oftentimes, though, they were crass. Cruel, even. One time Sean Rooks, the backup center, tried to put on one of his shoes, only to find O'Neal's feces-stained toilet paper stuffed inside. Shea Seals, the rookie from Tulsa, once refused a veteran's order to fetch him a Gatorade. "Rook," O'Neal barked, "get the drink."

Seals, a prideful man, shook his head no.

"Is that how it is?" O'Neal said, scowling.

"It is," Seals replied.

A few hours later, Seals emerged from the shower. Upon returning to his locker, he was surprised to see that his suit had vanished. "Rudy," he said to Garciduenas, "where'd my clothing go?"

He shrugged.

Seals did a one-man hunt through the room. "Finally," he said, "Rudy grabs my suit out of the bottom of a dirty locker with a bunch of shoes. It was dirty and wrinkled, and smelled really bad."

When O'Neal spotted Seals, he said, "Do what I say," and walked off.

"I learned not to mess with Shaq," Seals said. "I wasn't gonna win that one."

When he and Bryant arrived on the scene in 1996, O'Neal envisioned a big brother–little brother relationship. He wanted to be needed; admired; turned to for advice and wisdom. Yet that wasn't Kobe Bryant, and as the season progressed and the second-year guard came off as increasingly self-assured, O'Neal recoiled. In perhaps the most infamous on-court moment from Bryant's career, during the All-Star Game, Karl Malone, Utah's star post player, set a pick for Bryant — only to have the second-year guard wave off the 13th-year forward. Afterwards, members of the West roster (O'Neal included) ripped the audacity of the child, then cringed as his quote ("I found it kind of funny," Bryant said of Malone's anger) made its way around the league.

Bryant simply refused to be a part of things. On flights, as the other Lakers played cards and talked trash, Bryant kept to himself, headphones firmly planted in his ears. "I remember he'd watch the movie *The Ten Commandments*," recalled one teammate. "That was unusual." Oftentimes he'd have a pen in hand, notepad on the tray table, scribbling down lyrics for his future hip-hop dominance. On the road, six, seven, eight Lakers would dine together. Kobe? Never.

"He was a loner," said Jon Barry. "He wanted to be great and had no time for anything else. Remember, he was 19. We're grown men with families. But did it turn people off? Yes."

"There was a lot of 'This guy is younger than me. Why is he such a dick?'" recalled Uhlenkamp. "Almost like 'What right did he have?'"

In his first documented shot at Bryant, O'Neal explained away an ugly March 2 loss at Washington by telling the media, "We've got a lot of Rex Chapman wannabes on this team," he said, referring to Phoenix's long-distance assassin. "Those off-balance, one-legged, fadeaway 3s won't get it done in this league."

He wasn't referring to Mario Bennett.

By the time the playoffs rolled around, the Lakers were the NBA's best worst best team. Their 61-21 record screamed, "We are contenders!" Their four All-Stars screamed, "We are contenders!" O'Neal's 28.3 points per game scoring average ranked second in the league behind Jordan, and five other players (Jones, Bryant, Van Exel, Fox, and Elden Campbell) averaged in double digits. The talent screamed, "We are contenders!"

"But we weren't ready," said Fox. "We were immature to think we were. But no. We weren't."

Los Angeles opened the playoffs as the No. 3 seed, and showed spunk in a convincing three-games-to-one cakewalk over Portland. The team advanced to play Seattle, and all Del Harris wanted (all he ever really wanted) was a workmanlike effort from his team. A professional approach. A get-in-there-and-take-care-of-business way of . . .

Dammit.

The series was scheduled to start May 4. One day earlier, O'Neal and six teammates were spotted at Rick's, a Seattle strip club known as a hot spot for prostitution. The players combined to drop $2,000 on table dances. Al Hansen, Rick's day manager, confirmed to the *Seattle Times*'s Jean Godden that several "7-foot-tall guys, basketball types," had visited the establishment. Dominique Weitzel, a salesman at the nearby Dodge dealership, was at Rick's and received autographs from the Lakers.

"I don't want to throw my boys under the bus," he said when Godden asked him to identify the athletes.

Wrote Godden: "[Weitzel] may have been thinking about Shaq's image. The basketball star just signed a contract with Scholastic Inc. to create a fairy-tale collection: 'Shaq and the Beanstalk and Six Other Very Tall Tales.'"

Harris was furious. And mortified. His star center was arguably the most recognizable athlete on the planet. Why in God's name would he frequent a strip club eight miles away from the area where he'd be playing a day later?

Meanwhile, the Sonics took Game 1 with a 106–92 triumph, made worse by Bryant coming down with a serious case of the flu that would limit his availability and O'Neal engaging in a silly war of words with Seattle coach George Karl, who whined to the officials one too many times. "He looks like a woman coach sometimes. I guess he's just trying to get into certain people's heads, but it won't work with me," O'Neal said. "Like a woman who coaches and cries all the time. He can't get in my head. He's a crybaby."

Like the strip club, this did not play well. Harris feared that his team was unfocused and unprepared, and he was correct. Fortunately, Seattle's weakness was far greater than a case of the flu or an ill-conceived journey to see bare breasts. The Sonics were old.

Save for Gary Payton, the 29-year-old point guard, and Vin Baker, 26, the power forward, Karl's rotation was composed primarily of geriatrics like Detlef Schrempf (35), Sam Perkins (36), and Dale Ellis (37). That was fine for much of the regular season, when rest could be offered on an as-needed basis. But against the Lakers, a club whose oldest contributor, Elden Campbell, was only 29, the Sonics looked slow, sluggish, overwhelmed. Before the 1996–97 season, they had paid $35 million to sign Jim McIlvaine, a 7-foot-1, 240-pound center, with the idea that he could serve as a Shaq deterrent. It didn't work — O'Neal had his way, averaging 30.6 points and 9.6 rebounds. "We need a big guy," Ellis said after the elimination.

He was correct.

The Lakers won the last four games, crushing the fatigued Sonics and advancing to the Western Conference Finals for another date with the

Jazz, the team that had dashed their hopes a year earlier. This time, they convinced themselves, things were different. O'Neal was better than ever. Fox added veteran savvy. Bryant was far more mature. But beneath the bluster, there was doubt. The embarrassment of four air balls followed the Lakers like a bad scent, and Utah — owners of 62 regular season victories and the NBA's best record — had improved.

"We're real good . . . when we show up," Nick Van Exel said. "If we continue to show up, we can go as far as we want to go."

It was not to be. On May 16, the Jazz thrashed the Lakers at the Delta Center, 112–77, and it wasn't as close as the 35-point margin indicates. Only two starters, O'Neal (19 points) and Fox (15 points), scored in double figures, and Fox tallied Los Angeles's only field goal in the game's first nine minutes. "We're not a team that handles success too well right now," Fox said. "We're not as good a team as we think we are."

Returning to his I-must-dominate-the-world ways, Bryant shot an exasperating 4 of 14 from the field. Wrote J.A. Adande of the *Los Angeles Times:* "The rest of the Lakers better hope no one accused them of committing a crime Saturday afternoon, because they can't claim they were playing basketball at the Delta Center as an alibi."

The next game, a 99–95 Utah win, was at least close, but the third contest, a 109–98 Jazz victory in Los Angeles, ended any legitimate hopes of the Lakers reaching the Finals. "We should be embarrassed," O'Neal said. "We just have to show a little pride."

There was a one-day gap between Games 3 and 4 of the series, and Harris called for a relatively short Saturday morning practice. By now it was fairly obvious that the Lakers weren't going to win the series. But while it's okay for fans to acknowledge such a truth, and it's okay for media members to acknowledge such a truth, it violates 800 different athlete laws to admit, openly, that your team has no chance.

That's why what happened next was so egregious.

Traditionally, as the players huddled to end a practice, the men would — in unison — place their hands in the center while chanting, "One, two, three — team!"

This time, however, Van Exel barked, "One, two, three — *Cancún!*"

The gym went dead quiet. Bryant looked at his teammate as if he'd just smelled spoiled milk. Fox was equally disgusted, whispering, "Can you believe this shit?" to O'Neal. Even Jones, Van Exel's friend, was taken aback. "What the hell was that all about?" he asked. Chick Hearn, the legendary Lakers announcer, was furious. "If I were the coach," he said, "I would have cut him on the spot."

Van Exel swore he was kidding. One year earlier, following the loss to the Jazz, he and Blount had spent a week together in Cancún, drinking cocktails, lounging on the beach, hitting the clubs. It was a joke. Ha ha. Get it? Just some fun. "Everyone who was in that locker room with me knows I'd never give up on the team," Van Exel explained. "Everyone."

O'Neal went directly to West's office to tell him of the incident, to which the veteran executive said, bluntly, "After this all ends, Nick is done here."

A day later in Salt Lake City, the Jazz completed the sweep, 96–92, as everyone but O'Neal (38 points) and Jones (19 points) took the night off. West watched from above in utter disgust. At the start of the season, he believed the Lakers were a legitimate title contender. Now, devastated by the setback, he wondered about his coach, about his veteran point guard, about his shooting guard, about himself, and whether it was time to retire.

"We had a couple of players that should be embarrassed," West said. "Players who are good players. We played with no confidence. We had guys that passed up shots that were unimaginable. There was no rhyme or reason to it. It was ridiculous."

Indeed.

Some drastic changes were in order.

7

Worm Food

In the weeks and months that followed yet another disappointing conclusion to a Los Angeles Lakers season, the NBA decided to lock out its players. This came after fruitless negotiations between ownership and the Players Association. At issue was a desire by the powers that be to make changes to the salary cap system, as well as to place a hard ceiling on maximum individual salaries. The players, for their part, opposed everything the owners sought, and also demanded pay *increases* for those earning the NBA minimum salary.

The end of days began on July 1, 1998, and teams were barred from making trades, signing free agents, or holding workouts. Exhibition games were canceled, training camps were postponed, headlines that once hailed dunks and wins now told the stories of accusations and briefings. Basketball fans didn't care much for nuance — it was millionaires fighting millionaires over money neither side deserved.

Unlike, say, Milwaukee or Cleveland, life in Los Angeles without the NBA continued relatively smoothly. No one was happy about the lockout, but there were distractions and, in regard to the Lakers, interesting subplots of varied importance to whet the celebrity appetite. For example, Magic Johnson, the team vice president and hoops legend, had been hired by 20th Television to host an hourlong talk show, *The Magic Hour*.

The program featured a comedy troupe, a house band fronted by Sheila E., and not one single shred of redeeming entertainment value. If Johnson isn't the worst host in television history, it's only because Gabrielle Carteris walks the earth. The show lasted eight weeks before suffering a necessary death. When it was canceled, a nation exhaled and returned to watching *Love Boat* reruns.

The indignity was profound. But at least Johnson's embarrassment was in a secondary field. The same could not be said for Shaquille O'Neal, who — around the same time Magic was landing that big interview with Vanessa Marcil — was facing a very public and painful rejection. After six years of paying him to be their superstar endorser of athletic shoes, Reebok cut the Lakers center loose. Dave Fogelson, the company's spokesperson, said Reebok and O'Neal had "mutually agreed" to not renew a five-year, $15 million sponsorship deal — and this was pure fib. What the company had learned through its failed partnership with the 7-foot-1, 325-pound mountain was that sneaker buyers don't relate very well to 7-foot-1, 325-pound mountains. When *Sports Marketing Newsletter* projected its top 10 endorsement earners for 1998–99, O'Neal was nowhere to be seen. He was cold product. Or, put simply, he was unrelatable to the average consumer.

It was that sort of run for O'Neal, who was also accused of grabbing a woman by the neck while waiting outside a club on the grounds of the Disney World resort. The charges were quickly dropped, but the PR blowback was harsh. Among peers, meanwhile, O'Neal was not making any friends with his I'm-rich-so-I-don't-care-about-the-lockout outlook on things. "I don't really know what they're fighting about," he told the Associated Press. "I make good money and I'm happy with my life."

All of this contributed to O'Neal's out-of-the-norm grouchiness. It hardly helped that, midway through the lockout, *Los Angeles Magazine* published a 4,646-word story headlined KOBE BRYANT: PRINCE OF THE CITY. The article, written by Mark Rowland, was a glowing puff piece about a man the publication was all but anointing the next Michael Jordan. Wrote Rowland:

> Right now, by NBA standards, Bryant is a pretty good basketball
> player. By the standards of marketing and entertainment, he's

a global superstar, the most popular commodity in the league after Mr. Jordan. His visage is omnipresent, hawking for Adidas, Spalding, Sprite, his own Nintendo game and God knows what else.

Already Bryant's story is the stuff of myth, proof biblical that even after Jordan, God's divine plan for his favorite sports league continues to unfold.

By now, O'Neal was no Bryant fan. He had tired of the selfish play, of the single-minded life approach that excluded any Laker not named Kobe. Peter Vecsey, the *New York Post* basketball guru, had it right when he wrote, "Kobe's all-around splendor is unquestionable and, obviously, he's willing to outwork anybody to improve. But because he's so good, he's impossible to play with, because he always feels he can beat his man. Everybody else gets to watch him hoist up pot shots, hurried shots and contested shots. That's not good when you've got Shaq, bigger than an industry, posted on the low blocks waiting impatiently to get plugged into the play."

O'Neal wanted to be the king, ruling over his loyal subjects. "Jerry West wanted that, Shaq wanted that," recalled J.A. Adande. "But Kobe always bristled at that. He was no man's little brother."

"You have to let people be who they are," O'Neal recalled years later. "Some people do different things to make it. He wanted to be the Will Smith of the NBA. He wanted to work out seven, eight, nine hours per day. That's fine. That's you. I wanted a relationship that he wasn't really interested in. I get it."

The animosity mounted. Not in Bryant's mind—he had bigger things to worry about than the big man's acceptance. But to O'Neal, the slights stung. A few months earlier, *People* magazine had featured Bryant in its World's Most Beautiful People issue, and the kid seemed to lap it up. "He's quickly becoming one of the main marketing tools of the NBA," Fox observed. "Which means that someone else isn't." Dating back to his rookie season in Orlando, no one rejected Shaquille O'Neal. If he offered to buy a rookie teammate a suit, the rookie teammate took the suit. If he wanted you to come over and party at his mansion, you came over and partied at his mansion. "As Shaq went, we went," recalled Fox. "It was his show. But Kobe didn't care about that. He just didn't."

In many ways, the lockout was a battle of agents. Leonard Armato, O'Neal's representative, was working behind the scenes to broker a deal, even hosting a meeting between David Stern, the NBA commissioner, and Billy Hunter of the Players Association. Arn Tellem, Bryant's agent, was not a fan of the approach. He felt that Armato was looking out strictly for his client, not the league's other players. The newspapers and TV networks began referring to *Shaq v. Kobe*. Or, at times, *Shaq's agent v. Kobe's agent*.

Without NBA games to turn to, players all across the United States spent a good amount of their time running high-level pickup at various gymnasiums and sports clubs. In New York, one might find scores of Knicks and Nets at the 92nd Street Y. And in Los Angeles, home to the Lakers and the Clippers, the place to be was Southwest College, a school of 8,200 students and an oft-available gymnasium.

One never knew who, exactly, would show up from day to day. It could be members of the UCLA and USC teams. It could be some players from UC Irvine or Long Beach State. It could be a handful of Clippers, a handful of Lakers, some NBA vets who lived in L.A. when they weren't deployed to Denver or Miami. Whatever the case, the games were ego-packed and highly competitive.

On one particular day, both O'Neal and Bryant arrived at Southwest College, ready to play. It was the first week of January, not long after the Kobe-is-the-next-Jordan piece ran in *L.A. Magazine*. Some other Lakers were in attendance, as was Olden Polynice, the veteran center who'd spent the preceding four and a half seasons with Sacramento. He was hoping the Lakers would sign him to a free agent contract, and had been told that Mitch Kupchak, the team's general manager, was planning on showing up. Though they'd battled for years, Polynice and O'Neal enjoyed a friendly relationship. "All I wanted to do was go there and play with Shaq," Polynice recalled. "The Lakers were my favorite team as a boy. It would have been a dream. I wanted to show Mitch I was serious."

The players straggled in, loosened up, stretched, shot some jumpers. They proceeded to divide into teams — some guys over here, some guys over there. O'Neal and Polynice — dueling 7-footers — were on different sides. "Kobe was on my squad," Polynice recalled. "Opposite Shaq."

It was just another run, until it was no longer just another run. As he was prone to do in pickup, O'Neal called a series of iffy fouls whenever he missed a shot.

Miss.

"Foul!"

Miss.

"Foul!"

"I'm tired of this shit," Bryant finally said. "Just play."

"One more comment like that," O'Neal snapped, "and I slap the shit out of you."

A few possessions later, Bryant drove toward the rim, leaned into O'Neal's body, and scooped the ball beneath his raised arm and into the hoop. It was a pretty move, but nothing otherworldly.

"Fuck you!" he screamed at O'Neal. "This is my team! My motherfucking team!"

It felt edgy. Everything stopped. "He wasn't talking about the pickup team," Polynice recalled. "He was talking about the Lakers."

O'Neal wasn't having it.

"No, motherfucker!" he screamed. "This is my team!"

"Fuck you!" Bryant replied. "Seriously — fuck you! You're not a leader. You're nothing!"

What did he just say?

"I will get your ass traded," O'Neal said. "Not a problem."

Several of the participants stepped in to separate the two, and the game eventually continued. But it no longer felt even slightly relaxed or friendly. "We probably went up and down the court two more times," Polynice said. "Kobe goes to the basket, scores, screams at Shaq, 'Yeah, motherfucker! That shit ain't gonna stop me!'"

O'Neal grabbed the ball in order to freeze action.

"Say another motherfucking word," he said, staring directly at Bryant.

"Aw, fuck you," Bryant said. "You don't kn —"

Smack!

O'Neal slapped Bryant across the face. *Hard.*

"His hands are huge," said Corie Blount, who was playing in the game. "The noise was loud."

Here is Polynice's recollection: "Then Shaq swung again at Kobe, but he missed. Shit! I run over and grab Shaq, because I'm big enough to do so. And Shaq keeps swinging, but everything's missing because I have his arms. I'm grabbing on to Shaq, holding on for dear life, yelling, 'Somebody grab Kobe! Seriously — somebody grab him!' Because I'm holding Shaq and Kobe's taking swings at him. At one point Shaq gets an arm loose and he pops me in the head. Seriously, no good deed goes unpunished. And I'm telling you, if Shaq gets loose he would have killed Kobe Bryant. I am not exaggerating. It was along the lines of an I-want-to-kill-you-right-now punch. He wanted to end Kobe's life in that moment."

Bryant was undeterred. "You're soft!" he barked. "Is that all you've got? You're soft!" Blount begged Bryant to stop talking. "You're not helping," he said. "Just shut up." The altercation was finally broken up when Jerome Crawford, O'Neal's bodyguard, walked onto the floor and calmed his friend down. O'Neal was furious. "You can't touch him in practice," he wrote of Bryant. "He's acting like Jordan, where some players thought you couldn't touch Mike. Whenever somebody ripped Kobe, he'd call a foul. After a while, I'm like, 'Listen, man, you don't have to start calling that punk sh**.'" As he walked from the court, Polynice looked at a shaken Kupchak and said, loudly, "You should sign me just for that."

He did not — Olden Polynice spent the 1998–99 season with Seattle.

"They were just two alpha males who couldn't coexist," Polynice said. "Shaq's mindset was 'This is my team.' Kobe's mindset was 'Nobody's gonna punk me.' You can't have two alpha males. It doesn't work."

He paused, reflecting on the insanity.

"It never, ever works. Even when it does."

At long last, in early January, a collective bargaining agreement was ratified by owners and players and the 191-day lockout came to an end. An abridged 50-game season would begin on February 5, meaning the Lakers didn't have long to get things going.

Nothing felt quite right.

First, in the aftermath of his (to understate) *poorly received* Cancún quip, Nick Van Exel was unloaded on Denver, ending a rocky five-year run in Los Angeles that produced a 100:1 headache-to-glory ratio. Jerry West organized, negotiated, and pulled off the trade, and while what he received was far below value for a 26-year-old All-Star floor general (the Lakers acquired forward Tony Battie and point guard Tyronn Lue, the recent 23rd pick in the NBA draft), ridding the organization of its biggest annoyance was addition by subtraction.

"I loved Nick," West recalled years later. "He's one of my favorite competitors. But it couldn't continue."

The trade took place on Wednesday, June 24. West reached out to Van Exel to let him know and to thank him for his contributions. Van Exel refused to take the call. On Wednesday. On Thursday. On Friday. On Saturday. On Sunday. *Ever.* "Fuck Jerry West," he told James Bryant, his agent. "You don't treat me this way."*

The Van Exel–less Lakers held a voluntary workout in early February at Southwest College, and a whopping five players — O'Neal, Eddie Jones, Sean Rooks, Derek Fisher, and Lue — attended. "I think we looked pretty good," Jones told the 20 reporters on hand. "I'm ready."

West has long been regarded as modern basketball's best organizer of talent, but the roster felt largely stale. Rick Fox decided to return on a one-year, $1.75 million middle-class exception, and Van Exel was replaced by free agent Derek Harper, a 16-year veteran who, at 37, was more important as a locker room leader than a producer of points and assists. Travis Knight, the backup center who played surprisingly well as a rookie in 1996–97, was reacquired from Boston in exchange for Battie — thereby setting off the longest whoop for joy in the history of human whoops for joy. "I was the happiest man in the world," Knight recalled. "Boston was

---

* "I'm very disappointed," West said. "I'd like to think his growth as a person, I helped contribute to that."

terrible, playing for Rick Pitino was just awful. He treated players like pieces of cattle. When they asked if I'd accept a trade to the Lakers, there was no delay. 'Yes! Send me! Now!'"

With Bryant prepared to start, there was increased pressure for Eddie Jones to be sent elsewhere. The Scottie Pippen talks resurfaced but died quickly when the Bulls requested Bryant, not Jones. (Kupchak's response to Chicago's Pippen-for-Kobe dream? *Ha ha ha ha*.) Before the scheduled opener against Houston, Los Angeles nearly reached an agreement with Minnesota on a Jones–for–Tom Gugliotta exchange. ("My agent was in regular contact with the Lakers, and they told him to hang tight, that they were about to make an offer the Wolves couldn't refuse," recalled Gugliotta, one of the league's top forwards. "I was so excited.") That also fell through.

When, at long last, the season commenced on February 5, with the Rockets visiting the Great Western Forum, the Lakers were a mess. The Associated Press was reporting that Bryant was set to sign a six-year, $71 million contract extension, upsetting many members of the roster. O'Neal was ranting about a new *USA Today* poll that had Los Angeles as only the fourth-best team in the Western Conference. Jones felt betrayed by the gossip, Robert Horry was diagnosed with an irregular heartbeat, the underwhelming Derek Fisher was back as starting point guard, and the tension from the Established Superstar (Shaq) vs. Rising Superstar (Kobe) brawl at Southwest College had yet to fully fade.

Plus, this was supposed to be a magical season. After 32 years, the Lakers would be playing their final campaign at the Great Western Forum, before moving downtown to the in-the-process-of-being-built Staples Center. The new arena promised to be everything the modern NBA offered fans: suites aplenty, endless concessions, prices through the roof. The Lakers would share the building with the Clippers and the NHL's Kings, and the money was sure to arrive in bundles.

So 1998–99 was a long-planned farewell to a home that had hoisted six championship banners and a court that had brought Southern California Magic and Kareem, Shaq and Kobe.

"It was very sad," said Jeanie Buss. "Like saying goodbye to your best friend."

The Lakers opened the 1998–99 season with a 99–91 victory over the Rockets, and afterwards Harris was downright giddy. O'Neal dominated with 30 points and 14 rebounds, and Bryant — an opening-day starter because of injuries to Fox and Horry — was just as impactful, adding 25 points and 10 rebounds. Houston's revamped lineup featured the legendary Pippen, recently acquired from the Bulls, and optimism was high. "The story was Kobe coming in and starting, going against Scottie Pippen, and I think nine out of 10 people would've thought Houston had the edge in that one," Harris said. "But Kobe played under control the whole game. We *know* he's an outstanding player."

By this point Harris could say, "I'm giving each man on this team $10 million and my nude pics of Halle Berry" and they would hear, "Blah blah blah blah blah blah blah blah Halle Berry blah blah blah blah." Now in his fifth season on the Los Angeles sideline, any lingering positives had worn off. The fans were tired of boring ol' Del Harris. The players were tired of talkative ol' Del Harris. O'Neal hated how Harris babied Bryant. Bryant hated how Harris held him back. "Del knew the game," said Harper. "But he expected guys to police themselves. It was a young team. A lot of kids, a lot of immaturity. Kobe and Shaq were too busy fighting each other, and he wasn't really the type of coach to handle it."

"Kobe didn't respect Del, and that was a problem," recalled Fox. "Kobe didn't listen to him. And Shaq didn't listen to him, either, mainly because he wanted Del to be harder on Kobe."

The glow of the opening victory faded as Los Angeles lost two nights later against Utah, won at San Antonio and Denver, lost a pair against Minnesota and Indiana. Excuses were made — shortened campaign, injury-depleted roster, chemistry problems. Harris, looking back, believed the squad was about to find itself. "We had the pieces," he said. "I needed a little more time."

The first sign of the sheer craziness that was about to envelop the franchise came on February 13, 1999, when subscribers to the *Los Angeles Times* opened to the front page of the sports section and spotted the headline RODMAN READY TO JOIN LAKERS.*

Read Mark Heisler's piece:

> Dennis Rodman, the game's greatest rebounder and its most disruptive force, has decided to join the Lakers, sources told The Times on Friday.
>
> The team has been in negotiations with Rodman's agent, Steve Chasman of International Creative Management, for almost two weeks, with owner Jerry Buss extending a personal invitation to play.
>
> The talks had been sidetracked for a week while Chasman discussed possible movie deals with Fox, which holds an option to buy into the Lakers as a 10% partner.
>
> Rodman had been laying low in his home in Newport Beach, refusing to talk to Laker officials until finally agreeing to meet with them Thursday. He has reportedly reconciled himself to the veteran's minimum of $1 million — pro-rated to $600,000 for this shortened season — plus another $3 million he'd get from his endorsement contract with Converse.

This was bonkers. No, bigger than bonkers. Dennis Rodman, 37-year-old cross-dressing, cigarette-smoking, body-coated-in-tattoos, shows-up-on-time-once-every-three-years power forward, had led the NBA in rebounding for the past seven seasons. But after helping the Chicago Bulls capture a third-straight title in 1998, he was a free agent, understandably unwanted by all 29 of the league's franchises because (strange as this sounds) in a sport that depends on communal accountability, an unaccountable cuckoo bird isn't all that appealing.

---

* A writer's note that feels appropriate. It is May 13, 2019, and as I write this an alert has just popped up on my laptop: DENNIS RODMAN ACCUSED OF STEALING 400-POUND CRYSTAL FROM YOGA STUDIO. Okay, back to your reading.

Rodman's biggest flaw was, well, everything, except for his geographic proximity (he lived in a Newport Beach duplex) and an innate ability to snatch basketballs off a metal cylinder. He once headbutted an official —and was suspended. He once cursed on a live postgame show—and was suspended. Over the seven previous seasons, he had been suspended on 14 occasions (not including a 14-game paid leave by the San Antonio Spurs).

That said, Jerry Buss, the Lakers' owner, was enamored with Rodman. Yes, for his rebounding. But also for the accompanying pizzazz. For good and for bad, Rodman garnered attention, and Los Angeles was an attention seeker's paradise. "Dennis is a talent on the floor," Buss said before the season opener. "As far as I can read the public, they want to win as badly as I want to win. They're very hungry for a championship. It's been a while."

The whole idea began via fluke. Shortly before the NBA tipped off, Rodman was entrenched in an all-out war with his longtime agent, Dwight Manley. Or, according to Manley: "I couldn't handle the circus any longer, so I quit working with him." Rodman employed an off-the-court representative, Steve Chasman of ICM, who helped with television, motion picture, and literary contracts. He had no experience as a sports agent, however, and had never aspired to enter the medium.

"I was talking to Dennis one night about his career, and we agreed to meet for dinner," Chasman said. "I made a reservation for 7 p.m." The agent arrived at the Palm, in Hollywood, at exactly 7. That turned to 7:30. Then 8. Then 8:15. Then 8:30. "Dennis shows up one and a half hours late," Chasman recalled. "He has this beautiful woman on his arm. I had no idea who she was, but she was gorgeous."

As they sat, Chasman told Rodman that if he wanted a multimedia career, he had to continue playing basketball. "Call Dwight," Chasman said. "Tell him —"

"Fuck Dwight," Rodman replied. "I don't wanna talk about that asshole."

Unbeknownst to either man, a few tables away sat Jerry Buss, accompanied by three scantily dressed women in their twenties. The Lakers' owner was 66. He approached Rodman, extended his hand, and said, "Dennis, I care about two things, in this order: I want to fill my arena and I want to win a championship." Pause. "I want you to be a Laker."

Rodman smiled and nodded toward Chasman. "Mr. Buss," he said, "you need to speak to my agent, Steve Chasman."

Um, what?

Within 48 hours, Chasman was meeting one-on-one with Buss inside a Marina del Rey restaurant, then driving to West's home in Bel Air. It was all a psychedelic whirlwind, made particularly strange by the fact that Rodman had not picked up a basketball in nearly half a year. "I didn't know what sort of shape he was in," Chasman recalled. "But he could always rebound."

Behind the scenes, Harris (to the shock of most everyone) endorsed the idea of bringing Rodman into the fold. He'd watched from afar the way Phil Jackson handled him in Chicago, and he believed that he, too, could get the most out of the Worm (his nickname dating back to childhood, when his mother noticed him wriggling around while playing pinball). But two days after the *Los Angeles Times* report of Rodman's imminent acquisition, the forward was nowhere to be found. Literally no one knew where Dennis Rodman went. Until, somehow, a couple of tourists spotted him in Las Vegas, shooting craps and downing beers and living the non-NBA life. Which caused an agitated Jerry West to rant to the *Chicago Sun-Times*'s Lacy J. Banks, "This is no way to do business!"

Laker players were torn. Derek Harper, the veteran guard, viewed Rodman as pure distraction. O'Neal, on the other hand, said, "Hey, I want me a thug!" One thousand miles away in Denver, Van Exel laughed at the idea. *He* had been a problem — but bringing in Dennis Rodman made sense? "If he comes in with all his antics and just thinking about Dennis Rodman the show," Van Exel said, "he's going to kill that team."

"The whole thing was such a reach," recalled Corie Blount. "That's what it felt like — 'We're having some problems and here's an idea that might work. It probably won't — but it might. So let's sign the crazy guy and see what happens.'"

At the same time the Lakers were trying to make sure Rodman wasn't lying dead in a gutter with three hookers and a needle protruding from his left nipple, Harris's grasp on the coaching job felt tenuous. On February 19, Peter Vecsey of the *New York Post* wrote that Los Angeles would be firing its leader within a matter of days, if not hours. "From what I'm told," he reported, "the players, almost to a man, are simply exhausted from standing around at practice and listening to Harris talk. And, because the players are repeating the same mistakes, it's the same speech over and over again."

On Sunday, February 21, the Lakers fell 92–89 to the mediocre Sonics. Polynice, Seattle's center, heard Los Angeles players bickering among themselves during the game. They lost again the next night, this time in overtime to Van Exel and the 1-8 Nuggets.

It was a strange game, one in which Denver shooting guard Eric Washington — a man few of the Lakers had ever heard of — scored 16 points in 48 minutes of play. But the mild unusualness of the defeat failed to rival the spectacular insanity of the happenings in Los Angeles, where Dennis Rodman — alive and well — was holding a press conference inside a Planet Hollywood to announce, um, eh, ah, hmm . . . nothing.

Really, *nothing*.

Roughly 30 members of the media showed up, believing the Lakers were about to anoint a new power forward. Rodman arrived 40 minutes late to his own event, accompanied by Chasman, model Carmen Electra (his wife for less than a year — in a silver dress the size of a Band-Aid), and his sister, Debra, holding a box containing four of Rodman's five NBA championship rings. He was wearing a white T-shirt, sunglasses, multiple nasal piercings, and a *Joseph and the Amazing Technicolor Dreamcoat*-inspired floppy cap. He might have been drunk. Or high. Or, perhaps, just sleep-deprived. Probably drunk and high.

"There are a lot of things that have to occur before I even step on the floor," he began, leaning into a Planet Hollywood microphone. And with that, all went haywire. With no prompting, Rodman ripped into some of the young Lakers, saying, "All these guys want to be basketball superstars, but everybody has to play a role." Then, also with no prompting, he added that his motivation wasn't a drive to win. "What got me over the hump," he said, "is I'm bored. I'm tired of not doing anything."

He rambled. Like a bored man with a microphone and too much free time. There was, everyone came to realize, no reason to be here. It was a circus arranged by the modern-day P.T. Barnum, sans elephants and tigers.

One media member had enough. The previous hour had not been a good one for Lisa Guerrero, the recently hired KCBS-TV sports reporter, who was better known for her time as a Los Angeles Rams cheerleader, then as a cast member of the short-lived Aaron Spelling show *Sunset Beach*. Eager to impress her new bosses, Guerrero arrived early and promised she would be ready for the live report as soon as Rodman confirmed he had signed a contract. Yet as the minutes passed and the Planet Hollywood filled, Guerrero began to lose her patience. "None of the other reporters know who I am, and they're staring at me," she recalled. "Someone said, 'Did they hand a model a mic?' Another guy started talking about my breasts. It was really uncomfortable. Finally, thank God, Rodman walks in."

She expected news. She got nonsense. "He smelled like a hangover," Guerrero said. "The combination of sweat, drink, and cigarette." Rodman talked about the terrific sex he and Electra were having; about random thoughts on intercourse. Then he uttered the words that changed everything. "He said, 'I just called this press conference to see if you would all show up, and you did,'" Guerrero recalled. "He's laughing and laughing, like it's funny. Well, enough was enough for me."

As the other reporters quietly lapped up the indignity, Guerrero stood, stared down Rodman, and said, "This is unbelievable. You've just wasted our time. You're telling us we're here for nothing? This is the most selfish thing I've ever heard of."

Silence.

"Are you kidding me, honey?" Rodman replied. "You're calling me selfish? I've been a team player, honey. I've been a team player for 13 years, I've got five championships, seven rebound titles, I've been in the Finals

10 years ... For you to say something like that, you got problems ... It's amazing, when Michael Jordan retired, he wasn't selfish. When Michael Jordan came back, you people right here kissed his ... All of a sudden, I do something like this and I'm selfish."

Then something truly unexpected unfolded: Dennis Rodman started to sob.

"I'm never going to win," he said between tears. "No matter what I do for this league, for the game of basketball, I'm never going to win." He opened a piece of paper, pointed to some letters. "I've got 10 charities here that I'm going to give $10,000 to. You tell me if that's selfish." He was holding a takeout menu.

"The next day, the story wasn't Dennis Rodman to the Lakers," Guerrero recalled. "It was the little girl who made him cry."

Soon enough, there was more crying. Or cheering — depending on the perspective. In one of the most bizarre two-day spans in the history of human breathing, on Tuesday, February 23, the Lakers finally signed Rodman, who agreed to the $1 million veteran's minimum (pro-rated to $600,000 due to the abbreviated season). That night, the Lakers suffered a 93–83 setback at punchless Vancouver that dropped the team to 6-6. "I've never been on a team that's 6-6," a glum O'Neal said. "We all just have to look in the mirror and evaluate ourselves rather than point the finger."

As soon as the game ended, Fox and Horry told Harris that there would be a players-only meeting inside the visitors' locker room at General Motors Place — no coaches allowed. It was an ugly scene. Tom Savage, an assistant public relations director, was lingering in the room when Harper, the veteran guard, screamed, "Get the fuck out!" Savage was humiliated, and O'Neal tapped him on the shoulder and said, "Basketball player or not, don't let anyone talk to you like that. *Ever.*" Once the session began, most of the participants pointed their fingers directly at their loquacious coach's plodding approach to an increasingly up-tempo game. In the era of Allen Iversons and Vince Carters and Kobe Bryants, it often felt as if the Lakers were participating in a walkathon. The meeting allowed players to let loose, without fear of agitating their leader. "I didn't have a say in that," Harris recalled. "Did I know some of the guys were unhappy? Sure. Did I think I'd get fired? No."

The following morning, West asked Harris to come to the team offices, where he was promptly dismissed of his responsibilities. West was crestfallen — he loved everything about Harris. "We were not playing up to our potential and we needed change," he recalled. "But that doesn't mean Del wasn't a terrific man. He was. Man and coach. Sometimes you just need a different look." Though he was shocked and disappointed, it was far from Harris's lowest moment. Both of his parents, Ed and Wilma, had died in the preceding months — his father from heart ailments, his mother after a five-year dementia nightmare that rendered her unable to state her own name. "She didn't know who I was for a long time," Harris recalled. "By comparison, what's basketball?"

Indeed.

Two back-to-back press conferences were held on February 24, 1999 — Del Harris saying farewell, Dennis Rodman saying hello. The juxtaposition was striking. Angel. Devil. Saint. Sinner. Only the pious one was being shown the door, while the man with a snake-circling-a-crucifix tattoo was being hailed as a savior. Harris was told he certainly didn't need to meet with the media, but he did so anyway. "Who attends his own firing press conference?" said Howard Beck, a writer for the *Los Angeles Daily News*. "But that was Del. He had dedicated the season to his parents, and he really wanted to win a championship for them. Then he's dismissed, and he comes to talk to us. He was always accountable and decent.

"And then," Beck added, "in walks the freak show."

Behind the scenes, West was apoplectic. Ever since joining the organization as the second overall pick out of West Virginia in the 1960 NBA draft, he had been the loyalist of foot soldiers. As a superstar guard for 14 seasons, he never took a game lightly. As the head coach for three seasons in the late 1970s, he lived and died with every matchup. As the general manager from 1982 to 1994, he spanned the globe seeking out any possible advantage, any obscure talent who might help the purple and gold. Now, as the executive vice president of basketball operations, all he wanted was for Los Angeles to return to its place atop the basketball

universe. That's why he took every step to sign O'Neal. That's why he surrendered one of his favorites (Vlade Divac) to score Kobe Bryant. That's
why he pulled out every stop to sign Rick Fox, to trade for Robert Horry,
to draft Eddie Jones.

This was too much.

Jerry Buss demanded the team sign Rodman, so the team signed Rodman. The owner viewed him as an electric mix of rebounding and pizzazz.
But West saw Rodman for what he was: an unreliable locker room cancer
with faded abilities and a narcissistic need for attention at all costs. In
public, West did his best to appear a team player — "[Rodman's] intelligence for the game amazes me," he said. It was pure BS. West abhorred
everything about the transaction. J.A. Adande, the *Los Angeles Times* columnist, penned a piece urging the team to ignore Rodman. On the afternoon it ran, West sought out Adande at practice. "That was an excellent
column," he told him. "You keep it up."

"Jerry went nuts when Rodman signed," said Tim Kawakami, the *Times*
beat writer. "Once they got Rodman, he basically disappeared, because he
wanted nothing to do with it."

In his excellent autobiography, *West by West*, West shared a letter his
wife, Karen, had written to Jerry Buss on April 17, 1999. A portion of it
read:

> As I am positive that you know, my husband is a very tormented
> individual. The greatest source of his torment in the last few
> years has been the Lakers. That I am sure you also know. But
> he seemed to have overcome that torment when the two of you
> worked things out last summer. I made him promise that he
> would be happy staying with the Lakers before he agreed on a
> contract extension and he responded that he had a renewed en-
> thusiasm and that he knew that the correct decision was to stay.
> He was raring to go. As long as Jerry was happy, I was happy.
>
> Well, everything has gone to hell. He is a man that if he were
> suicidal would be gone. The fact that some major decisions
> have been made that he did not agree with and that this once

most-respected team is now, as he says, the "laughing stock of the league" has put him in a downward spiral that is almost as self-destructive as Rodman.

It was *that* bad.

With Harris out, the Lakers needed a replacement. On February 25, they beat the Clippers 115–100 in Anaheim with Bill Bertka, the long-time assistant, filling in and Rodman sitting out. The next day West announced that Kurt Rambis, the 41-year-old former power forward who won four titles as a Los Angeles player in the 1980s, would serve as the interim head coach. It was a curious pick, in that Larry Drew, the onetime Kings point guard, had been Harris's top assistant, while Rambis occupied the second chair. Though he was somewhat quirky and scattered, players liked Rambis. But he struck most as neither head-coach-like nor the type of man you spend time listening to. "Kurt was very smart," said Howard Beck. "But at that point I don't think he had the stature to confront Shaq and Kobe. There was a lot that came with the job. He probably wasn't there yet."

The Lakers' initial practice under their new coach was held at Southwest College on the morning of Friday, February 26. One of the first players to greet him was Rodman. The initial conversation went thusly . . .

RODMAN: Hey, Kurt. How are you doing?

RAMBIS: Hey, Dennis. I'm fine. How are you?

RODMAN: I'm fine, but I need a couple of weeks off. I wanna go to Vegas and get my head right.

RAMBIS: What?

RODMAN: Yeah. I need to go and get focused and prepared.

Rambis didn't know whether to laugh or cry. Was Rodman being serious? The new coach couldn't tell. Rambis asked Corie Blount, the backup forward, to walk Rodman through the offense, step by step. "The dude was weird as shit," Blount recalled. "I was not even a little bit comfortable around him. He had a vibe that didn't work for me."

That night, the Lakers and the Clippers were scheduled to meet again for a 7:30 tipoff at the Forum. Players were required to arrive by 6 p.m., but a few hours later, with the clock at 6:06, and then 6:07, and then 6:08 . . .

Rodman entered the building. Wrote Adande: "He finally arrived, with his people, illuminated by mini-cam lights, walking into the locker room and quickly disappearing into a back room . . . Classic Rodman, right off the bat. Close enough to the appointed time to avoid being a major problem, over the edge just enough to show he's a nonconformist. With Rodman, the infractions always start off small, growing until he finds out just how much he can get away with."

With Jerry Buss watching from his regular perch in the stands, it felt as if a scripted series — *As the Worm Turns* — was coming to life. Rambis, a crumpled napkin of a dresser during his playing career, looked resplendent in a fitted dark blue suit and gray-and-white tie. He was greeted by the 17,505 fans with a standing ovation — in part because he represented the Showtime glory of not all that long ago, in part because he was *not* Del Harris.

The Clippers were the perfect meal for the occasion — an 0-11 crosstown non-rival with a 15-pounds-overweight Sherman Douglas at point guard and Michael Olowokandi, deemed one of the worst No. 1 picks in NBA history by the *Washington Post*'s Neil Greenberg, starting at center. Rodman arrived at the Forum with his hair painted black, yellow, and purple — like an amoeba mixed with banana extract. Carmen Electra, wearing a midriff-baring crème outfit, chomped on gum while signing autographs from her seat four rows off the court. It was just like the good ol' Showtime days, and with 6:03 remaining in the first quarter and the score 12–11 Lakers, Rodman rose off the bench to replace Travis Knight. A thunderous roar filled the building.

A few seconds later, he tapped a loose ball to O'Neal, who accepted the gift by slamming a powerful dunk. On the next trip down the floor, Rodman gobbled up his first offensive rebound as a Laker, then hit O'Neal for another basket. Shortly after that, he batted away a pass on defense. Los Angeles went on a 7–0 run, and in the 26 minutes Rodman was on the floor, the Lakers outscored the Clippers 59–37. The Worm's line for the night was emblematic of his career — 0 points, 11 rebounds, 3 personal fouls, burns and scrapes across his elbows and knees. The Lakers won 99–83, and afterwards it felt as if the greatest basketball gift had arrived. "He's definitely a very special player," Harper raved. "Tonight he gave us instant energy. The minute he came in, positive things started happening."

"So," asked Tim Kawakami of the *Times*, "everything with Dennis Rodman will work out?"

Harper smiled.

"So far," he said. "Just wait, though. We'll see."

The wait didn't take long.

Dennis Rodman's debut was on a Friday. Two days later, he arrived 30 minutes late for his first full-squad Laker practice, telling the team that he was stuck in traffic on the 405. "He's a free thinker," Rambis explained to the media. "And if he wants to do things different, I do not have a problem with that."

Being a first-time head coach is hard enough without a crazy person. With one, it's nearly impossible. Rodman missed another practice. And another practice. He arrived reeking of alcohol and cigarettes on multiple occasions. "We had one practice where, immediately afterward, we were heading for the airport," said Tom Savage, the assistant public relations director. "Dennis didn't show up. Well, I let the media in for the final 10 minutes, and right when that happens Dennis enters in the side door. It was like angels singing, the timing. His shoes were tied at the very ends — knots at the tip of the laces. He had pajama bottoms on, and his sneakers were slung over his shoulders."

Under Rambis and featuring Rodman, the Lakers won 10 in a row and found themselves with a 16-6 record. Yet it was a balloon on the verge of popping. O'Neal had been the biggest advocate of signing Rodman, but he didn't understand the man. Rodman would come to practices and, midway through, lie down on the court and appear to nap. He showered before games, not after. Sean Rooks, a reserve center, blew off a weekday practice to make the point that "If Dennis can come and go, why can't I?" A journalist from the London *Times* reported that Rodman was cheating on Electra with another woman in room 821 of the Four Seasons hotel in Beverly Hills. "Whatever the room," Rodman recalled, "I was having a large time." On one occasion inside the Laker locker room, Rodman removed his uniform and slipped into a woman's dress. "I was like, 'Did this dude *just put a dress on?*'" recalled Erikk Aldridge, the PR assistant. Rodman spoke to no one — not O'Neal, not Bryant, not Rambis. He would engage the media only after an hour of weight lifting, which meant he never engaged the media. "One time, we were getting on a bus and it was raining," said Savage. "He said, 'Hey, Tom, be careful. The stairs are slick.' I was shocked."

On March 12, after playing but eight minutes in a win over the Warriors, Rodman was granted an indefinite leave of absence. When asked when the player would return, Rambis shrugged. "You're asking me hypothetical questions," he said, "for which I have no answer." There were rumors that Rodman had $600,000 in gambling debts and needed to come up with a method to settle. There were rumors that he and Electra — who had wed while Rodman was intoxicated* — were getting a divorce. There were rumors that Electra was cheating on Rodman with Mötley Crüe drummer Tommy Lee.

"He was all sorts of mess," said Harper. "He showed up, he didn't show up. It was more headache than anything else."

On April 16, the Lakers released their power forward. When all was said and done, Dennis Rodman — who told *Newsweek* the team "depends on me to keep this ship afloat" — played 23 total games for the Lakers, averaging 2.1 points and 11.2 rebounds while landing 13 technical fouls and an infinite number of quizzical headlines. "Am I a genius?" he asked

---

* Rodman recounted the romantic way he proposed in his 2005 autobiography, *I Should Be Dead by Now*. Wrote the bard Dennis: "It was five o'clock in the morning and my right-hand man Thaer Mustafa and I were playing blackjack, winning for a change, at the Hard Rock. We had been up all night, of course, and I was pretty much wasted. Carmen had gone to bed hours before. 'Go get Carmen,' I suddenly said to Thaer. 'I want to talk to her.'"

during an interview. "Am I a miracle worker? Am I a God? No — but I have a gift."

Kurt Rambis wasn't prepared.

He admitted as much some two decades later, and without a second's pause for debate. "I just don't think I was ready to be a head coach," he said. "The preparation, the player management, putting a system together that fit offensively and defensively. We all probably think we can coach, but then you're asked to do it. And, you have to remember, that was no ordinary season."

The shortened schedule made preparation nearly impossible. Rodman's antics made normalcy nearly impossible. Then, on March 10, you had the trade.

No — *the Trade*.

After no fewer than 9,353 Eddie Jones–to–(*fill in the blank with any NBA team*) rumors, the Lakers finally unloaded their small forward, sending him, along with Elden Campbell, to Charlotte for small forward Glen Rice, power forward J.R. Reid, and point guard B.J. Armstrong (who was immediately waived). Two days earlier, Jerry Buss had approached Jones in the locker room and said, bluntly, "We are not trading you."

"Really?" Jones asked. "Because I hear . . ."

"Eddie," Buss said, "you have my word."

Within 48 hours, Jones was on the phone with Jerry West, who wished him luck and broke down the logistics of a relocation to North Carolina. In Charlotte, meanwhile, Rice had mixed emotions. On the one hand, he was a small-town kid from Jacksonville, Arkansas (pop. 28,364), and the bright lights and nonstop buzz of Hollywood weren't his thing. On the other hand, Rice was seeking a contract extension, and the Hornets wouldn't touch his $14 million price tag. "I loved Charlotte, but we weren't in position to contend," Rice recalled. "With the Lakers, I walked into a team that was pretty loaded."

A three-time All-Star and former first-round draft pick out of Michigan, Rice showed up having not played all season after recovering from surgery to remove loose particles from his right elbow. That said, he was thought to be the missing piece. Under a stream of illogical gibberish re-peated by team executives, then the local media, Jones and Bryant were too similar and could never truly play together. ("That never made sense to me," Jones said years later. "It just wasn't true.") Rice, on the other hand, was a dead-eye outside shooter who would open up the court and give op-posing defenses all sorts of problems. "He's going to bring us a dimension we haven't had here for a long, long time," West raved. "I've heard from a number of people in the NBA today who thought we did well."

Rambis was told, repeatedly, how impressive the new forward would be. Dave Wohl, an assistant coach, had once worked with Rice when both were with the Miami Heat and spoke nonstop about his shooting range. Lakers scouts insisted Rice was in terrific shape. "I knew he had a lot of talent, but I was worried about integrating a third offensive player into the game plan," Rambis recalled. "I'm thinking about all this — *How will it work? How will our team change?* — and then, on his first day, Glen comes walking through the tunnel."

Rambis was standing alongside Bill Bertka, the assistant. "Whoa," he said, "Glen is fat."

"How can you tell?" Bertka replied.

"Because," Rambis said, "I can see the rolls in his neck."

In his top condition, Rice, who was 6-foot-7, weighed 215 pounds. He reported to the Lakers at 240. Maybe 245. He made his debut against Golden State, coming off the bench to score 21 points in an 89–78 victory. "It was a great feeling," Rice said afterwards. "A lot of good things are go-ing to happen with this team."

The optimism was real. The reality was not. "Glen came with a *huge* ego," said Kevin Ding, the *Orange County Register* beat writer. "He had expectations that couldn't be met." The 10-game winning streak faded as the team lost five of its next eight. Rice's adjustment was anything but seamless. A 23.5-points-per-game scorer in his three years with the Hornets, he averaged but 17.5 with the Lakers. Teammates were dumb-founded by his inability to create off the dribble or pick up basic offensive ideas. "Glen was really one-dimensional," said Harper. "Great shooter. But if he's not making his shots, he's not valuable. He can't defend, he doesn't make other players better. Eddie was the exact opposite — he defended, he scored in the open court, he created opportunities for other people. I was adamant that was a bad trade to make. But who was listening to me?"

Rambis longed for the lithe, smooth Jones, who was busy establishing himself as Charlotte's new star. "There were times in games when I'd be on the sideline, right behind Glen," recalled Rambis. "He's getting these wide-open shots, and as soon as it's leaving his hands it's clear the ball has zero chance of going in. I said to Dave, 'What the fuck? What is this?'"

Wohl could only shake his head. "I know," he'd reply. "I've never seen anything like it. I don't know what to tell you. He's not the same guy."

Over the next four games, Rice — slow and fat and out of sorts — shot a putrid 26 for 65 from the field. "He was very bad," said Rambis. "Not the player I thought we were getting."

A bigger problem, though, was an out-of-his-depth new head coach confronted with rotten team chemistry. "Many of the writers had been around Kurt when he was a player, and he was quippy, he was funny," said Kawakami. "But as a head coach he lost that. He was humorless and angry and took things very personally." The lack of a regular training camp ruined any chances of player-to-player bonding, and the firing of a coach, the additions of a lunatic rebounder and a pudgy outside gunner — it was all too much. Plus, there was the continuing saga of "the boy wonder," which was O'Neal's new, not so lovely designation for Bryant. When Rambis was assisting Harris, he often found himself sitting on the bench alongside Bryant, trying to explain the professional game to Los Angeles's young phenom. He believed that Harris, for all his positives, failed to take time to help Bryant along, so Rambis filled that void. Now, as the man in charge, he was still whispering sweet nothings into Bryant's ear. It was pissing people off. Rambis simply refused to punish Bryant for selfish play or chide him for poor decisions. "He let Kobe do whatever he wanted to do," recalled O'Neal. "No questions asked. Kurt would defend everything he did instead of just being man enough to tell Kobe, 'Look, this is what you got to do if we're going to win.' The truth is nobody wanted to play with Kobe."

Though J.R. Reid was a 10-year veteran near the end of his career and a mere throw-in in the Jones-for-Rice swap, West liked the way he communicated with other teammates. That's why, one day shortly after the trade, he pulled the power forward aside and requested a favor. "I notice that you and Derek Harper get along great, that you and Shaq and you and Rick Fox and you and Travis Knight all get along great. Can you do me a favor and try and teach Kobe some of that?"

"Some of what?" Reid asked.

"Try and get him to understand this isn't a one-on-five sport," West said. "Educate him on how to be a teammate."

He would have been better served teaching Bryant to speak Pirahã. The third-year guard averaged 19.9 points over 50 games for the Lakers, but where O'Neal's team-leading 26.3 points per game were achieved efficiently, Bryant was a self-detonating nuclear bomb, too often looking off his teammates in an effort to break down defenders and attack the rim. When he was great, he was spectacular. Bryant lit up the Magic for 38 points on March 21, and did so on 15-for-24 shooting. But too often, it was 4 for 14 from the field (March 10 against the Clippers) or 5 for 15 (April 3 against Golden State) or 8 for 21 (April 11 against Seattle). If there was an hourlong 1999 Glen Rice highlight reel, 57 minutes of it would be devoted to him standing outside the three-point line, waving his arms and waiting for passes that never arrived. On multiple occasions, Rambis begged his veterans to encourage Bryant, only to be rebuffed with blank stares and disinterested shrugs. "They'd all say, 'We tried, but he doesn't listen,'" said Rambis. "And I'd think, *You tried one time. Once. How about trying two times? How about three?*" Having come along during the Showtime era, Rambis was accustomed to Magic Johnson taking Vlade Divac under his wing; Michael Cooper educating Byron Scott. But those were different men of a different age. Tom Savage, the assistant public relations director, recalled an agitated O'Neal pulling him to the side and saying, "What do you think of No. 8? Don't you think he needs to pass more?"

Before a game at Sacramento in April, O'Neal called for a players-only meeting in the Arco Arena visiting locker room. One after another, Lakers stood up to insist they were fed up with "the golden child" — O'Neal's term again — receiving special treatment. "Kobe just sat there," O'Neal recalled. "He didn't say anything."

It was an opportunity for the men to vent their frustrations. "I have an idea," Harper said. "Shaq, Kobe — why don't you two motherfuckers go at it on the floor? You keep arguing about whose team this is, and we all clearly don't mean shit. We're just the people passing you the fucking ball. So go at it. Please." The suggestion was greeted with awkward laughter. Then, midway through the session, Rambis — who was eavesdropping outside — entered the room and screamed, "Well, you guys were young and selfish once!"

It did not play well. "Once Kurt said that," O'Neal recalled, "it became clear to all the veterans we aren't going anywhere with this guy as our coach."

Were Bryant digestible off the court, perhaps the hoggish behavior could be forgiven. Many of his teammates, though, were now in their third year of witnessing his standoffish arrogance, and enough was enough. Bryant continued to turn down any and all invitations to team functions, player parties, birthday gatherings, bowling alley treks. In Miami, O'Neal took the entire roster out to a fancy seafood restaurant. Bryant was the lone Laker not to attend, but 30 minutes into the engagement he entered the restaurant, only to sit at his own table with a book.

Derek Fisher, supposedly his closest friend on the squad, had not so much as visited Bryant's house. Once, while the team was on the road, Bryant encountered Robert Horry and Rick Fox sitting together in a restaurant. The Lakers had a game the following night, and Horry was nursing a beer. "How can you drink when we have to play?" Bryant asked — as much lecture point as question. "Don't you wanna be your best?"

Horry just laughed. "I'll be okay, Junior," he said. "Worry about you."

"Lord knows I gave it a go with Kobe," recalled Reid. "We'd be on the plane and I'd say, 'Kobe, come on back here. We're playing cards.' No. 'Kobe, we're shooting dice.' No. 'Kobe, wanna talk —' No. He'd be all alone, reading *The Art of War* and trying to figure out how to kill opponents. It was not a way to be a team player." Unbeknownst to teammates, Bryant sometimes wandered to the nearby UCLA campus, where he would sit in the student center and pretend he belonged. "I think he was sad," said Harper. "Lonely."

The one Laker he somewhat confided in was Harper, whose 17-year age difference made him feel more uncle than teammate. Now in his 16th NBA season, Harper was desperate for a championship, and Bryant's hunger spoke to him. The youngster was the first teammate he ever had who taped up before practice, then again after practice for a second work-out when everyone else left the gymnasium. It was impressive.

"We'd eat," Harper recalled. "We'd sit down, have a bite, talk. Kobe doesn't let you up on him. He keeps people back. Sometimes he will look right through you, like you're not even there. And other times you sort of see the real guy."

One day O'Neal approached Harper in the locker room, confused expression plastered on his face.

"Yo," he said, "where do you and Kobe go?"

"To eat," Harper replied.

O'Neal shook his head. "Well," he said, "it's good to know he talks to someone."

When the regular season ended, the Lakers were 31-19 and a disappointing No. 4 seed in the Western Conference. They missed Eddie Jones's intensity, Elden Campbell's below-the-basket muscle. Rodman was gone, Rice was fat, Bryant was out of control, and the three rookies (Sam Jacobson, Tyronn Lue, and Ruben Patterson) rarely contributed. O'Neal was the best big man in the game, but when he was off, the Lakers were in trouble.

After ousting Houston in the first round of the playoffs, Los Angeles was swept in four games by a far superior, far more cohesive San Antonio team featuring David Robinson and Tim Duncan manning the blocks. "They were better," Harper said. "By a lot." The last game of the series, a 118–107 setback, was also the final regular season game inside the Great Western Forum. A building that had served as home to some of the greatest teams in NBA history was closing with a sad, pathetic thud. The banners hanging from the rafters seemed to taunt the current players as they shuffled off the court. *You're not good enough* . . .

Many in the sellout crowd of 17,505 headed for the exits with five minutes left and the Lakers — called "bumbling" and "inept" by an accurate *Newsday* piece — down 13 points.

It felt like a new low.

8

Phil the Void

H e was hanging there.

Everyone in Los Angeles knew it.

Everyone in Los Angeles felt it.

Everyone in Los Angeles wanted it.

Everyone in . . .

Stop.

Hold on.

Not *everyone*. Just mostly everyone.

In the aftermath of yet another Los Angeles Lakers playoff disappointment, it became increasingly clear that something drastic needed to happen to escape a black hole of good-not-great mediocrity. In Shaquille O'Neal and Kobe Bryant, the team boasted two cornerstone pieces, both in their twenties. From Rick Fox and Robert Horry to Glen Rice and Derek Fisher, there were quality role players galore. A brand-new arena, the Staples Center, was opening in downtown Los Angeles, and Jerry Buss, the team's owner, was 100 percent committed to winning, price be damned.

There was just the teeny-weeny issue of the head coach.

If the Lakers had learned one thing in the era since Pat Riley departed after capturing four NBA crowns, it was that the power of a great leader could not be understated. Yes, those Showtime teams of Magic Johnson and Kareem Abdul-Jabbar and James Worthy were loaded, but a loaded team sans guidance is rudderless. Mike Dunleavy, Riley's immediate replacement, took the franchise to one Finals appearance but otherwise did little with much. He was followed by Randy Pfund, whose biggest accomplishment was sporting a *P* alongside an *F* in his last name. Magic Johnson took over for 16 nightmarish games, then Harris and, lastly, Rambis. Some were awful, some were good, some (specifically, Harris) were better than good. But, man after man, the consensus was that, while a team could win a championship with (*fill in the name*) as head coach, it wouldn't win a championship *because* (*fill in the name*) was head coach.

So, again, he was hanging there — and everyone in Los Angeles knew it.

Not that Philip Douglas Jackson was, from the day the 1999 season ended, a shoo-in to take over the Lakers. There were complications. First, Jerry West, executive vice president for basketball operations, believed that Rambis was on the threshold of becoming a quality NBA coach. He knew there were problems with the interim's relations with certain players, but he also believed Rambis was the ideal man to help Bryant reach his full potential. West and Rambis weren't mere friends and colleagues. They were Lakers who bled the purple and gold. To West, that meant something.

Second, Jackson was a wanted man. His coming to Southern California would be no slam dunk. New York was interested. New Jersey was interested. "He had to be on the top of any list," recalled Ray Chambers, who led the Nets' coaching search. "Certain coaches exemplify winning. That's Phil Jackson."

Third, he would be expensive. The average NBA coach was making $2.6 million in 1999. Jackson would demand, at the least, $5 million per season.

Fourth ... *hell*, where to begin? For the most part, the NBA is not a complicated league populated by complicated men. Sure, everyone comes attached to a backstory, often accompanied by a rise from poverty, a local playground, a weathered ball, a high school renaissance, a college campus, a snazzy suit on draft night. But the single-mindedness of the professional basketball pursuit generally results in participants who — in *Brady Bunch*–speak — fit the suit. They are what you expect when it comes to standard Xs and Os, and for decision-makers like Jerry West there is a comfort in that.

Such does not apply to Phil Jackson.

At the time, he was known best for what he had most recently accomplished — namely, guiding the Chicago Bulls of Michael Jordan and Scottie Pippen to six NBA titles over a nine-year span. To even his biggest detractors, Jackson was a coaching genius, a savant who could read players, understand what made them tick, push without being pushy, and instruct without talking a guy's ear off. He was known for presenting his men with literary classics that meshed with their personalities, then (gasp!) expecting the books to be read. He insisted that his teams meditate, engage in yoga, develop themselves beyond the court. When, in 1995, the Bulls signed Dennis Rodman following nine tumultuous years with the Pistons and Spurs, naysayers said it was akin to inviting a wild pig inside a reading room. Jackson coached Rodman to the three greatest seasons of his career — and three rings.

Yet with Phil Jackson, there was a whole lot of X factor. Born in tiny Deer Lodge, Montana, to a pair of Assemblies of God ministers, he was raised watching his mother, Elisabeth, and father, Charles, preach every Sunday. There was no television in the Jackson home, which was built by his dad. Phil attended Williston (North Dakota) High and didn't see his first movie until his senior year. He never danced — literally *did not* dance — until his freshman year at the University of North Dakota. "One of the first things my parents would ask when I came home and told them of some new friend I had met was, 'Is he a Christian?'" Jackson recalled. "We were taught a disdain for any other type of religion." Cigarettes were of the devil. So was alcohol and, of course, premarital sex. ("I was curious about the female body," he once wrote, "but I had no idea how women functioned.") He began driving a car at 12, because the Jacksons lived in the middle of nowhere and, well, someone needed to drive. The main activity for many years was picking cherries (called "lugs" by the locals) with his aunt Katherine in Missoula, then returning home and having his mother can and sell them. "It sounds like a deprived childhood, but I don't see it that way," Jackson said. "My father was a really great image for me growing up. Once he had to fire a minister who was having a relationship outside his marriage with a member of the congregation. He did it in such a subtle manner. It was very honorable."

When Jackson was 13, his dad devoted an unusual amount of time to counseling a parishioner who had caused a horrific car accident with his grain truck. The man would arrive at the Jackson household, shoulders slumped, tears streaming down his face, and he and Charles would retreat to the study. "One day our phone rings," Jackson said. "I was just a kid, but I answered it because Dad was busy. It was the man's wife. He'd gone into the bathroom and committed suicide. I've never forgotten that."

The isolation. The spirituality. The intimacy. It all contributed to an unusual man. Young Phil paid attention to human interactions, to the way people responded to his parents. He was a student of engagement, even without knowing it.

He also happened to be an otherworldly athlete. As a 6-foot-1, 150-pound high school sophomore, Jackson — nicknamed "Bones" by classmates and once described as "having the physique of an upside-down hanger" — played varsity baseball, football, track, and basketball, excelling at all four. He loved the attention sports brought, as well as the thrill of a body in motion, but his parents recoiled. That same year, Jackson was baptized in a river, and what was supposed to follow was a full devotion to Christ. Instead, Jackson said, he "started taking shortcuts" — pretending he loved God when, in fact, he wasn't certain such an entity existed. Jesus's teachings were well and good. But they could wait.

As a senior, Jackson was arguably the best prep athlete in North Dakota. Every day, a different letter arrived at the principal's office — recruiting pitches from basketball coaches all across America. He wound up picking the University of North Dakota, where he would play for an up-and-coming head coach named Bill Fitch. By now Jackson was 6-foot-8, with the wingspan of a pterodactyl, and the Fighting Sioux's full-court pressure defense was perfect for his intensity and athleticism. In four years at the school, he was twice named a Division II All-American while garnering a new nickname, "the Mop," for his propensity for falling on the floor to chase loose balls.

College was also the place where Jackson learned to open his mind to new ideas. Having been raised in a cultural bunker, he considered himself an archconservative — both socially and politically. In the university setting, he saw a different light, majoring in a combination of psychology, religion, and philosophy, dabbling in Buddhism, and diving into Nikos Kazantzakis's *The Last Temptation of Christ*.

In 1967, Jackson was picked by the New York Knicks in the second round of the NBA draft. He had never traveled to the Big Apple, and on his introductory visit he was greeted at the airport by Red Holzman, the team's chief scout, and his wife, Selma. On the drive along the Long Island Expressway into the city, Jackson — whose arms stretched from Tulsa to Prague — broke out his best party trick, simultaneously rolling down both rear windows. Then, without warning, someone threw a rock into the car windshield. For a kid whose hobbies included fly-fishing and canoeing, it was a jarring introduction to Metropolis. "That's nothing," Holzman told the startled rookie.

The Knicks were coached by Dick McGuire, but when he was fired that December New York hired Holzman to take over. He loved everything about Jackson — his appreciation of literature, his free-flowing game, his Woodstock sensibilities, a mustache the size of (in the words of the *New York Daily News*'s Vic Ziegel) "a blackboard eraser." Led by the superstar play of Willis Reed, Bill Bradley, and Walt Frazier, the Knicks went on to win the 1970 and 1973 NBA titles, and Holzman established himself as an all-time great coach. Jackson was a member of both teams, but he was far from the most important Knick, averaging 6.8 points in New York. It was the proximity to Holzman, however, that proved invaluable.

More than any other player on the roster, Jackson paid attention to every move. Due to a crippling back injury and spinal surgery, he was forced to miss the entire 1969–70 season, but the devastation of sitting out a championship run (the Knicks beat the Lakers in the Finals) was lessened by an invitation from Holzman to serve as an unofficial assistant. Jackson sat by his role model's side, absorbing as much information as possible, asking 1,001 questions. "I'll always remember the first day of practice," Jackson recalled. "Red took these plays — maybe three sheets, 12 in all

— and told the team, 'You can wipe your ass with this stuff,' before throwing it in the garbage can. He said, 'We're gonna play full-court pressure defense, today and every day.'" He was equally impressed by Holzman's away-from-the-court disposition. On other teams, players lived in fear of a disciplinarian coach, a disciplinarian owner, fines and suspensions. With the Knicks, the rules were simple: *Go where you want, stay out until you're tired — just don't interrupt Holzman's late-night scotch and don't show up unprepared.* Once, when asked how he would have reacted had the Knicks won a particularly important game, Holzman replied, "I'd go home, drink a scotch and eat the great meal Selma is cooking." Then, asked what he was going to do following the loss, he said, "I'll go home, drink a scotch and eat the great meal Selma is cooking."

"I learned that he usually had an Alka-Seltzer before the game," Jackson said. "He had a great sense of humor. He always said that basketball isn't rocket science. It's a pretty basic thing. You stay in front of your man defensively and on the offensive end, hit the open man . . .

"But he had a lot of common sense about people. I think that's more than anything else what I picked up on."

Following the 1978 season, Jackson was traded to the Nets, where Kevin Loughery, the head coach, saw him as an at-the-end-of-his-run veteran who would be most valuable working with the team's younger players. Jackson agreed, and on the 14 occasions the volatile Loughery was thrown out of games by the referees in 1978–79, Jackson took over. The next year, when Loughery threatened to quit over a dispute with management, he recommended Jackson as a replacement. "I was a little stunned when I heard this," Jackson recalled. "But it felt good to know someone of Kevin's stature thought I could handle the job."

His final game as an NBA player came on March 30, 1980, when he scored 4 points in a meaningless New Jersey loss to Washington. What followed was a riveting off-the-grid barnstorming coaching journey. Between 1982 and 1987, Jackson led the Albany Patroons of the Continental Basketball Association — making $25,000 per season to coach the immortal likes of David Ancrum and Abdur-Rahiim Al-Matiin. In addition to designing plays and setting rotations, Jackson drove the team bus. To keep costs in check, the Patroons traveled with only nine players. Following the 1984 championship series, Jackson demanded the Patroons increase his road per diem by $3. They agreed. "When I asked him why he didn't make the players drive, he explained that there was more legroom in the driver's seat," said Jim Coyne, the Albany owner. "The CBA was rough, nothing luxurious. It was a tough learning experience. He really paid his dues." Come the off-season, Jackson flew to Puerto Rico and scored another $20,000 to coach the Piratas de Quebradillas (1984 and 1987) and the Gallitos de Isabela (1984–1986) of the National Superior Basketball League. "All those experiences surely made Phil the coach he became," said Lowes Moore, a player with the Patroons. "We had a wild cast of characters in Albany — guys of different temperaments, intelligence. Getting us to play together was no simple task. But Phil did. Even back then, he understood the dynamics of human nature."

At the same time Jackson was completing his third season in Puerto Rico, the Chicago Bulls were naming Jerry Krause their general manager. A longtime scout for four different NBA franchises, Krause was brought to the Windy City to turn around an operation that had been tidal-waved by drug addiction, indifference, and chronic losing. He first interviewed Jackson in 1985, when (coincidentally) Loughery was being fired as the Bulls' head coach. The job wound up going to Stan Albeck, who lasted one year before being replaced by Doug Collins, the feisty former Philadelphia 76ers guard. Two years later, Krause was back speaking with Jackson after an assistant coaching slot opened. The news of his hiring was barely news at all — beneath a minuscule headline, PHIL JACKSON SIGNS AS BULLS' ASSISTANT, the *Chicago Tribune* ran six paragraphs on the seventh page of its sports section. Jackson was merely another retired ex-player sitting along the sideline, scouting opposing teams and looking busier than he actually was.

Before long, though, Collins and Krause were mortal enemies. The GM wanted to be deeply involved in the Bulls' day-to-day operations. Collins — "strung tighter than a piano wire," in the words of the *Tribune's* Sam Smith — wanted Krause permanently reassigned to the Guam office.

On July 6, 1989, Collins was fired and replaced by the 43-year-old

Jackson, who was handed a four-year, $1.2 million contract and asked to coach a group headlined by Michael Jordan, the gifted and egomaniacal superstar, now in his sixth year. He immediately brought calm to a frenzied scene, presenting each player with a book (the first he gave Jordan was *Song of Solomon,* by Toni Morrison), lowering expectations, cutting back on Collins's intensity, letting the men express themselves as individuals. He also did something that, at the time, seemed relatively insignificant but wound up changing basketball.

One of Collins's other assistants was Tex Winter, a 67-year-old basketball lifer and the high priest of an offensive system referred to as "the triangle." Under Winter's ideal, perfected over four decades of coaching at various levels, the Bulls' attack would be a more balanced, more nuanced system based largely upon spacing and open spots. He repeatedly urged Collins to embrace the idea — then was banished to a spot alongside the Gatorade jug.

Jackson, however, was all in. Despite Jordan's initially referring to the triangle as "that equal-opportunity offense," the new coach urged him to give it a chance, to score a bit less and distribute a lot more. He wanted the Bulls to be a free-flowing offensive machine, where defenders could no longer triumph simply by double-teaming the league's best player. "The important thing," he told Jordan, "is to let everybody touch the ball so they won't feel like spectators. You can't beat a good defensive team with one man. It's got to be a team effort."

Over the course of his nine seasons running the Bulls, Jackson's teams captured six titles. It was part triangle, part understanding Jordan and his primary sidekick (the mercurial Scottie Pippen), part operating with an open mind and eternal inquisitiveness. "There was something about Phil that caused you to buy into what he was saying," said Corie Blount, a Bull from 1993 to 1995. "It never felt like bluster coming from him. He had a plan for everything."

Following Chicago's sixth championship, in 1998, the glory ended. The Bulls were deconstructed, a product of Krause's mounting resentment of Jackson, Jordan's desire to retire, Dennis Rodman's weirdness. Pippen was traded to Houston, Jackson retreated with his wife, June, to their new home in Woodstock, New York, and the NBA's 28 other franchises were thrilled to have a dynasty set to the side. For the first time in nearly 20 years, Jackson was blessed with a year to himself to fish and read and take long walks and . . .

Yawn.

Be bored.

Really bored.

His marriage to June 24 years strong — ended in divorce.

He tried giving speeches.

He volunteered for Bill Bradley's failed presidential campaign.

He returned to his home in Montana.

"I was searching for something," he recalled. "But I wasn't sure what that was."

When the Lakers called, it wasn't a shock.

Throughout the disappointing 1998–99 run, Jackson's name appeared in the Los Angeles media, oh, 50 times per month. First as a speculative replacement for Del Harris. Then as a speculative replacement for Kurt Rambis. He had infuriated many members of the Lakers' front office in the spring of 1998, when *ESPN The Magazine* published excerpts from his diary. One of the passages featured Jackson musing about coaching the Lakers and wondering whether O'Neal had the intellectual capacity to play in the triangle offense.

Harris, in particular, was agitated. There are things you do in the professional coaching world and things you don't do. "You don't campaign for another person's job," he recalled years later. "What Phil did — it was classless. It wasn't right."

Jackson didn't see it the same way. He was merely discussing a hypothetical — *What would O'Neal be like in the system?* West, too, was upset. He and Krause had been close since their time together with the Lakers in the 1970s, and during the Jordan dynasty the Bulls' GM would often call his Los Angeles counterpart to complain about Jackson's arrogance, dismissiveness, rudeness. "[Jerry] told me in no uncertain terms that Phil was trouble," West recalled. "That we should stay away from him." Krause thought Jackson to be more than merely manipulative. He considered him mean.

Having faced Jackson during their playing days, West didn't have to be told twice. During the 1972 NBA Finals, between the Knicks and the Lakers, West was walking off the floor after one of the games when his face came into direct contact with Jackson's elbow. "Phil . . . broke the guy's nose," recalled Walt Frazier, New York's point guard.

There was also the matter of Jackson's recent criticism of the Lakers' handling of Rodman. He felt the team didn't give his former star enough of an opportunity, and said so. "Apparently we don't do things right," West fired back.

That's why, when West was asked during his team's playoff loss to San Antonio about the possibility of hiring Jackson, he said, curtly, "Fuck Phil Jackson."

Yes, *Fuck Phil Jackson.*

There was, however, a reality West and Jerry Buss couldn't ignore. Bryant had made it clear he wanted to play for Phil Jackson. Rice had made it clear he wanted to play for Phil Jackson. O'Neal had made it clear he wanted to play for Phil Jackson — going so far as to present his agent, Leonard Armato, with a list of the coaches he would deem acceptable going forward. One was Chuck Daly. One was Bob Hill. The third — and most desirable — was Jackson. "We couldn't go on with Kurt," O'Neal recalled. "Nice guy, but a Kobe guy all the way." Within a week of the end of the 1998–99 season, O'Neal made a demand of Armato. He called him and said, "Listen, tell [West] I'm not playing for Kurt. Nobody wants to play for Kurt. If Kurt's coach next year, I ain't playing."

The Los Angeles Lakers were not supposed to be an operation that developed coaches and provided them with time to learn on the job. No, the organization — what with its 11 championship banners and nine uniform numbers dangling from the rafters — was all about excellence. Plus, the new Staples Center would be open for business come October 17, 1999. Everything concerned winning in the present. *Absolutely* everything.

In June 1999, West sucked up his pride (as well as his commitment to Rambis) and flew to Chicago to meet with Todd Musburger, Jackson's agent. That same week, he reached out to Jackson via phone, the first meaningful conversation the two had ever had. What began as awkward and stilted flowed into awkward and stilted. But useful. "We have talent here," West told him, "we just lack leadership and maturity. It's probably not all that different than what you walked into with the Bulls. This team is ready."

Jackson told West that he always felt unappreciated in Chicago; that this call meant the world to him. He said he had been watching the Lakers, and he, too, believed they were of championship ilk.

Several weeks later, at the invitation of a friend named Mark Bilski, Jackson was in Alaska, fishing with his sons, Ben and Charlie, on Iliamna Lake. The rainbow trout and northern pike weren't biting, so they stashed their poles and traveled up the river to take in breathtaking Petrof Falls. Upon returning to the village a few hours later, the three Jacksons were surrounded by a handful of youngsters.

"Are you Phil Jackson?" a boy asked.

"Yes," he said. "Why?"

"I hear you got the job with the Lakers," the youth replied.

"What?" said Jackson. "How do you know that?"

"We got a dish," he said. "It's on ESPN."

Oh.

The introductory press conference was held on June 16, 1999, at the Beverly Hilton. With a room overflowing with media members and with Jackson's five children in attendance, West stepped to the microphone and invited forward the newest coach of the Los Angeles Lakers, a man who would be paid $6 million per season for five years, plus a $2 million bonus for each NBA championship.

There was no containing the giddiness. Bryant—who paid an unannounced visit to Jackson's hotel room before the press conference and asked him to autograph his book *Sacred Hoops*—would now be playing for the coach who made his hero, Michael Jordan, a ring-collecting NBA force. Rice would now be playing for the coach who understood the value of spacing and spreading the offensive wealth. Rick Fox would now be playing for the coach who used small forwards as stewards of the offense.

At his home in Newport Beach, Dennis Rodman — a thrice champion with the Bulls under Jackson — was convinced his phone would be ringing any day now. "They ain't gonna win with what they've got, I'll tell you that," he told a reporter. "I know what's going to happen. They'll wait until the last minute, and then they'll call me." (He was incorrect.) No one was more euphoric than O'Neal, whose first seven years in the NBA were spent under five different head coaches — none of much note. Jackson and his new center chatted via phone shortly after the press conference but didn't meet until several weeks later. That was when O'Neal, visiting Kalispell, Montana, for a concert to promote his fourth studio album, *Respect*, decided to take the 10-mile drive to Jackson's home in Flathead Lake. In his autobiography, *Shaq Talks Back*, O'Neal writes that he and his bodyguard, Jerome Crawford, arrived at the coach's house unannounced. Jackson said that is simply not true. "I knew he was coming," he said. "I was given a heads-up and I thought it was great. I wanted to meet him."

O'Neal showed up earlier than anticipated, and Jackson wasn't home. But Chelsea and Ben, two of his children, were, so O'Neal spent the next 25 minutes jumping with them atop an enormous trampoline. "I go in the house, he's got all these Zen books and all the championship balls, and his rings right there," O'Neal recalled. "Then . . . I decide I'm gonna take a swim. [June] gives me some shorts. I jump in the lake. It's freezing. So I start doing flips off the dock. They were laughing at me because I'm not completing my flips, landing on my back like some knucklehead at the community-center pool." Before long, dozens of boats congregated near Jackson's property, awestruck by the sight of the Kazaam genie soaring through the air.

When Jackson arrived, he was greeted by O'Neal gazing at the championship trophies. It was a scene out of a corny sports movie — the glory-deprived star staring longingly at a pane of glass as the sunlight's reflection creates a holy glow. "You know," Jackson said, "you can get one of those if you listen to me."

"I believe you," O'Neal replied.

"But before we start," Jackson said, "I could use your help with something."

"Okay, Coach," O'Neal said. "Name it."

He walked his new center toward the edge of his property, which ran adjacent to a lake. An enormous fallen tree was lying along the shore, and Jackson needed it relocated. He tied a rope around one end and attached the other end to his boat. "He's there pulling it with the boat," O'Neal recalled, "and I'm pushing the tree."

Jackson told O'Neal to hang on to the tree, so he did — as the boat kept going and going. It distanced itself from the shore — "and then I had to swim back from this damn island," O'Neal recalled. "It was far — I don't know how far, but it was far. And you know what I'm thinking? This man is challenging me."

Later on, Jackson looked over the 350-pound goliath standing before him. Frustrated by one lost season after another, O'Neal spent the summer lifting weights, watching what he ate, ingesting creatine and other supplements. "I was huge," he said. "Solid bulk."

"How much you weigh?" Jackson asked.

"I don't know," O'Neal replied.

"I want you to lose about 15 pounds," Jackson said. "The bigger you are, the harder it's gonna be on your knees, and I want you playing 40 minutes a game."

"Okay," O'Neal replied.

With that, Shaquille O'Neal departed the property and, soon enough, found himself back in Los Angeles, trying to shed the weight and prepare for what he believed would be the season of his life. Along with the addition of Jackson, the off-season had been a remarkable one for the Lakers, where "reinvention" was the buzzword and the name Del Harris felt like a long-ago ghost. The first thing Jackson concerned himself with was the painful lack of cohesion. Yes, Rick Fox was a stand-up guy, and Horry's gravitas was undeniable. ("Rob wasn't outspoken," Fox recalled. "That wasn't his thing.") But for all the flash and sparkle of O'Neal, Bryant, and Rice, none of the three were tremendous leaders. They were stars who needed to be stars. Important. Hell, essential. But not leaders. In his nine years with the Bulls, Jackson was blessed with the rarity of his best player also being the NBA's greatest front man. But Michael Jordans were once-in-a-century creatures. There were no Michael Jordans to be found in Los Angeles.

The team underwent a hefty makeover. Ron Harper, the 36-year-old shooting guard who had spent the past five seasons with Jackson in Chicago, was signed as a free agent — "one bum knee, ugly shot, old body," recalled Travis Knight. "But so important to winning." A.C. Green, also 36 and the Lakers' power forward from 1985–93, was acquired via trade from Dallas for Sean Rooks and a future draft pick. Not because he had much left in the tank (Green averaged 4.9 points for the Mavs), but because he played with heart and drive and never hesitated to throw himself on the ground in pursuit of a loose ball. Brian Shaw, the 6-foot-6 guard with 10 seasons (and six teams) under his belt, was brought in as a free agent to serve as Bryant mentor and locker room lawyer.

"We added guys," Bryant said with a laugh, "I looked at when I was like 4 years old."

The most fascinating (in a watching-two-grandpas-argue-over-a-bingo-game sort of way) training camp battle would be held between Benoit Benjamin, the long-ago No. 3 pick in the 1985 NBA draft, and John Salley, a key member of the Detroit Pistons' Bad Boys dynasty of the 1980s. Jackson very much wanted a sage basketball guru as his last man off the bench, and while Benjamin's résumé could be read as *sage basketball guru* (he was a 14-year veteran who had played for eight different teams and averaged a respectable 11.4 points over his career), he was a notoriously lazy player who once brought two left shoes to a game and, as a member of the Lakers back in 1993, missed the playoffs with a torn toenail.

Salley, though, was an even bigger enigma. He'd last played in the NBA in 1996, a veteran buried on the bench for Jackson's Bulls as they beat Seattle for the NBA title. With the ring, Salley retired — then un-retired six months later to sign a one-year, $2 million deal with Panathinaikos of the Greek Basket League. "I thought, *Why not?*" Salley recalled. "It could be a great experience. See the world, different cultures, different foods . . ."

After arriving in Greece, Salley met with Božidar Maljković, the Panathinaikos head coach, who shook his hand, offered a couple of kind words — then told him Michael Jordan was an average player who *might* average 16 points per game in Europe. "At that moment," Salley said, "I knew it'd be a short stay."

He lasted seven weeks.

The next two and a half years were a blur. Salley tried his hand at broadcasting, at acting, at going vegan, at raising two daughters. He moved to Los Angeles and gave his all to being a sunglasses-wearing someone. He reached out to a handful of NBA teams, but the market for a mid-thirties non scoring rebounder who couldn't cut it in Greece wasn't fierce. "I was in the worst depression in the world," he recalled. "I thought I'd ruined everything for me and my family. I left Europe, I couldn't get a job playing basketball. What was I?"

Not long after the 1999 NBA playoffs, Salley tracked down a phone number for his old coach. Jackson answered, a deep "Hello" in that trademark gravelly voice.

"It's John," Salley said. "Did you watch the Lakers series? That was just shit."

"Who have you been talking to?" Jackson replied.

"What do you mean?" Salley said.

"I think I'm about to be offered the Laker job," he said. "But nothing's final yet."

Salley was giddy.

"There's no way you're gonna let Shaq and Kobe not win together," he said. "That's not happening." Then a pause for impact. "You know, Phil, I live five doors down from Shaq . . ."

"You do?" Jackson said.

"Yeah, I do," Salley replied. "And you're gonna need someone to teach him the triangle offense in English . . ."

Though the coach was bringing in two of his assistants from Chicago

(Tex Winter and Jim Cleamons), teaching the Bulls' Way wouldn't come easy. So he told Salley he was welcome to come to camp but that he would have to beat out Benoit Benjamin for a roster spot. He then heard Salley snort. Literally, he snorted. "Benoit Benjamin?" he replied. "Why not give me a bigger challenge — like beating out a folding chair?"

Salley wound up making the team, but helping out with Winter's triangle was only slightly more challenging than helping out with the Lakers' two superstars. When Salley and Jackson were together with the Bulls, Jordan and Scottie Pippen coexisted as A and B+. There was a king, and his sidekick never so much as aspired to the throne. Yet what was transpiring with the Lakers was a combination of confusing, uncomfortable, and exasperating. "The players on that team didn't seem to like each other," said Cleamons, the assistant coach. "There was a lot of raw talent, but I'd never played for a good team where the players didn't get along. And in Los Angeles, there was very little sense of that. The tension was real."

Training camp was held at UC Santa Barbara, and in the lead-up Jackson made it a priority to sit down with O'Neal and Bryant together — with Harper in attendance as a buffer. Jackson had heard — from West, from Rambis, from various players and officials — that the two returning stars were oil and water, and he wanted to nip it in the bud. "Every great team has a one-two punch," Jackson said. "This is your team, Shaq. And Kobe, you're gonna be our floor leader. You guys don't like that, let me know now and I'll trade you now. You're gonna do what I say, and if you don't, you're out of here."

O'Neal was thrilled. Bryant was less than thrilled. The center saw the guard as a not-ready-for-prime-time player who thought himself superior to his peers. O'Neal had extended 800 olive branches to Bryant over their first three seasons together, and time after time the efforts were rebuffed. Bryant saw the center as a fat, indifferent wannabe megastar who couldn't hit a free throw to save his life (in this regard, he was correct). "It was different than anything I'd ever seen," said Devean George, the team's first-round pick out of Augsburg College. "They had the same goals on the court, and they played well together. But the personal relationship was rough."

"Everyone accepted and embraced Shaq as the key guy," said Knight. "Except for Kobe. He chose not to. And that's his personality — the unwavering belief that he was the best. Which is fine, I guess. But he definitely antagonized the situation."

"How do you convince people who are so strong and egocentric and believe in themselves so much to join in?" Jackson said years later. "It's a mystery."

Save for the players who had been with Jackson in Chicago, picking up Winter's triangle offense was the equivalent of picking up the intricacies of *The Brothers Karamazov*. Nobody knew this better than Cleamons, Jackson's assistant for seven years in Chicago, who had recently spent a season and a half as the head coach of Dallas. The Mavericks had been blessed with three young stars (Jason Kidd, Jim Jackson, Jamal Mashburn), and none were willing to adjust their games to try running the triangle. Why? "Because players get comfortable doing what they know," said Cleamons, who was fired with a 28-70 record. "Change is uncomfortable." Salley and Harper were strong tutors, but by now most of the Lakers had spent the majority of their basketball lives as stars or, at the very least, standouts. Even Knight, the least-skilled member of the roster, was a Gatorade High School Player of the Year in Utah, who went on to appear in three straight Sweet Sixteens. Now, without preparation or much warning, Winter was teaching stubborn wealthy men a completely new way of thinking about offense. With his gray hair and wide eyes, he was a nutty basketball professor, barking terms they had never before heard.

Explained Frederick C. Klein in the *Wall Street Journal*:

> The Triangle's basic setup — the one that gives it its name — involves putting three players on the same side of the lane — one near the sideline, one near the free-throw circle and one down low, near the basket. The player with the ball can drive to the hoop or shoot if those opportunities present themselves, or pass, usually to one of his triangle mates. Once he passes, he can move to the hoop for a return pass, or to an unoccupied part of the court. In the latter case, the triangle re-forms around the new

ball handler, who repeats the same options. The overloading of one side of the floor is a key to the system's effectiveness.

Shaq was sold from the get-go — "An offense where everyone feels involved?" he said. "Terrific." Knight, too, found it refreshing and invigorating. "Really, it's just spacing," he said. "You put guys in spacing, and when someone moves someone else fills the spot. Not hard."

Others, though, were not so happy. Los Angeles's preseason was a carnival of fools. "We were running into each other," O'Neal recalled, "turning the ball over and looking awful." George, the first-round pick out of Division III Augsburg, experienced his initial taste of the triangle during the Lakers' summer league play. In college, his life had been *dribble-rebound-shoot-create*. No longer. "You go from being the dominator to sharing," he recalled. "It wasn't natural. I remember Jerry West storming into our locker room during a game and just blasting me — 'This is an embarrassment! You're our No. 1 pick!' It wasn't that I wasn't strong enough or athletic enough. It was the triangle. A new language to learn."

Glen Rice was to the triangle what pecans are to a desk lamp — completely disconnected. He always seemed to be in the wrong place. Or forgetting to move. He arrived in shape, but Jackson quickly saw that he couldn't fit in. Rice wanted the ball and he wanted to shoot. The triangle demanded that he pass and forgo regular thinking.

As soon as Jackson was hired, he urged Mitch Kupchak and Jerry West to find a way to trade Rice for Scottie Pippen, who was on the market after spending the 1998–99 season as an unhappy Houston Rocket. Pippen had been the perfect triangle player in Chicago — a 6-foot-8 small forward who could run the offense — and Jackson and Winter cherished the idea of him wearing purple and gold, dribbling up-court, Bryant roaming the perimeter, O'Neal planted down low. Los Angeles offered the Rockets a package of Rice and Robert Horry but were rebuffed. "The Pippen talk really got to me," said Rice. "All I heard was 'He wants Scottie Pippen. He wants Scottie Pippen.' If you want Scottie Pippen, get his ass in here. Look, I love Scottie. He's a friend, and he was phenomenal. But if you're not gonna get him in here, excuse my French, but shut the fuck up. To hear that shit day after day was not fun." The Lakers then tried convincing the Knicks to exchange Latrell Sprewell, a Pippen-like player in both skill and temperament, for Rice. New York had no interest.

The worst triangle offender was Bryant, who didn't care to understand that the new Lakers offense ran through the center, and that it fell apart every time he dribbled, dribbled, dribbled, dribbled — then shot. Bill Plaschke of the *Los Angeles Times* asked whether Bryant was "rhythmic enough to fit his cymbal-like skills into a triangle" — and it was a fair question. Practices were a maddening chorus of exasperated sighs and exaggerated moans, of O'Neal muttering, "Fucking Showboat . . . ," and Winter demanding, aloud, for Bryant to explain what, precisely, he was thinking when Fox was wide open, Horry was wide open, Fisher was wide open — and he hucked up a 30-footer.

"I had my man beat," Bryant would start to say. "So what I did was —"

"Jesus Christ, Kobe," Winter often replied. "It's not *that* hard."

"Kobe wanted to chase the ball," said Cleamons. "The triangle is about spacing and ball movement, not ball chasing. You don't have to chase the ball. Be patient. But Kobe didn't feel that. He's like Keyshawn Johnson: *Just give me the ball. Just give me the ball. Put the ball in my hands.*"

The frustration was real. So much so that O'Neal and his teammates came up with a hand signal — a twitching downward motion of the thumb — that meant "No more passing to Bryant." The kid never caught on.

Los Angeles — and Winter — received an unexpected gift on October 13, when the Lakers and the Washington Wizards traveled to Kansas City, Missouri, to open the exhibition season. While reaching for an errant rebound in the first quarter, Bryant slammed his right hand into an opposing player. He thought little of it, scored 18 points, shrugged off the 88–84 loss — then learned that the appendage was broken and he would miss four to six weeks. The news was devastating to a point. With the shooting guard sidelined, the other players were able to work out a complicated system, and Bryant was able to watch the other players work out a complicated system *without him.* "I try to keep [my anxiousness] under control," he told the *Los Angeles Times* on October 29. "But I'm getting very anxious, yeah. I'm ready to burst out of the cage."

On November 2, 1999, Jackson's Los Angeles Lakers kicked off the regular season with a visit to Utah, where a Bryant-less squad opened up a 25–18 first-quarter lead, en route to a 91–84 triumph. It wasn't pretty (the Lakers committed 16 turnovers and shot a mediocre 43.4 percent from the field), but the team rebounded well, O'Neal tallied 23 points and 13 rebounds, and Rice — receiving far more looks without Bryant around — led the way with 28 points while shooting 5 of 6 from three-point range. "I thought we performed okay down the stretch," Jackson said afterwards, then noted that the team was still "rusty."

One night later, the $375 million Staples Center debuted as the official home of the Lakers. A crowd of 18,997 paid upwards of $1,000 for tickets (the team's average ticket price jumped from $51.11 to $81.89), and in exchange for the piles of dough, they received the rare and precious gift of watching the Vancouver Grizzlies (straight off an 8-42 season) try and play basketball. The early reviews of the new building were mixed. It was big and filled with restaurants and concession stands and located in the heart of a revitalized downtown Los Angeles. However, it also felt cold and impersonal and lacking the Great Western Forum's charm and warmth. Team employees — including Jeanie Buss, the owner's daughter and Lakers' executive vice president of business operations — seemed unwilling or unable to hide the truth: This wasn't home. Bill Plaschke, the *Los Angeles Times* columnist, nicknamed the building "the Superstore." The Lakers had captured six titles playing in Inglewood, and now they were co-tenants with the Clippers. *The Clippers?!* It didn't feel right. "The energy was really weird in the first half," O'Neal said of the building. "Everything was really weird."

"The practices we've had here, I think guys have understood what this building brings," Jackson said, "as far as the context, the depth, the size, the immensity of the backdrop that you've got to work against."

The Lakers won 103–88, with O'Neal's 28 points and 10 rebounds setting the pace, then captured nine of their next 13. When Bryant made his season debut on December 1 against Golden State, he was joining an 11-4 team that sat atop the Pacific Division standings. Jackson insisted he was happy to have Bryant back, just as O'Neal insisted he was happy to have Bryant back. Yet even though he played well in a 93–75 rout of the Warriors (he collected 19 points, 6 rebounds, and 3 assists coming off the bench), Bryant's presence was an irritant. Suddenly Rice was once again a spare part, longing for passes that never arrived. Suddenly O'Neal found himself fighting for position down low, only to look up and see Bryant soaring toward the hoop. Were they better with health? Yes. Los Angeles won four in a row with Bryant in the lineup, dropped a game at Sacramento, then went on a 16-game winning streak that cemented their status as the NBA's elite operation.

Yet there had never been a less happy 31-5 team. O'Neal was fined $10,000 for verbally slamming officials. Rice told his agent, David Falk, to seek out a trade, and calls were made to the New York Knicks and the Miami Heat. (So desperate was Falk to move one of his star clients, he told organizations that, should they acquire Rice, his other players would be more likely to come to their franchise.) In a game against the Nets, Jackson signaled for a play involving Horry, but it fell apart. Afterwards Horry told his coach, "I didn't hear your call" — to which Jackson replied, "The sheep know their master's voice. It's all about recognizing the master's voice and responding to his call." The use of "master" did not sit well with the team's African American players, and Jackson (who said it in a biblical context) was embarrassed.*

The darkest cloud hovered above Jerry West, everyone's favorite Laker icon. Whether he was in a great mood or an awful mood, upon arriving at the office West always — *always* — greeted co-workers with a warm "Hi!" and a couple of questions about his or her life. It was the way he did things, stardom and name recognition be damned. You treated people with compassion, with kindness, with humanity. Jackson, though, was a different bird. "One of the problems I had with Phil was this," West recalled. "His office was right near mine, and when he would arrive in the

---

* This was not Jackson's strong suit. During the 1999–2000 season, Jackson enraged several of the African American Lakers when, during a practice, he looked at guard J.R. Rider and said, "You gonna go down to Crenshaw and get a haircut after practice?" Rider was furious and snapped, "I'm not afraid of my people."

morning, he would walk right past and never even bother to wave or duck his head in to say hello.

"Phil and I had no relationship. None. He didn't want me around and had absolutely no respect for me — of that I have no doubt."

In the moments following one home loss, West entered the locker room to speak with his players. It was something he often did, a way of staying connected with the team he'd assembled. Jackson, however, had yet to complete his postgame chat, and he was enraged. "Jerry, get the fuck out of here!" he screamed. "What the fuck are you even doing in here?"

West was as sensitive as he was talented ("He let things fester," Jackson recalled), and he slunk out of the room, hurt and humiliated. He had mixed feelings about hiring Jackson from the get-go, and now it felt as if the franchise was slipping away. "What he didn't understand is I came from an organization [Chicago] where I kicked everyone out of the locker room," Jackson said. "I kicked out Jesse Jackson, I kicked out movie stars. The locker room is a sanctuary." West didn't buy it. These were players *he* acquired. This was an organization *he* bled for. A shockingly egoless man who requested zero credit and zero spotlight, West simply wanted the team to win. "I don't interfere with the coaches," he said. "I always tried to get players who would work best with what we were doing. I never wanted to overstep or get in the way."

It did not help that Jackson was now dating Jeanie Buss, the owner's daughter and executive vice president of business operations. The relationship had blindsided West from the very beginning — Jeanie had been a vocal proponent of keeping Kurt Rambis as head coach. "I was actively *against* hiring Phil," she said. The two had first met in September, waiting in Vancouver International Airport for a flight to return from league meetings. Jackson was simultaneously perplexed and impressed that Buss was flying coach (he was in first class). A few weeks later, on September 26, Jeanie was presented an in-office cake for her 38th birthday, and she had a slice delivered to Jackson's office. Later that evening, he asked her out for dinner. "We were eating and I laid it out," Buss recalled. "I liked him a lot. He had a sparkle in his eye. But I said, 'Look, I'm not going to have an affair with you. I'm not doing anything hidden. Because it'll compromise the Lakers organization, and if you try to keep something secret, people own you. So if we're going to date, it has to be in the open.'" Jerry Buss was fine with the relationship. Jerry West was not. "There's a fucking million women in this town," he said to Jackson. "Why would you end up with Jeanie?"

How, West wondered, was this okay? Didn't there need to be some sort of separation of church and state? What if Jackson proved the wrong coach? What if he needed to be disciplined? Or fired? West was all business — the Lakers were the Lakers; his family was an entirely separate entity. That's the way it was supposed to be. "I never wanted to have a pissing contest with the coach," West recalled. "That's not who I was. Even when maybe I should have."

On the court, meanwhile, Bryant was scoring at will — 27 points against Sacramento, 30 at Atlanta — and each time he released the ball, it felt like a punch to his teammates' faces. Without him in the lineup, Lakers players believed the offense was smooth and efficient and relatively egalitarian. "[When Kobe returned], the offense wasn't flowing as smoothly as it had," Jackson recalled. "Kobe was having a difficult time staying in the triangle and would frequently go rogue, which annoyed his teammates." In the immediate aftermath of a January 19 win at Cleveland, during which Bryant shot 6 for 15 in 41 minutes of play, O'Neal entered the locker room and instructed his teammate to "grow the fuck up and pass the fucking ball."

"Fuck you," Bryant replied. "Make some fucking free throws."

O'Neal had shot 5 for 13 from the line that game — and was hitting at a 52 percent rate for the season. It was not an area he enjoyed discussing.

"Are you fucking talking to me?" O'Neal said. "Are you really fucking talking to me?"

Bryant backed down.

"There was a lot of hatred in [O'Neal's] heart," Winter later said. "He was saying really hateful things. Kobe just took it and kept going."

In the coming days, several members of the team asked Jackson for some alone time. He knew, as soon as the request was made, what topic would be broached. Whether it was Rice feeling obsolete on the perimeter or Fox wondering why he existed just outside the paint or O'Neal slamming his head into a brick wall, they all desperately wanted Bryant to either pass the ball or vanish into the abyss. Jackson had gone through a similar circumstance when he coached a young Michael Jordan with the Bulls. "But Michael was receptive to criticism," Jackson said. "He wouldn't always agree, but he would hear you out. Kobe didn't have that. I did a lot of studying about juvenile narcissism, and juvenile narcissists are the worst, because they think they only deserve the best. They want to be the leaders. They don't accept counseling or advice. You can't criticize them. Kobe was a juvenile narcissist." Around this time, Bryant requested a meeting with Jerry West to ask how — back in 1961–62 — both he and Elgin Baylor had averaged more than 30 points per game for the Lakers. West told Jackson of the question, and it agitated the coach. Why was it always about points? What about learning? *Winning?* At one point, Michael Jordan — now retired as an active player — attended a Lakers-Bulls game in Chicago. Afterwards Jackson brought Bryant into a rear room for a discussion with his idol. "Michael's back there smoking a cigar," Jackson recalled. "And Kobe comes in and the first thing he says — the very first thing — is 'I can take you one-on-one.' It wasn't said jokingly. And Michael said, 'You probably can. You're 22 and I'm 36.' It was weird."

On an afternoon in late January, Jackson held a meeting inside a video room at Southwest College, the organization's practice spot. The coaches lined up four rows of chairs for the players, and the front seats were filled by O'Neal, Fox, Fisher, Harper, and Shaw. Bryant was all alone in the rear, the tip of his sweatshirt's hood covering his eyes. Jackson once again explained that the triangle relies of selflessness and wide-open eyes to succeed. "You can't be a selfish player and make this offense work for the team's good," he said. "Period."

When he was done, the head coach opened the room for comments and questions. There were a few seconds of silence. Awkward silence, but silence nonetheless. Then O'Neal, who had griped about Bryant to teammates, cleared his throat. "I think Kobe is playing too selfishly for us to win," he said. "I'm tired of it."

Open the floodgates . . .

"How many times have we been through this?" Fox added.

"The best teams I've ever been with," Shaw said, "were teams that shared the basketball. You can't win one against five. Ever."

It was ugly. Years later, Jackson noted (correctly) that were he to pre-side over a players-only vote — trade Kobe Bryant or keep Kobe Bryant — the kid would have been banished without a second's thought. And it wasn't merely the refusal to adapt to the offense. Now in his fourth NBA season, the 21-year-old guard had yet to mature or understand that the Lakers weren't his team. He was a piece. An important piece. But that's where it ended for the other members of the squad.

Jackson asked whether Bryant had anything he wanted to say. "Kobe finally addressed the group," the coach recalled, "and in a calm, quiet voice he said he cared about everyone and just wanted to be part of a winning team."

Salley, the veteran forward, devoted himself to helping Bryant under-stand camaraderie, and years later acknowledged it was a herculean task. During the season, he invited the young guard out for a night of party-ing on Miami's South Beach. Bryant begrudgingly agreed to accompany his teammate, and the gasps and smiles that greeted him inside the var-ious clubs made Salley giddy. *Finally*, he thought, *Kobe is having some fun.* Not so fast. After an hour, Bryant tapped Salley on the shoulder and asked that they talk outside, away from the loud music. It was maybe 10:30 p.m. "I've gotta go," he said. *What?* "I need to train in the morn-ing." An exasperated Salley retrieved his car and drove Bryant back to the Ritz-Carlton South Beach. "He was single-minded," Salley explained. "You had to understand that."

Few Lakers did. In the aftermath of Jackson's January all-hands meet-ing, the team lost four of their next five, including a disheartening 105–101 double-overtime crusher at Utah and a 24-point spanking at the hands of San Antonio. After starting the season 33-5, by February 1 the Lakers stood at 34-11. Jackson believed his built-to-win operation was crumbling apart, and couldn't possibly be saved.

The glory? The rings? They seemed out of the question.

9

Turning Around

As Los Angeles began falling apart, and turmoil threatened to overtake talent, Jerry West and Mitch Kupchak were working the phones, desperately trying to find a way out of the worst Los Angeles acquisition of recent note.

Sure, by measure of statistics Glen Rice appeared to be a perfectly fine Laker. He was averaging 16.7 points per game, which certainly wasn't embarrassing. Yet, from West and Kupchak to Phil Jackson and Tex Winter, everyone could see that he was the wrong player for the wrong system for the wrong team. In Charlotte, Eddie Jones was averaging 20.1 points per game and leading a revival. "I don't think anyone knew how great Eddie Jones would be," recalled Rick Bonnell, the *Charlotte Observer* writer. "He was a giant upgrade over Glen." At the same time, the man he'd been traded for was mopey, flat, ornery, ineffective. He had been a superstar with the Heat and a superstar with the Hornets, and he thought himself a superstar here. "Huge ego, saw himself as a prime-time guy," said Kevin Ding, the *Orange County Register* scribe. "Without the game to match it." Rice was the Lakers' third option. And a flabby one at that. Who couldn't shoot without dribbling first. Who played mediocre defense. Who was surprisingly feeble with his left hand. Who seemed to have aged 10 years overnight. Who didn't take to teammates. Or coaching. Or criticism. "David Falk [Rice's agent] called me one night and just went off on the team and the way they treated Glen," recalled J.A. Adande, the *Los Angeles*

Times writer. "I asked Mitch Kupchak about it and he said, 'That guy's just trying to manage the damage.'"

The Jones-for-Rice swap was a blunder, but now the Lakers would be cleaning the mess. After working the phones for days, a deal was all but in place that would send Rice to the Philadelphia 76ers as part of a three-team trade also involving Detroit. In return, the Lakers would get Larry Hughes, the explosive second-year Sixers shooting guard, and the expiring contract of retired center Bison Dele. Hughes was hardly the next Iverson — in many ways, the hyperkinetic 21-year-old was a poor man's Eddie Jones. But it would be addition by subtraction, and Los Angeles believed Rick Fox or Robert Horry could step in and up the scoring once Rice departed.

First, though, there was a game to be played.

Three days after a demoralizing 105–81 setback at the hands of the defending champion Spurs, during which Rice scored a mere 5 points and Tim Duncan lit up the Lakers for 29 points and 18 rebounds (wrote Tim Kawakami of the *Los Angeles Times*, "The Laker Recession of 2000 continues"), Los Angeles hosted the Jazz — aka the squad that had tormented them for the past half decade. As always, Utah was one of the NBA's elite operations, with point guard John Stockton and power forward Karl Malone continuing to execute offensive perfection. A week and a half earlier, the Jazz had numbed Los Angeles with a 105–101 double-overtime triumph, another reminder that O'Neal, Bryant, and Co. had yet to master pick-and-roll defense.

So the Jazz arrived at the Staples Center, at the seemingly perfect time to take a baseball bat to the knees of a wobbling franchise. Jackson wasn't happy with Bryant. Bryant wasn't happy with O'Neal. Nobody was happy with the one-foot-out-the-door Rice. "We were at our bottom," recalled Fox. "Sometimes, in the course of a season, you wonder if maybe this just isn't going to work. That's where we were."

Then everything changed.

The Jazz began the game by shooting 1 for 14 — brick after brick after brick. Some of this was fatigue (one night earlier, Utah had hosted Milwaukee), but most was attributable to the genre of suffocating defense

Jackson had preached throughout the season. Bryant, too often an offense-only ball hog, was all over the court. O'Neal, never pleased by the sight of Jazz center Greg Ostertag, swatted away five shots — several violently. Los Angeles forced 14 first-half turnovers, resulting in 21 points. After one quarter, the Laker lead was 33–14. At halftime it was 56–21. "We pretty much did what we had to do, and we came out with a lot of energy," O'Neal said afterwards. "We kind of needed this game."

The final score, 113–67, was greeted by America's sportscasters as some sort of misprint. Was that 87? Maybe 77? "It's just one game," Stockton said, following his 14-minute, 2-point night. "You find out a little bit about yourself after something like this."

Indeed.

Three nights later, the Lakers triumphed again, this time a 106–98 victory over Denver. Then they won again, a 114–81 takedown of Minnesota. Then they won again — 88–76 at Chicago. And 92–85 at Charlotte (Rice scored 21 in his return; Jones tallied 18 against his old team). And 107–99 at Orlando. Before long, the same franchise that had been on the verge of a collapse was piecing together a breathtaking 19-game winning streak. The trade talk — dead. The turmoil — shelved. The Lakers were the hottest team in basketball, a turnaround powered by talent trumping discord and (as always) the presence of the world's greatest post player.

Throughout his first seven years in the league, O'Neal had been both the NBA's most awe-inspiring and most maligned presence. By now, wasn't he supposed to have a championship ring? At least one? O'Neal was a dominating force. He was an awful free throw shooter. He made teammates better. He was an awful free throw shooter. The media loved him. He was an awful free throw shooter. O'Neal had shot 59 percent from the line as a rookie with Orlando in 1992–93, and it was presumed, with time, he would get better. Only he never did. Excuses were made — oversized hands, fatigue, nerves, anxiety, the lasting impact of a childhood accident that had resulted in a broken wrist. Every year it seemed a new free-throw-shooting expert would be brought in to change the world. Once, a University of South Florida–St. Petersburg American foreign policy professor named Dennis Hans mailed Kupchak a series of articles he'd penned on O'Neal's problems at the line. "One day I got an e-mail from Mitch, and he told me he passed my writing on to Phil and Shaq," Hans recalled. "He made a little progress and I felt good about that. But it didn't last." Another time, the Lakers enlisted a private shooting coach, Ed Palubinskas, who diagnosed O'Neal as overly stiff and intimidated by the rim. Rick Barry, the retired Hall of Famer who shot free throws underhanded, to the tune of an 89 percent success rate, suggested aloud that O'Neal, too, shoot underhanded. (The big man wouldn't dare.)

The only diagnosis — the correct diagnosis — belonged to Derek Harper, the veteran guard who had played with the Lakers in 1998–99. "He didn't work at it hard enough," Harper said. "That's the simple truth. Anyone who works on free throw shooting can become at least a decent free throw shooter. Shaq was one of the best players to ever step on a court. But he didn't devote himself to something he needed to devote himself to. He was all about power and force. Not free throws."

Two decades removed, Harper recalled a 1999 game against Seattle that had gone down to the wire. Coming out of a fourth-quarter time-out, Kurt Rambis drew up a play for O'Neal. "We're walking back onto the court and Shaq goes, 'What am I supposed to do? Who is that play for again?'" Harper said. "I was like, *Oh, he doesn't want the ball because he might get fouled.* I told him to get the ball right back out to me. I'd take care of it. It's incredible — someone of that stature to come out of a time-out and not want the ball."

There was a growing concern that, toward the ends of tight games, opposing coaches would foul O'Neal and place him at the free throw line. Jackson always felt the threat lingering, as did Bryant — who simply did not understand (and wondered aloud) how a man with so many skills couldn't hit six out of ten unencumbered shots. During the streak, though, the Lakers came up with a temporary solution: Beat the snot out of opponents so they'd never have reason to place O'Neal at the stripe. Over 19 games, Los Angeles's margin of victory was an average of 14.1 points. The close contests weren't even that close — often the margins got tighter only late in the fourth quarter, when Jackson rested his starters.

On March 6, O'Neal celebrated his 28th birthday by — in the words of the *Los Angeles Times*'s Lonnie White — ripping "through the Clippers' collection of big men as if they were wet food stamps," en route to 61 points and 23 rebounds in a 123–103 win. Upon arriving at the Staples Center three hours before tipoff, O'Neal was told by the Clippers staff that his request for extra seats for family members had been denied. If he wanted his relatives to attend, he'd have to pay just like everyone else. O'Neal couldn't believe it. This was *his* building. *His* court. "Don't ever make me pay for tickets," he said afterwards. "Ever." Before tipoff, he had pulled aside point guard Derek Fisher and said, "Man, can a brother get 60 on his birthday?" Translation: *Get me the ball, and get it to me often.*

Fisher nodded. "Absolutely," he said. "Let's make it happen."

O'Neal would play 19 NBA seasons, but never quite at the level of 1999–2000. He averaged 29.7 points, 13.6 rebounds, and 3 blocks, and set a career high in assists (3.8). He was in the best shape of his life, desperate to please a new coach with a track record. "Shaq is in great condition," Brian Shaw said late in the year. "He's blocking shots and rebounding like never before. I played with him for three years in Orlando, and he didn't get after it on defense like this."

The Lakers finally lost on March 16, dropping a 109–102 nail-biter at Washington. But two games later, something happened that both pleased Jackson and solidified the Lakers — *these* Lakers — as a different breed than their immediate predecessors. On March 19 the team returned to California to host the Knicks, a legitimate title contender whose coach, Jeff Van Gundy, had little good to say (or think) about his Los Angeles counterpart. Before accepting the Lakers job, Jackson had been in light discussions with the Knicks, and Van Gundy rightly believed it crossed a line. As Del Harris repeatedly noted, one doesn't vie for a job held by a peer.

Even without any hostility, the Knicks weren't a team to mess with. Their roster was a Who's Who of NBA brawlers. Larry Johnson, the 6-foot-6, 250-pound power forward, regularly dropped opponents to the floor. Latrell Sprewell, the athletic small forward, had famously choked his head coach, P.J. Carlesimo, two years earlier. A backup power forward named Kurt Thomas was widely considered the most physically intimidating (non-Shaq) man in the league, and Patrick Ewing, the center in his 15th season, still possessed a scowl that froze boiling water. The hardest rock on the roster was also one of the smallest — 6-foot-3, 195-pound point guard Chris Childs.

A product of Boise State University, Childs went undrafted out of college in 1989, where his solid production (he averaged 13.6 points per game) and Flash-like quickness were obscured by his beyond-the-spotlight life as a fifth-generation alcoholic. He bounced around basketball's minor leagues and took his last drink on June 26, 1993. A year later, Childs was a member of the New Jersey Nets. He parlayed strong play into a six-year, $24 million deal from the Knicks, and before long he was the starting point guard for an elite NBA franchise. "Chris took no shit," said Jayson Williams, his teammate on the Nets. "He was small, but he played big."

The one thing Childs had no patience for was arrogance. In Kobe Bryant, he saw arrogance. He liked nothing about the kid, despised how he acted as if he walked on air and played as if he were better than the men who had been around far longer.

That's why, in the third quarter of Knicks-Lakers, Childs took particular exception to Bryant twice elbowing him in the head as he dropped back on defense.

"Did you see that?" Childs whined to Ted Bernhardt, the referee. "Are you gonna do something about that bitch and his bullshit?"

Bernhardt shook his head.

"Okay," Childs said. "No problem." He leaned into Bryant and said, "I don't mind elbows from the neck down. But do that to my head one more time, young fella, and it's on."

Bryant laughed. "You ain't gonna do shit," he said.

The Laker stood 6-foot-6, 210 pounds. He was taller, thicker, more muscular. But, across the league, few found Kobe Bryant even slightly intimidating. Seconds later, Bryant elbowed Childs again. It was mild, but enough was enough.

"He hit me with a chicken wing," Childs said. "I hit him with the two-piece and a biscuit."

Childs drew back his forehead and brushed it into Bryant's face. Momentarily stunned, the Laker paused, then came back with a meek forearm to the face. ("Pussy shots," Childs recalled.) Childs fired off a straightaway right and a left cross, both of which connected with Bryant's cheek. Finally, with Bryant unleashing a fury of punches (none of which connected or even came close to connecting), Bernhardt stepped in and broke the men up. As Jim Cleamons, the assistant coach, dragged him away from the scrum, Bryant scrapped and clawed and screamed for more of Childs. "Fuck you!" he bellowed toward the Knick. "Fuck you, pussy!" Moments later, in the tunnel leading to the locker room, Bryant made another move at Childs, but to no avail. When asked about the exchange, Childs told Marc Berman of the *New York Post*, "Tell him I'm at the Four Seasons, Room 906."*

Both players were ejected in the 106–82 Los Angeles win, but it was what happened next that felt remarkable. Rick Fox barked at Childs as he left the court. O'Neal shoved Ewing. Jackson scowled at Van Gundy. In the locker room afterwards, one Laker after another whispered into Bryant's ear, assuring him they all had his back. "That's our little brother right there," Fox said. "As big brothers, you don't let somebody pick on your little brother."

"Everyone knows Kobe's a clean-cut guy," O'Neal added. "But he had somebody punching in his face, he had to do something about it. I was just trying to protect my little brother. If something crazy would happen, I would defend him . . . But Kobe's a tough kid, he protected himself."

The next morning's *Miami Herald* featured the headline FIGHT MARS LAKERS WIN OVER KNICKS. Only, for Los Angeles, the fight marred nothing. Ever since Bryant arrived in the league four years earlier, Laker coaches and administrators had tried everything to make him part of the team. But here, in standing up to one of the NBA's feistiest players, perceptions had changed. Bryant was suspended one game and fined $5,000, and it was well worth the cost. He would never be fully embraced, for he

---

* He was not inviting Kobe Bryant over for room service and a movie.

was not embraceable. But as the Lakers headed toward the playoffs, they were — at long last — unified.

"Thanks to me," Childs said years later. "Me and my stupid temper."

The Lakers wrapped the season with an NBA-best 67-15 record, and while O'Neal (29.7 points per game), Bryant (22.5 points per game), and Rice (15.9 points per game) stood out on the statistical sheets, the key was Jackson. The veteran coach somehow kept a roster overflowing with egos and arrogance in one piece; somehow convinced O'Neal to ignore Bryant's cockiness; and somehow convinced Bryant to accept life in the shadow of a larger-than-life big man. He used Rice wisely, leaned on veterans like John Salley and Ron Harper to keep the locker room happy, forbade the hazing of rookies. "He was the greatest studier of people I'd ever been around," said Salley. "He knew exactly which buttons to push." In what, decades later, remains one of the more impressive tricks in modern coaching history, Jackson's staff *included* Kurt Rambis, his predecessor on the sideline. It is one of the few times a new coach dared employ an exiled coach, but Jackson made it work. "It wasn't easy at first," Rambis said. "I felt on some level he took a job that should have been mine. But I came to like Phil, Phil came to like me. We had trust."

The Lakers opened the playoffs by beating the eighth-seeded Kings in five games, then moved on to play the overmatched Suns, who predictably fell, four games to one. It was during the series with Phoenix that two distractions caused Jackson to silently question his team's focus.

First, on May 9, O'Neal was named the NBA's Most Valuable Player. He was, beyond debate, the league's best player and led the NBA in both scoring and field goal percentage. Yet while the initial reaction was unbridled giddiness ("The first thing I did was call my mother and father," he said. "My father started crying"), that changed when it was learned that 120 of 121 voters had selected O'Neal first. Yes, the 99.2 percent was the highest in league history. Yes, his 1,207 points dwarfed the 408 of Minnesota's Kevin Garnett, the runner-up. But how did someone fail to place O'Neal atop his ballot?

Within hours, the promised confidentiality of MVP voting was set aside and the world learned that Fred Hickman, the veteran CNN/SI anchor, had voted for Philadelphia's Allen Iverson first and O'Neal second. The backlash was fierce — from the Laker players (said Robert Horry, "I heard some guy at CNN didn't vote for him. Did he ever play?"*), from West ("God, I feel sorry for the guy who didn't vote for him"), from media members (Fox's Marques Johnson: "What happened? Some of Allen Iverson's boys had his daughter tied up in a Brooklyn basement, there was some extortion going on?").

"It was bad," recalled Hickman. "To this day I don't know how my name got out, because the vote was supposed to be anonymous. I was Steve Bartman before Steve Bartman. That reaction was *really* intense. Really angry. I was getting threats, which was a first for me. *Threats?* All because I thought Iverson was more important to his team than Shaq was to his."

O'Neal bit his tongue and said little. Years later, however, he admitted that the anger was real. "Do I hold a grudge about that? Yeah — I do," he said. "Some fucking dickhead kept me from being the first unanimous MVP. Some asshole who doesn't know shit gives his vote to Iverson and fucks up history. I never forgot that."

The hullabaloo passed, but days later an even bigger bombshell hit the Staples Center: Kobe Bryant was engaged.

To be married.

To another person.

With a pulse.

Really.

The Associated Press was first to report the news, and few Lakers believed it. For four years, Bryant had been a brick wall when it came to his personal life. Other members of the team were well-known partiers and womanizers, happy to hit the town and return to the hotel with your dime-a-dozen large-breasted, big-haired groupie. Though this was no longer the 1980s, when females lined the lobbies as Magic, Worthy, and Co. came to town, the Laker players hardly had to work to acquire late-night company.

---

* Hickman attended Coe College, in Iowa, where he did not play any varsity sports.

Bryant's personal life, though, was pure mystery. The last anyone heard of him dating someone had been in the summer of 1996, when he was accompanied to the Lower Merion senior prom by Brandy Norwood, the chart-topping pop singer, whom he (ahem) didn't actually know.

The stunt had been arranged by Michael Harris, a local sports promoter who thought the idea of the soon-to-be NBAer attending the big event with a superstar would be marketing gold. On the night of May 25, 1996, with dozens of media members in attendance and cameras flashing left and right, Bryant ("looking debonair in a tuxedo and banded-collar shirt, no tie," wrote Jennifer Weiner of the *Philadelphia Inquirer*) and Norwood ("in champagne Moschino, flawless maquillage and shoulder-skimming braids") ascended the marble stairway of Philadelphia's Bellevue Hotel. Hundreds of spectators watched from a nearby sidewalk, some calling out for autographs.

"It was super weird," recalled Weiner. "In a way it was the closest Philadelphia has ever come to having a Grammys or Oscars happening here. *People* magazine was there, all sorts of onlookers were there. But it wasn't real. It was a show."

Indeed, at night's end, Bryant received nothing more than a kiss on the cheek and some solid PR sizzle. As the years passed, there were (count them) zero rumors about his dating life. No paparazzi camped outside Madonna's house, expecting a Kobe sighting. No visits to the Men's Club of Dallas with Michael Irvin and Tony Tolbert. Fox, the veteran forward and well-regarded ladies' man, was married to a superstar singer/actress named Vanessa Williams, and their lives were perfect *Jet* magazine cover fodder and photographer-in-the-bushes stakeouts. But not Kobe Bryant. As far as anyone knew, he was locked inside his Pacific Palisades home, curled up with a bowl of Fritos and a Candace Bushnell novel. Some on the team wondered whether he was a virgin. Hell, if Bryant were as awkward with women as he was with teammates . . .

But now, thanks to the Associated Press, came the bombshell. Not only was Bryant engaged to be married, but he was engaged to be married to an 18-year-old high school senior from Garden Grove, California, named Vanessa Urbieta Cornejo Laine. She was, word leaked out, a dancer. A sexy dancer. A sexy dancer who had appeared as an extra in a handful of music videos.

In truth, however, Laine was really just an ordinary, middle-class teenager with a warm face and a couple of flirty moves. On August 15, 1999, while attending the 92.3 the Beat Summer Jam concert in Irvine, California, she was approached by a man who said he was seeking "pretty girls" to appear in music videos. Within two months she could be spotted — scantily dressed, body greased up — in a Krayzie Bone music video, then a video for Tha Eastsidaz's "G'd Up" featuring Snoop Dogg. An impressed Bryant hired her to appear in his never-to-see-the-light-of-day debut music video — and was immediately smitten.

He acquired Laine's phone number, paged incessantly, repeatedly pulled up at Marina High School in his black Mercedes to offer rides. Once, in a burst of romance, Bryant ordered dozens of roses and had them sent to the school's main office. Laine was summoned via the PA system to pick them up, and cooed to classmates, "They're from Kobe."

"It was just Kobe this and Kobe that," one friend recalled. "It got so that that was all she or anyone could talk about."

Bryant's presence at Marina High turned into such a distraction that school officials finally asked Laine to complete her senior year via independent study. Meanwhile, neither Kobe's nor Vanessa's family members knew exactly how to feel. Was it weird, Laine's parents wondered, for an adult to be scoping out a high school kid? Was it immoral? "He was an adult and she was only 17," recalled Stephen Laine, Vanessa's stepfather. "It was like *Hey, wait a minute . . .*"

Joe and Pam Bryant had their own issues to sort through. Ever since Kobe entered the NBA in 1996, his parents had been (literally) by his side. Having played eight NBA seasons, Joe Bryant knew the pressures and issues of being a professional, and he desperately wanted to steer his son out of trouble. That's why he and Pam relocated from the East Coast to supervise his life, run his affairs, keep his home in order, make sure no outsiders were taking advantage. They initially lived in his six-bedroom house, then moved to a significantly larger spot on the same street. Much of Kobe Bryant's solitude was due to the repeated lectures administered by his folks: *Be your own man. Make your own mark. Don't get sucked in.*

In Vanessa Urbieta Cornejo Laine, the Bryants saw everything they had warned against. She was a groupie. *Had to be* a groupie. Look at her — big breasts, too much perfume, clothing three sizes too small, rap video gigs.

Also, she surely saw their son for what he was: a walking, dribbling ATM machine. While Kobe was making $9 million in salary and nearly double that in endorsements, Vanessa was living under the roof of two people (mother Sofia and stepfather Stephen) who were mired in credit card debt and car loans. Sofia had been laid off from her shipping clerk job two years earlier, and a chronic back injury kept her unemployed. While the clichéd storyline about Kobe always involved his father and the family's basketball pedigree, Pam was the true behind-the-scenes gate-keeper. She was the daughter of a U.S. Army private and a graduate of Villanova University; tough as rust and unwilling to take nonsense from anyone. "Pam runs that family and has always run that family," said John Smallwood, the longtime *Philadelphia Daily News* writer. "If Pam hadn't been who she was, calling the shots, making sure everything runs as it should, there would be no Kobe."

Like her husband, Pam wasn't hearing any nonsense about some poor teenager marrying into the empire. It also pleased neither father nor mother that Vanessa was Latina and not African American. First they urged their son to reconsider. Then they urged their son to wait. Then they urged their son — *begged* their son — to sign a prenuptial agreement. *No way*, Kobe Bryant said. *No possible way.*

None of his Laker teammates could believe this was happening. They had never seen this girl before. Had certainly never seen Kobe Bryant with a girl before. And now he was engaged to be wed? "Bryant has always struck me as mature beyond his years," wrote Dana Parsons in the *Los Angeles Times.* "To give up groupies at age 21 is laudable, and one hopes he can pick a bride as well as hit a game-winner."

Eventually, the relationship — consummated in an April 18, 2001, wedding at St. Edward the Confessor Catholic Church, in Dana Point — would drive a wedge both within the Bryant family (none of Bryant's relatives attended, and Pam and Joe moved back to Philadelphia) and within the Laker family (a grand total of zero teammates and coaches were invited).

But that was a ways off.

First, Los Angeles had to survive the biggest challenge of the year.

Heading into the Western Conference Finals, the Portland Trail Blazers didn't give a crap about Fred Hickman's MVP vote, and they certainly didn't give a crap about Kobe Bryant's engagement. They weren't interested in Phil Jackson's Zen teachings, Glen Rice's trade talk, Rick Fox's marriage, or Robert Horry's outside shooting.

No.

The Portland Trail Blazers cared only about kicking the snot out of Los Angeles.

This was personal.

For far too long, the Blazers existed as mere gnats to the Laker lion. The two teams, located 962 miles apart and situated side by side in the Pacific Division, both boasting storied histories, featuring huge names and heady days. Yet in an Annie Oakley–Frank Butler modus operandi, anything the Blazers could do, the Lakers could do better. The Blazers' all-time greatest center was Bill Walton, the UCLA legend. The Lakers' all-time greatest center was Kareem Abdul-Jabbar, the UCLA icon. The Blazers' 1980s superstar was Clyde Drexler, a wonderful player. The Lakers' 1980s superstar was Magic Johnson, a transcendent player. The Blazers proudly hung the 1977 NBA championship banner from the rafters. The Lakers proudly hung the 1972 NBA championship banner from the rafters. And the 1980 championship banner. And 1982. And 1985. And 1987. And 1988.

Now, entering the series, the Lakers were once again expected to triumph. They were the No. 1 overall seed, facing a third-seeded Portland squad that had won eight fewer regular season games and lacked anyone of O'Neal's physical stature. Yet, unlike top-heavy Los Angeles, the Blazers' $73.9 million roster was uncommonly deep. Mike Dunleavy, the veteran NBA coach, regularly used nine of his players, and in forwards Rasheed Wallace and Scottie Pippen and center Arvydas Sabonis he had at his disposal the league's best frontcourt.

"We were the better team," recalled Antonio Harvey, a Blazer forward. "Yes, they had Shaq and Kobe, and those guys were fantastic. But, top to bottom, we were far more skilled. I was pretty sure we were winning."

The series began on May 20 in Los Angeles, and the Lakers destroyed the Blazers, jumping out to a 21-point halftime lead en route to the 109–94 win. The game itself was an exercise in frustration and, for the 18,997 fans inside the Staples Center, boredom. With 5 minutes, 29 seconds remaining in the fourth quarter and his team down 13, Dunleavy had his men commence the infamously named and executed Hack-a-Shaq — aka *Foul O'Neal whenever he touches the ball and hope he bricks his free throws.*

The tactic failed. O'Neal connected on 12 of 25 fourth-quarter attempts, shattering the playoff mark for free throw tries in a quarter, finishing with 41 points total, and causing the Portland players to look toward their coach with exasperated glares. "Anything that works, I'm fine with it," Pippen said with a sigh. "Shaq did what he had to do. He stepped up and made them, which makes everything look kind of stupid."

Two nights later, Portland annihilated the Lakers, 106–77, setting up what would go down as one of the all-time classic playoff series. Sabonis, the Portland center, was 35 years old and far past his prime. A decade and a half earlier, while the Kaunas, Lithuania, native had starred in Europe and for the Soviet national team, most basketball experts had placed Sabonis alongside Patrick Ewing, Hakeem Olajuwon, and Ralph Sampson for big-man greatness. He was quick and strong and passed like a mountainous Pearl Washington. By the time he arrived in the NBA for the 1995–96 season, though, Sabonis was hobbled by arthritic knees and a battle-wounded body. "He was *so* talented," said Kerry Eggers, who covered the Blazers for the *Oregonian.* "He couldn't run anymore, but he was one of the very few NBA players who matched strength with Shaq."

In Game 3 at Portland, Dunleavy kept Sabonis on the court for 35 minutes, hoping (praying) he would wear down O'Neal with unyielding physicality. For a spell, it seemed to work. The Laker center ended the first quarter with no points or rebounds, and the Blazers led by 14 in the second quarter and 10 at halftime. Sabonis wasted no chance to give O'Neal an elbow to the ribs, a forearm to the chest. Inside the locker room, a furious Jackson pulled his star aside and said, bluntly, "You're playing terribly."

"[He] said I wasn't being aggressive enough," O'Neal said. "He was right."

Unlike Bryant, who did not need a coach's anger to get him going, O'Neal could be a Porsche without its engine. He required an enemy. A rival. Someone to piss him off. For years, he told people that Ewing was a jerk who treated him rudely. He told people Alonzo Mourning hated him. He told people David Robinson, the Spurs' sublime center, had refused to sign an autograph for him as a teenager.

This time, still licking his wounds from the Jackson tongue-lashing, O'Neal convinced himself that Sabonis was a world-class whiner who had the officials' ears. "It's kind of funny to me," he later recalled, "how a guy 7-foot-3 who weighs almost as much as me starts crying to the officials."

The second half was all O'Neal, who scored 18 of his 26 points while gathering 12 rebounds. What he did best was beat down Sabonis. O'Neal had punished his rival the way he punished all his rivals: with blunt force trauma and excessive weight. With 13 seconds remaining and Los Angeles up 93–91, Portland guard Damon Stoudamire drove through the lane past Bryant, then kicked it out to Sabonis, who stood just inside the three-point line. Portland's center pump-faked, sending O'Neal flying, and dribbled glacially one time toward the hoop. As the center released the ball, Bryant — eight inches shorter — leapt through the air and swatted it away.

With that, the clock expired, Lakers players swarmed Bryant in a congratulatory group hug, and the team held a two-games-to-one series lead. Inside the Los Angeles locker room, there was little doubt that the Blazers were about to roll over and die. "Now the pressure's on Portland," Jackson said. "Because if we put another notch in our belt Sunday, they're really at death's door, and they know it."

He was speaking to Chuck Culpepper of the *Oregonian*. Truly, though, he was speaking to the Blazers — a group of uber-talented players who, with the exception of Pippen, were better known for choking than celebrating. There's something draining about hearing how gifted you are, then failing to capitalize on that gift. Steve Smith, the Portland shooting guard — no rings. Stoudamire, the point guard — no rings. Detlef Schrempf, an elite scorer for 16 seasons — no rings. Sabonis, the giant with the soft touch — no rings. Wallace, feisty but productive — no rings. Dunleavy, the head coach in his ninth season on a sideline — no rings. "You have to have something to show for your efforts," Fox said. "Otherwise it's just rhetoric."

Yet *these* Blazers weren't *those* Blazers. After losing Game 4 at home, 103–91, to go down three games to one, they somehow staged a remarkable bounce back, winning the next contest in Los Angeles, 96–88. Three days later, back home at the Rose Garden, Portland won 103–93, evening the series at three games each. O'Neal looked like a deadwood ghost of his MVP self, scoring just 17 points, lumbering up and down the floor, hitting a putrid 3 of 10 free throws. For the second-straight game, he was barely existent in the fourth quarter. He scored just 4 points, taking a single shot — a measly four-foot hook. Over the game's final 5:25, he did (almost literally) nothing but watch as players whizzed past. When asked afterwards about his partner's ineffectiveness, Bryant could barely conceal his irritation. "There was a lot of bumping and shoving going on," he said. "But Shaq's a big, strong guy. He'll be ready to play on Sunday."

Jackson wasn't so sure.

When the game ended and the media cleared out, he sat down with his coaches and wondered — truly wondered — whether the series was a lost cause. In all those years with Chicago, Jackson knew, come crunch time, Michael Jordan would be there to carry the team.

But now, the coach wondered, did that even exist?

Did the Lakers have what it took to survive?

On April 7, 2001, slightly less than a year after the Lakers-Blazers series, Shaquille O'Neal authored a book titled *Shaq Talks Back*. It sold fairly well and spent a bunch of weeks on the *New York Times* bestseller list, but it is hardly ranked alongside Jim Bouton's *Ball Four* or Pat Jordan's *A False Spring* as a classic athlete tell-all. Like many books, it came, it went, it found itself selling for $1.98 on Amazon.*

Which is a shame, because over the course of 276 pages, O'Neal — who teamed up with Mike Wise of the *Washington Post* on the project — bared his soul in unusual and remarkable ways.

O'Neal wrote, at length, about his disdain for Bryant, his mistrust of Del Harris. He touched on insecurities, fears, plagues, heartache. Page after page, it's O'Neal speaking truth to power in ways very few athletes ever do.

Nearly two decades after the release, O'Neal told a reporter† that the book was a mistake — that he'd said too much and the backlash wasn't worth the paycheck. "I didn't even read it," he admitted. "I just didn't like the reaction."

In particular, O'Neal might have been referring to page 229, when he admitted that, following the Game 6 defeat to Portland, he was quite certain the Lakers were about to fold. Wrote O'Neal: "Walking off the court after Game 6, I didn't feel good at all ... I was remembering all those people who kept badgering me about the Lakers not having a killer instinct. As much as I hated to admit it, they were right. It was the truth. We couldn't put the nail in the coffin."

There have been times throughout his life when O'Neal seemed to enjoy exaggerating things for the sake of explosiveness, headlines, bullet points. He was P.T. Barnum in a basketball jersey, and the rap albums, grade-D films, T-shirts, hats, commercials, self-appointed nicknames — Shaq Fu, Shaq Diesel, the Real Deal, the Big Daddy, the Big Aristotle, the Big Galactus, Mayor McShaq, Wilt Chamberneezy, M.D.E. (Most Dominant Ever) — were all part of the show. "He used to say he had 52 moves on the lower box," said Andy Bernstein, the Lakers' photographer.

This, though, was no act. The man was genuinely concerned that his

---

* Really, it's $1.98 on Amazon!
† It was me — Jeff Pearlman.

NBA résumé was about to include the harrowing update EIGHT SEA-SONS, NO CHAMPIONSHIPS.

Truth be told, to be a Laker — any Laker — in the aftermath of the 103–93 setback was to be a man plagued by a severe sense of self-doubt.

"Did I think we were going to win that seventh game?" John Salley, the 12th man and 11-year vet, asked decades later. "Honestly, I don't think so."

"It was," added Rice, "not looking very good."

The Portland Trail Blazers entered the building determined to put the Lakers to sleep. Historically speaking, seventh games tend to go to the team with the greatest depth. It makes sense — you're beaten down, you're worn out, legs are Jell-O, feet are hot coals, minds are pudding. If there are two or three or (gasp!) four guys who can come off the bench and do damage, the odds shift to your favor. Why, a mere 13 years earlier, Los Angeles had made a February trade with San Antonio, adding (long-time Portland) forward Mychal Thompson to a somewhat thin bench. The result? An NBA title.

These Blazers were stacked. Perhaps that's why, when asked about Game 7, Dunleavy told the assembled media, "The team that plays the full 48 minutes is going to win."

The words would prove prophetic.

A sellout crowd of 18,997 entered the Staples Center, with tickets going for as much as $1,200 in the secondhand market. The Lakers had last reached an NBA Finals series in 1991, a short span for most cities but an eternity in a metropolis spoiled by success. As the starting lineup for the home team was introduced — first Bryant and Harper at the guard slots, then A.C. Green and Rice as forwards, then O'Neal in the middle — the noise was deafening. The Staples Center lacked the acoustical oomph of the now shuttered Forum, and sound tended to get lost in the high ceiling. But here, at this moment, it was as loud and explosive as a stadium could be.

This was the return of Showtime.

The return of the dynasty.

The return to NBA dominance.

The . . . worst.

The opening tip went to Portland, and seconds later Wallace — lithe, quick, confident — hit a turnaround jumper over the earthbound A.C. Green. Harper answered quickly with his own jumper, and as he bounded back down the court, he bobbed his head, skipped backwards. In hindsight, it can be read two different ways. Either:

A. "Yeah, we're ready!" Or:

B. "Guys, come on! Wake up!"

It was B.

Los Angeles *needed* to wake up. Portland opened up a 23–16 lead, and at halftime the advantage was 42–39. Which, while only 3 points, felt closer to 30. Much had gone right for Los Angeles (Bryant had 12, O'Neal 9), and they still trailed. In the locker room, Fox — the emotional leader of the squad — went off. "Here we go again," he said, standing in the center of the rectangle. "Everybody's got a blank look on his face. So what are we going to do about it? Are we going to let the referees dictate the terms of the game? Are we going to be passive and get blown out again? Or are we going to stand up on our own feet? Are we going to provide support for each other?"

Tex Winter, lingering alongside Jackson, said, "Phil, you better tell him to shut up."

"No," the coach replied. "Somebody's got to say these things."

In a movie, the Lakers charge back onto the court and dominate. A John Williams song plays, Bryant soars through the air, O'Neal swats shot after shot.

This was no movie.

Portland exited its locker room looking like the 1995–96 Chicago Bulls. Powered by 10 points from Steve Smith and 6 from Wallace, they went on a 21-to-4 spurt. The boos rained down. Horry, the veteran with two rings, looked numb. *What the hell is going on?* Fox recalled thinking. *Who are we?* Wallace, in particular, couldn't be stopped, spinning past O'Neal (who was scoreless in the third period) on multiple moves to the hoop. "Rasheed Wallace is working harder for better position than Shaquille O'Neal," Bill Walton, broadcasting the game for NBC, noted. "He knows he's gonna get the ball. Shaq works hard and doesn't get it. Rasheed does."

With 20 seconds remaining in the period, Pippen hit a three-pointer over a lunging Shaw, giving his team a game-high 71–55 advantage. The arena's occupants let loose a collective groan and Walton said, in a rare dose of seriousness, "The Lakers need something big here to try to fire the crowd up over the quarter break."

Shortly after the words were uttered, Bryant found himself holding the ball atop the key, Bonzi Wells in his way, Pippen drifting in from his right. Everyone knew the kid would shoot, because, with history as a guide, the kid always shot.

Dribble.

Dribble.

Dribble.

Off to the side stood the most nondescript of Lakers. At 6-foot-6 and 190 pounds, with sleepy eyes and a longish neck, Brian Shaw wasn't one to be noticed on or off the court. He was only a member of the team because, three days after Houston acquired him in an October 2, 1999, trade from Portland, he was unceremoniously released. The Lakers signed Shaw for a mere $510,000 — chump change for a reserve with a long résumé of solid play and team-first mechanisms. "He's been a quality player in this league for a number of years," Jackson said at the time. "He's been down for a couple of years now and this is an opportunity to get a player . . . who can play a big guard."

"Brian always wanted to be a Laker," said Jerome Stanley, his agent. "He was a California kid, loved the team. When they were interested, he wanted me to jump on it. So we did."

Shaw wound up averaging 4.1 points in 74 games and served an important role as the clubhouse peacemaker and love guru between O'Neal and Bryant. In a room overflowing with stars and established veterans, his voice carried the loudest. Part of it was the gravitas of 10 NBA seasons: Stanley refers to his client as a 1990s "NBA Zeitgeist — he played with Shaq in Orlando, played with Larry Bird in Boston, was on the Warriors when Sprewell choked the coach, was with the Celtics when Reggie Lewis died." But it also had something to do with his status as a survivor. Seven years earlier, while a member of the Miami Heat, Shaw was at home in Oakland, preparing for a June 26, 1993, barbecue, when his phone rang. He picked up and was told — by the Nevada's coroner's office, in the bluntest of terms — that his mother, father, and sister had been killed in a one-car crash en route from Northern California to Las Vegas. The lone survivor was his 11-month-old niece, Brianna.

Shaw hung up and immediately called Stanley.

"They're all dead!" he wailed.

"Who's dead?" Stanley said.

"Everybody!" he replied. "My whole family is dead. They died in a car accident."

Silence.

Somehow, Shaw was able to recover. He and his wife, Nikki, adopted Brianna. When she was finally old enough to ask about the tragic day, Shaw told her, "Your mommy went to live with God and left you here for me to take care of you."

Now, seven years later, Shaw feared nothing. A bad pass? Big deal. A moment of laziness on defense? Ho-hum. A key shot with 4.4 seconds on the clock and his team down by 16 to the Portland Trail Blazers in Game 7 of the Western Conference Finals?

Bring it.

Bryant took a dribble toward the hoop, then shoveled the ball back to Shaw, who stopped, squared up, and banked a three-pointer over the outstretched arms of Wells.

The shot wasn't a game winner, but it was, in hindsight, a game changer. As his players congregated along the sideline to begin the fourth quarter, Jackson had something important to say. "You know what," he growled. "They're kicking our ass. They are absolutely kicking our ass. I don't know what's going on, but let's just get it over with. I'll see you guys next year. To hell with this."

O'Neal shook his head. "Fuck that," he said. "Fuck that."

What happened next is NBA lore. Or, put differently, the high-flying, free-flowing, confident-to-the-point-of-cockiness Portland Trail Blazers were run down by a Mack truck. Jackson told his players — begged his players — to shoot. Dunleavy had the Blazers double-teaming O'Neal, and the forced passes down low were too often being batted away. "Kobe, fire away," Jackson said. "Brian, fire away. When you're open, take it."

"We started getting mad," O'Neal said. "Kobe was mad, B-Shaw was mad. That's exactly what we needed: that anger. That was the one time all year when they really saved my ass, because I was getting quadruple-teamed and playing like shit. I needed help in the worst way."

"You're talking about the ultimate warriors," Rice recalled. "Our team was made up of guys who never gave up."

The Blazers started the fourth quarter with Steve Smith driving to the hoop for an uncontested runner, and the boos rained down. Walton, from the booth, said, "Twelve minutes to do something in your life. This is where you just blast through all the pain, and know that if you come up big . . ."

With 10:06 left, Shaq took a pass down low from Horry and hit a layup over Sabonis. 75–62, Blazers.

No big deal.

On the next Blazer possession, Bryant emphatically swatted a Bonzi Wells shot, grabbed the ball, and pushed it up the court. Shaw, standing alone in the corner, received a swing pass from Horry and drained the three. 75–65, Blazers.

Still, no big deal.

Portland called a time-out. NBC's microphone picked up Jackson's sideline instructions. "Get yourself in position to shoot the ball," he said. "And shoot good shots. Forget about Shaq. If he's open, throw it in. If he's not, don't force things just to go into him. And loosen up."

The Blazers brought the ball up-court and Pippen bricked a three-point attempt. The ball found its way into the hands of Bryant, who soared to the hoop and was fouled on the way up by Wells. Bryant licked his lips, à la Michael Jordan, and walked to the line. He missed the first free throw, then made the second. 75–66, Blazers.

Nine minutes left in the game.

Still, no big deal.

"We have the lead," recalled Elston Turner, a Portland assistant coach. "We have veteran guys who can't make plays — guys with a resume of making big plays."

The Blazers again had the ball. Wallace shot — and missed — a jumper. Wells collected the offensive rebound, passed it back down to Wallace, who shot — and missed — another jumper. Shaw gobbled the rebound, pushed the ball up-court, and passed it down low to O'Neal. He was elbowed by Sabonis, who whined, moaned, griped — and left the court with his fifth foul. This was, for the Lakers, a blessing. Portland's center was a big, strong, physical thorn in his side. Now that thorn was shuffling toward the bench, replaced by the smaller Brian Grant ("who has been completely ineffective," as Walton said when he entered the game).

Fox fired a three and missed, but the rebound was corralled by the suddenly liberated O'Neal, who went back up and was hacked by Wallace. O'Neal bricked the first free throw attempt, then made the second. 75–67, Blazers.

Still, eh, um, not a particularly big deal.

Only, eh, um, it was starting to feel like a big deal. The crowd was now cheering. The Portland players looked stiff. "We weren't built for it the way we thought we were," Antonio Harvey, a Portland reserve, said. "The only player on the roster ready for the moment was Scottie, but he wasn't the Scottie of the Chicago Bulls, a guy equipped to carry that load when he was with Michael Jordan. Rasheed was the best player on the roster, but at that point in his life I'm not sure he was ready to carry that load. Steve Smith was a great player, but physically he wasn't what he once was. We were an ensemble cast of former great players, but nobody was in the moment at that time."

The teams exchanged misfires on their following possessions, and with 7:30 on the clock, Shaw casually brought the ball up the court and passed to Horry, who passed to Fox, who passed back to Shaw, who bent his knees and bricked a three. Horry somehow grabbed the rebound, dribbled out behind the three-point line, and, in a moment of laziness from Wallace, let loose a wide-open shot that floated through the air before slicing into the net. Dunleavy, nervously pacing the sidelines, licked his lips — a telltale sign of coaching anxiety. 75–70, Blazers. A hair more than seven minutes left.

"It just snowballed," said Joe Kleine, Portland's backup center. "It was a real shitty feeling."

Action needed to be taken. A time-out. A substitution. Give the winded Wallace a quick breather. Get Stoudamire, stuck to the bench in favor of Wells, back on the floor. Find time for the sharpshooting Schrempf. Something. Anything.

Instead, Portland's coach froze. Pippen misfired yet again, and Shaw stole the rebound out of Grant's hands. When the officials called a charge on Horry, Portland was blessed with a much-needed television time-out. Los Angeles was in the midst of a 10-0 run, and the Blazers were shooting 1 for 7 in the quarter. The needed moment of rest would help the experienced Blazers regroup and . . .

Nope.

Wallace missed yet another turnaround jumper, leading to an O'Neal rebound and Bryant drifting into the lane and nailing a short jumper. The score was 75–72, with 5:40 left and everything going right for Los Angeles. "The attack came from all angles," Jackson recalled.

During his 11 years as a Bull, Pippen was considered one of the NBA's five or six best players — an elastic, do-everything superstar with an inevitable future in the Hall of Fame. But here, with the ball in his hands, he seemed uncertain. Having coached him for nine years, Jackson knew his former pupil's shortcomings. Desperate to escape Jordan's ghost, Pippen played as a man without a map. The need weighed on him. Controlled him. Now, when the Blazers required a hero, their go-to guy was anything but. Pippen passed up several possible shots, and with 5:08 left he got the ball to Wallace, who yet again misfired.

The Lakers failed to convert, and as Pippen dribbled the ball, Walton, sitting courtside, could not hide his indignation. "Slash to the hoop if you're Scottie Pippen!" he yelped. "Forget the fade-away jumpers! Forget the double clutches!" Pippen wasn't listening. He passed down low to

Grant, whose shot was swatted away by O'Neal, then dished to Wallace, who missed another jumper. By now it was clear: Scottie Pippen did not want the game in his hands.

Los Angeles finally tied things at 75 on a Shaw three-pointer, and the building erupted as it had never erupted before. Then, moments later, it turned 1,000 times louder.

With the home team up 83–79 and 56 seconds showing on the clock, Pippen misfired on a three-pointer. O'Neal gobbled the board and Bryant was handed the ball. Guarded by the now exhausted Pippen, he charged into the paint as all five Blazer defenders collapsed around him. Then —*pow!*

Without looking, he looped the ball toward the rim, where O'Neal soared through the air and slammed it, one-handed, over a helpless Wallace. It was athletic, explosive, dynamic, and O'Neal dashed back down the court, mouth agape, pointing toward the bench and darting past Bryant, the teammate he loathed/loved. "That was the defining moment for us," O'Neal recalled. "For Shaq and Kobe. For the two of us. Once he did that, anything bad was forgotten. It was fucking magic."

Dunleavy called a time-out, but it was too late. The modest final score, 89–84, failed to tell the story of one of the most euphoric nights in franchise history.

The Los Angeles Lakers were heading to the NBA Finals.

Glen Rice is a nice man.

This needs to be said, because occasionally capsules in time suggest character traits that are temporary, not eternal.

So, again, Glen Rice *is* a nice man. He's an attentive father, a warm friend, a person who has helped more than his fair share of those in need. "Glen was fun to cover," said Rick Bonnell, the *Charlotte Observer*'s Hornets beat writer during Rice's time there. "There was nothing not to like."

With that out of the way, it is equally fair to note that as the Los Angeles Lakers headed into the NBA Finals, Glen Rice was a *major* pain in the ass.

Sure, he was glad the franchise had advanced past Portland and, sure, he was happy to be receiving the extra dough that came with the post-season success. But where were the touches? The shots? The attention? In the Portland series, he averaged but 11 points per game and a paltry 8.9 attempts. When Rice arrived from Charlotte a season earlier, he had known that O'Neal and Bryant were offensive options A and B. But he would be a B, too, right?

No.

"I didn't *need* to be *the Guy* in Los Angeles," Rice recalled. "I really didn't. But I'd always had a scorer's mentality, and they didn't need that as much from me as the other teams. So it was . . . different."

Unlike the Blazers, a loaded outfit with a roster of stars, the Eastern Conference champion Indiana Pacers were a largely blue-collar operation in the mold of their blue-collar coach, the legendary Larry Bird. Their small forward, Reggie Miller, was a dynamic (and loquacious) player who averaged 18.1 points, and Jalen Rose, the shooting guard best known for his time as a member of Michigan's Fab Five, had averaged 18.2 points and emerged as a legit NBA standout. Otherwise, Indiana's rotation was as dull as the team's blue-and-gold uniforms. Center Rik Smits, a 7-foot-4, 265-pound beanpole, was steady. Point guard Mark Jackson, in his 13th season, was steady. Power forward Dale Davis, 6-foot-11 and strong as oak, was steady. The team won 56 games, but few inside the Los Angeles locker room felt particularly concerned.

"Playing the Pacers in the Finals was almost anti-climactic," O'Neal recalled. "They were a scrappy team . . . but we were just better."

The series began with Game 1 in Los Angeles, and if ever an omen existed, it was the sight of one of the Pacers' buses stuck in rush-hour traffic en route from the team hotel in Santa Monica. By the time the vehicle — carrying Bird, Miller, Rose, Jackson, and point guard Travis Best — arrived at Staples Center, less than an hour remained before tipoff. "Reggie was a complete creature of habit," recalled Best. "He had to get to an arena early, get all his shots up. He'd usually be waiting in the locker room while we all warmed up, because he did his work already. It was the way it had to be."

Now, after sprinting through a tunnel and into the locker room, then changing into his uniform, then taping, then stretching, Miller had approximately five minutes to shoot. "That," Best said, "didn't help."

The massacre that followed surprised no one on the Pacers. Miller, one of the great gunners in NBA history, went 1 for 16 from the field, and his team trailed for all but 1 minute and 41 seconds of the 104–87 setback. Of greater concern for Bird was O'Neal, who totaled 43 points and 19 rebounds in a methodical decimation of Smits, Davis, and Derrick McKey. When asked afterwards how he would defend himself, O'Neal laughed. "I wouldn't," he said. "I would just go home. I would fake an injury or something."

The teams met two nights later, and while the score was closer (111–104), the Lakers once again exploited a preposterous mismatch. This time O'Neal was held to 40 points (with 24 rebounds), and the Pacers could merely watch and wonder how this series might possibly turn around. "We kept trying to give Shaq different looks, but it didn't work," said Davis. "You tried to push him away from the basket. But look at his size and look at my size. It's like trying to move a mountain."

The only glimmer of hope for Bird's club came with 3:26 remaining in the first quarter, when Bryant hit a 17-footer from the right wing, then crumbled to the floor after his left foot landed atop Rose's. This was no random mishap — the Indiana guard intentionally tried to injure his nemesis. "I'm not proud," Rose later admitted, "and I don't think it's cool or cute to say, but he didn't accidentally hurt himself." Bryant's ankle turned over grotesquely, and the crowd of 18,997 grew silent. Bryant was helped off the court, not to return.

Fortunately, Rice stepped up and scored 21 points, tying his playoff high. "A lot of people say I'm the third option," he said after the game. "It was a matter of getting looks. Once I hit a couple, the confidence went up."

Rice sounded optimistic and engaged. He looked optimistic and engaged. But then, two days later, the series shifted to Indiana, and the Bryant-less Lakers fell, 100–91. Thrust into the spotlight as the man who needed to pick up the slack, Rice appeared awkward, ordinary, and a wee bit confused. In 27 minutes, he shot 3 of 9 from the field for 7 points and watched angrily as Harper, Shaw, Fox, and Horry received more time. Rice played a total of four second-quarter minutes, during which Indiana outscored Los Angeles 30–27. "I never really got into the offensive flow," he said later. "Once I went to the bench I never got back in it." For much of the season, he had silently stewed in a broth of his own self-pity. Rice wanted to be the guy launching threes. Now, even when duty seemed to call, the Lakers were holding him back.

On the morning following the setback, Jackson gathered his team for a workout. Afterwards, players were made available to the media, and the normally bland Rice, whose quotes often devolved into take-one-for-the-team cliché blather, longed to unload. He was tired — damn tired — of not being used properly, and if Jackson hoped to hang on to the series lead, he'd be wise to let the three-time All-Star do his thing. "I definitely think we would have had a better chance to win with me on the floor," Rice said. "I really think I need to be in there for us to succeed . . . I'm trying to be as positive as I can. I'm not trying to be negative or be the bad apple in the bunch. I'm just asking to be involved a little more."

When asked if he would talk to his coach, Rice shook his head. "I'm not going to him," he said. "He's going to do what he's going to do."

The words were bad. What was uttered 2,067 miles away in Southern California was worse. Bill Plaschke, the *Los Angeles Times* columnist, spoke with Cristina Fernandez Rice, Glen's wife, about her thoughts on what was transpiring. Why was her insight important? Hard to say. Was it worthy of 700 column words? Also hard to say. But Mrs. Rice didn't hold back:

> Jackson has never wanted Glen, he's always wanted somebody like Scottie Pippen, and this is his way of getting back at management for not letting him make a trade. This is Jackson's way of showing the people on top of him who is in control. It's crazy.
>
> Glen shined, so Jackson had to put him back in the dark again. It's all a mind game. It's all about control. Jackson did not get his way with the general manager or the owner about trading Glen, so who pays for it? Glen does. You have Kobe out,

it was Glen's one chance to step up and contribute to the team, and Jackson wouldn't let him do it.

Back in Indianapolis, Rice wanted to hide. Yes, he believed everything his wife had said. But . . . did she have to say it? An already awkward coach-player relationship turned even more awkward. "I told her, 'You can think all that stuff, but you can't *say* it,'" Rice recalled. "Especially to a reporter."

Coach and shooter didn't discuss their differences or the words, and when the Lakers and the Pacers resumed the series on June 14 at Conseco Fieldhouse, Rice was still in the starting lineup, standing alongside O'Neal, Green, Harper, and a taped-up, back-from-the-dead Bryant, who'd had Gary Vitti, the Los Angeles trainer, pop the ankle into place so he wouldn't miss what would normally be an extended amount of time.

This was Rice's chance to prove his coach wrong. O'Neal was tired. Bryant was injured. The team was coming off a defeat and needed a boost. The Indiana fans — 18,345 strong — were as loud as any in the league. Jackson, the coach always seeking a mental edge, knew Rice was hungry.

He played 39 minutes, third most on the Lakers.

He scored 11 points.

For those focused on Rice's plight, it was a pathetic reminder of a falling star falling fast. For those focused on the Lakers as a whole, it was a night of ecstasy. Bryant's return was startling. After hobbling onto the court, limp slight but noticeable, he scored 28 points on 14-for-27 shooting. When regulation concluded with a tie at 104, Bryant shifted to a higher gear. Or, as Peter May of the *Boston Globe* wrote, "This game may well be remembered as 'The Night Kobe Bryant Came Out.'"

With 2:33 remaining in overtime and the Lakers up 112–109, O'Neal picked up his sixth foul, walking off the court to elated cheers. He was replaced by Salley, the 36-year-old deep reserve trying to become the first man to win titles with three different franchises. *This game,* Bryant thought, *just became a lot more interesting.* Salley had averaged 1.6 points in limited regular season action, and in the moment his job was simple:

In the early days of the Lakers dynasty, Shaquille O'Neal fancied himself as a big brother figure to his teammates. Though most bought in, a young Kobe Bryant wasn't feeling it.
AP Photo / Victoria Arocho

Both selected in the first round of the 1996 NBA draft, Derek Fisher (above left) and Kobe Bryant (right) shared a kinship that extended through the entirety of their careers. When Bryant was appearing in court on rape accusations, however, there was nothing Fisher could do to help his teammate.

Nick Van Exel (above left) and Eddie Jones (above right) were considered the building blocks of the mid-1990s Lakers. With the arrivals of Shaquille O'Neal and Kobe Bryant, though, their days were numbered. Rick Fox (below center), here slugging it out with Sacramento's Doug Christie (second from right), brought needed toughness to Los Angeles.

Alamy / Sinartus Sosrodjojo / UPI

Laker role players came in myriad shapes, sizes, and attitudes. Glen Rice (above left) was a blockbuster acquisition, but arrived out of shape and out of sorts. Mike Penberthy (below left), a scrappy guard from Master's College, pretended to be Allen Iverson to prepare the Lakers for a 2001 NBA title clash against Philadelphia. Robert Horry (below right) was persona non grata in Phoenix after throwing a towel in his coach's face. But his clutch shooting made him invaluable.

Getty Images / Vince Compagnone / *LA Times*

Alamy / Bryan Patrick / ZUMA Press

AP Photo / Icon Sportswire / Matt A. Brown

AP Photo / Mark J. Terrill

The athleticism and scoring talents of J.R. Rider (above left) made him an exciting 2000 acquisition, but his eccentricities and inconsistencies doomed him to the margins. Dennis Rodman (above right), a Laker for 23 games in 1999, was the only player anyone knew who'd shower before games. A gifted scorer with an enormous ego, Cedric Ceballos (left) nicknamed himself "Chise" — short for "Franchise." It did not go over well.

AP Photo / Eric Draper

Del Harris (above) was a wonderful man and coach who was admired by players — but who also talked and talked and talked the Lakers to sleep. The arrival of Phil Jackson (below center) brought immediate respect and gravitas to the franchise.

Kobe Bryant's other-worldly athleticism (left) resulted in countless comparisons to the legendary Michael Jordan. Shaquille O'Neal (below, dunking) was the most physically imposing player of his generation—and maybe of any generation.

Though they bickered, griped, whined, and even exchanged blows, Shaquille O'Neal and Kobe Bryant were an artful and devastating duo on the court. Getty Images / Andrew D. Bernstein

Creaky knees, sensitive feet, minimal vertical be damned — guard Smits as best he could and get out of Kobe's way.

Three seconds later, Smits tossed an easy hook over Salley's head. The lead was sliced to a single point.

The clock was approaching two minutes. Bryant was charged with everything. He dribbled the ball up-court, guarded closely by Miller. The crowd chanted "Dee-fense! Dee-fense!" Horry rose from the paint to set a pick, then rolled. Any point guard worth his salt dumps the ball to Horry, who was open and free. Bryant didn't glance his way. Not for a second. He dribbled and dribbled, just as he'd always dreamed of dribbling and dribbling, then crossed over Miller before releasing a jumper from inside the three-point line. The ball soared through the air and cut through the net, and Los Angeles was up three.

The Pacers came back down and, once again, Smits scored over the outgunned Salley, who could only stare longingly toward O'Neal on the bench. With 1:34 left, the score was 114–113. The Pacers needed one stop.

Bryant had the ball, this time guarded by the old, slow, and overweight Mark Jackson. Horry liked the mismatch, and came up to set a pick. It was perfectly done, and Horry then rolled — all alone, in the way one is all alone when he has hepatitis C and is coughing uncontrollably — toward the basket. All Bryant had to do was throw an easy pass and Horry would score. But no. Bryant pulled up and uncorked another jumper that swooshed through the net. "How good is this kid?" marveled Bob Costas to NBC's viewers.

Miller's two free throws again sliced the lead to one, 116–115. The next time down the court, Bryant's shot was blocked out of bounds by Smits. Rice had the ball a second later, and his air ball (yes, air ball) was grabbed by Shaw, who put it in the hoop.

Smits answered with two free throws, and the game clock read :28. There was no mystery here — Bryant would surely have the ball, and the game, at his disposal. Shaw advanced up the court, Jackson before him, and tried getting it to the star. Only he couldn't. Miller was all over him, refusing to let Bryant get free. So, with six seconds on the shot clock, Shaw scooted toward the basket. His shot bounced off the rim when — *swoosh* — Bryant soared through the air and put it in the hoop, back facing the rim.

When Miller's three-point attempt hit the front of the rim and bounced out, the Lakers had a 120–118 win and a three-games-to-one series lead. O'Neal and Bryant embraced on the court shortly after the final buzzer sounded — a big man thanking a smaller man for bailing him out. Asked afterwards about the importance of the win, Bryant, who had 8 points in overtime and could barely hide the pain of a now pulsating left ankle, was blunt.

"In our mind," he said, "this is the championship."

He was right.

The Pacers won the next game at Conseco in a 120–87 fluke blowout, before which members of the home team saw bottles of champagne being wheeled toward the Lakers' locker room. (Said Mark Jackson: "That was disrespectful to us and the character we have on this basketball team.") But there was no way Indiana was going to travel to Los Angeles and take two straight road games.

On June 19, 2000, the Lakers captured the NBA championship, winning 116–111 behind O'Neal's 41 points and 12 rebounds and Bryant's 26 points and 10 rebounds. In the fourth quarter of a tight contest, the stars teamed up for 21 points and 7 boards. When it finally ended, O'Neal — battered, exhausted, in need of a long nap — stood in the middle of the Staples Center floor, surrounded by teammates and fans, and bawled.

"I held emotion for about 11 years now," he said. "Three years of college, eight years in the league, always wanting to win. This is what I wanted to come to the NBA for. It just came out."

Moments later, O'Neal cradled the Larry O'Brien Trophy in his lap. He rested his shaved head against the golden ball, a man at peace with his place. He was the Finals MVP, which was wonderful and dandy.

But this was about far more than an individual accolade.

This was about legacy.

10

Someone Shoot J.R.

In the aftermath of the June 21 parade to celebrate the Lakers' 2000 championship, Phil Jackson and Co. immediately returned to the job of keeping the winning alive. Some major changes were in order, beginning with the departure of Jerry West, the executive vice president of basketball operations whose 35 years with the franchise would be coming to an end. West put on a good face, telling reporters it was simply the moment to depart. He was tired. He needed some time away from the game. "I was going to sleep and every dream I was having was about the Lakers," he explained. "That was sad."

Truth be told, West simply could no longer coexist with Jackson and his profound arrogance. The two were polar opposites, and West was tired of having his feelings hurt by an outsider who'd been ushered in to shake things up. This no longer felt like home to the franchise's greatest ambassador. He needed out, and some two years later was hired by the Memphis Grizzlies to serve as general manager.

"I didn't like being around someone who didn't want me there," West later said of Jackson. "I hated the idea that he was uncomfortable around me. I hated being a sore spot. I wanted to finish my career as a Laker, but that wasn't going to happen. And that's okay. Change can be good."

There were other shifts. John Salley retired. A.C. Green signed with Miami. Glen Rice and Travis Knight were dealt to New York, netting Los Angeles Horace Grant, the veteran power forward. The team nearly signed New Jersey swingman Kendall Gill to a two-year, $4.5 million free agent contract, and even presented him with a No. 12 jersey to hold up at the scheduled press conference. When, at the last minute, the Nets offered $7 million for one year, Gill stayed put. "Such a regret in hindsight," Gill recalled. It was largely run-of-the-mill off-season stuff — accented by one of the most bizarre and puzzling acquisitions in franchise lore.

Or, perfectly stated in six words via Rick Fox, "some crazy, crazy, *crazy-ass shit.*"

Enter Isaiah (J.R.) Rider.

It seemed like a good idea. Or, rather, it didn't seem like a bad idea. At least not an awful idea. Sorta. Kinda. *Maybe.* Jackson, a noted kook himself during a decade-long playing career that featured all manner of facial hair and 1970s recreational experimentation, loved finding a square peg and shoving it into a round hole. Hell, while his greatest grand achievement in basketball was guiding the Bulls to six championships, his greatest micro-accomplishment was taking Dennis Rodman — the unwanted cross-dressing, attention-starved, multi-pierced, alcoholic, drug-addicted, smells-like-sewer-rot power forward — and molding him into a key piece of Chicago's dynasty.

So when Rider, a 29-year-old free agent shooting guard with an 18.1-points-per-game career scoring average and Kobe-esque athleticism, became available, Jackson and Mitch Kupchak weighed the pros and cons.

The pros: Rider was supremely talented and (at $736,000 for the season) cheap.

The cons: Where to begin?

In seven NBA seasons (the first three with Minnesota, then three more with the Blazers and one in Atlanta), Rider had been late for dozens of practices, team meetings, team functions, media appearances, personal appearances, and games. Why, after being selected fifth overall out of UNLV in the 1993 NBA draft, the rookie arrived nearly two hours tardy for his Timberwolves *introductory press conference.* "First we were told it'd just be a few minutes, then more than a few minutes," recalled Steve Aschburner, who covered the event for the *Minneapolis Star-Tribune.*

"Then we're told he's flying out of San Francisco and the traffic on the Bay Bridge was terrible. Then we were told he needed a later flight."

That season, Rider dazzled fans with one phenomenal play after another. Spins. Glides. Twirls. Jams. He won the All-Star Weekend Slam Dunk contest with something he called the "East Bay Funk" and averaged 16.6 points and 2.6 assists for a franchise in dire need of pizzazz. That said, he was an off-the-court nightmare. His lateness excuses were straight out of an eighties sitcom—*frozen pipes, flat tire, got lost, taxi never arrived.* One day, after a reporter named Ray Richardson, of the *St. Paul Pioneer Press,* asked an unflattering question, Rider said, "I don't need to talk to you no more." Then, as Richardson began to walk away, he added, "I know people who can take you out."

The words might have been laughed off had Rider not, in fact, known people who could take Richardson out.

Born and raised in Oakland, young J.R. was 12 when his father, Isaiah Sr., abandoned the family, leaving Donna Rider alone with four children to care for. They moved from a house to Parrot Village, an Alameda housing project. Within a year J.R. had smoked marijuana for the first time. He loved the taste.

When he was a student at Encinal High, Rider's teachers were wowed by his natural intellect and infuriated by his indifference. He attended one class, skipped two, attended three, skipped two. Some of his closest friends were gangbangers. He was considered among the best schoolboy basketball players in Oakland history, and accepted a scholarship to Kansas State, where Coach Lon Kruger couldn't wait to add a man of such skills. Yet Rider was forced to miss his senior year of basketball because of multiple Fs, and—after he attained his GED—Kruger covertly smuggled him to Allen Community College, in Iola, Kansas, where he promptly landed Fs in 15 units and was charged with felony burglary for stealing the jewelry of a fellow athlete named Anthony Shaw. "I saw him wearing my ring and confronted him," Shaw recalled. "J.R. smiled at me, took the ring off his finger, put it in his pocket, and said, 'I don't have no ring on me.'" Kansas State wanted no part of this, and Rider's next stop was Antelope Valley College, in Lancaster, California. Playing for a coach, Newton

Chelette, who saw him as more than mere poker chip, Rider led the nation in scoring with 33.6 points per game and did enough in the classroom to snag a coveted UNLV scholarship.

Las Vegas, though, was everything a young man of Rider's ilk didn't need. "He was *always* in trouble," recalled Paul Gutierrez, sports editor of the *Rebel Yell*, the student paper, "and always late." Coach Jerry Tarkanian ran a program that lacked discipline and ethics, and over the course of the 1992–93 year, his star recruit engaged in a fight with a police officer, threw a strawberry milkshake in the face of a Jack in the Box cashier, then submitted a paper for his "Prevention and Management of Premenstrual Syndrome" class that was written by another student. (The giveaway: Rider's first name was misspelled.) That last transgression resulted in Rider's suspension for the 1993 postseason, which mattered little to the nation's second-leading scorer (who averaged 29.2 points per game for the Rebels). He knew the NBA awaited.

Rider and professionalism were an *awful* match. The Timberwolves were coached by Sidney Lowe, a basketball lifer who believed there was a proper way to approach the game. Rider, who was making $25.5 million over seven years, didn't care. He ignored Lowe's instructions, ignored his directives. Once, while coming off the court, he spit on the hardwood, drawing his coach's ire. "J.R. walked right past him," recalled Richardson. "He had no respect for authority."

The Wolves tolerated Rider, but it was never easy. In the summer after his rookie year, he was robbed at gunpoint in East Oakland, and the assailant took his most prized possession, a gold No. 34 pendant that hung from his neck. Rider and a friend drove to a nearby crack house, where they suspected the thief could be found. The Timberwolves' marquee player entered the building armed with a pistol. He emerged with the necklace.

By 1996, Kevin McHale, Minnesota's general manager, knew he needed to make a change. Rider had been arrested on multiple charges, including drugging and raping a woman, driving illegally with tinted windows, and possession of stolen phones. He was peddled to the Blazers for two forgettable players and a low-first-round draft pick, and while in Portland he stood as one of the NBA's truly terrific shooting guards. He also became the face of a lawless operation.

Bob Whitsitt, the team's general manager, assembled a roster filled with gifted players who, one way or another, had dogged or drugged their way out of other cities. Rider, though, was the king. If he wasn't late, he was absent. If he wasn't abusive, he was rude. He usually played hard, but not always. He was arrested for smoking marijuana out of a Coca-Cola can. He ignored the directive of Coach Mike Dunleavy and once refused to enter a game.

In his excellent book *Jail Blazers: How the Portland Trail Blazers Became the Bad Boys of Basketball*, Kerry Eggers recalls the lowest lows . . .

> On March 5, Rider missed the team's charter flight to Phoenix by about 15 minutes. Blaming Flightcraft officials, he badgered them to supply him with another plane. When they refused, according to police reports, he became angry and abusive and challenged four employees. They said he screamed obscenities at them, got in their faces, behaved in a threatening manner, and spit in one man's face from a distance of four to six inches away. He also spat at another employee, who turned to avoid being hit. Rider then grabbed a third employee's cell phone and smashed it to bits on the pavement.

In his three seasons with the Blazers, Rider averaged 16.9 points and helped the team to the 1999 Western Conference Finals. But when enough was finally enough, and Atlanta offered guard Steve Smith in a package for Rider, the Blazers leapt at the opportunity.

Pete Babcock, the Hawks' general manager, was horrified by the trade, which was ordered by ownership. "I told people in the media, off the record, that we were trading Steve Smith for the anti–Steve Smith," Babcock recalled. "J.R. was a likable guy, actually. But he was so moody, and I just got tired of fining him all the time."

Rider played 60 games for the very bad Hawks, averaging 19.3 points but embarrassing himself and the franchise with repeated intolerable antics. It was all too baffling for words: Rider put his sister Michelle through a master's degree program at Northwestern. He built two recreation centers in Oakland's low-income neighborhoods with then-Mayor Jerry Brown. He often displayed a huge heart. "You saw the kindness," said Babcock. "You truly did."

On Friday, March 17, 2000, Rider arrived 10 minutes late for the Hawks' home game against Boston. As he began to change into his uniform, Babcock approached. "J.R.," he said, "don't get dressed today."

"Why?" Rider asked.

"Let's just talk after the game."

Rider watched on a television monitor from a side room. He summoned Babcock in the first quarter. "Pete," he said, "I'm so sorry. This will never happen again."

Babcock nodded, excused himself.

Rider summoned Babcock again in the fourth quarter. "Pete," he screamed, "fuck this shit! Just get me the fuck out of here! I hate this fucking team and you're a fucking twat."

He was released that Friday night and sat out the remainder of the 1999–2000 NBA season.

Then the Lakers called.

Shaquille O'Neal couldn't believe it. Kobe Bryant couldn't believe it. It wasn't that the two superstars were upset, or even overly disappointed. At the Lakers' behest, O'Neal had actually reached out to Rider suggesting (hesitantly) he join the show. But having survived the Dennis Rodman fiasco of 1999, the actuality came as a surprise. For all his quirks, at least Rodman was the owner of three NBA championship rings. Rider had never won a thing.

When training camp opened in El Segundo on October 3, all eyes were on Rider, and how he would fit in, and whether he would behave, and . . .

Blllllleeeeecccchhhhh!

He barfed.

"It's maybe the first or second workout, and our gym is a sweatbox," recalled Rudy Garciduenas, the equipment manager. "We cleaned it up for practices and made it look pretty, but when the heat was unbearable and the humidity rose up, it was just a sauna inside.

"So we're practicing, and I look around and I don't see J.R. anywhere. The next thing I know, the guys who help me are coming to get me, sort of in a panic. I asked what's wrong. 'It's J.R! He's outside in the gutter, puking his guts out!'"

Over the course of his first seven NBA seasons, Rider thought he understood competitiveness. But he had never experienced anything like *this*. Though Laker camps (as a whole) tended to be relatively tame under Jackson, Bryant viewed Rider as a direct threat — a veteran of similar size, similar skills, a Slam Dunk championship (Bryant won the contest in 1997), and three seasons with the loathed Blazers.

"He wanted to cut my heart out," Rider recalled. "Then eat it."

The two had never before met, yet as soon as Rider arrived, Bryant was begging him/goading him/pleading with him to play one-on-one. It was a nonstop, two-or-three-times-per-day conversation. Usually one that went thusly:

BRYANT: C'mon, man. Play me.
RIDER: When I'm in better shape.
BRYANT: Seriously, let's go.
RIDER: When I'm in better shape.

"Obviously, it was personal for Kobe," Rider recalled. "He just asked far too many times. So one day I looked at him and it was like 'Okay, fine. Let's go.'"

J.R. Rider and Kobe Bryant finally played.

The game was held after a practice, and the other Lakers gathered around, eager to see what happens when the world's most competitive man does battle with the world's biggest basketball fuck-up. According to roundball mythology and foggy memories and good old-fashioned exaggerated hype, what transpired was a slaying of epic proportions. Bryant didn't merely beat Rider — he embarrassed him, ridiculed him, stole his manhood. Sixteen years later, in a piece for *The Players' Tribune*, several Laker veterans wrote of the game. Here is a snippet . . .

Brian Shaw: They played to 10 by ones. Kobe just absolutely demolished him.

Ron Harper: Kobe destroyed him.

Brian Shaw: This is 22-year-old Kobe. Crazy athletic. Unlimited stamina. I mean, he kicked his ass. He pulled out everything in his bag — dunk, up-and-under, pull-up, crossover.

Devean George: Fade-away. Left hand. Right hand. Blowing by him.

Brian Shaw: We were on the sidelines gassing it up. People are laughing, yelling, "Hey, J.R., be careful what you wish for."

It's not true. Any of it. Bryant and Rider played two games to five. There was a fair amount of trash talk, but it never turned heated, and neither battle was a blowout. "I don't even think some of the people who've talked about it were watching," recalled Mike Penberthy, a rookie guard. "I saw the whole thing, and it was close. J.R. wasn't just a good player. He was great. Sometimes we make things bigger than they are. That was the case here. Kobe won, but it wasn't anything ridiculous."

"It actually makes me really angry," said Rider. "The story that I was talking smack to him from Oakland, that we played in front of the whole team, that it was this huge deal. Nope. We played, he won, it was cool. That's it."

Sadly, for Rider, the Kobe matchup — preposterous hype be damned — was probably the highlight of the season. The Lakers may well have believed enough in Rider's future redemption to have him pose for October promotional shots with O'Neal, Bryant, and Jackson, but he was too far gone to save. "Once in my office he broke down and started to cry," said Jackson. "I was telling him he wasn't playing to his potential, and he got very emotional. It was . . . different. When you have a player with ADHD who needs to smoke dope to stay grounded, you've got a problem."

In 67 games with Los Angeles, he averaged career lows in minutes (18) and points (7.6), while off the court it was one pratfall after another.

There was the time when he was late to practice, and Penberthy heard someone pounding — *bang-bang-bang!* — on the rear gymnasium door. "I open and it's J.R.," Penberthy said. "And he's wearing slippers and a sweat suit. He threw on a jersey over the sweat suit and practiced in slippers."

There was the time in San Antonio when he was late for another practice and arrived 20 minutes behind schedule with a note from the desk clerk at the hotel: DEAR COACH JACKSON: IT WAS OUR FAULT FOR FAILING TO GIVE J.R. A WAKE-UP CALL. DON'T BLAME HIM. SINCERELY, CHARLES OUBINA, MARRIOTT.

There was the time . . . well, let Shaquille O'Neal tell it. "This is no lie," he said. "He lived in the team hotel, which was right here. And the back door of the gym was right here — facing the hotel. Yards apart. Motherfucker didn't come to practice for three straight days because of a flat tire."

There was the time when a scribe named Tim Brown from the *Los Angeles Times* spotted Rider engaged in a screaming match with Mitch Kupchak, then had the audacity to (gasp) write about it. That day, after practice, Rider approached Brown's car in the facility lot.

"You wrote that fucking story?" he said to Brown.

"Yeah. I did."

"Why would you write that story?" he said.

"Because," Brown replied, "it was true."

"You know," Rider said, "I know where your family lives. I know where you live."

He drove off.

There was the time — the absolute best time in the history of times — when the Lakers were leaving Toronto after a game with the Raptors. The players and coaches had to pass through customs at Pearson International Airport, and as they approached the checkpoint, an officer's German shepherd barked wildly at Rider.

"J.R. decides he's going to pet the dog," recalled Rick Fox. "And the guy goes, 'Sir, please don't pet the dog.' And the dog did everything short of pointing at J.R. and saying, 'This motherfucker has drugs and you should search him right now.'"

The guard ordered Rider to follow him to an interrogation room, where he was detained as the Lakers boarded their chartered plane. Jerome Crawford, O'Neal's bodyguard and constant companion, left the aircraft after 30 minutes to see what was happening. He returned with a smiling, laughing Rider, who said, "I'm clean! I told those fuckers I'm clean!"

With Rider out of earshot, Fox asked Crawford what had transpired. "He smoked so much weed his tracksuit smelled of the stuff," Crawford said. "So they stopped him."

Years later, Fox still cackled at the memory. "He literally got pulled over because his clothes reeked of weed," he said. "It was the tracksuit he wore for the entire trip, and all J.R. did was sit in his hotel room and smoke out."

Asked in 2019 whether Fox's take was correct, Rider chuckled. "Well," he said, "I did like my weed."

Winning the NBA title changes things.

It *always* changes things.

In the course of an NBA off-season, across the league players come and go, coaches shuffle jobs, executives are hired, fired, retire.

But when you capture a championship, something shifts. It's like watching a boxer go from a top 10 contender to heavyweight champion of the world. Walk turns to swagger. Promises turn to guarantees. You look the same, but you're different. *Forever* different.

The 2000–01 Los Angeles Lakers were different.

The biggest change came via the two biggest stars. With the burden of a ringless hand now lifted and his status as the NBA's most dominant force solidified by his regular-season and Finals MVP awards, O'Neal considered himself (more than ever before) the unambiguous leader of the Lakers. This was his team in his town, which meant his teammates were his soldiers under his guidance.

Shortly after signing a three-year, $88.5 million contract extension in October, O'Neal drove to Beverly Hills, purchased $150,000 in Rolex watches on his American Express card, and presented the jewelry to 18 teammates and four staff members. The message wasn't so much *I'm rich* as *I'm rich and I'll watch over you*. It came from a sincere place.

"When I was young with the Orlando Magic, nobody really took care of me," O'Neal said. "Nobody looked after me. That's not right. I come from parents who are big on respect and also who are big on treating everyone with love. No race, no religion, no culture — none of that matters. You're a person: you deserve respect. I was in a position to make people feel good and welcome and loved. Why wouldn't I act on that?"

O'Neal was good with teammates like Fox and Robert Horry and Derek Fisher — established veterans with money and job security. But he was phenomenal to those who most needed the love. The Los Angeles roster was largely a Who's Who of NBA names, men from major college programs born to be professionals. In between the cracks, however, were guys like the two new rookies in town — Mark Madsen, the 6-foot-9 forward from Stanford, who was rough and rugged but as athletic as a mug; and Mike Penberthy, a 6-foot-3, 185-pound guard from a place called Master's College.

Yes, Master's College.

From his early days in Los Angeles, Madsen was an O'Neal favorite. The Lakers were panned for wasting the 29th pick on such a run-of-the-mill player, and the star center took it personally. First, he escorted the rookie on a shopping spree. "[H]e took me *car* shopping," Madsen recalled. "He literally said to me, 'I'm putting the down payment on whatever car you want.' I told him I wouldn't let him, but he negotiated a great deal for me on a Chevy Tahoe."

After that it was time for new duds. Recalled Madsen: "He drove us up to Beverly Hills and we went to a big-and-tall clothing store. I found a pair of jeans that fit and Shaq said to the store worker, 'He'll take eight of each color!' I said, 'All I need is one of each color.' When Shaq kept piling on Italian sweaters, I told him I didn't need all the stuff, but he told me it was a welcome gift and to relax while he paid the $2,500 bill."

Unlike his teammates, Madsen was a devout Mormon who was saving himself for marriage. Some 15 years earlier, A.C. Green, the born-again Christian forward, had been drafted out of Oregon State and subjected to nonstop ridicule from Magic Johnson, Byron Scott, and the gang. This time, with Madsen, O'Neal would not allow it. In fact, he turned into his new teammate's personal MormonMatch.com service. On one team flight, the two men were sitting side by side when a pretty stewardess approached. "Are you Mormon?" O'Neal asked.

"No," she replied. "Why?"

"Never mind," O'Neal said.

Recalled Madsen: "A few weeks later, a single member of the Lakers' front office came up to me at the Staples Center and said, 'The most interesting thing happened last night. I'm sitting in a restaurant in Redondo Beach and Shaq was in there asking some of the girls if they were Mormon because if they were, he wanted to set them up with you.'"

Like Madsen, Penberthy was a perplexing addition. Unlike Madsen, nobody — *absolutely nobody* — had heard of him.

As a senior at Hoover High, in Fresno, California, Penberthy averaged 21 points per game, and was recruited by such Division I schools as Cal and Utah. But he weighed 160 pounds, and coaches insisted he'd need to redshirt and gain weight. So instead of waiting, he committed to Master's College, an 850-student NAIA school that was founded in 1927 as Los Angeles Baptist Theological Seminary by John Dunkin — Penberthy's grandfather. In four seasons with the Mustangs, the guard emerged as one of America's best players, division be damned. As a senior in 1996–97, he led the NAIA, averaging 27.5 points per game, and while no teams considered drafting him, he was on the radar. Penberthy's daily workouts were Kobe-esque — 500 shots in the morning, 500 shots in the afternoon, 500 shots in the evening. Then he'd play five-on-five pickup. "He was committed to reaching the NBA, but I didn't see it happening at first," said Ray Farrell, an assistant coach at Master's. "It was a stretch, because of his size, his athleticism. But he would do anything. He'd get up at 6 and work before anyone else was up. He'd study, he'd run. He knew how hard it would be, coming from Master's, but he was hungry. And he could *really* shoot.".

Penberthy was invited to camp with the Indiana Pacers in 1997 but tore his hamstring beforehand and couldn't participate. He spent the next few years bouncing from Idaho to Germany to Venezuela, always returning to Southern California and playing in various summer leagues. In June of 2000, Penberthy played for the *Slam* magazine entry in the LA Pro Summer League, which held its games inside the Pyramid at Long Beach State as opening acts for NBA summer league games. One day, Jim Cleamons, the Lakers' assistant, was waiting for his game to start when he found himself transfixed by this small white kid who looked like Richie Cunningham, dribbled like Tiny Archibald, and shot like Craig Hodges. He told Kupchak that — *holy shit* — this whirling dervish of a player was worth checking out, and before long Penberthy scored an invitation to training camp. "Mitch said to me, 'Enjoy your week here — you've earned it,'" Penberthy recalled. "Well, that set me off. I figured I had nothing to lose, so I just went off. I played exactly like I did in college, shooting threes, finding open guys. I learned the triangle in three days, so that helped, too. At the end I figured they'd either cut me because I shot too many threes or keep me because I made them all,"

The Lakers were scheduled to open the season on October 31 at Portland. That morning, Penberthy found himself in the team offices, waiting to learn his fate. The team brought in a pair of veteran guards (Shawn Respert and Emanual Davis), and Penberthy outplayed both. Fisher, the regular point guard, was injured and out for most of the season with a stress fracture in his right foot. "They were looking for somebody to play," Penberthy said. "I really wanted it to be me."

Finally, after waiting for what felt like 200 hours (but was probably 15 minutes), Penberthy sat across from Kupchak and Jackson, his basketball existence hanging by a thread.

"Well," Jackson said, "we're keeping you. You've done a good job for us. Keep doing what you're doing."

The Laker who expressed the greatest happiness for Penberthy was O'Neal, who congratulated him with a spine-snapping hug and an offer he could not refuse. On the flight from Southern California to Portland, Penberthy noticed that all his teammates wore stylish, custom-made suits, many of which cost upwards of $2,000. "I had no suits and no money," Penberthy said. "I went to a Nordstrom in Portland by the hotel, but they had nothing in my size. So I went to a Banana Republic and grabbed some slacks and a shirt. I wore them with a jacket that didn't fit. I thought I looked good."

Penberthy tried entering the Rose Garden for the game and was stopped by security. It was humiliating.

From a short distance, O'Neal observed what was transpiring with his terribly dressed new teammate. When no one else was around, he asked for a moment with Penberthy. "You don't have any suits, do you?" he asked.

"Nah," Penberthy replied. "But it's . . ."

"I'm taking you to get suits," O'Neal said.

The next morning, the center worth more than $100 million picked up the guard worth $3.76 and took him to his personal tailor. Penberthy left with six suits.

"He's the best teammate I've ever had," said Penberthy, who averaged 5 points in 53 games. "He was like having a big brother with a huge bank account. Every time we'd go into a city he'd shoot me a text — GOING TO DINNER. And he'd always pay. I can't overstate this. There are good people, there are great people, and then there's Shaq. Or put it this way: when my father died, Shaq offered to pay for the funeral. He's *that* kind of guy."

Madsen and Penberthy were hardly the only two to feel the love. O'Neal's generosity was Santa-like, his heart the size of Saturn. From treating teammates to fancy meals and $1,000 bottles of wine to (in 2001) flying the parents and two sisters of rookie Joe Crispin from New Jersey to Los Angeles to see their loved one's NBA debut, few escaped the big man's warmth.* The team once enlisted the services of a deaf ball boy, who hung a sign in the locker room soliciting money for a trip to a tournament for hearing-impaired teens. As soon as he saw the posting, O'Neal said, "Take that down!," opened his wallet, and handed the boy the requisite sum in cash. Another time, an assistant public relations director named Tom Savage was offered a pay raise to work for the WNBA. When

---

* "He insisted, and I ignored it," Crispin recalled. "Finally he said, 'They're coming, I'm paying — that's final.' Then he booked them first class."

O'Neal heard the news, he approached Savage and said, "How much more are they giving you?"

"About $20,000," Savage said.

"I've got the cash in my locker," O'Neal said. "Stay and it's yours."

Though touched, Savage left.

For all his empathy and decency, as well as a profound need to be loved, O'Neal had two Kryptonites.

One, free throw shooting, would haunt him throughout a 19-year NBA run.

The other, Kobe Bryant, was far worse.

Over the first four years of the guard's career, teammates recoiled at his arrogance, his indifference. But between the end of the 1999–2000 season and the start of the 2000–01 season, something changed. It was akin to watching a middle-aged person with bad habits become a senior citizen and having those habits turn significantly more pronounced. A loud talker grows louder. An argumentative curmudgeon becomes increasingly curmudgeonly. Though Bryant was only 22, he behaved as if he were a 10-year veteran. Especially galling was his treatment of rookies. The Lakers were not a team that harassed newcomers. Never had been. But Bryant lacked the maturity to know better. Penberthy, for example, was four years his senior, yet Bryant took pride in barking at him, belittling him, showing him what was what. "He wanted people to be scared of him," Penberthy said. "I got knocked out of a game in Venezuela by some crazy former prison guy because I scored 27 in the first half. There were defected Russian players who hated America and wanted me dead. Kobe? I wasn't scared of Kobe."

Penberthy earned his stripes when Bryant missed a couple of free throws during a practice. "C'mon," the rookie said, "you've gotta make those."

"Shut the fuck up," Bryant replied. "If you played some defense, you'd get more minutes."

"Okay, Kobe," Penberthy said. "Talk trash to a rookie. It's what you do."

The back-and-forth continued, and when the session ended, Penberthy followed Bryant to the locker room.

"You wanna say something?" he barked. "I'm right here."

Bryant walked off, head down.

Once upon a time, O'Neal loved the big brother–little brother model, where he'd guide and mold and encourage young Kobe in a sort of Batman and Robin setup. But now he realized it was an impossibility. Bryant was, truly, unbearable. The way he needed to challenge J.R. Rider from the day he arrived. The way he needed to belittle Penberthy. The way he, once again, was hogging the basketball, dribbling without looking up, turning the triangle into a piece of warped cardboard. Bryant wanted other players to share his intensity, but *no one* shared his intensity. O'Neal, in particular, had spent the months after his first ring celebrating as he had never celebrated before. "While Kobe shot jumpers," the author Elizabeth Kaye wrote, "Shaq feasted on the fried shrimp, mayonnaise, ketchup, and cheese concoctions he called Shaq Daddy sandwiches. He took his posse to Las Vegas, gave them $10,000 for the gambling tables, and kept hours that gave him headaches . . . That summer, as Shaq sightings occurred at what he called gentlemen's clubs and at Fatburger at three in the morning, that notion — you are what you repeatedly do — still had application."

The Lakers opened their title defense with a 6-4 record; the locker room felt cold, hostile, detached. O'Neal refused to hide his disdain for Bryant, especially after the kid launched 31 (yes, *thirty-one*) shots in a 91–81 loss to San Antonio. "We need to play smarter," O'Neal said to the assembled reporters — a not so subtle euphemism for "It'd be lovely if the child passed the ball on occasion."

Thus commenced one of the most interesting internal mini-dramas of the season — the Shaq v. Kobe Media Shuffle. After every game, reporters entered the locker room and encircled one of the stars. Then, when that man was done talking, they'd shuffle to a nearby stall and encircle the other star. Usually, O'Neal spoke first, and he'd subtly (and occasionally not so subtly) rip Bryant for selfishness, for childishness. Some of it would be off the record. Most would be on. Then Bryant would be told of O'Neal's words and subtly (and occasionally not so subtly) respond. It was the most passive-aggressive teammate-to-teammate behavior scribes had witnessed, not unlike two toddlers arguing over a lollipop. O'Neal's locker and Bryant's locker were separated by approximately 15 feet. They could have directly uttered the complaints to each other while rolling on deodorant. That, however, would take courage. "It was babyish, and it was really more Shaq," said J.A. Adande, the *Los Angeles Times* writer. "Shaq would say to us, 'You guys know what's really going on' all the time. He didn't want to come out and say it, so he'd have us do the dirty work. Kobe wasn't as cryptic. He'd bide his time, then unload."

Writers were quickly designated "Shaq guy" or "Kobe guy," based upon perceived allegiances. Ric Bucher, the *ESPN The Magazine* writer who covered a large amount of Laker basketball, was once in the running to co-author O'Neal's autobiography. Then he wrote a piece deemed sympathetic to Bryant. "From then on I was a 'Kobe guy' to Shaq," Bucher recalled. "That was it for me with him. I didn't want any allegiances. But in Shaq's mind you were with him or you were with that guy."

Adande was considered "a Shaq guy," and with good reason. "I tried not to take sides at first," he said, "but they forced you to. So I was on Shaq's side, mainly because for that team they were better off when the ball went through him. And Shaq was more accessible and — despite his size — more relatable. I also was closer in age to Shaq, I knew him longer. He allowed me in. Kobe never really did."

Said the *Times*'s Plaschke:

Kobe had nobody. He had a bodyguard, but that was it. So I would wait and walk him to his car. Every night when I was there. The same competitiveness that made him great on the court kept people away off the court. He was always snarling. Always biting. And he would see who you were talking to. You had to pick a side — Kobe or Shaq. And I picked Shaq. You would be talking to someone about Kobe and Shaq would be listening. I'll never forget one time I was talking to Rick Fox about Kobe in the hallway. And Shaq came bursting through the curtain: "What are you talking about? What's going on?" After the games they would see who you went to first. They were watching after shootarounds to see who you went to. You had to clearly choose.

Shaq was jealous of Kobe. Kobe wasn't jealous of Shaq. Kobe just wanted to kick everybody's ass.

Those who knew both men well found the dynamic fascinating, in that what people thought they were observing wasn't entirely accurate. Because he was bigger, stronger, more accomplished, more boastful, O'Neal was largely considered the secure veteran dealing with the insecure kid. In reality, O'Neal could never fully get past Bryant's refusal to embrace him. Everyone loved Shaq. So why didn't Kobe? He was supposed to come and seek advice — but never did. He was supposed to sing O'Neal's praises — but never did.

Even worse, Bryant didn't give two craps what O'Neal said or thought about him. O'Neal could ramble on about Bryant's flaws, and it felt raw. Bryant's replies, though, were often accompanied by shrugs and smirks. The body language screamed: *Seriously? Who cares what he thinks?* — and it drove O'Neal insane. Before every game, the Laker players huddled in the hallway leading to the court, and O'Neal would lead them — in the words of Bucher — "into a bouncing frenzy, bodies ricocheting off each other turning the circle into a mosh pit." Every man participated, from Fox and Horry to Penberthy and Madsen. But not Bryant. Never. Why? Well, why should he?

Jackson, for his part, kicked back and let it unfold. Though he preached Zen and had his players sit in rooms together as incense burned, the coach was a firm believer in letting conflicts play out organically. He actually believed there was value to *Shaq v. Kobe*, in that two angry stars oftentimes brought the ferocity to the court. If they were mad in the locker room, wouldn't they be mad against Portland and Sacramento? Jackson didn't like the word "manipulation," but it was manipulation.

Unlike his days in Chicago, however, it wasn't working here. The Lakers entered the month of December with a 11-5 mark, and most of the wins were a by-product of talent overcoming selfishness. Yet even when Los Angeles ran off five-straight triumphs midway through the month, it never felt right. "There were these stretches on the court when Kobe was really immature," said Greg Foster, the backup center. "Even when we were playing well. He just was brash. And sometimes brash is good, and sometimes brash is not even a little good."

In a December 12 home loss to Milwaukee, Bryant shot 8 for 31 from the field and entered the locker room to deafening silence. To the shock of teammates, he stood, cleared his throat, and said, "Fellas, that was my fault."

What?

"I missed a lot of shots," he said. "I missed shots I normally make. But I took some bad ones, too. It was my fault."

Fox, the sage veteran now in his 10th season, had long been one of Kobe's more sympathetic colleagues. He appreciated his talent, felt sympathy for his isolation. Fox knew that Bryant's family had returned to Philadelphia after his engagement. He knew he was largely alone.

"Look, you made some mistakes," Fox said. "So what? If you're responsible for tonight, you're also responsible for the 15 wins we got."

Bryant nodded appreciatively. Then, one night later, he fired off 25 shots in a loss to Portland. Then 18 more shots in a win against Vancouver. Then 29 more shots in a squeaker over a mediocre Toronto squad. Then 24 more shots in a narrow triumph against Miami. Then 26 more shots in Houston. In an overtime setback to Golden State, O'Neal and Bryant ran the pick-and-roll on five straight possessions late in the fourth quarter. Not once did Bryant pass to his teammate. "Drop it the fuck off," O'Neal moaned during a time-out. He would do no such thing. Against Philadelphia, Jackson berated Bryant for a series of dumb shots. The player argued, and Jackson snarled, "I don't want to hear that shit from you!"

"Well," Bryant screamed, "I don't want to hear that shit from you, either!"

Bryant shot and shot in the way Del Harris once talked and talked. Yes, O'Neal was a teammate, but so was Fox, one of the NBA's top midrange shooters, and Horry, a three-point legend, and Horace Grant, a terrific guy to have in the blocks, and Ron Harper, one of Michael Jordan's favorite teammates with the Bulls. Bryant ignored them all, because in his mind this was how it was supposed to be.

"He was a shooter," said Penberthy, "who believed his job was to shoot."

In his defense (sort of), Bryant looked around the league and saw peers firing away from all angles. The uber-athletic Vince Carter had the green light in Toronto, as did Allen Iverson in Philadelphia, Tracy McGrady in Orlando, Paul Pierce in Boston. There was an understandable sense of jealousy from Bryant, who aspired to not merely lead the league in scoring but fulfill an image he couldn't possibly live up to. "There was a game against Toronto when Kobe decided he needed to go one-on-one against Vince," Jackson recalled. "He had no space to operate, and he kept going right at him. Nothing kills team spirit like that."

Jackson observed a Bryant who felt haunted by an NBA he failed to fully relate to. He looked the part, but he wasn't the part. "The thing about Kobe, truly, was a search for street. He had no street in him. I don't even think he's attracted to African American girls. It was a search to be something."

At the time, the hot publication covering the NBA was *Slam*, which merged basketball and hip-hop culture into 12 yearly issues. *Slam* was all about trash talk, tattoos, Snoop Dogg and Wu-Tang verses, dangling gold chains and baggy shorts and FUBU ads. It was Iverson blowing out his cornrows, Carter leaping over Frédéric Weis, Stephon Marbury crossing over Rod Strickland. On four occasions between his rookie year and 2001, Bryant found himself on the cover, usually glaring in that I'm-a-hard-street-balla-about-to-dunk-on-yo-ass sort of way.

But it was an astrophysicist slipping into a black leather biker jacket. "Kobe just wasn't cool," said Elizabeth Kaye, the Laker biographer. "There's no coolness to him at all." His Adidas shoes, first the EQT Elevation, then the KB8, then the KB8 II, never sold particularly well, in part because Bryant had 0.00 percent street cred and in part because the brand wasn't Nike or And1. ("The second Kobe shoe looked like a toaster," said Russ Bengtson, who covered footwear for *Slam*. "Nobody wants to play basketball in toasters.") One model of "the Kobe" had a depiction of Kobe's profile on a gold coin gracing the inner lining. It was preposterous. "I remember growing up in Connecticut, pre-Internet, the only black kid in class, trying to hold on to any semblance of black culture," said Cheo Hodari Coker, who profiled Bryant for *Slam*. "It was the same thing for Kobe. He'd be trying to find a way to identify himself with the larger black diaspora and basketball. And he has all this skill, all these athletic gifts. But he doesn't have the relaxed street cred of an Iverson or a Stephon Marbury. He was always isolated in this me-against-the-world way."

"His level of sophistication didn't jive with *Slam*," said Tony Gervino, the magazine's editor. "He wasn't particularly cool; he was very polished. Slam was *never* polished. We were the opposite of polished."

Bryant tried compensating. Boy, did he try. As a rookie dealing with the media, he was always polite, inviting. *Yes, sir. No, ma'am.* Now, with the championship and the stardom and the engagement to the teenager and the estranged family back in Philadelphia, he was different. Bryant scored a 1080 on his SAT and was a B student throughout high school. He was never — literally never — someone who cursed for the sake of cursing, or eschewed "isn't" for "ain't." But now he was broaching out the fake street — not merely cursing, but cursing with forced attitude. "Fuck all y'all" and "Ah, fuck no." It was preposterous. In his 2011 autobiography, O'Neal recalled the new Kobe suddenly responding to people in a team meeting with "Y'all my n— —-s, y'all like brothers to me." Wrote O'Neal: "I was looking at him and wondering, What the hell is this?"

"I visited with him his second year, and he was the best," said Ronnie Zeidel, *Slam*'s associate publisher. "He felt blessed to be in the NBA. Just so happy. I went back in 2001. It was striking. He knew who I was and we talked, but he was aloof and really entitled. Kind of angry. It was like meeting a different person."

People who knew Bryant well chalked up some to much of the metamorphosis to Vanessa Urbieta Cornejo Laine, the 18-year-old he would be marrying in April. Though his family was now on the East Coast, Bryant received nonstop advice to sign a prenuptial agreement — a suggestion he considered to be an indictment of his judgment.* Also, Vanessa was everything Bryant was not (at least publicly). She was rude, standoffish, difficult. "Thank you" were words that rarely left her lips. Friends later

---

* It was an indictment of his judgment.

said the newfound fame and wealth had changed her, and not for the better. When Vanessa and Kobe went out, they were accompanied by bodyguards. When they went to a movie theater, they insisted upon blocked-off seats after the lights went down. Why? Shawn Hubler, who has written extensively about the relationship for the *Los Angeles Times*, says it was likely two kids lost in the whirlwind of celebrity. "How much psychological development did Kobe really have growing up?" Hubler said. "He was a kid made to be an athlete, and kids like that have no time for life. Figuring out who you are is trial-and-error. If you don't have that, and you're left with a singular skill, who are you? You're unfinished."

One thing Bryant's fiancée excelled at was telling her man he was the best. While Joe Bryant often focused on the negatives and the flaws, Vanessa was all about the talent. Like Kobe, she saw O'Neal as overweight and indifferent; saw Jackson as a coach who didn't fully appreciate the gift he had before him. What Kobe Bryant received from Vanessa was the one thing he did not need: encouragement to remain steadfast and stubborn.

So he remained steadfast and stubborn.

On January 22, 2001, Bryant's face appeared on the cover of *ESPN The Magazine*, alongside the headline THE ONE and the subhead KOBE SAYS HE'S SECOND TO NOBODY (YEAH, INCLUDING SHAQ). The issue first hit newsstands more than a week before the publication date, and the accompanying article — written by Bucher off of an interview conducted in the early days of the new year — was hardly the best thing to happen to a team trying to defend its title. Wrote Bucher:

> This is about which one captures your attention, your imagination and, yes, your respect, however grudgingly it may be given. It's about a player who has a vision of himself atop the basketball universe and will accept nothing less than that realization. It's Kobe's team; in fact, it's Kobe's league. If and when Shaq and the rest of the Lakers come to grips with that will determine if they can repeat as champions.

It got worse. When asked whether he needed to let the offense flow through O'Neal, Bryant said, "Turn my game down? I need to turn it up. I've improved. How are you going to bottle me up? I'd be better off playing someplace else." When asked about the Lakers' makeup, he said, "I trust the team. I just trust myself more. Yeah, we won last year with the offense going through Shaq. But instead of winning series in five and seven games, this year we'll have sweeps."

Brian Shaw, the veteran point guard who was respected by O'Neal and Bryant, tried explaining to the kid that his words were unwise. Fox, also respected by both, did the same. It mattered not. Jackson was furious, and in a closed-door meeting he told the Lakers he had erred in giving them too much freedom. "I tried to let you guys figure it out," he said. "Now I'm going to have to instill more discipline. You don't get the respect of being champions." But what did that mean? Would Jackson change anything? Would the approach shift? Answer: Not really.

O'Neal, meanwhile, was told of the article's contents and decided he was done turning the other cheek. He would always take care of guys like Fox and Horry and Penberthy and Madsen. They were *his* people. But Kobe? Fuck Kobe. As the media gathered around after a practice, O'Neal spoke intentionally loudly with Jerome Crawford, his bodyguard.

"Did you know they pay more taxes in Canada?" he said.

"Like in Vancouver?" Crawford replied.

"Hmm, Vancouver," O'Neal said. "Isn't that where Kobe's gonna get traded to?"

Moments later, surrounded by the beat writers, O'Neal made himself clear. "I don't know why anybody would want to change," he said, "except for selfish reasons. Last year we were 67-15, playing with enthusiasm. The city was jumping up and down. We had a parade and everything. Now we're 23-11.

"You figure it out."

They figured it out.

Not *they*, actually.

He.

Sixty-two games into the season, the Lakers' record sat at 41-21 — fifth best in the Western Conference. Worst of all, nothing had been resolved. O'Neal hated Bryant. Bryant hated O'Neal. Jackson talked of love and peace but presided over hostility and anger. Frustrated by what he felt was unfair treatment, O'Neal went on an out-of-character two-week media boycott. In back-to-back early March games against the Raptors and the Spurs, Bryant took a drunk-man-throwing-bottlecaps-into-a-garbage-pail 67 shots — 34 vs. Toronto, 33 vs. San Antonio. He shot 40 percent. "It was hard for Phil to rein me in," Bryant admitted years later. "Because by nature I'm a No. 1." The loss to the Spurs was particularly galling, as O'Neal was limited to four attempts in the fourth quarter and overtime, while Bryant had 11. "Kobe was out of line Friday," Jackson moaned. "He was out of line."

Then — *a miracle.*

Well, perhaps not a miracle per se. Miracles tend to appear out of nowhere, and Derek Fisher was, like Bryant, in his fifth season with the Lakers. But *unlike* Bryant, he had largely been relegated to the background, a pass-first, shoot-rarely point guard who, at 6-foot-1 and 200 pounds, was exceptional neither by stature nor skill. When Los Angeles grabbed the Arkansas–Little Rock senior with the 24th overall selection in the 1996 draft, there were few to no expectations, and early in his career Fisher met them. He never averaged more than 6.3 points or 23.1 minutes, and when he sat out the first 62 games of the 2000–01 season after undergoing surgery for a stress fracture in his right foot, no one seemed to flinch. Jackson had Ron Harper, Brian Shaw, Mike Penberthy, and Tyronn Lue — all capable of deftly dribbling a basketball.

But, to the shock of Jackson and Co., Fisher's absence was crippling. He wasn't the fastest, the strongest, the quickest. But Harper and Shaw were battered goods, Penberthy's defense was atrocious, and Lue was small and fragile. Fisher, on the other hand, was a rock.

"I think of him as the Laker backbone," said Travis Best, the veteran Pacers point guard. "He was a very strong physical player with tremendous leadership skills. You need Derek Fishers to win in the NBA."

He made his season debut on March 13 against Boston, and the impact was immediate. On the same day Bryant was sidelined with a viral infection, Fisher stepped in as the starting point guard and tallied 26 points and 8 assists. The ball movement reminded some of vintage 1980s Lakers, when Magic Johnson's first priority was feeding Kareem Abdul-Jabbar down low. This time, O'Neal scored 28 points, Fox scored 21, and Horace Grant added 16. There was no standing around watching Bryant dribble; no frustrations. Fisher's priority was to pass. His second priority was also to pass. His third priority was to play defense — which he did very well. (Randy Brown, the Celtics' point guard, was held to 3 points and 1 assist in 23 minutes.) "We lacked leadership without him, to be honest," Jackson said afterwards. "It was an incredible game. That's a remarkable game."

The timing was perfect. The Lakers were in dire need of sane leadership, and Fisher was the definition of sanity. He liked both O'Neal and Bryant, and served as the perfect buffer. Shaw, Harper, Fox, and Horry were all excellent locker room lawyers, but they were elders. Fisher *was* Bryant and O'Neal. A peer. Three years earlier, he and Bryant had appeared together on LL Cool J's television show, *In the House*. They spent a lot of time talking, commiserating. O'Neal, meanwhile, loved Fisher's desire to dump the ball down low. He was a point guard who knew the value of a dominant big man. What wasn't to like?

With Fisher now running the offense, Los Angeles won 13 of its final 18. And while it would be a stretch to say Bryant changed his ways, he at least temporarily *altered* his ways, averaging 21.4 shots alongside Fisher (as opposed to 29.6 without him).

One factor was health. For one of the rare times in Bryant's life, he was battered and bruised. Throughout the season he had suffered a sprained right ankle, a sore hip, a sore right shoulder, and a sore right pinkie. He actually re-strained his ankle in a March 21 game against the Bucks and had to sit out nine contests — seven of which Los Angeles won. "That," Jackson noted, "made him come face to face with his own vulnerability."

O'Neal called Bryant's time away "the best thing that happened to us." Why? "He's a smart guy," O'Neal recalled. "He's watching us win eight of nine games, he notices that when the ball is moving and everyone touches it, we're a better team. Give him credit. When he came back after his injury, he was a different guy."

Were the Lakers the same juggernaut of a season earlier? Hardly. They wrapped the regular season with a 56-26 mark and entered the playoffs as a No. 2 seed, widely perceived to be crippled by petulant infighting and embarrassing skirmishes.

Surely they were in for tough times.

"If you had to bet," said Fox, "you probably weren't betting on us."

Mike Penberthy was Allen Iverson.

That sounds sort of weird, doesn't it? Penberthy: the undrafted white kid from Master's College. Iverson: the No. 1 overall pick from Georgetown, cornrows and hip-hop and the projects of Hampton, Virginia.

Mike Penberthy was Allen Iverson? Makes no sense.

Yet in the leadup to the 2001 NBA Finals, with his team about to come face-to-face with a 6-foot, 165-pound guided missile, it was the best Phil Jackson could muster.

Despite the turbulence of a season gone crazy, the Lakers stormed through the playoffs, stomping past an overmatched Portland in a three-game sweep, then stomping past an overmatched Sacramento in a four-game sweep, then stomping past an overmatched San Antonio in a four-game sweep. Now, after wrapping the Spurs series on May 27, they had 10 days to wait for the winner of Milwaukee-Philadelphia to emerge from the Eastern Conference.

The presumption — the ultimately proven-to-be-wise presumption — was that the Lakers would meet the 76ers, a 56-win squad and the No. 1 seed out of the underwhelming Eastern Conference. Top to bottom, Coach Larry Brown's team was somewhere between solid and okay. The roster was largely an ode to so-so journeymen and so-so future journeymen. Aaron McKie, the shooting guard and NBA's Sixth Man of the Year award winner, had averaged a career-high 11.6 points during the regular season, and Jumaine Jones, the small forward, checked in at 4.7 points per game. Tyrone Hill, an able rebounder and defender at power forward, was a 9.6-points-per-game scorer, and the bench relied heavily on the contributions of Eric Snow, Raja Bell, Kevin Ollie, and Matt Geiger. Try recognizing any of those men in a shopping mall.

Philadelphia's starting center was the 7-foot-2 Dikembe Mutombo, beginning the downside of his career. A solid player, an excellent shot blocker, the league's Defensive Player of the Year. But a concern? Against O'Neal? No.

What they did have, however, was Iverson (as described by *Sports Illustrated*'s Phil Taylor: "six feet of scar tissue").

In 71 starts, the point guard led the NBA with 31.1 points per game. He also averaged a league-best 2.5 steals and was widely regarded as the quickest player anyone had ever seen. Which, in and of itself, doesn't do the NBA's Most Valuable Player justice. "He was special," said Brown, the longtime head coach. "The most special player I ever had on a team."

Iverson was basketball's knuckler—you thought you saw him, then (*whoosh!*) you didn't. You figured he was contained, then (*dribble, dribble*) he was gone. Though one of the league's smallest men, he somehow found his way past opponents like Bryant, over opponents like O'Neal. "He could play 40 exhausting minutes and still attack you for your life," said Tony Delk, the veteran NBA guard. "He looked for your weakness, and grabbed a knife to carve you up."

The Sixers toppled the Bucks in seven games, and the series against the Lakers would begin on June 6 in Los Angeles. Leading up to the postseason, Jackson had pulled Penberthy aside to say, bluntly, "I don't play rookies in the playoffs, so I'm deactivating you." The news was devastating, but he quickly adapted. In practices, Penberthy was always the opposing team's star point guard—Portland's Damon Stoudamire, Sacramento's Jason Williams, San Antonio's Avery Johnson. Mimicking Iverson was, hands down, the most fun.

He was 21 again, a star at Master's, shooting from every spot on the court. Jackson demanded that Penberthy *be* Allen Iverson, so he became Allen Iverson. "Mike," Jackson said on the first day of Iverson 101, "I'm giving you the green light. Go out there and gun." Penberthy was a whirling dervish of energy and emotion. All the discipline of the triangle could be — *needed* to be — set aside. Day after day, he beat up on Fisher, beat up on Lue, pulled up on Kobe and fired. "Guys would say, 'Mike, you're an amazing player!'" Penberthy recalled. "It was so much fun to break out."

By the time Game 1 arrived, Los Angeles felt ready. Plus, the Sixers were damaged. George Lynch, the onetime Laker, was Philadelphia's starting small forward until he broke his left foot against Toronto. Geiger, Mutombo's backup, had tendinitis in his knees.* McKie's recurring shoulder tendinitis was acting up. Snow was playing on a broken ankle. Mutombo had a broken finger. Iverson's bruised tailbone caused him to miss Game 3 against Milwaukee. Bell, the rookie guard from Florida International, was signed in April as a free agent out of a Miami, Florida, YMCA. He had actually been eating at a Denny's in Sioux Falls, South Dakota, when Philadelphia called with a roster spot. Now, two months later, he would be playing key minutes in the NBA Finals. "We had a lot of guys you'd never heard of, but I thought we could beat them," said Brown. "Things just had to go right."

A capacity crowd of 18,997 entered the Staples Center, and 15 minutes before tipoff, a chant of "Sweep! Sweep! Sweep!" filled the arena. Moments earlier, a clown wearing a Bryant jersey had crossed Figueroa Street toward the arena, carrying a broom. The thinking was understandable — on paper, the Lakers were Goliath, the 76ers David's pinkie toe. Oddsmakers had Los Angeles as 18-to-1 favorites, and the spread on the first game was 11½ points — "against a [Lakers] team that brings a 19-game winning streak and SUV-loads of confidence into the opener," wrote the Associated Press's Chris Sheridan.

Iverson dug the sounds of arrogance; of presumptuousness. "Sweep! Sweep! Sweep!" was symphonic to a man who, one day earlier, had told the assembled media, "We're supposed to come to this series, get swept and go home for the summer, I guess. Takes a lot of pressure off us." He also loved how Harper said that Lue, Los Angeles's backup point guard and a man who would be trying to shadow the Philadelphia star through-

---

* Years later, Brown told Kent Babb, the noted Iverson biographer, that Geiger's injury "was bullshit." He considered the center more lazy than hurt.

out much of the series, may well be the fastest man on the court. *Tyronn Lue?* Who the hell was Tyronn Lue? Iverson read the quotes in the *Philadelphia Inquirer* while on the toilet, and emerged enraged. "He was like 'It's on,'" McKie said.

Los Angeles jumped out to a 16–5 first-quarter lead, and all the predictions seemed prophetic. But Iverson did not care. He drove left, he spun right, he spewed trash talk toward Fisher and Bryant, he hit shots humans don't hit. His 30 points at halftime came on but 11-of-23 shooting, and it mattered not a penny. Bryant's nonstop chucking nearly ruined the Lakers; Iverson's nonstop chucking *made* the 76ers. Philadelphia led 56–50 at the half and extended it to 73–58 with 5:23 left in the third quarter. "You're getting outcoached!" Tex Winter screamed at Jackson along the bench. "You're getting outcoached!" Los Angeles ultimately battled back, and Lue — inserted for Fisher with his team down big — did a masterful job. A man who'd averaged just 12.3 minutes per game during the regular season was Elmer's Glue. Wrote Kent Babb: "Lue, nipping and grabbing, pushing Iverson away from the ball and staying in his way, was like a persistent gnat in Iverson's face." In 22 minutes of Lue time, Iverson was held to 10 points. At the end of regulation, the game was tied at 94, and in overtime Los Angeles built a quick 5-point lead. "I really thought we were going to win," said Pat Croce, the 76ers' owner, who was sitting courtside. "So to watch it all fade away . . ."

The MVP took over. With the Lakers up one and 1:19 remaining, Iverson hit a three, giving his team a 101–99 lead. Moments later, following an errant pass from Fox to O'Neal, Iverson received the ball from Bell on the right side of the key. Lue trailed close behind, like a mouse following a peanut butter trail, and Iverson took one dribble toward the baseline, pulled back, and fired a 16-foot jumper. As the ball fell through the net, Lue tripped over Iverson's feet and fell, butt first, onto the hardwood. In a slice of time that belongs frozen in Philadelphia sports lore, Iverson looked toward the Lakers' bench and took two dramatic, knee-to-belly-button steps over his fallen adversary. It screamed: *Who's my bitch?* "The whole game, people sitting near me were talking all sorts of garbage," said

Croce. "When Allen stepped over Lue, I stood up and turned to [actress and Laker fanatic] Sharon Stone, who was loud and near me, and said, 'In your face, Sharon! In your face!'"

The Sixers won, 107–101, and Iverson's 48 points on 18-for-41 shooting were an ode to resiliency, to never surrendering, to a gang of ragamuffins toppling a den of superstars.

"We've been in different wars, like, all season," Iverson said afterwards. "We got heart. We gonna play with that first. Play with talent second."

Translation: The Philadelphia 76ers were here to win.

Reality: The Philadelphia 76ers had no chance of winning.

They just didn't, and over the next four games Los Angeles sort of figured out an approach toward its game-yet-overmatched rival. Namely, let Iverson score his 100 points and dare anyone else to shoot the ball. Years later, Brown bemoaned the absence of Lynch, suggesting that with his presence Philadelphia was a different team. But it was wishful thinking — one doesn't stop an in-the-making dynasty with a journeyman 8.4-points-per-game scorer. The Lakers took Game 2 at home, 98–89, behind Bryant's 31 points and O'Neal's 20 rebounds, then moved to Philadelphia, where the third and fourth games were both fairly easy Laker triumphs. "What I'm starting to feel like now," Iverson said after a 100–86 Game 4 loss, "is that the way to beat those guys is to really blow them out to have a chance. And the way things are going, that's just not going to happen."

He was right.

On June 15, on the court of Philadelphia's First Union Center, the Lakers finished off the series with a punishing 108–96 win. Iverson went down fighting, and his 37 points led all scorers, but the outcome was a foregone conclusion.

Shortly after the buzzer sounded and Iverson went out of his way to hug his combatants (even Lue), O'Neal found himself strolling down a back hallway, cradling his second-straight Finals MVP trophy in his arms. The air was filled with a sweet scent, a by-product of the bottles of Dom Pérignon that had been popped and poured in the locker room. The Lakers had gone 15-1 in the playoffs. *Fifteen. And. One.*

"Smell that?" said O'Neal, who averaged 33 points and 15.8 rebounds in the five games. "That's what winning smells like."

Off in a side room, Jackson and his four assistant coaches were smoking cigars and embracing a moment of quiet contentment. Without warning, the door opened and in walked J.R. Rider — the forgotten (and chronically late) faded superstar. He had been deactivated for the postseason, glued to the bench for each game in a suit and dress shoes. Now, surrounded by celebratory excesses, he was looking for a private place to cry. Instead, he was face-to-face with the man who had marginalized him.

"I congratulated Phil and left," Rider recalled in 2018. "A personal dream of mine had been to win a championship, and it wound up being the lowest moment of my career, maybe my life. The guys tried telling me I was a part of it, but I knew I wasn't. Kobe was huge, Shaq was huge. What did I do? I sat there like a loser."

All these years later, has he worn the ring?

"Never," he said. "Never, never, never. It's barely mine."

11

The Coaching Job

Kobe Bryant is a fucking psychopath."

The sentiment is spoken in 2018, 17 years removed from the last time Paul Murphy Shirley, 6-foot-10, 230-pound forward out of Iowa State, wore the uniform of the Los Angeles Lakers. But even with the passage of time — with a professional basketball career that took him from (take a deep breath) Panionios to Yakima to Atlanta to Joventut to Kansas City to Chicago to Kazan to Phoenix to Beijing to Menorca to Unicaja — he vividly recalls his three weeks in camp with the two-time defending champions.

"We were in Hawaii," said Shirley. "Which is amazing, because who doesn't love Hawaii? But Kobe Bryant . . ."

A pause.

"I mean — 'psychopath' is the word I intentionally choose."

There is an accompanying story, Shirley assures you. "A pretty good one." After a two-year hiatus, Phil Jackson's squad was indeed back in paradise, once again holding its camp inside a gymnasium on the University of Hawaii campus. As always, there had been some tinkering to the roster, but nothing excessive. J.R. Rider was (praise Jesus) gone, as were Horace Grant, Ron Harper, and Tyronn Lue. Mitch Richmond, a six-time All-Star shooting guard now in his 14th season, was added for depth, and former Seattle center Jelani McCoy, former Spurs forward Samaki Walker, and veteran guard Lindsey Hunter were also brought into the fold. Mainly, though, it was familiar faces mixed in with a bunch of long-shot invitees: Dennis Scott, the veteran outside shooter/Shaquille O'Neal pal; Isaac Fontaine, the guard out of Washington State (whom Jackson repeatedly referred to as "Isaiah" — never a good sign); Dickey Simpkins, marginal Chicago Bulls bencher; Peter Cornell, once-upon-a-time Loyola Marymount center.

And Paul Shirley.

Of the 20 men in camp, he was the least likely to stick. Yet to Bryant — 23, newly married, a three-time All-Star — Shirley was a threat. Because, in the world of Kobe Bryant, every basketball player was a threat. They were trying to take what was his. They were trying to dent his status. They were trying to crush his legacy.

"Honestly," Shirley recalled, "I was just trying to make the damn team."

One afternoon, in a full-court scrimmage between five men wearing purple singlets and five men wearing gold, Shirley drove toward the hoop and put up a flimsy layup attempt that fluttered toward the rim. From behind, Bryant swooped in and — *pop!* — swatted the basketball behind the baseline. An off-balance Shirley crashed to the ground, and Bryant straddled over his crumpled corpse while staring down toward his pelvic region, both hands pointing at his groin. "Get that fucking weak shit out of here!" Bryant screamed. "You fucking pussy!"

Shirley was neither scared nor insulted. He was merely confused. "Kobe was such a bully," Shirley recalled. "But in a sadistic way, not a good-natured, normal way. Almost like he was play-acting the part. I remember I was at the free throw line once, and he tried calling me 'French Lick,' after Larry Bird. But it made no sense — I'm not from Indiana, I'm from Kansas. He had zero authenticity. It was as if he saw himself in a movie, writing his own dialogue. The kid was a tremendous talent, but I'd rather be me than him. He was embarrassing."

Shirley wasn't alone in his confusion over Bryant. McCoy, straight off three seasons in Seattle, recalled his new teammate as coming "from a vindictive place. Some guys just need to go home and smoke a fucking joint." Cornell was a 1998 college grad, and in the three ensuing seasons he had bounced around to a couple of NBA camps, and enjoyed stints in a handful of smaller leagues. On the night before the first practice in Hawaii, the Lakers treated all the players and coaches to a fancy dinner. At one juncture the rookies were asked to stand and introduce themselves, so Shirley said his hellos, Fontaine said his hellos . . .

"This was my third camp, so I didn't say anything," recalled Cornell. "And Kobe said, 'What about the big fella over there? You're a rookie.' It was just to humiliate me. He was such a dick. Such an absolute dick."

On another occasion, Jackson interrupted a practice and told the players to hydrate. As Bryant leaned against the base of the goal, Cornell walked toward a cooler to grab a bottle of Gatorade.

"Hey rook!" Bryant yelled — making certain everyone heard him. "Rook, you know I need a Gatorade! Grab me one!"

Cornell picked up a 12-ounce bottle of red Gatorade. He extended to hand it to Bryant.

"Come on, rook!" he said. "I need a big bottle!"

Cornell returned to the cooler and dug out a 32-ounce Gatorade. It was red.

"Rook!" Bryant yelled. "Rook! You must not realize I only drink orange!"

To O'Neal, defender of the little man, enough was enough.

"Yo, Kobe!" he hollered. "Chill the fuck out!"

That ended that.

Bryant had arrived at camp with bodyguards. Multiple bodyguards. One to stand in the hotel lobby, near the elevator. Another to stand by the elevator bank of his floor. A third to stand in front of Bryant's door. "Sometimes he had a bodyguard positioned on the hotel roof," said Fontaine. "I'm no security expert, but I don't think snipers were after Kobe Bryant." O'Neal found this delightful in all its egomaniacal splendor. "Kobe," he said on an early bus ride, "why the fuck do you need three bodyguards? Or even one bodyguard? Who exactly is coming to kill you?"

"He was just wacko," said Cornell. "You're in Hawaii. You need a bodyguard?"

Such was life as a Laker in 2001–02, a season unlike any other. Bryant's out-of-control ego was more out of control than ever before, and would culminate in the now infamous fight with Samaki Walker on the Cleveland bus trip. O'Neal, approaching his 30th birthday and happy as ever to devote his off-season to cookies, tropical drinks, and naps, reported looking like the Kool-Aid Man, not a superstar center. "He had said he was going to come in at 300 pounds," recalled Mark Heisler of the *Los Angeles Times*. "He literally came back weighing closer to 400." Three key returnees — Rick Fox (32), Robert Horry (31), and Brian Shaw (35) — were on the wrong side of the aging fence, and the draft had yielded a grand total of zero players.

This would be the greatest challenge of Phil Jackson's career.

It would also be his greatest success.

The knock on Jackson throughout his first 11 years as a head coach had always been stated along the lines of "Well, who couldn't win with those players?" Which could be expanded to: "You had Michael Jordan, Scottie Pippen, and Dennis Rodman in Chicago, and you have Shaquille O'Neal and Kobe Bryant in Los Angeles. You *were supposed to win . . .*"

Jackson did, in fact, boast a buffet of transcendent future Hall of Famers. Yet any coach worth his or her salt will tell you that talent is only a small part of what makes a team work. Dating back to his time with Albany of the Continental Basketball Association, Jackson's gift had been an ability to somehow convince his men to stay on the same page. Even when they hated one another. Even when times were particularly tough. Yes, he deserved credit for having the wherewithal to let Tex Winter implement his triangle offense. And, yes, his demeanor was agreeable and placating. But the Lakers functioned as a unit even when all logic suggested they shouldn't have functioned as a unit; when the two superstars detested each other; when the supporting cast was old; when Hollywood's temptations had ruined far less impressive collections of talent. "He was an absolute master of tweaking and poking," said Fox. "Every single day he was poking somebody, getting someone in line. There was always a bigger meaning behind his methodology. But you had to look for it." In particular, Fox recalled the team's ritualistic "Indian runs" — the players lined up and ran laps around the gym, and the person at the rear needed to sprint to the front. "We're all made to be so competitive, so we're sprinting as hard as we can, then we're at the front of the line, running insanely fast," Fox recalled. "But we realized eventually we needed to work together, pace ourselves together, be a unit. Not rocket science, but a very Phil approach."

It didn't take Jackson long to see that this season — and this team — would be a greater challenge than the previous two. The obvious issue was O'Neal, who (to the organization's great chagrin) waited until August 29 to undergo surgery to relieve pain in his left toe, and would spend much of the season battling the malady. (He wound up appearing in just 67 games.) But it was more than that. The splashiest addition into the fold was Richmond, with his dead-eye outside shot and 22.2-points-per-game lifetime scoring average. Yet the six-time All-Star was now 36 and had appeared in just 37 games with Washington in 2000–01 because of a hyperextended knee. "I knew I could contribute," Richmond recalled. "I reported in great shape, I still had my skills. I was ready."

What quickly became apparent was that the Richmond who'd gained fame and fortune from his high-flying days alongside Tim Hardaway and Chris Mullin in Golden State was a shell of his old self. He could still shoot, but not quite as well. He could still move, but minus the burst. "He was thick-legged," recalled Jackson. "So it took him four or five minutes off the bench to get going, and all the while you have Kobe sitting so Mitch can get his body warm. I didn't know what I could do with him."

He was forced to look elsewhere. Throughout the first two championship seasons, Los Angeles fans would gaze toward the bench and know all was right in the world when Devean George's rear end was planted to it. He was a guy you'd see on the court only if (a) the score was lopsided or (b) a whole bunch of Lakers were in deep foul trouble.

Back in 1999, when the Lakers used the 23rd pick in the first round to select a Division III forward no one had ever heard of, the reaction was one of modest optimism. Jerry West, after all, had earned the benefit of the doubt, so if he said Devean George would be something special, who were the team's loyalists to argue?

Only, well, Devean George wasn't something special. At least he didn't seem to be. Not all that long ago he had been a nobody 6-foot-2 senior guard at Benilde–St. Margaret's high school in St. Louis Park, a Minneapolis suburb. Though he averaged 25 points and 8 rebounds as a senior, the competition was a joke, and he was ignored by every major college and nearly every minor college.

He had recently seen his brother's best friend, a boy named Byron Phillips, get killed in a drive-by shooting, and all he wanted was to escape a tough neighborhood. But how does one escape when nobody knows of his existence?

Dave Johnson, his high school coach, started making calls on his player's behalf, and reached out to Augsburg College, his alma mater, where a man named Brian Ammann ran the program. "He told me he had a guy I absolutely had to recruit," Ammann recalled. "I get these calls all the time, and mostly they're nonsense. But he was very insistent." One line in particular caught Ammann off guard. "Brian," Johnson told him, "he's only 6-foot-2. But he's about to grow four inches."

What?

"Seriously, he has an older brother who sprouted up. Trust me—it'll be worth it."

Ammann offered George a spot, and immediately regretted it. His new player—"*maybe* 140 pounds soaking wet," Ammann recalled—was stubborn, obnoxious, and overly confident for his talent level. So the coach stuck him on Augsburg's junior varsity team, then watched as George scored 40 points in each of his first two games.

Because Division III schools do not have athletic scholarships, George's parents were paying most of the $20,000 annual tuition. His mother, Carol, owned a beauty salon and took a second job cleaning an airport. His father, Eddie, worked at Cato's Shrine, a neighborhood nightclub, and also drove a truck for a construction firm.

George's freshman year was forgettable, and his sophomore season hardly much better. The team took a trip to Germany to play a series of exhibitions, and George was physically beaten down by the bigger, tougher opponents. They would elbow his ribs, punch his head, crunch him on picks. George would all but slink from the court toward a screaming Ammann. "Where's your heart?" he yelled. "Do you even know the difference between injury and pain? Do you want this?"

Then, as Johnson had promised, he grew.

In the blink of an eye, Augsburg College was home to a 6-foot-6 athletic phenom with a 7-foot-1 wingspan. Suddenly he was being beckoned by Division I programs, offering an NBA future one couldn't possibly attain from the Division III level. *Transfer and we can make your dreams come true. Transfer and leave the bush leagues behind.* After much debate, George stayed, and as a senior finished third in scoring (27.5 points) and seventh in rebounding (11.3) in Division III while leading the Aggies to the Minnesota Intercollegiate Athletic Conference title.

The Augsburg staff tried getting their star invited to various showcases, but to no avail. Finally, when a player had to drop out of the annual Portsmouth Invitational, a three-day pre-draft camp for prospects, George was granted one of 64 spots. He posted double doubles in his first three games and by the session's end was being besieged by agents looking to add him as a client. Over a seven-day span, he worked out at the facilities of eight different NBA organizations. One of his final appearances was in Los Angeles with the Lakers. Jackson had agreed to coach the team a handful of days earlier, and an early task was to observe George performing alongside Leon Smith, a highly touted prep-to-pros kid out of Chicago's Martin Luther King High.

With Mitch Kupchak and Jackson sitting side by side, George hit his first 15 jump shots and owned the outmatched Smith.

"I thought you said this kid had no pull-up," Jackson said to the general manager.

"Phil, I was under the impression he didn't," Kupchak replied.

Without saying a word to George or Smith, Jackson rose, gathered his possessions, and left the building. "It was weird," George said. The Lakers called a few weeks later and invited George back for a second appearance. His hot shooting continued until Jackson stepped in. "Why don't we stop this," the coach said, "because you're getting really lucky."

"Mr. Jackson," George replied, "this isn't luck. I can shoot the ball this good. I can do other drills if you'd like."

"No, no," Jackson said. "It's luck. I don't need to see this."

When the workout concluded, Ammann received a phone call from Jerry West. ("I'm a stupid Division III coach," he recalled. "And Jerry West is on the phone!")

WEST: Coach, how did you get this kid? Is he a thug?
AMMANN: No.
WEST: Does he have a criminal record?
AMMANN: No.
WEST: There has to be something . . .

There wasn't. Devean George was a late bloomer who fell through the cracks.

Regrettably for West and the Lakers, the buyer-beware factors of selecting a low-level player quickly came into focus. George's first summer league was an utter disaster, so much so that the team considered trading him before every other franchise learned of the non-player at hand. He was clueless when it came to positioning, timing, spacing. "I was overthinking everything," George recalled. "I really believed I could make the leap from small college basketball to playing against guys like Shaq and Kobe. But it's not just a different level. It's a different planet."

George wasn't ready. He spent his first season playing just seven minutes per game, and the next season was largely the same. Some of the freakish athleticism that made him stand out on the Division III level no longer seemed so freakish. Plus, he was assigned the worst adjective one could bestow upon an NBA player: *soft*.

Fox, the owner of the lineup spot George presumed he would one day fill, admitted years later that he'd refused to help the newcomer. "I would beat the shit out of him," Fox recalled. "Remember, I grew up playing for the Celtics. Xavier McDaniel was my teammate. We fought for three years, and he raised me to play angrily. Devean was too nice. We were a bunch of sharks. He was a guppy."

The tone was set early in George's rookie year when, during a trip to Ames, Iowa, for an exhibition game, he was asked by O'Neal to stay after the shootaround for a chat. "He said they wanted to show me something," George recalled. "I was a rookie. I had to listen." One by one, the veteran Lakers surrounded George, ripped off his clothing, duct-taped his hands and mouth, forced him to the ground, and duct-taped his entire body to the court. Then they boarded the bus and left. Generally, the Lakers were a no-hazing operation. Or at least a hazing-lite operation. But this was a special circumstance. George's softness didn't merely make him a ripe target. It made him someone who, to the veteran Lakers, *needed* to be abused and hardened. "Phil was very strict about people not watching our practices, so I was there for a long time," George recalled. "They didn't even know the practice was over." At long last, a maintenance man entered and — to his great shock — saw a 6-foot-8 athletic specimen adhered to the hardwood. "He cut me out, and I got a ride back to the team hotel," George said. "I was naked."

For a team that hazed its newcomers only in the mildest of manners, this was dramatic stuff. But while Bryant would have fought back and thrown punches, and Derek Fisher would have fought back and thrown punches, and Mike Penberthy would have fought back and thrown punches, George meekly accepted his fate.

"He was fragile," O'Neal said. "Looking back, he was terrified of me and Kobe, because Kobe stayed on him and I stayed on him. I wish I'd known he was like that, but I misread him, and I think it hurt his development. He couldn't take it, and he played scared."

Yet now Jackson needed George to emerge. Fisher, who had come of age as a legitimate NBA point guard during the 2001 postseason, was out for three weeks after surgery to repair a stress fracture in his right foot, and the roster looked painfully thin. When the team opened its title defense at home against Portland on October 30, the starting lineup featured O'Neal, Bryant, a 32-year-old Fox, and two unfamiliar journeymen (Hunter at point, Walker at power forward). The bench was George,

McCoy, and a gaggle of residents from the nearby assisted living facility. "Improvising was the only way we could get through the 2001–02 season," Jackson later noted. "Nothing that happened followed any pattern I'd seen before."

With a hobbled O'Neal and a selfish-as-ever Bryant, Los Angeles somehow beat the Blazers, 98–87, then won six more in a row (by an average of 11.5 points) before arriving in Phoenix for a game against the Suns. Though the season was but 18 days old, Jackson hadn't felt his players' body language during the previous day's 98–97 triumph over Houston. Everything just seemed flat and blah. Jackson knew the Lakers were far more talented than the Suns, but he also knew any NBA team could beat any other NBA team on a given night. So when the Lakers were outscored 23–19 in the second quarter, then 32–21 in the third, he . . . watched. He didn't berate. He didn't suspend time. He didn't snarl, pace, whine, mope. Joe Crispin, a rookie guard from Penn State who'd grabbed the final roster spot, was on the bench alongside Hunter, dumbfounded. Where was the panic? "Lindsey," he said to Hunter, "is Phil letting us lose?"

Hunter nodded, the way a veteran would nod. "Yeah," he said. "Might be."

When the game ended with a 95–83 Suns triumph, Jackson stood before the locker room and said, "We didn't show up with the right energy. That was good for us. We needed that."

Crispin, who in 2016 was named the men's head basketball coach at Division III Rowan University, never forgot the lesson. "Sometimes," Crispin said, "a team wins by losing."

Two days later, the Lakers kicked off a nine-game winning streak, leaving Jackson's squad at an NBA-best 16-1 on December 5. For most basketball fans, the success was greeted with the ho-hum-ness of a team that (yawn) always wins continuing to win. But what was transpiring was masterful. Walker, new to the scene after spending the past two seasons under Gregg Popovich in San Antonio, wasn't overly dazzled by the triangle, which he found relatively easy to understand and master. But the way Jackson coached a roster was breathtaking. "There were so many egos, and he worked it," Walker recalled. "It wasn't that people put their egos aside for Phil. They certainly didn't. But he understood how the guys thought and worked, and he just nudged them in positions to succeed. Pop would go at guys. Phil was so cool, he didn't. It was more subtle, but genius."

George, playing significant minutes for the first time in his career, was evolving as a lockdown defender who could run the court alongside Bryant. Walker, a disappointment since leaving Louisville early for the 1996 draft, was a big body, ideal when the Lakers needed to physically challenge stronger clubs. In Fisher's absence, Lindsey Hunter ran the offense with seamless efficiency — a shock even to the coaching staff. Once upon a time, in the summer of 1993, the Jackson State shooting guard was the hot, out-of-nowhere prospect entering the draft. At barely 6-foot-2, he had to make the switch to point guard, and the jump from small college to the professional ranks would be daunting. But when the Pistons grabbed him 10th overall, it was widely believed the franchise had found itself Isiah Thomas's heir apparent. "This is fantastic," Hunter said at his introductory press conference. "I'm like in a dream. And this is just the beginning."

It was the beginning of a fairly ordinary career that saw him spend seven years with the Pistons during what would go down as perhaps the least interesting span in the franchise's history. Like most of his teammates, Hunter was pleasantly mediocre. He played hard, worked doggedly on defense, struggled to shoot better than 40 percent, never fully adapted to passing. He was, in the words of Helene St. James of the *Detroit Free Press*, "shunned as a true point guard," and his 2000 trade to Milwaukee was greeted in Motown with a yawn. When the Lakers sent backup forward Greg Foster to the Bucks for Hunter on June 28, 2001, it was deemed nothing more than garbage for garbage. Perhaps Hunter would stick. Perhaps he would not.

Instead, he excelled. Earlier in the summer, Hunter's younger brother Tommie was killed in a single-car accident after he lost control of his vehicle and slammed into a tree. He was 19, and about to begin his freshman year at Jackson State. Lindsey was home in Raymond, Mississippi, at the time, and when he received the call he rushed to the hospital. Alas, his sibling had already died. Lindsey heard the news and started vomiting. Just a few hours earlier they had been shopping for a Father's Day gift for Lindsey Sr., then running the stairs at Jackson State's Memorial Stadium. When Tommie went out that night to see his girlfriend, he was wearing his brother's shirt. This wasn't merely the death of a relative. Tommie had been like a son. What Lindsey did, Tommie aspired to do, too.

The result was a darker, more serious Lindsey Hunter. He came to Los Angeles not with a chip on his shoulder but with a weight on his heart. "I'm different [now]," Hunter told the *Los Angeles Times*. "It's not like I want to be different. But, it's a struggle. Eventually, I'll get better. But there's nothing I can do about it. Of course, I talked to counselors, to other people, trying to get some perspective about it. I can't understand it. That helps a little, but they all tell me the same thing, that you've got to go through what you've got to go through."

No one knew what to expect, especially when Hunter became the starter. But his head-down, be-professional, life-is-more-than-basketball approach to running the team was pitch-perfect. He was happy passing to Bryant, passing to O'Neal, winning or losing (preferably winning, of course), then returning home at day's end to his wife, Ivy, and their three children. When, in the fourth and fifth games of the season, he had back-to-back 16-point gems in wins over Utah and Memphis, he showed no great pleasure. When, a few weeks later, he was held to a single bucket in a whitewashing of the Clippers, he showed no despair. His go-to move — a Grandpa-Stan-at-the-YMCA pump fake that worked every time — was artistic in its simplicity. He didn't need Hollywood or the palm trees. He certainly didn't care whether it was Shaq's team or Kobe's team. "He was the Man," said Crispin. "Lindsey took great care of me as a rookie. He was a leader without attitude or ego."

These Lakers, flawed and prime for a letdown after back-to-back titles, were grittier than before, more likable than before. Despite what one might read in the Bryant-fawning *ESPN The Magazine* (one particularly laughable cover headline: CRACKING KOBE: HOW SHAQ, PHIL, VANESSA AND THE LAKERS BROKE THROUGH), it had nothing to do with the maturation of the star guard, who was more detestable and selfish than ever. When Kobe and Vanessa were married on April 18, 2001, inside St. Edward the Confessor Catholic Church, in Dana Point, no Laker players or coaches were invited. Which surprised no one and relieved most everyone. ("Do you think the guys wanted to go?" said Walker.) They only learned of the event at practice the next day. It was merely Bryant's way.

That same season, when Los Angeles made a trip to the City of Brotherly Love to play the 76ers, Bryant's high school — Lower Merion — announced that it would hold a ceremony to retire the uniform number of its all-time greatest player. Ever since he left for Southern California in 1996, Bryant's relationship with his hometown had been strained. He was viewed as something of a sellout; an inauthentic, Italy-raised suburbanite who could never match the adopted Allen Iverson for grit and hustle. After Game 3 of the 2001 NBA Finals at Philadelphia, he told a fan, "We're going to cut their hearts out," and the comment was received badly. ("What's he supposed to say?" asked Anthony Gilbert, a *Hoop* magazine scribe. "'I grew up there so I'll lay down'?") Eight months later, at the 2002 All-Star Game, also in Philadelphia, he was booed while accepting the MVP trophy, a blow that bled scarlet. As he walked off the floor, Bryant was greeted by Scoop Jackson, the *Slam* magazine writer whose cozy relationships with players crossed the athlete/journalist line. "Scoop, I don't understand it," Bryant said, tears streaming down his cheeks.

Jackson offered a hug. "That's the first time I'd ever seen anything get to him," Jackson said. "That got to him. We were literally standing there for five minutes, and he straightened the fuck up. I was, like, hitting him in the chest and saying, 'Fuck, man, they don't get it. They'll get it one day.'"

Like the All-Star Game, the high school ceremony was a meaningful night. Bryant even invited teammates to attend — the same people who weren't asked to his wedding. Those who showed up were struck by the awkwardness of it all. Brian Shaw, the veteran guard, sat in the gymnasium bleachers alongside Samaki Walker and said, "You're about to see some real shit now."

"What do you mean?" Walker said.

"Just watch," Shaw replied.

Joe and Pam Bryant entered the building and sat to their son's right. Vanessa Bryant entered the building and sat in front of her husband. Cool glances were shot between one and the other. The event was uncomfortable from start to finish — a handful of people honoring a man they didn't much care for. "It was sad," Walker recalled. "Kobe told me that a bunch of guys from high school reached out to him before that trip to see if he wanted to hang out. Kobe said to me, 'Are they stupid? Are they silly? Why do they think I'd hang out with them?' That tells you everything."

None of it mattered. Truly, none of it. O'Neal was a father of three children, and with age and maturity he appeared genuinely less interested in the back-and-forth clubhouse minutiae. Jackson had often gone hard on Bryant during his first two seasons, but this year there seemed to be some surprising on-court growth. The coach pulled back. "I'm not going to say he turned 180 degrees," Jackson said in December. "But there's certainly been a 90-degree swing of character." Though Richmond averaged only 11 minutes and 4.1 points per game, his presence was important. He realized early on that the majority of his time would be spent on the bench, yet he continued to practice hard, cheer hard, encourage and educate. He proved his worth during a February journey to New York when Jelani McCoy, frustrated by inactivity and limited court time (he averaged 5 minutes in 21 appearances), chose a team practice inside a Manhattan gymnasium to vent. A California kid who starred at UCLA, McCoy joined the Lakers expecting glory and sunshine. Instead it was the misery and humiliation of friends asking, "What the hell happened to you?"

"So we were scrimmaging there in the Big Apple, and enough was enough," McCoy recalled. "I'd gone out the night before, and I was still vibrating from the partying. I started abandoning the triangle. Just — fuck that offense. Fuck it. I was tearing everybody's ass up who played my position. Madsen. Slava Medvedenko. I was talking shit, going up and down the court, blocking shots, goaltending."

Put differently, McCoy was acting like a jerk.

"Yeah," McCoy said years later. "I really was."

Richmond, a member of McCoy's squad during the practice, leaned over toward his teammate during a water break. "Young fella," he said, "you've gotta chill."

"Fuck that!" McCoy bellowed. "This ain't my fault! Ain't nothing wrong with me! They have me fucked up, sitting on the bench, acting like I can't play this motherfucker!" He returned to the court and continued to perform with a wild-eyed, Lyle Alzado–esque intensity. It was one of those moments when Jackson, instead of inserting himself or banishing McCoy to the team hotel, kicked back to see what would unfold. As soon as the practice wrapped, Richmond sat McCoy down in the corner. This would not be a friendly chat. This was principal to truant. "Listen," Richmond said, "you fucked up. And you didn't just fuck up a little. You *really* fucked up. Phil is just testing you . . ."

"Well," McCoy said, "let him test me, because I'm fu —"

"No," Richmond said. "You're smarter than this. If you ever want to vent, just walk to me. But don't go about displaying your skills in that way. It only makes you look like an idiot."

Years later, McCoy considered it to have been the most important lesson of his career.

"Great teams need leaders," he said. "Mitch was the best leader."

12

Kings Without a Crown

The Los Angeles Lakers won 58 times in 2001–02, and from both a statistical and a clinical standpoint, all seemed well and good. O'Neal's toe injury healed, and he averaged 27.2 points and 10.7 rebounds per game. Bryant played his best basketball to date, as his 25.2 points per game and career-high 5.5 assists attested to. Fisher missed 12 games but came back to sport a second-best scoring season (11.2 points per game) and establish himself as one of the West's better point guards. Jackson pulled out every tool in his kit to keep things cohesive, and it mostly worked.

They were a good team.

A strong team.

A tested team.

But — if we're being honest here — the 61-win Sacramento Kings were better.

And it wasn't all that close.

The idea itself was preposterous. Or, put differently: Were a Kings fan from the early to mid-1990s to wake from a coma and be told that his organization was superior to the Los Angeles Lakers, he'd either laugh, cry, or wonder what drugs had been injected to propel Mike Peplowski and Duane Causwell to NBA superstardom. "Everything about that franchise was unstable," said Mitch Richmond, a King from 1991 to 1998. "We were the dysfunctional laughingstock of the league."

Ever since relocating from Kansas City in 1985, the Kings had served as a regular pro sports sinkhole. Over 17 seasons, they finished above .500 four times — and the franchise hadn't won a title since 1951, dating back to its time in Rochester, New York. If it wasn't the awful drafting (the team used the No. 1 overall selection in 1989 on Louisville center Pervis Ellison), it was the awful trades (Otis Thorpe to the Rockets for Rodney McCray and Jim Petersen in 1988 still stings). The low point (of endless low points) came during the 34-win 1996–97 season, when the franchise was prepared to relocate to Nashville before receiving a last-gasp $70 million loan from the city.

"You wondered sometimes whether we even belonged in the NBA," said Walt Williams, a Sacramento small forward in the early 1990s. "Nothing ever went right."

Almost nothing. In 1994, the organization hired Geoff Petrie, the professorial former Princeton standout who had once starred for six seasons with the Trail Blazers, as its new general manager. The team all but begged him to take the position, and when Petrie told Jim Thomas, the owner, that a major roster upheaval would be implemented ("Like, a *major* upheaval, Jim. *Major*"), he was met with a solemn nod and an open checkbook.

Over the next few years, Petrie dug the franchise out from under the rubble of hoops hell. His debut draft yielded an excellent young power forward, Brian Grant of Xavier, and a year later the Kings snagged Corliss Williamson, an even better power forward out of Arkansas. The real turnaround commenced in 1998 — first with the trade of Richmond (and Thorpe) to Washington for a 6-foot-9 forward/center named Chris Webber, then with the hiring of Rick Adelman as head coach. In his five NBA seasons, one with Golden State and four more with the Bullets/Wizards, Webber had become known as a prolific performer whose moodiness, pettiness, and inconsistencies could ruin an organization. His most infamous gripe came when he went to the D.C. media to complain about the food served on the team's chartered flights ("You got this little thing right here with beef on it. I don't eat beef") and a sincere if misguided gripe turned into a neon museum exhibit for the modern coddled athlete. In hindsight, though, that was nothing. During his time in the nation's capital, Webber was arrested on marijuana possession and assault charges and went through a separate grand jury investigation into a sexual assault complaint. In breaking news of the transaction, an Associated Press piece led with "The Washington Wizards yesterday traded a problem child for two veteran gentlemen."

Petrie, however, was willing to take the risk. Webber was 25, gifted, and the type of star a starless franchise needed but never obtained. Desperate times called for desperate measures.

"Chris actually had some real reservations about coming to Sacramento," said Petrie. "We were coming off of a 27-win season, and he didn't know if we'd ever have enough to contend. It took some salesmanship to get him to give us a chance."

Webber was immediately the most talented big man the franchise had ever employed, and shortly thereafter Petrie did himself a huge favor by signing Vlade Divac, the former Lakers center, to a six-year, $62.5 million contract. At 7-foot-1 and 243 pounds, Divac was a legitimate presence in the middle and — just as important — stood out as the league's best locker room leader. Having spent the first two years of his career playing alongside Magic Johnson in Los Angeles, Divac possessed a master's degree in team cohesion, along with the quirky unpredictability of a man who smoked half a pack of cigarettes a day. (Really, he smoked *half a pack* of cigarettes per day.) "Vlade was the most beloved player I ever covered," said Ailene Voisin, the longtime *Sacramento Bee* columnist. "He had no ego. He didn't need to score, didn't need the attention. He just wanted to win. I'm not sure anyone helped Chris mature more than Vlade."

Piece by piece, Petrie cobbled together a potential powerhouse. He sent Jason Williams, the flashy yet limited point guard known as "White Chocolate," to the Grizzlies for the steady, productive Mike Bibby and added the best defensive shooting guard in the league, Doug Christie, in a deal with Toronto. Peja Stojaković, a small forward from Croatia, was drafted with little fanfare in 1996 (one pick after the Hornets took Kobe Bryant), and by 2000 he was a sharpshooting gunner averaging 20 points per game.

"We were becoming something special," recalled Bibby. "You could see it all happening. There was a time when nobody in the NBA wanted to go to Sacramento. But when my agent asked me where I'd want to go were I traded, it was the first place I mentioned. They had all those pieces, they played the right way. It was basketball heaven."

In 1998–99, Adelman's first season in Sacramento, the Kings went 27-23, a huge boon to a franchise that rarely won. The next year, their record improved to 44-38, then 55-27. Now, with an NBA-best 61 victories, Sacramento (pop. 407,018, with both a Target and a Walmart) was the center of the basketball universe. The Kings graced the covers of *Sports Illustrated, ESPN The Magazine, Slam*. Their players were landing endorsement deals, and for a nation of people who hated the *fucking* (their word) Los Angeles Lakers, they were deemed sports saviors. In Sacramento, the Lakers were even worse than the Cowboys or the Yankees. They were the organization that owned the state; that dwarfed the Kings the way a tidal wave dwarfs a puddle. For far too long, the Lakers had been Magic and Kareem, the Kings Jim Les and Wayman Tisdale. The Lakers were palm trees and the Beverly Wilshire. The Kings were strip malls and Wendy's. "Los Angeles had Jerry West, Kirk Gibson, Magic Johnson," wrote Laura Loh in the *Los Angeles Times*. "Sacramento had just the hand-me-down memories of other towns." When, two years earlier, Phil Jackson dismissively referred to Sacramento as "a cow town," residents of the state capital had recoiled — in part because he was speaking truth. When he added another harsh zinger ("I coached basketball in Puerto Rico, where when you won on a visiting floor, your tires were slashed and you might be chased out of town with rocks breaking the windows of your car. I mean, it's a different environment, entirely. You're talking about semicivilized Sacramentans. Those people up there may be redneck in some form or fashion"), it got even worse.

"We were jealous, plain and simple," said Sean Cunningham, a longtime Sacramento sports radio personality. "They had everything, we had nothing. It sucked."

"God, Phil Jackson was such an asshole," said Marcos Bretón of the *Sacramento Bee*. "Such a fucking asshole."

Now it was time for revenge.

The Lakers cruised past Portland in the opening round of the playoffs, just as the Kings cruised past Utah. The semifinals were equally devoid of drama — Los Angeles crushed San Antonio, four games to one, while Sacramento manhandled Dallas in five games. It was two heavyweight fighters preparing for the clash of the century. In the lead-up to their epic 1971 battle at Madison Square Garden, Muhammad Ali battered Oscar Bonavena, Joe Frazier destroyed Bob Foster. They were dust-offs en route to something monumental.

Wrote John Nadel of the Associated Press:

> As preposterous as it sounds, the two-time defending NBA champion Los Angeles Lakers consider themselves underdogs to the Sacramento Kings in the Western Conference finals.
>
> At least that's what several of them are saying.
>
> Don't believe it, because they don't. It's just talk.
>
> And considering the Lakers have won a playoff-record 11 straight road games, 23 of their last 25 postseason games and 19 of the last 20 they've played at Staples Center over the past three months, they're probably quietly offended anyone would consider them underdogs.
>
> Following his third straight clutch fourth-quarter performance against San Antonio on Tuesday night that helped eliminate the Spurs from the best-of-seven series in five games, Kobe Bryant placed the Lakers in an underdog role against the Kings.
>
> But asked if he really felt that way, Bryant paused and replied: "I never feel like an underdog. It's irrelevant. All that matters is how we feel as a unit, how we feel as a team and our togetherness."

The series was scheduled to begin on May 18 in Sacramento, and a couple of days beforehand, Jackson cut out a photograph of Divac and pasted it alongside a quotation assigned to the Kings center from earlier in the season. It read: "If [the Lakers] don't have homecourt advantage this year, they're not going to win it."

Was Los Angeles's coach offended? Not even slightly. Were the words said maliciously? Vindictively? With an ounce of . . . anything? No. They were mere words, an excerpt from an extended quotation. The NBA season was a long one, and players chirping this and chirping that was all part of the drill. Hell, back during his days as a Knicks forward, Jackson was hardly one to hide his feelings about opponents. It was never anything personal. Just chatter. Regardless, he knew a good piece of motivational chum when he saw it. This was stellar.

Jackson hung the piece of paper in O'Neal's locker without uttering a peep. When the Los Angeles big man saw it, he smiled widely. He had recently given himself a new nickname — "the Big Deporter" — for his treatment of foreign-born centers like Divac. Now he spun and told a reporter standing nearby, "I hear and see everything. I'm the police."

Translation: *It's on.*

Despite their status as the West's second-best squad, the Lakers were as cocky as ever. O'Neal, in particular, was convinced that his team was destined to three-peat. The playoffs tended to be a unique span for the big man, who used the time to set aside his jovial regular season self for a more serious, determined entity. Local writers knew O'Neal to be a largely agreeable chap who was prone to bouts of dark moodiness. The postseason brought that out in droves. During the Spurs series, for example, O'Neal had lit into Devean George after a sloppy late-game mistake. He took his sniping from the court to the locker room and — in front of the other Lakers — openly questioned George's manhood. Brian Shaw stepped in, screaming, "If you'd used that much energy blocking out under the boards, you would have gotten yourself a rebound!" O'Neal was in no mood. He attacked Shaw, grabbing his torso and dragging him through the locker room until his knees began to bleed. It was a scary moment that left onlookers shaken. "Shaq was a big puppy," recalled Richmond. "Until the games mattered."

By now the Laker players ran the triangle offense to perfection. Their defensive roles were well defined. None of that needed to be reviewed, sharpened, toned. But what Jackson deemed vital was convincing his players that the Kings were soft tissue paper, likely to wilt under pressure.

For the past year, Sacramento had been America's media darling, piling up easy win after easy win. The narrative was mindless and digestible — finally, an outfit built to stomp the Lakers.

Ten years earlier, Jackson had guided the Chicago Bulls to a six-game Finals series win over the Adelman-coached Portland Trail Blazers, and he knew (truly knew) his rival was no sideline match. Adelman's rotations were strange. His substitution patterns — limited in scope — often made little sense. He went long spans when it seemed he genuinely forgot that certain players were on the bench. His offensive schemes (knockoffs of assistant coach Pete Carril's old Princeton offense) were predictable. The Kings usually had three guards on one side of the court, with Divac and Webber on the other. ("We went through Chris and Vlade," recalled Stojaković. "Those two guys were our point guards, basically.") Time after time after time. Same stuff. Adelman wasn't a bad coach. But he was ordinary; Jackson was a genius. "Rick had some moments," said Lawrence Funderburke, a Kings forward. "But his communication skills were lacking." If you were in the rotation, Adelman was your best friend. If you were on the bench, you failed to exist. Jim Cleamons, the Lakers assistant, scouted the Kings throughout the regular season ("They were *my* team," he recalled), and his No. 1 takeaway was simple and to the point: "I told Phil the truth," Cleamons said. "They were legitimate competition. But I don't think they believed they could beat us. They knew we were the better team. When it came to Sacramento, I could damn near tell you what they had for breakfast in the morning. They were good and I respected them. But were they going to beat us? No."

That said, Jackson knew these Kings weren't the old Kings. Sure, Shaq was far superior to Divac, and Bryant would get his points over the lanky Christie, who relied on sharpened elbows and elastic limbs to blanket rivals. But like few teams in modern history, Sacramento could fill up the basket. A whopping seven members of the roster averaged double figures in scoring, led by Webber (24.5) and Stojaković (21.2) but also including reserves like guard Bobby Jackson (11.1) and Hedo Türkoğlu (10.1). On paper, Sacramento (even without a limited Stojaković, hobbled by a right ankle sprain and out the first four games) was more talented. "We wanted to use our five guys to beat their two," said Carril, referring to O'Neal and Bryant. "We had depth. The question was whether depth could trump superstars."

In the spirit of a long-deprived fan base desperate to exact revenge on a loathed opponent, 17,317 loud, angry, obnoxious, cowbell-clanging fans filled Arco Arena for Game 1, desperate to watch the beginning of the inevitable Laker destruction. The decibel level inside an otherwise forgettable arena (Marcos Bretón of the *Sacramento Bee* called it "an old, ugly barn") was measured as high as 112 — the equivalent of a jet engine. The noise never seemed to die off.

What Kings fans witnessed, however, was a wire-to-wire thumping. The Lakers scored the first — and final — basket of a decisive 106–99 win, and while O'Neal and Bryant combined for 56 points, the brilliance belonged to Robert Horry, who scored 18 points and added 8 rebounds in 42 minutes of play. The 10th-year power forward slotted seamlessly into Adelman's coaching soft spot. The Kings, their leader decided, would dare Los Angeles to beat them with someone other than its two superstars. Swarm O'Neal down low, trap Bryant as he heads toward the hoop, and, um, hope the rest struggle. So Horry — wide open, happy to fire, and confident times 1,000 — went 6 for 12 from the field. Sacramento had no answer. "That clanging heard at the Arco barn wasn't cowbells," wrote Bill Plaschke of the *Los Angeles Times*. "It was escort sirens."

If one needs to grab a bite to eat while visiting Sacramento, he can do far worse than Dawson's Steakhouse, a city dining institution dating back to 1988.

Deemed a prestigious "four diamond" establishment by the American Automobile Association, Dawson's offers such scrumptious delights as pan-seared scallops, pork schnitzel, mushroom ravioli, and lobster bisque.

It also has, for $20, a hamburger.

But not merely any hamburger.

The "Dawson's Burger" features SunFed beef, butter lettuce, heirloom tomatoes, red onions, pickles, secret sauce, and a slice of Fiscalini bandage-wrapped cheddar cheese.

It is thick and delicious and wonderful, and after eating one inside his Hyatt Regency Sacramento hotel room on the night of May 19, 2002 (Dawson's, situated inside the lobby, provided room service for the Hyatt), Kobe Bryant discharged vomit and diarrhea for hours.

And *hours.*

That's why, when he arrived at Arco Arena for Game 2, Bryant's skin was the hue of a moldy green olive. Beads of sweat coated his forehead. He kept a trash can nearby at all moments, just . . . in . . . case . . . he . . .

Blech!

. . . needed to vomit yet again.

When Bryant explained to teammates about the burger and the illness, antennas rose. Had this all been planned? Was it old Red Auerbach-inspired trickery? Mix some ipecac syrup in with the ketchup and eliminate Kobe Bryant? "I was upset and I was mad," said Devean George — convinced of the conspiracy. "At the same time, I was scared. I was like 'Are these people really taking this that seriously where they would put something in this man's food?' I can just remember how he looked. It was nasty."

For all his flaws, Bryant was a fighter. About thirty minutes before tipoff, he detached from the IV drip set up in the training room and jogged/shuffled onto the court. He played a team-high 40 minutes, and while his 9-for-21 shooting wasn't ideal, his 22 points and 6 rebounds were a pronounced "You won't keep me down!" to both Sacramento and America's cheeseburger distributors.

The Kings won, 96–90, riding 21 points from Webber and another 20 from Bibby to overcome O'Neal's 35. But no one with the defending champions was genuinely concerned about falling short. With a healthy Bryant, the thinking went, Los Angeles would have been up 2-0. The Lakers had lost only two home playoff games in two years, and the Kings owned an 0-6 lifetime postseason mark in La La Land. "Honestly, we chalked up the loss to Kobe being sick," said Fox, who scored 10 points in the setback. "We respected them, because you respect other NBA players. But we didn't have the appropriate amount of fear. We won two straight championships. It was, 'Yeah, we've got this. No problem.'"

. . .

The two squads had three full days off before shifting to the Staples Center, and Divac — dean of the Kings and averager of just 11.1 points per game during the regular season — was more important than ever. He had been a young, dumb member of the Lakers team that lost the 1991 NBA Finals to Chicago, and the experience taught him about the thin line between winning and losing. Despite the rival presence of Michael Jordan, Divac believed (truly believed) that Los Angeles was destined to topple the Bulls. When the series was settled in five games, he was crushed.

Now 34, with a couple of gray specks in his beard and 13 NBA seasons under his belt, Divac had the perspective of a basketball sage. He could look around at kids like Webber and Bibby, with their egos and entourages, and remind them how fragile this all was. He urged his younger teammates to jump on the opportunities at hand before they faded away. Divac knew the Lakers would not go easily. "If we lose [Game 3]," he told the media, "we have a one percent chance of winning the series."

In what still goes down as perhaps the greatest game in franchise history, the Kings annihilated the Lakers, leading 32–15 at the end of the first quarter and turning 18,997 spectators into mummies. The score was 52–40 at the half, and with 9:21 remaining, the Kings led by 26. At one point, after he stole an inbounds pass and hit a short jumper, Bibby let loose with a primal yell that could be heard from the highest seats. His team would go on to a shocking 103–90 triumph and a two-games-to-one series lead. "I can't explain it," Bibby said afterwards. "We felt really strong out there, like we could execute our game plan all the time."

"They definitely handed it to us," said Samaki Walker. "There are no ifs, buts or ands about it."

It was panic time. Only it wasn't panic time. Because if there was one thing Phil Jackson didn't do, it was panic. On the day after the defeat, he reported to work wearing a baseball cap that read, "Blah, Blah, Blah," and when asked to assess his team's suddenly iffy fortunes, he grinned, looked at the Associated Press's John Nadel, and said, "We think we're okay." Which was true — he did think the Lakers were okay. They had been here before. Maybe not in such a dire circumstance, but struggling, grasping.

Throughout all the Shaq-Kobe drama, when reporters asked 10,000 variations of "Can your team survive this?," Jackson refused to squirm. He would not squirm now, either. Nor, for that matter, would his players. "Well," Bryant said, "we're not bored now."

"Are you in trouble?" a reporter asked an incredulous Fox.

"Are we in trouble?" he replied. "I immediately think of school, like we're in detention. We'll be in trouble if we continue to do what we've done in the last two games."

Though it went unsaid, the Laker veterans — Fox and Horry, Bryant and O'Neal — doubted Sacramento's resolve. Divac was an experienced player who knew how to handle tough circumstances. But Bibby had spent the majority of his career in Vancouver, land of losers. Webber was a me-first crybaby. Stojaković, expected to return later in the series, had never hit a big shot when it mattered. During Game 3, Adelman repeatedly whined to officials about O'Neal stepping over the line too soon after releasing free throws. The superstar responded — first by dismissively saying, "Rick Adelman's over there taking a shit . . . ," then offering up a hip-hop verse, written for the Kings coach: "Don't cry / Dry your eyes / Here comes Shaq / With those four little guys."

"I think we all doubted whether they had the resolve to take us out," Fox said. "Whether they were strong enough."

Game 4 seemed to answer that question.

Playing once again before a hostile crowd in a hostile city, the Kings jumped out to a (warning: this is not a misprint) 40–20 first-quarter lead. It was a show of brute basketball force — Webber forcefully dunking over Fox, Bibby charging toward the hoop, Hedo Türkoğlu (starting for Stojaković) positioning himself in the corner and nailing two three-pointers. At one point Grant Napear, the Sacramento play-by-play announcer, leaned toward his microphone, listened to the non-sounds of a quiet arena, and said, "This is like the Los Angeles Public Library." Anyone who watched enough basketball could recognize the body language of the Sacramento players. It was confidence. Big, bold, arrogant confidence. "We were the better team," said Bibby. "Not even a doubt. We were the better team."

With 10:18 remaining in the second quarter, a three-pointer from

Christie put Sacramento up 46–22, and when Lindsey Hunter missed his own three on the next possession, all was lost. The Kings were about to take a three-games-to-one series lead, with two more games back home. It was as over as a midway-through NBA game could possibly be. The crowd was dead silent. The team was dead. "We're like, 'Oh, shit, this is for real,'" recalled Fox. "We need to get our shit together."

And then . . .

Well, how to explain it?

The Lakers made a third-quarter run. They outscored the Kings 22–15 in the period and entered the fourth trailing 80–73. What had been discussed ad nauseam seemed to be happening. To be a Laker was to sense the panic along the Sacramento bench. The Kings' verbal chippiness had ceased. Laughs and guffaws morphed into furrowed brows. Adelman urged/begged/pleaded with his men to stay calm, stay composed — "*Do what we always do!*" But they had never been in this position. For all of his basketball accomplishments, Webber, the most important of Kings, was known first and foremost as a choker. That dated back to 1993, when the then–University of Michigan star called a late time-out his team didn't have in a national championship game loss to North Carolina. The blunder's legacy followed Webber like toilet paper on the bottom of his shoe, and still followed him into the 2002 playoffs. Was Chris Webber a winner? No one knew — but when ESPN's Bill Simmons wrote that "watching C-Webb figure out ways to eradicate himself from crunch-time possessions was the most intriguing subplot of the playoffs," few came to his defense.

Christie, the shooting guard, was no better. He had once been a Laker hotshot — a 1992 first-round draft pick by Seattle who was traded to Los Angeles midway through his rookie year. But after his second season, the Lakers grew fatigued. For all his athleticism, Christie was frustratingly erratic — "trying to make the highlight-reel move instead of the high-percentage play," wrote Scott Howard-Cooper in the *Los Angeles Times*. So he was shipped off to the Knicks, and ultimately made his way to Sacramento. He was a good regular season fit, an acrobatic trash talker who would fight at the drop of a hat. But Christie vanished in big moments.

When the Kings needed a shot, he languished in the shadows. It was a problem. Because, on the Lakers, nobody languished in the shadows.

The fourth quarter was, drama-wise, one of the greatest 12-minute stretches in modern sports. With 6:33 remaining, Horry received a pass from Hunter and drained a 23-foot three-pointer to cut the Kings' lead to 88–84. Webber answered with a short jumper, matched seconds later by Bryant's own jump shot. It was hard to tell where this was going, especially when, over the next 2½ minutes, Los Angeles suffered two Bryant turnovers, a George turnover, and an O'Neal miss as Sacramento upped the advantage to 94–86. Türkoğlu, a 23-year-old from Istanbul in just his second season, took a pass from Christie, dribbled twice, and drained a leaner over Bryant with 1:52 left, and the Kings' 96–90 lead felt somewhat secure.

As Fisher dribbled the ball back up the court, Marv Albert and Bob Costas, calling the game for NBC, raved about Sacramento's offense, momentarily forgetting the action before them. That's when Fisher drove toward the paint and whipped the ball to Fox, standing behind the three-point line. The pass was a smidge high, and as Türkoğlu approached, Fox — in one seamless motion — caught the pass, spun his torso, and whipped it to Horry, alone in the corner.

With enough time to tie his shoes, research solar energy, shake Jack Nicholson's hand, and listen to all 42 minutes and 46 seconds of Kiss's *Music from "The Elder,"* the Lakers' best outside shooter bent his knees, leapt into the air, and drained the 24-foot shot, the ball rattling inside the rim. It was now 96–93. The arena, silent less than an hour earlier, was a blizzard of noise, and as Bibby methodically set up the Sacramento offense, no one dared sit.

Over the next 1 minute and 24 seconds, the teams exchanged blows — a Bryant jumper, some O'Neal free throws, some Divac free throws. With 11 seconds remaining, Los Angeles called a time-out, down 99–97 and in possession of the ball. When play resumed, Fox inbounded to O'Neal, who popped out from the paint to the three-point line. He quickly tossed to Horry, who then gave it to Bryant, shadowed by the pesky Christie, whose fluid body was perpetually shape-shifting. The clock read 9 seconds. Bryant sashayed his torso, retreated one and a half steps, then dribbled to the right of Christie and toward the rim. As Divac approached, right arm raised, Bryant let loose the type of off-balance, one-footed, *have-you-learned-nothing?* shot that drove teammates to imbibe. O'Neal grabbed the miss and put up his own quick shot, which somehow hit the side of the rim. Divac, the smartest and wisest of Kings, could have gripped the basketball. He *should* have gripped the basketball. Instead, thinking back to the 1991 Western Conference Finals against Portland, when Magic Johnson snared a final-moment rebound and threw the ball down the court to let the clock expire, he batted it out of the paint, toward the top of the key. That was precisely where Horry awaited behind the three-point line. The ball bounced into his hands and, with less than one second remaining, he fired a straight, flat arrow that . . .

"Horry for the win!" screamed Marv Albert.

Slow motion.

Slow motion.

Slow motion.

Slow motion.

. . . cut through the net.

Albert surely said something. Probably "Yes!" Perhaps "Where's my ferret?" Whatever it was, the explosion of audible joy in the arena banished his words to the dungeon of verbal nothingness. Horry was mobbed by his teammates, Bryant wrapping him in his arms, Walker rubbing his short hair. He had scored 11 of his 18 points in the fourth quarter, when they were needed most. Horry was no Chris Webber and no Doug Christie. After every practice, he and Richmond stayed behind to launch between 200 and 300 three-pointers. He would shoot the ball under any circumstance — "Worst-case scenario, I miss," he later said. "So what?"

"Thank God Robert's mother met his father," O'Neal cracked afterwards. "Or we wouldn't be here."

Bibby and his stunned teammates walked off the court and into the tunnel, silent and dumbfounded. The point guard had played his guts out, totaling 21 points, 4 assists, and one broken heart in 46 exhausting minutes. "I made a good pass," Divac later deadpanned, "to Robert Horry." When he elaborated by referring to the shot as "lucky," Horry was ready for a reply.

"I've been doing that all my career," he said. "So [Vlade] should know — he better read a paper or something."

Had the Kings won, the series was theirs — and they knew it.

Had the Lakers lost, the series was hopeless — and they knew it.

"That was a miraculous finish," Phil Jackson said afterwards. "Sometimes you wonder if you've done everything right and luck falls on your side. That's a victory from the jaws of defeat. That was an incredible finish. And I didn't draw it up like that, so don't ask me."

Marcos Bretón, the *Sacramento Bee* scribe, was staying at a Holiday Inn near the Staples Center. He woke up in the middle of the night, groggy and disoriented. "Did I just dream that?" he asked himself. "Or did the Kings really lose?"

Where was this headed?

No one was entirely sure, and with good reason. It was conceivable that the two teams would return to Sacramento for Game 5 and the traumatized Kings might roll over and die. It was also conceivable that the Lakers — battered, fatigued, older than their rivals — would fall to the floor and collapse into a heap of skin and hair.

By this point in the season (any season), O'Neal's arms and legs were covered with scratch marks and bruises. His feet ached, his head pounded, his hands were swollen. He was both the most physically dominant man in the league and its most attacked. Ice was his constant companion. Heating pads were never out of reach. "He took so much," said George. "Every night."

The prognosticators seemed to suspect that Game 5 would be lopsided — one team feeding on the festering wounds of the other. Hell, every series had to have one or two duds, right? Such was not the case. Los Angeles jumped out to a 33–27 lead, but foul trouble plagued O'Neal, and with 3:22 left in the fourth quarter and Los Angeles up 85–84, he picked up his sixth infraction. Bibby, the Kings' best player throughout the series, drained a 22-footer with 8.2 seconds remaining, and Sacramento's 92–91 nail-biter placed them one game away from a trip to the Finals.

Afterwards, Jackson and his players fumed about the officiating, which they thought lopsided toward Sacramento. Some of the fouls called on O'Neal seemed phantom in nature. Webber's physical play hadn't drawn whistles. On the last possession of the game, Bryant released an errant jump shot as Kings guard Bobby Jackson yanked his jersey from his shorts.

"I'm pretty sure I did foul him," Jackson admitted a decade later.

"You can't pull a guy's shirt off and it not be a foul," Fox said afterwards. "But in this league, a lot of that is left alone down the stretch."

The words would prove haunting.

The sixth game was slated for May 31 in Los Angeles, and the Kings were once again on a high. They possessed two shots to dethrone a wounded champion and collectively assumed it would happen ASAP. "I thought the series was over, just the way we were playing and how everything was rolling," Bibby recalled. "Going into Game 6, we were unbeatable, really."

That night, the telephone in O'Neal's house rang at 2:30. He was fast asleep, infant daughter Amirah resting atop his torso, and the noise stirred him from his slumber. A 2:30 a.m. call meant emergency. *Was someone sick? Dead? Was there an accident of some sort? His mom? His sisters?*

"Hello?" a groggy O'Neal said.

"Yo, Shaq. It's me — Kobe."

Um . . .

"Big fella," Bryant said.

"Yeah," O'Neal replied. "What's up?"

"I need you tomorrow," Bryant said. "Let's make history."

Click.

O'Neal wasn't the type of person who required pep talks. Especially from Kobe Bryant. And — in normal circumstances — it would be notably bizarre for his young teammate to randomly call in the wee hours. Or, truly, any hours. But this *felt* different. *Heavier.* The season had been a rough one, and now the Kings — suddenly cocky, arrogant, disrespectful — were primed to take Los Angeles out. It didn't feel right.

The next afternoon, the Shaquille O'Neal who arrived at the Staples Center was clear-eyed and intense. He told Phil Jackson to feed him the rock, then feed him the rock again. He was fed up with Divac's nonstop flopping. He was fed up with Scot Pollard, the backup center, taking injurious shots when the refs looked away. "Give me the ball," he said. "Ride me."

Much like in the previous engagement, Los Angeles opened Game 6 with O'Neal (11 points) and Bryant (9 points) teaming up to give the Lakers a 28–26 first-quarter lead. But also as in the previous engagement, Sacramento's players didn't care. The loud fans didn't bother them. Bryant's trash talk didn't bother them. They fought back to snag a 56–51 halftime advantage, and at the end of the third quarter the teams were deadlocked at 75.

And then three new NBA stars emerged onto the scene. Their names:

- Dick Bavetta
- Ted Bernhardt
- Bob Delaney

They were the night's officials.

Years later, after the sweat and blood of the evening had vanished, a disgraced former NBA referee named Tim Donaghy was charged with fixing some of the games he'd officiated. On June 10, 2008, his attorney filed a court document that explained how Donaghy had learned, among other things, that two of the referees attempted to tilt Game 6 in Los Angeles's direction, a covert effort to give the NBA another night of moneymaking action. Read the brief: "Tim knew Referees A and F to be 'company men,' always acting in the interest of the NBA, and that night, it was in the NBA's interest to add another game to the series."

"Sacramento had the best team in the league," Donaghy said in 2017. "But the referees/league didn't allow the better team to win."

Was Donaghy, a man as trustworthy as a street-corner huckster, telling the truth? Unlikely. But that many believe him speaks to the hideousness of the referees' work. What occurred over the course of the game's final 12 minutes was the most lopsided officiating anyone had ever seen. First, after playing just 11 minutes, Pollard fouled out. Then, toward the end of regulation, Divac fouled out, too. With three minutes remaining and the Kings up 92–90, Webber caught the ball on the left elbow and, facing the basket, drove on Horry. His floater fell through the hoop, but it was nullified because Sacramento's star was deemed to have charged into Horry with his left shoulder. It was preposterous — a feather running over a brick. "This," said NBC's Bill Walton, "is a terrible call."

A few possessions later, Bryant scooted baseline past Christie and had his shot swatted away by a soaring Webber. Yet instead of the Kings taking possession, Christie was called for a phantom foul.

The worst transgression came with 12.6 seconds left, when the Lakers were up 103–102 and inbounding the ball. As Horry stood along the baseline, looking to make a pass, Bryant charged in from the foul line and pummeled Bibby, slamming his right elbow into the point guard's nose. Delaney observed this from inches away. It could not have been more obvious had Bryant been dressed as a fully padded Mark Gastineau, but the foul was called — *on Bibby*. "You're watching Mike get absolutely plastered in the face by Kobe," said Pollard, "and it's a foul on Mike Bibby. And you're just sitting there, trying to laugh it off." Blood streamed from Bibby's nose. He withered in pain on the floor. It was an NFL-level tackle, violent and delivered with bad intentions. "Kobe Bryant," said an incredulous Walton, "*ran over* Mike Bibby to get that ball."

Moments later, as the Kings' bench pleaded with Bavetta and Bibby had gauze shoved into his left nostril, Bryant sank two free throws, giving the Lakers a controversial 106–102 win. Los Angeles attempted 27 free throws in the fourth quarter, compared with 9 for Sacramento. With Pollard and Divac handcuffed and sent to the bench, O'Neal tallied 41 points and 17 rebounds. Wrote ESPN's Simmons: "Rumors that David Stern wanted to pull a Vince McMahon and declare himself 'The special guest referee' for this game prove unfounded."

No one with the Kings had the energy to laugh.

• • •

There was a seventh game.

People tend to forget this, years later, because *Lakers 106, Kings 102* was so thunderous. But following a single day of rest, the teams returned to Arco Arena for the final chapter of an enthralling clash that, wrote Chris Dufresne of the *Los Angeles Times,* "might be the most riveting series on TV since *The Sopranos.*"

Coming off the improbable triumph, Los Angeles's players were oozing confidence.

Coming off the devastating defeat, Sacramento's players were . . . terrified.

Not all of them, mind you. Divac and Bibby were ready to go, as were Bobby Jackson and Scot Pollard. But while the Lakers were loose and relaxed inside their locker room, the home bunker was tense. Los Angeles had actually spent the past 24 hours slinging as much yang as a team could sling — telling reporters near and far that the Kings were about to choke yet again. It was all part of Jackson's master design. "We knew all those guys were reading the papers, so we wanted them to know how little we thought of them," said Fox. "We knew they would tighten. They just weren't mentally tough." Members of the media were struck by the difference in tone and texture, as well as some Kings' refusal to move past the Game 6 officiating. "They were still whining and moaning about how they got screwed," said Voisin, the *Sacramento Bee* columnist. "I understood, because it was bad. But come on, man. You have a game to play." Early in the first quarter, during a pause in the action, a troop of child break-dancers took the floor for a 60-second performance. The King players, intently listening to Adelman's instructions, failed to notice. The Laker players, loose as can be, watched the entire gig, pointing and chuckling. "They were so calm," said Voisin. "And the Sacramento guys were so tight."

The game was exhausting. Exhausting to play, even exhausting to observe. A packed and thunderous Arco begged, pleaded the Kings to victory. Los Angeles wanted the win, but Sacramento *needed* it. All those years wandering the desert. All that haplessness.

It nearly worked. Through 19 lead changes and 16 ties, the Kings hung tough, and with 13 seconds remaining in the fourth quarter, the perfect scenario presented itself. The Lakers were up 99–98, but when Türkoğlu dribbled past Brian Shaw and into the paint, Fox made the boneheaded mistake of leaving his man unguarded in the corner, just beyond the three-point line. ("We called Rick 'Blondie,'" Jackson recalled. "Because sometimes he didn't think.")

That man was Peja Stojaković.

Even with a bum right ankle, he was the best shooter on the court — a dead-eye outside gunner who would play in three All-Star Games and rank in the top 20 in three-point field goals made in seven different seasons. "He wasn't the No. 1 guy on the Kings," Fox said. "But he was the one guy you didn't want shooting from that spot."

Türkoğlu found his teammate all alone, and the pass was perfect. As soon as Stojaković received the ball, the Arco crowd began its roar. Everything was perfection. The knee bend. The angle. The pump. The release.

The ball rose . . .

And rose . . .

And rose . . .

And hit — *nothing*. Wide right.

"Air ball!" yelled a shocked Albert. "Peja Stojaković came up with air!"

A few seconds later, Bibby's two free throws sent the game into overtime, but Sacramento was spent. They were soldiers nearing the end of a first combat tour, emptied of ammo. In the extra period, Webber wanted nothing to do with the basketball, and Bobby Jackson — as confident as any King — was left by Adelman on the bench. The biggest problem was Christie, who shot 2 for 11 from the field and looked clumsy, nervous, and indecisive. The Kings trailed 108–106 with 24 seconds on the clock when Bibby found him all alone behind the three-point line. Christie ("He wants no part of this shot!" said Walton) fired the brick of all bricks — a rocket that skidded off the backboard and into the arms of Horry. It would have been funny were it not so pathetic.

"I knew some of them were nervous," recalled Fox. "Maybe it's talked about too much, but experience matters. We had a lot of experience."

In the end, the Lakers walked off with a 112–106 victory and a trip to a third-straight NBA Finals. The collective feeling was relief, not bliss. Sure, they escaped. But to cite Rocky Balboa describing his fight with Ivan Drago, "He broke things in me that ain't never been fixed." Los Angeles players were relieved, exhausted, sweat-drained. "That series," recalled Mitch Richmond, "was pure pain. I played seven years in Sacramento, and we always sucked. Now I get to the Lakers and the Kings are gonna knock us out? No, no, no. I probably played five minutes that whole series, but my jersey was covered in sweat the whole time. It was scary, but at least we won. It could have been worse."

Indeed.

Seventeen years later, the Kings are still without a trip to the NBA Finals.

Three days after eliminating Sacramento, the Lakers hosted New Jersey in the first game of the NBA Finals.

Yawn.

Yes, yawn.

This was eating at Burger King following a nine-course bonanza at Per Se. The Nets were a 52-regular-season-win team with one superstar, point guard Jason Kidd, and a slew of *mehs* who would be sixth and seventh men in Jackson's rotation. Their leading scorer, power forward Kenyon Martin, averaged 14.9 points per game, and their second-leading scorer, forward Keith Van Horn, averaged 14.8. A single occupant of the planet Earth, TNT's Charles Barkley, predicted the Lakers would be upset. No one else (literally, nary a soul) thought the Nets had a chance. Hell, even the Nets didn't think the Nets had a chance.

"Did we truly believe we could win?" Kerry Kittles, the veteran shooting guard, asked years later. "I don't know. Probably not."

For Brian Scalabrine, a rookie reserve forward out of Southern Cal, the dire reality of the situation hit during Game 3, played at the Continental Airlines Arena in East Rutherford, New Jersey. Midway through the third quarter, the Nets — behind 2-0 in the series — found themselves trailing 70–59 when (*bam!*) everything clicked. Kidd started nailing jumpers and pushing the ball past Los Angeles's defense. Kenyon Martin was using all sorts of low-post moves. Richard Jefferson dunked, then dunked again. "We were running them off the floor," Scalabrine recalled. "It was some of the best ball we'd ever played, just basketball at a high level. Then I looked up at the scoreboard."

With 8:48 remaining in the game, the Nets led 90–83.

"And that's when I realized we weren't beating these guys," he said. "We were playing the best we could possibly play, we're disrupting what they wanted to do, and it wasn't nearly enough. It felt like we should have been up by 30. We just weren't of their class."

Scalabrine was right. The Nets lost 106–103, and one game later the Lakers wrapped the most forgettable of Finals with a sweep. O'Neal, averaging a team-best 36.3 points and 12.3 rebounds, spent the four games feasting on New Jersey's three biggest men (Jason Collins, Aaron Williams, and Todd MacCulloch), who could merely watch and shrug as he won a third-straight Finals MVP trophy.

"Sometimes you're not good enough," said Collins. "That was us — not good enough."

The Lakers were the first team to win three straight NBA titles since Jackson's 1996–98 Chicago Bulls.

The goal was now four.

13

Gettin' Bored with It

O n June 25, 2002, Will Smith (aka the Fresh Prince) released his third solo studio album. In its first week, the humbly titled *Born to Reign* sold 60,000 copies and sat at No. 13 on the U.S. *Billboard* 200 chart. The people at Columbia Records were moderately pleased.

Then (*poof!*) it vanished.

There were a handful of reasons. The opening single, "Black Suits Comin' (Nod Ya Head)," may well be the worst hip-hop song in the history of hip-hop songs. The second single, "1,000 Kisses," is a dog excrement milkshake put to a beat. The CD came out just a month after Eminem dropped the fantastic *The Eminem Show*, and there was now precious little interest in Smith's upbeat messaging and goofball rap stylings.

More than anything, though, people were simply fatigued.

For the last decade and a half, Smith had been a ubiquitous rapper, actor, and late-night television guest. We'd seen him as one half of DJ Jazzy Jeff and the Fresh Prince, we'd seen him in *Independence Day* and *Bad Boys* and *Wild Wild West*, we'd heard "Gettin' Jiggy wit It" approximately 17 million times on a merciless pop radio loop. After a while, the schtick simply grew stale, because, inevitably, all schticks grow stale.

In the summer of 2002, at the same time *Born to Reign* was being ridiculed as laughingstock garbage, the Los Angeles Lakers' schtick grew stale.

It was, like Smith's nonsense, all too much. The back-to-back-to-back titles. The parades. The Shaq-Kobe drama. The Phil Jackson Zen master stuff. Randy Newman's hackneyed "I Love L.A." blaring inside Staples Center after every Laker win. Jack Nicholson sitting courtside. Dyan Cannon sitting courtside. Leonardo DiCaprio sitting courtside.

Sure, it played well in La La Land. But around the NBA, patience was wearing thin. Few opposing players had anything good to say about Bryant. Even fewer opposing coaches liked Jackson. And while O'Neal was a beloved Care Bear of a man, he had changed. On August 5, 2002, Chick Hearn, the iconic Lakers broadcaster, died at age 85 — and the normally thoughtful O'Neal skipped out on paying his respects. His excuse ("family emergency") was dismissed as tone-deaf and cruel. From Kareem Abdul-Jabbar to Magic Johnson to James Worthy to Byron Scott to Pat Riley, seemingly every member of the Laker universe made sure to be there for Hearn's family. But not Shaq. Wrote Bill Plaschke in the *Los Angeles Times:* "Few who attended [Hearn's] funeral will soon forget that Kobe Bryant was there but O'Neal was absent."

If that wasn't bad enough, O'Neal waited more than three months after the conclusion of the 2001–02 season before scheduling necessary surgery on his arthritic right big toe. This infuriated Mitch Kupchak, Phil Jackson, and Bryant, none of whom could fathom how the organization's centerpiece would willingly miss part of the upcoming season when it could have been avoided. Like his reason for failing to attend the funeral, O'Neal's justification ("We had to get three different opinions because this is my future, my life, we're talking about") was baloney. Simply put, he was a man who valued his off-seasons, and he didn't want to spend the summer in a cast. So — $23.5 million salary be damned — he waited, and insisted on handling the malady on "company time."

"What kind of athlete would ever say that?" said Peter Cornell, the journeyman center who attended 2001 training camp with the team. "No true competitor would ever say that. But Shaq took a different approach."

"He first said he wanted another opinion," Jackson recalled. "Then he fessed up and admitted he was having too much fun in the off-season."

According to several teammates and coaches, the hunger that once motivated O'Neal toward the three straight titles had slipped away. Bryant's past complaints over his co-superstar's indifference had usually been crumpled and tossed into a trash bin. But now, as training camp opened in Hawaii, it was hard not to listen. Not only was O'Neal sidelined for nine weeks post-surgery — he was fat and lumpy and clearly unprepared to play. His off-seasons were devoted to eating, to drinking, to endorsement opportunities, to hip-hop albums, to club openings and movie premieres and late nights and extravagant travels. As soon as the final buzzer sounded, he suspended his identity as Los Angeles Laker and started his identity as Shaq Fu, larger-than-life cartoon character. It was Kazaam come to life.

"He was around the team rehabbing," recalled A.J. Guyton, a guard in camp. "But was Shaq lifting weights? No." When the Lakers expected O'Neal to walk the treadmill or stretch or do other unenjoyable tasks, he was hit-or-miss. Sometimes he'd listen to the advice of Gary Vitti, the head trainer. Other times he'd ignore him as he would a pesky autograph seeker.

When there was fun to be had, O'Neal was all in — foot pain or no foot pain. One day, midway through camp, the Lakers bused their players to a nearby Army facility for a paintball battle. Bryant and O'Neal were anointed team captains and drafted their squads. What followed was a hyper-intense military standoff to the death. "I was with Kobe's team, and he and Shaq *wanted it bad*," recalled Jannero Pargo, a rookie Laker guard out of Arkansas. "It was just paint guns, but at one point Kobe looked me square in the eyes, pointed two fingers to his eyes, and screamed, 'Go! Go!' He was a paintball leader, with no regard for my life. Shaq was the same. They needed to win."

Beginning in 2002, O'Neal was paid by a sponsor to host a party in every city the team visited. Even when he was inactive, he made certain to attend. "It was wild," Pargo said. "We'd get to the hotel, he'd throw his bags in his room, there'd be a cab waiting, and he'd go to the party for 30 minutes, get paid, and leave. It'd be called SHAQ'S PARTY or something, and people just wanted to be near him. Crazy days."

O'Neal was having the time of his life. But other franchises smelled blood. In a chronological sense, O'Neal was in the prime of his career.

Sure, centers wore down faster than guards and forwards. But a 30th birthday was far from a death knell for the dominant big man. If anything, it was a peak. At 30, the great low-post scorers were at their greatest. At 30, Bill Russell was averaging 14.1 points and 24.1 rebounds for the 1964–65 world champion Boston Celtics. At 30, Wilt Chamberlain was averaging 24.1 points and 24.2 rebounds for the 1966–67 world champion Philadelphia 76ers. At 30, Kareem Abdul-Jabbar was averaging 25.8 points and 12.9 rebounds for the 1977–78 Lakers.

O'Neal, however, didn't take care of himself — and everyone knew it. With each Laker season he seemed a bit slower, a bit less athletic, a bit more injury prone — still otherworldly 85 percent of the time, but not 100 percent of the time, as once had been the case.

That was a big reason why on August 6, 2002, the New Jersey Nets — recently vanquished by Los Angeles — had sent forward Keith Van Horn and center Todd MacCulloch to the 76ers for Dikembe Mutombo, the four-time NBA Defensive Player of the Year. The *Asbury Park Press*'s headline read NETS UNVEIL ANTI-SHAQ DEVICE, and upon completing the transaction, Rod Thorn, the New Jersey general manager, told the media that the new center could make the difference between a Finals appearance and a Finals triumph. "We have a chance," Thorn said, "to be the best defensive team in the NBA."

About a week later, the Sacramento Kings signed Keon Clark, the 6-foot-11, 220-pound free agent center, to a one-year, $4.5 million contract — "another big man to square off against the Lakers' Shaquille O'Neal," read an Associated Press article.

The most noteworthy knock-Shaq-on-his-rear addition took place on June 26, 2002, when the Houston Rockets used the first pick in the NBA draft to select Yao Ming, the 7-foot-6, 310-pound center who had recently averaged 38.9 points and 20.2 rebounds per game in the playoffs with the Shanghai Sharks of the Chinese Basketball Association. Though he was just 21 and unfamiliar with high-caliber competition, Yao's arrival was considered a direct challenge to O'Neal's reign as the NBA's mightiest big man. Sure, Shaq was tall. But he wasn't *this tall*. Within weeks, a song titled simply "Yao Ming" was being played on Houston radio stations, and Steve Francis, the Rockets' superstar guard, was being introduced to audiences as "Yao Ming's teammate." There was talk — only half in jest — of a Ming dynasty.

Put simply, the NBA's 28 other franchises were doing their all to shove the Lakers off their perch. If that meant copying elements of the triangle offense (as many teams attempted to do), so be it. If that meant adding Mutombo or Clark, so be it. If that meant importing China's greatest center, so be it. And if that meant throwing punches — well, let's go.

On the evening of October 23, 2002, six days before the season openers for both franchises, the Kings and the Lakers met in an exhibition game at Staples Center. It was supposed to be nothing more than a harmless warm-up — a final opportunity to work on rotations, to give rookies some experience, to let Phil Jackson and Rick Adelman get comfortable with what their general managers had given them.

Instead, it turned into World War III.

The game began with Doug Christie, Sacramento's off guard, manning up against Rick Fox, the Los Angeles small forward. And even though the night would count for nothing, Christie refused to hide his fuck-the-Lakers-and-everything-they-represent feelings. Only five months had passed since the Kings were eliminated in the worst possible way, and the bruise remained raw. Christie, in particular, had been one of the goats of the playoffs, a shooting guard minus the accurate shooting. So now, here in hostile territory, Christie affixed himself to Fox, behaving as if this were Game 8 of the Western Conference Finals. Fox did not enjoy it. "He was all up in my shit," Fox recalled. "I was like, 'Ugh, dude, come on. Back up a little. It's just preseason. Chill.'"

Christie was relentless with his badgering, and Fox came to the realization that his rival was trying to set a tone for the upcoming season. "The last thing I wanted," Fox said, "was Doug Christie thinking he had the upper hand." Hence, with a little more than two minutes gone by in the first quarter, Fox grabbed a loose ball and swung his right elbow into Christie's chest. The King flopped backwards, stood, and walked toward his rival, who then jabbed Christie in the chin with a stiff left. Christie fired back with a left of his own, and Clark — doing the most he would all season to earn his paycheck — stepped in to break things up.

Both players were ejected, and Fox thought to himself, *It is time for me to kill this dude.* Especially when he spotted Christie celebrating with his teammates, basking in the glory of taking on the enemy. Only, well, Fox couldn't kill this dude on the court, with the presence of three referees. So he waited. Christie exited the court through one tunnel, Fox through the other. Fox walked casually, almost at a saunter, until he was deep enough into the darkness of the Staples Center bowels. Then — a sprint. Fox dashed through the hallway and toward the other tunnel, where he spotted Christie yukking it up with Kings security guards. Without a thought, he charged Christie, leaping through the air in an attempt to break out the Bruce Lee flying dropkick. It didn't quite work. "Doug caught my foot as I hit his chest," Fox recalled. "So now he's holding my foot and I'm hopping around on one foot and a Kings security guard starts grabbing me and Doug's wife [Jackie] is swinging her purse. Doug is taking swings at my body, I have him in a headlock, the Staples Center security guards come in and grab me, trying to separate us. But in grabbing me they're giving Doug all these free shots at me. I'm backed up into the rear of the bleachers, it's not going very well, and then, out of nowhere . . ."

Shaquille O'Neal arrived.

Still recovering from toe surgery, he had been sitting in a chair along the sideline, decked out in a baggy blue-and-beige checkered outfit that reminded one of a 1970s grandfather's pajama set. When Fox started down the tunnel, O'Neal was tapped on the shoulder by Jerome Crawford, his bodyguard, who whispered, "Rick's about to get into it."

O'Neal bolted from his spot and sprinted to the rear of the arena. As soon as he saw the Christie-Fox fisticuffs, he revved up his deepest of baritones and screamed, "What is going on?!" It was reminiscent of André the Giant coming to save Bob Backlund during their WWF heyday, and the fighting immediately ceased. Christie backed off. Christie's wife backed off. Fox gave a final shove and walked alongside O'Neal, who escorted him to the Lakers' locker room.

"Dude, you were crazy," O'Neal said. "What were you thinking?"

Fox barely flinched.

"I was thinking," he said, "that we need to defend who we are."

It wouldn't be easy.

With the exception of two marginal rookies, Pargo and Kareem Rush, and the addition of a veteran small forward named Tracy Murray, the 2002–03 Lakers were largely the same cast of characters as the 2001–02 Lakers. Which meant that an already aged roster was merely aged a bit more. Now five members of the team were 30 or older, and it was a legitimate concern. Basketball is a young man's game, unkind to ancient legs.

The season began on October 29 against San Antonio at Staples Center, with O'Neal situated on the bench in street clothes and a starting lineup featuring Derek Fisher and Kobe Bryant at guard, Robert Horry and Devean George at forward, and Soumaila Samake in the middle.

Hold on.

Hoooooold on.

Soumaila Samake?

Yes, Soumaila Samake. Not to be confused with Saylac, Somalia, or the Nakajima Sakae, or a legitimate NBA center. Born and raised on a farm in the small town of Bougouni, Mali, Samake was first discovered by American basketball seekers in 1997, when Joby Wright, University of Wyoming head coach, was looking for obscure international players to join the Cowboys. Instead of coming to the United States, Samake joined Geoplin Slovan, a professional Slovenian club, so that he could make money to support his family. One year later, Scott Spinelli, assistant coach at American University, was attending the African Games when he spotted a tall, gangly Manute Bol–esque man playing on an outdoor court with thousands of bats flying overhead. The creatures swooped left and right, high and low, yet Samake — standing at 7 feet and weighing about 200 pounds — barely seemed to notice, swatting one attempted shot after another from overmatched opponents. Within 18 months, Spinelli was an assistant coach with the Cincinnati Stuff of the minor league International Basketball League, and Samake — selected in the 12th round of the IBL draft — was his starting center.

Playing against people who weren't very good, Samake was named the 2000 IBL Defensive Player of the Year, averaging 2.7 blocks per game, along with 9.7 points and 7.6 rebounds. In the June NBA draft, he was selected by New Jersey with the 36th overall pick, and Nets GM John Nash offered one of the great non-praises in modern sports history, telling the press, "He does not have a variety of moves, but he has decent hands."

Samake's 34-game, 1.4-points-per-game year in New Jersey was perfectly summarized by Steve Adamek of *The Record*, who gave the center an F in his season-end Nets report card: "The difference between this guy and Manute Bol, another one-time long-term project? Six inches."

He spent the next season in Italy, then joined the Lakers' 2002 Summer Pro League team in Long Beach. Though Samake averaged just 3.8 points and 6 rebounds per game, he was, um . . . eh . . . very tall. And with O'Neal shelved, tall was better than not tall. "He'll be OK," O'Neal said. "He's young. So he's going to be all right."

As Laker fans quickly learned, Soumaila Samake was not going to be all right. The Spurs jumped out to a 24–18 first-quarter lead, with David Robinson and Tim Duncan, the team's twin tower low-post superstars, attacking the rim without pause. Samake, meanwhile, played as if his knees were glued to each other. His first field goal attempt as a Laker was an 11-foot jumper — brick. His second field goal attempt was an uncontested layup — brick. His basketball instincts were brutal: a buffet of mistimed jumps and unanticipated passes. To Samake, the pick-and-roll was something to watch unfold from afar.

When he was mercifully replaced by Tracy Murray with four minutes left in the first quarter, the 18,997 in attendance offered a mock ovation. As the dust cleared and the game ended with a 87–82 San Antonio triumph, Samake exited the arena with a 13-minute, 2-point, 6-rebound dandy. His uniform number (0) felt appropriate.

Los Angeles lost again one night later, this time a 102–90 slogger at Portland, then won two straight before going on a four-game losing streak that turned into seven setbacks in eight games. On November 20, following a 95–88 defeat at San Antonio, Los Angeles's record was 3-9, and the team sat at the bottom of the Pacific Division, 5½ games behind Seattle. The four main culprits were (1) O'Neal, who was out because of a surgery he should have scheduled months earlier; (2) Samake, a poor man's John Shasky whose ignoble Laker career came to an end in late November after the 230-pounder was suspended for testing positive for (of all things) steroids; (3) Bryant, who saw O'Neal's absence as a golden opportunity to shoot sans conscience; and (4) Jackson, who did nothing to stop him.

The head coach's sudden impotence was jarring. Throughout his 13 years running the show in Chicago and Los Angeles, Jackson never shied away from conflict with a player. If he needed to admonish Michael Jordan for dominating the ball, he did so. If he needed to lecture O'Neal on fitness, he did so. Now, however, with his center shelved and his team on the ropes, Jackson remained taciturn. He had one hope, and it was Kobe Bryant. Flawed, annoying, stubborn Kobe Bryant.

Organizations, he believed, sometimes needed to figure themselves out. Yet the Lakers were figuring nothing out. Murray, fresh off two seasons under Lenny Wilkens in Toronto, was stunned by his new coach's unwillingness to step up and express himself. During the club's early struggles, Murray asked Jackson whether they could discuss his place in the rotation.

"When I have time to talk to you," Jackson snapped, "I'll talk to you."

Hmm.

"It was a two-minute conversation, and there was never a follow-up," Murray recalled. "Phil never talked to me. Or a bunch of the guys. It wasn't what I was expecting when I got there."

What perplexed Murray most wasn't his limited role (he averaged a mere 6.2 minutes per game), but the team's obsessive reliance on Bryant to do everything. Horry was a proven scorer. Fox was a proven scorer. Devean George was uber-athletic, and Samaki Walker had low-post moves. Derek Fisher, the point guard, certainly knew his way to the hoop. There were men who could help make up for O'Neal's absence.

But . . . no. Jackson knew that Bryant, now 24 and in his seventh season, wanted the ball, and he was presented with it. This was actually his dream come true — a chance to prove that the Los Angeles Lakers could thrive without O'Neal clogging up the middle. What transpired, though, was misery. A *USA Today* headline read, WITHOUT SHAQ, LAKERS ARE LOSERS, and it was inarguable. A system created to run inside out was now perimeter-oriented. The other players spent much of their time standing on the court, bored and disinterested. Bryant shot 8 for 21 in a loss to Washington, and Jackson uttered nary a complaint. He shot 8 for 22 in a loss to Atlanta, and Jackson uttered nary a complaint. He shot 18 for 40 in a win over Golden State, and Jackson uttered nary a complaint. Ball movement, a supposed staple of the triangle offense, barely existed. "A whole lot of dribbling," said Murray. "Very little passing." No game screamed *Somebody do something — please!* quite like the November 7 trip to Boston. Having grown up a Magic Johnson diehard, and possessing an encyclopedic knowledge of the history of the Lakers-Celtics rivalry, Bryant always got geared up for Beantown. Earlier in the day, six hours before tipoff at the FleetCenter, O'Neal could be seen in the lobby of the Four Seasons Hotel Boston, wearing a T-shirt and shorts while sliding down the banister and shouting, *"Heeeeerrrre coooommmmes Shaaaaaq!"* It was preposterous — the last thing a man nursing a toe injury should be doing; the most joyful thing a man nursing a toe injury should be doing. When he learned of O'Neal's antics, Bryant let out a sigh. *This,* he thought, *is the reason I'm the Man around here.*

That night, the Man launched 47 shots, connecting on just 17 while committing 5 turnovers and scoring 41 points in a 98–95 overtime loss. It was typical Bryant, who viewed Boston's Paul Pierce in much the way he viewed Philadelphia's Allen Iverson and Minnesota's Kevin Garnett — not merely as rivals, but as MOST ELECTRIFYING PLAYERS IN THE GAME obstacles that needed to be scaled. So he fired away, and afterwards he whispered to Pierce, "That was fun. Just like the old days."

Only it wasn't fun for the four other telephone poles standing on the court. The Lakers stunk, and Jackson seemed frozen. Truth be told, he was a victim of the same plague that had infected others who came into prolonged contact with Bryant — an inevitable surrender to the ceaseless force that identified itself as *"Give me the ball. Give me the ball. Give me the ball. Give me the ball.*" Bryant had entered the NBA believing he was the greatest talent on earth, and that feeling was 100 times more powerful now. "It's rare to have what Kobe had," said Rush, the rookie guard. "I love basketball. But Kobe was at a different level, and that could definitely be overwhelming." Jackson, like Del Harris before him, was rendered largely mute and useless. He would watch Bryant dominate the ball, and after-wards — when confronted by reporters — sort of sigh and explain it away as "part of the process." Only there was no process. Jackson felt numb and detached. Like most of the other men in the locker room, he was a "Shaq guy," and Bryant knew it. Jackson would say things, offer sugges-tions, design plays — but without much conviction. It hardly helped that Tex Winter, the triangle architect and Jackson's cohort for more than a de-cade, had been marginalized and largely ignored by the head coach. There was a not-so-secret secret to much of Los Angeles's success, and it was the genius of Winter's offensive mind. Jackson — whose ego "could not be any bigger," according to Larry Brown, the veteran coach — was cer-tainly aware that there was an asterisk alongside his success, a universal acknowledgment that, sans triangle, he probably goes down as the win-ningest coach in Albany Patroons history. So as the accolades mounted and the deification increased, Jackson set Winter aside, asking him to no longer sit beside him during games, but on a rear, out-of-the-way seat. Wrote Roland Lazenby: "Jackson explained the move as being made out of consideration for Winter's age. But Winter wondered if Jackson hadn't become overly concerned with making sure he got the credit for the team's success."

Now, minus O'Neal, the Lakers were a crappy one-man show with the franchise's worst record in 36 years.

On the night of November 19, after the host Dallas Mavericks im-proved to 11-0 with a 98–72 thrashing of Los Angeles, Bryant teed off. "I look around the locker room and I don't see any fire in anybody's eyes," he said. "Everybody's just kind of dozing off a little bit. I don't know if they're waiting for Shaquille to get back or whatever. I don't know. But there's just no intensity."

It was Tone Deafness 101. Bryant took 21 shots against the Mavs, hitting a mere 7 and committing 5 turnovers. He failed to see the agitation in the faces of his teammates, the frustrated glares toward the bench. "When Kobe didn't look to get other guys involved, it could be really tough," said Fox, who scored 11 in the setback. "Sometimes you wanted to say to him, 'Kobe, you know we're all out here, right?'"

Shaquille O'Neal made his return to the court on November 22, bounding off the bench to replace Samaki Walker with 5:43 remaining in the first quarter against the visiting Chicago Bulls. The fans greeted their savior with a pronounced standing ovation: a hero back from the depths and ready to help Los Angeles — 4-8 and still in the Pacific basement — regain its rightful spot.

That, at least, was the hope.

The O'Neal who walked onto the Staples Center hardwood, however, was a faded copy. He looked the same, what with the gold No. 34 jersey and the cheek-to-cheek grin. But while he scored 17 points in the 86–73 victory, O'Neal played sluggishly. Twice he had his shots swatted away by Donyell Marshall, a subpar 6-foot-9 forward. (Wrote J.A. Adande in the *Times:* "One was a straight-up block of Shaq's baseline jumper, something I've never seen before.") When Fox tossed him a perfect alley-oop late in the fourth quarter, O'Neal struggled to get his right hand above the rim, barely stuffing the basketball into the hoop. Somewhere Soumalia Samake, soon-to-be backup center for the Greenville Groove, chuckled.*

The idea that the Lakers would once again dominate the NBA seemed increasingly fantastical. Bryant's selfishness remained a problem. O'Neal's limited health — also a problem. At age 33, Fox's athleticism was waning, and at 36 Brian Shaw was more assistant coach than viable point guard option. More than anything, though, the team seemed to suffer from limited heart. Devean George, now playing major minutes, was considered soft by teammates. Horry, 6-foot-9 but a lover of life beyond the three-point line, rarely mixed it up down low. The scrappiest Laker was Pargo, a

---

* Yes, the Greenville Groove — pride of the NDBL (National Basketball Development League).

6-foot-1, 175-pound point guard who barely made the team and saw every practice as a chance to show his worth. Upon arriving in Los Angeles, Pargo rented a Marina del Rey apartment and invited a University of Arkansas teammate, Teddy Gipson, to live with him. Throughout the season, the two would wake up Saturday mornings, head down to Venice Beach, and play pickup on the outdoor concrete courts. Nobody with the Lakers had the slightest idea, and it violated a solid 30 clauses in his contract. "I'd never wear any team gear," Pargo recalled. "Headband on, regular black Nike shorts. I just loved the game *that* much. I wanted the action."

Pargo was an exception. In many ways, the 2002–03 Lakers are best represented by Walker, the power forward who, one season earlier, had been popped in the head by Bryant on the bus in Cleveland. When the team signed him to a two-year, $3 million free agent deal in the summer of 2001, it was with the belief that the 6-foot-9, 240-pounder would add toughness and snarl. But Walker wasn't tough, and he lacked snarl. He was lazy and sloppy and inconsistent, the basketball equivalent of a roll of Charmin. When the Lakers placed Walker on the injured list with a strained lower back, Bryant was rightly incredulous. "He's not hurting any more than I am," the guard said. "I'm out there playing my butt off every single night. He should be as well." It was the rare area where Bryant and O'Neal agreed. "Talk to the fuckers who ain't doing nothing," O'Neal said after a loss. "Don't talk to me."

The fuckers was a singular fucker — Walker.

Years later, Walker conceded that both men were correct. He was 26 and single and living in Santa Monica *as a Laker.* "It was crazy," Walker said. "There were so many distractions." One day, back during his rookie season with Dallas, Walker arrived at the facility reeking of alcohol, still slightly hungover from a night on the town. The behavior was nothing new. Walker often returned home at 6 a.m., took a quick nap, forgot to brush his teeth, then darted off for practice with the scent of Budweiser and Bar Hag IV on his breath. This time, A.C. Green, the starting power forward, pulled Walker aside and lectured him on the finer points of NBA responsibility. "You're not special here and neither am I," Green told him.

"You have to give everything to the game if you plan on lasting." Walker listened — kind of. He imbibed less, slipped into bed earlier. But the devotion to the craft never caught on. Such was the by-product of being born with athletic gifts and never feeling compelled to work on them. In high school, then at Louisville, Walker was rarely challenged. His 60 percent was another player's 100 percent. So why go hard?

"I didn't take care of my body and I could be pretty soft," he said. "I had superstar ability without superstar determination. When I guarded Shaq in practice, I held my own. I had that natural ability. But looking back, I needed to care more. That's on me."

Bryant and O'Neal tried to act as if the power forward's laziness were some sort of manageable disease. Only it was not. With Walker either inactive or benched or counting the imaginary butterflies fluttering atop his head (he averaged just 4.4 points per game), Jackson turned toward Mark Madsen, the former first-round draft pick out of Stanford.

Which presented its own complications.

In a world of 6.36 billion people, not a one disliked Madsen. He was polite, funny, quirky, endearing; a devout Mormon who had done his requisite missionary work on the Costa del Sol in Spain but never felt comfortable trying to sell his teammates on faith. Bryant — a man who considered few *Homo sapiens* worthy of his presence — enjoyed Madsen so much that, when it came time for the Lakers' annual secret Santa gift, he exceeded the $100 maximum and bought the forward two suits. Throughout most of his first two NBA seasons, Madsen's primary task was to serve as O'Neal's practice dummy, and he attacked the job with gusto. "I was going 100 percent every day," he recalled, "and Shaq had to save himself for Hakeem and Alonzo Mourning. I had to find the balance of going hard on him but not trying to wear him down for the games." Yet league-wide respect didn't come easy. Nicknamed "Mad Dog," Madsen was always being compared to the long line of tall, white, unathletic stiffs who occupied many an NBA bench in the 1980s — men like Greg Dreiling, Stuart Gray, Uwe Blab, and Paul Mokeski. Why, heading into the 2001–02 season, *Sports Illustrated* rated Madsen the NBA's worst player, a designation that deeply wounded the recipient after the *Los Angeles*

Times picked it up and ran a front-of-the-sports-section piece on his hap-lessness. "It was so painful," he recalled. "It was a picture of me sitting on the bench with my hands on my face, looking sad. I didn't appreciate it. But I'm a big boy, and the media had their job to do."

Many of the Lakers defended Madsen, insisting that he most certainly was not the NBA's worst player. And (thanks, Lavor Postell) he wasn't. But he rarely played, and back-to-back seasons of 2.0 and 2.8 points per game hardly inspired confidence. Now, though, Jackson decided it was time to set the vastly more talented Walker aside and give Madsen a chance. Worst-case scenario, he'd last a game or two before being sent off to bunk with Soumaila at the Greenville Motel 6. Best-case scenario, he'd light a fire beneath a team sitting on damp kindling.

On February 18, with the Lakers in the midst of a two-game losing streak and slipping away at 26-25 and 8½ games behind Sacramento in the Pacific, Madsen played 28 minutes against Houston, contributing 9 points and 5 rebounds off the bench in a 106–99 triumph. One night later, with O'Neal home in Beverly Hills resting his sore toe and Walker injured early on with a sprained right ankle, Madsen scored 7 points in 22 min-utes of a 93–87 win at Utah. In what was considered the biggest triumph of the season, the Lakers hosted Portland (35-18 and two games out in the Pacific) on February 21, and Madsen's 6 points, 4 rebounds, and rugged interior defense on Rasheed Wallace made all the difference in a 92–84 win.

Yes, the headlines rightly belonged to Bryant, who was in the midst of a phenomenal run that saw him score 40 or more points in nine straight games (including 51 against Denver and 52 vs. the Rockets). But Bryant was a known quantity — with O'Neal still struggling to fully recover, he was expected to shoot and score with gusto. What Madsen brought was something far more intangible: toughness, intensity, spirit, selflessness. He was inserted into the starting lineup by Jackson on February 23, and in that night's 106–101 win against Seattle played 22 minutes, scoring 5 points and grabbing 6 rebounds. His name appeared in none of the following day's newspaper recaps (Bryant scored 41, O'Neal 27), but his impact was legitimate. "You knew he was going to play hard every night," said Adande. "That wasn't something you could say for everyone on that team."

Madsen wound up starting 22 games, averaging career highs in minutes (14.5), points (3.2), and rebounds (2.9). Nobody would argue that he was the centerpiece of the franchise, or even a primary piece of the franchise. But Los Angeles won 17 of his starts, and the team concluded a rocky season with a 50-32 mark and the fifth seed in the Western Conference.

They were a wounded three-time defending champion . . .

. . . whom no one wanted to play.

They were all vanquished.

Shaquille O'Neal never had any doubt, but the rest of the league sure did. Heading into 2002–03, several teams looked at the Laker center and saw fat, lazy, injured, vulnerable. So you had the Mutombo trade to the Nets, the Keon Clark signing in Sacramento, the Yao arrival in Houston. They were all supposed to shift the balance of power, to inject a silver bullet into the heart of the slam-dunking vampire.

Alas, none of it really worked. Though O'Neal was limited to 67 regular season games, and though it was widely accepted that he wasn't quite as explosive as in seasons past, he was well aware of what was transpiring, and he refused to cower. That's why, in his first meeting with Yao, O'Neal outscored his new rival 31 to 10, taking great pride in physically punishing the rookie. ("The league still no doubt belongs to O'Neal," wrote the *Los Angeles Daily News*' Howard Beck in the immediate aftermath.) That's why he repeatedly destroyed Clark, whose heavily hyped arrival was undermined by minimal abilities, a little-known drinking problem ("I never played a game sober," he later admitted), and a 6.7-points-per-game scoring average. That's why he laughed as Mutombo missed both games against the Lakers with a wrist injury and had minimal impact in New Jersey.

O'Neal was a mountain to be toppled, and as Los Angeles commenced its pursuit of a fourth-straight title with an opening-round four-games-to-two beatdown of the Timberwolves, one had to wonder whether we were witnessing the inevitable continuation of a dynasty. The Wolves threw a bevy of bodies at O'Neal, including a 7-foot, 248-pound block of manhood named Rasho Nesterović, and it barely registered. He averaged 28.7 points and 15.3 rebounds against overmatched Minnesota, and after gobbling up an eye-popping 17 boards in the 101–85 Game 6 clincher, O'Neal turned toward the assembled reporters and grinned widely. He was still the Diesel.

"Everything went through the monster," Kevin Garnett, the Wolves' star forward, said of O'Neal. "And it was over."

After the game ended, as his players showered and ate and celebrated their accomplishment, Jackson approached the dry-erase board inside the locker room, picked up a black marker, and wrote: THE # IS 12.

It sounded so simple. A mere 12 wins and Los Angeles could make its claim to being the greatest basketball dynasty of all time. Yes, the Chicago Bulls won six rings under Jackson, but never more than three consecutively. And, while Boston captured eight straight from 1959 through 1966, the league then was a shell of what it now was. Those Celtics — small, slow, mechanical — wouldn't win a game in the modern NBA.

So, yes, the Lakers were on the verge of history.

But was it as easy as THE # IS 12? No.

The San Antonio Spurs, a 60-22 regular season juggernaut, awaited, and for one of the rare times during Jackson's tenure, the Lakers were underdogs. Los Angeles would be playing without Rick Fox, out for the postseason with a torn tendon in his left foot. San Antonio would be play-ing *for* David Robinson, its 10-time All-Star center, who was retiring at season's end. Los Angeles, as the lower seed, lacked home court advan-tage, and San Antonio had won all four regular season meetings.

Most important, the Spurs featured a nuclear weapon named Tim Duncan.

He was easy to miss, but tough to ignore. Since entering the league as the first overall selection in the 1997 draft, Duncan had established him-self as an impossible-to-stop low-post force. Physically, he was no more or less remarkable than other NBA power forwards — tall, long-armed, a bit slouched even. He also happened to speak in the hushed tones of a suburban librarian. There were never any boasts or wild predictions. Yet Duncan was a five-time All-Star who had been named the 1997–98 Rookie of the Year, the 1999 Finals MVP, the 2000 All-Star Game MVP, and the 2001–02 NBA MVP. He had yet to average fewer than 21.1 points or 11.4 rebounds per game, and his repertoire of low-post moves was something out of a Kevin McHale/Adrian Dantley mashup video. "He was the best player we faced," said Devean George. "And the one who talked the least about himself."

Much of the lead-up hype concerned Duncan and Bryant, two of basketball's transcendent young stars. Much of it also concerned O'Neal and Robinson — for years, the Laker center had expressed disdain for his San Antonio counterpart, insisting that the Admiral (as he was nicknamed for his time at the Naval Academy) had turned a boyhood signature request into a nightmare. Wrote O'Neal: "One time I asked him for an autograph. He wrote his name real quick and was like, 'Yeah, come on, hurry up.' He kind of dogged me out. He was my favorite player. That's OK. I said to myself, 'When I see you, I'm gonna get you.'"

Was the story true? Not even close. Robinson was a kind and gentle man whose charitable donations and appearances topped the NBA. But O'Neal needed a reason to motivate himself, so he created the fable of the slight. "Was it exaggerated?" O'Neal said years later with a chuckle. "Yeah."

Beneath the headlines and the bluster, Gregg Popovich, San Antonio's veteran coach and a man mockingly referred to as "Popobitch" by Jackson, had a two-pronged plan. First, with the Los Angeles bench already decimated by Fox's injury, he wanted the Laker reserves to take as many shots as humanly possible. Mark Madsen? Fire away! Kareem Rush? The floor is yours. It wasn't that he disrespected the backups, it was . . . yes, he disrespected the backups. They were untested and underwhelming, and Popovich thought the ball should be in their hands.

Second, because the Spurs were loaded with stars (Duncan, Robinson) and rising stars (point guard Tony Parker, shooting guard Manu Ginóbili), it was easy to overlook one of the team's secret weapons. Yet sitting there on the bench, wearing uniform number 31 and looking like a fire hydrant with legs, was a key to keeping O'Neal in check. He was a (listed) 6-foot-7, 250-pound small-college power forward who stood closer to 6-foot-5. His name, Malik Jabari Rose, wasn't a household one, and 99 of 100 Americans had never heard of his alma mater, Drexel University. Since being tabbed by Charlotte with the 44th overall pick in the 1996 draft, Rose had averaged a pedestrian 7 points and 5 rebounds per game.

He was, by all measures, ordinary.

But while the vast majority of NBA centers struggled to figure O'Neal out, debated whether to front him or back him, use arms or legs, elbows or knees — Malik Rose knew a not-so-secret secret.

"Get under him," Rose said years later. "And stay under him."

There were, Rose will admit, conditions: One needed superhuman strength. And superhuman toughness. One needed to accept — with unwavering certainty — that the ensuing pain would be severe. That the next morning would feature a broken back, a pounding headache, cracked kneecaps, and a large helping of Extra Strength Tylenol. "I was willing to do whatever it took," Rose said. "When I was in there, my job was to keep Shaq in check."

The series began on May 5 in San Antonio, and the Spurs — unlike Minnesota — were unintimidated. They were of not-so-long-ago championship stock, loaded with confidence, and the Lakers were the annoying bully deserving of a punch to the face. With Duncan's 28 points leading the way, and Rose's feisty physicality contributing to O'Neal's muted 24 points on 10-for-20 shooting, Popovich's team won 87–82, then grabbed the follow-up game two nights later with a 114–95 blowout. IMPENDING GLOOM read the *Los Angeles Times* headline, and the accompanying story described the rest of the NBA (and NBA fans) writing off the Lakers. They were done. Toast. Old news. "Some people view us as a bleeding dog, just lying there, waiting to die," Bryant said. "We don't feel that way. We don't think that's the case."

The Lakers bounced back to even things with two victories at Staples Center. Of particular note was the second win, which came without Jackson. Midway through the Timberwolves series, he felt tightness and pain in his chest. He ignored it at first, because that was Jackson's way. How can you ask players to sacrifice body (and ego) when you don't do the same? But as the discomfort intensified, and jolts of agony shot through his torso, Jackson started to fret. He was a father of five, grandfather of eight. There was much to live for. Hence, he went to see Dr. John Moe, a team internist and cardiologist at Centinela Hospital Medical Center, who conducted an examination and concluded that one of Jackson's coronary arteries was 90 percent blocked.

The coach was immediately scheduled for surgery, and on the morning of May 10, a little more than 24 hours before Game 4, Jackson was anesthetized, then had a balloon threaded into the clogged artery. The blockage was placed aside, and a stent was inserted to prevent future problems. He was released Sunday morning, but Dr. Phillip Frankel, who performed the operation with Dr. Vern Hattori, insisted that coaching that same day was out of the question.

Jim Cleamons, the longtime assistant, spoke with Jackson before tipoff, then coached the Lakers to a 99–95 victory. With the series knotted, the narrative shifted. "Don't underestimate the champs," wrote Mickey Herskowitz of the *Houston Chronicle*. "[They] have the look of miracle workers."

It was illusion.

In Game 5 at San Antonio, the once-again-led-by-Jackson Lakers fell behind by 25, only to go on a Kobe-fueled 41–18 run. With 14.7 seconds remaining and the hosts up 96–94, the ball wound up in Horry's hands. As the time ticked away, the greatest clutch shooter of the decade stood on the left wing, just beyond the three-point line. His shot flew through the air, a dove in perfect flight, then — *clang!* It hit the rim and bounced off. Game over. "It was so disappointing," he said afterwards, "it made me want to shed a tear."

Back in California two days later, the dreams of a fourth-straight crown came to a harsh end. At the conclusion of three quarters, the Spurs led 78–69, but Jackson insisted to his men that they were still in this thing. "Those guys are tired," he said of San Antonio. "I assure you, we have a run in us." He wanted to see emotion. He wanted to see oomph. Instead, he later admitted, he saw deadened eyes and fatigued bodies. Defending a title is exhausting. Defending two titles is excruciating. Defending three titles — when the world is sick of your existence and people everywhere seek your demise and the hunger you once possessed has been satiated by caviar and lobster — is nearly impossible. You stop wanting it the way you once wanted it. Someone punches, and you don't have the energy to duck. You're Mike Tyson against Buster Douglas. The upstart possesses the edge, because the upstart is edgy. The endless praise softens you. The free meals fatten you. Jackson's plea was wishful thinking, minus the willpower.

Behind Tony Parker's 8 points and Rose's battering defense, the Spurs outscored Los Angeles 32–13 in the fourth, taking home a 110–82 clincher. With the outcome all but determined, Jackson summoned Samaki Walker off the bench for meaningless garbage time. "I'm not fucking going in," Walker barked. "Fuck this shit."

Afterwards, in the embarrassed Lakers locker room, O'Neal scowled at media members, Bryant kept his eyes glued to the floor, and Fisher sobbed openly.

"Whoever wins this championship" — that would be the Spurs — "will get to feel what we have felt for three years, and they better enjoy it," O'Neal said. "Because it doesn't last forever."

14

Room 35

On the afternoon of February 4, 2003, Geoff Wong was sitting at a desk inside his Sacramento office when he opened up a letter from Kobe Bryant's attorney.

A few days earlier, Wong had been quoted in a *Sacramento Bee* article concerning Bryant's case of food poisoning during the previous year's Kings-Lakers playoff series. According to the piece, Wong — co-owner of a restaurant named Chanterelle — had witnessed Bryant having a few cocktails inside his establishment, and "he had obviously been (out having fun)."

Although a good chunk of time has passed since the story ran, Bryant never recovered from the anger. Despite reports, he had *not* been drinking that night. He hadn't even left his room inside the Hyatt. The information was pure fiction. Wong later admitted it was bad gossip from an unreliable source.

Hence, when Timothy J. Hoy, attorney at law with the SFX Basketball Group, sat down to type out his note to Wong, he held nothing back . . .

> If you made these clearly false statements for publication, you were committing a libel against Mr. Bryant as well.
>
> Lies such as these are not without consequences, Mr. Wong. Mr. Bryant takes very seriously his position with the Lakers and

his reputation in the community. He is known as a responsible person, one who does not consume alcohol and lives a clean family-oriented life.

Geoffrey Wong loves that letter.

They could have stayed at a different hotel.

That's the first fact one should know, because it *changes absolutely everything* about this story and its 100,000 ramifications.

So, to repeat: They could have stayed at a different hotel.

On the afternoon of June 30, 2003, Kobe Bryant and three of his bodyguards (Michael Ortiz, Jose Ravilla, and an off-duty Los Angeles police officer named Troy Laster) chartered a private plane to ferry them from Southern California to Eagle County Regional Airport, near Vail, Colorado. There, one day later, the Laker star was scheduled to undergo arthroscopy on his right knee at the Steadman-Hawkins Clinic. Fed up after a long, fruitless season, Bryant told no one with the Lakers of his plans. He booked the jet, he scheduled the (seemingly minor) procedure. It was his business, not the team's.

The flight, as scheduled, took approximately two hours, and when the plane landed, its inhabitants shuffled down the steps and into an awaiting SUV, which drove the four men to the front entrance of the Lodge at Vail.

Exactly four years later, Apple would release its first iPhone, and a world of wayward travelers would never again find themselves lost. On this evening, however, either someone had written down the wrong establishment or the driver was a misguided summer employee unfamiliar with the area. Whatever the case, the Lodge at Vail — while a spectacular property, featuring plush terry cloth robes for every guest and breathtaking views of the mountains — was not where Bryant and Co. had booked their reservations. This small detail was learned when, upon trying to register at the front desk, Bryant was told, "Sir, we don't have a booking for you."

That was the bad news.

The good news, however, was that Kobe Bryant — *the* Kobe Bryant, five-time NBA All-Star and a man recognized on all seven continents of the world — would be welcomed at the Lodge at Vail with open arms. There were certainly enough rooms available. And when a celebrity of this stature walks through a resort's front doors, said resort finds a way to make it work.

"We can make it work," the man at the front desk said.

This is a moment.

A sliver of a moment that, in *Sliding Doors* tradition, makes an eternity's difference. If Kobe Bryant nods and says, "Okay, that sounds good," his night is almost certainly one of rest and boredom. He remains at the Lodge at Vail, orders room service, kicks back in bed, dials up a movie. Maybe that film is *The Air Up There*, maybe that film is *Apartment Wife: Moans from Next Door*. Whatever the case, the next morning he wakes up, eats a quick breakfast, and goes in for surgery — no mess, no fuss.*

Instead, Bryant and Co. figured out that they had been booked by a travel agent to stay 20 miles to the west in Edwards, at the Lodge & Spa at Cordillera. Ortiz called the correct hotel to tell the front desk clerk that the party of four was nearby, and Bryant would prefer that his keys be ready in the lobby so he could retreat to his room sans paperwork.

The men returned to the vehicle, made the trip, and, at approximately 10 p.m., entered through the grand front doorway. As is generally the case with celebrities, Bryant never registered with his own name. There is a long history to this. Actor Tom Hanks was "Harry Lauder." Red Sox pitcher Roger Clemens was "Red Glare." Michael Jackson was "Doctor

---

* According to Bill Zwecker of the *Chicago Sun-Times*, there was another potential scenario that, had it gone that way, would have resulted in Bryant not being at the hotel. Several months earlier, he was offered a cameo role in the Snoop Dogg film *Soul Plane*. He turned down the opportunity because the day of filming conflicted with his scheduled knee surgery. Ironically, Bryant's presence is still felt. In a scene where Tom Arnold's on-screen daughter is hit on by an older man, Arnold barks, "She's only 17! Back off, Kobe!"

Doolittle." Guns N' Roses guitarist Slash was "I.P. Freely." And Bryant, at least on this day, was "Javier Rodriguez."

The Lodge & Spa at Cordillera was a 56-room resort that catered to the rich, the famous, and the rich and famous. The 7,000-acre grounds featured four golf courses, two ski-in/ski-out clubs, indoor and outdoor pools, elevation-relief treatments, a five-star spa, and mountain views from every window. The least expensive room cost $300 per night, and it was a steal. The most expensive room cost $700 per night, and it was a steal, too. "Everything about that place was amazing," said Doug Winters, an Eagle County detective. "If you haven't gone there, you need to."

Javier Rodriguez was assigned Room 35, a first-floor luxury suite at the end of a long hallway, placed (via request) alongside a vacant room. (Two rooms for his bodyguards — numbered 18 and 20 — were registered under Ortiz's name.) The key, as instructed, was waiting at the desk.

As was a bellman named Bob Pietrack.

As was a front desk employee named Jessica Mathison.*

She was a local girl, a 2002 graduate of Eagle Valley High who had been a member of the cheerleading squad, sang in the school choir, and had a special place in her heart for the Broadway musical *Les Misérables*. In November 2002, Mathison and a friend named Lindsey McKinney took a break from their freshman year at the University of Northern Colorado to drive 14 and a half hours to Austin, Texas, and audition along with 3,000 others for the TV show *American Idol*. Standing before the regional judges, Mathison belted out Rebecca Lynn Howard's "Forgive." She failed to make the cut.

Now, living at home with her parents and a month and a half into her summer job, Mathison found herself decked out in the resort uniform of black dress, black blazer, and white name tag, staring at Kobe Bryant (aka Mr. Rodriguez), the first celebrity she had ever encountered. A few weeks earlier, Bryant had sat down for an interview with Lisa Guerrero of Fox Sports Net, who asked the basketball star how he never got into trouble.

---

* Not her real name.

"Well," Bryant replied, "I have a spidey sense for that. I stay out of bad situations."

Now, in a request that—in the world of opulent resorts—was hardly unusual, Ortiz asked Mathison (and specifically *not* Pietrack) to escort the men to Room 35. So that's what she did—Mathison grabbed the key and led the way down the hallway. She was an attractive young woman, about 5-foot-9, slender, blond hair, light brown eyes. A bit nervous, but only because she was in the presence of fame. She opened the door, and the four men entered. Ortiz and Ravilla did what bodyguards do, and as they checked under the bed, inside the closet, inside the bathroom, Bryant looked at Mathison and said, softly, "Any chance you'd come back in 15 minutes and give me a tour of the hotel?"

"Sure," she said. "I can do that."

At approximately 10:30 p.m., Mathison took the back way to Room 35—out the front door of the lobby, turn left through a door into the employee cafeteria, take another left with a ramp up to the second floor, walk to the nearby elevator, and return to the first level. She had been instructed to knock, so she knocked. What transpired was a fairly ordinary tour. Mathison showed her guest the spa, the exercise room, the outdoor pool, the outdoor Jacuzzi. She brought him back to the lobby to observe the terrace, where Pietrack was standing and the Chipowskis, an elderly couple who frequented the facility, were sitting. The entire walk lasted 15 minutes, and when Mathison was done, Bryant inquired, quite politely, whether she could return him to the room.

"Of course," she replied.

They walked back the conventional way, and a couple of steps in, Bryant asked, "So, do you have a boyfriend?"

Silence.

"You know," he added, "a beautiful girl like you should really have a boyfriend."

When they reached Room 35, Bryant invited her in, closed the door, then suggested she sit on a couch. He was wearing a white T-shirt and blue nylon track pants. He unfolded into an adjacent chair and, according to Mathison, admired the musical-notes tattoo on her back. He asked her to open the Jacuzzi for their use that night. She replied by noting that her shift was over and she was done. Bryant urged her to clock out, then return in 15 minutes. She agreed but later said, "I told him I would just so I could get out of there and then I was just gonna leave and not come back."

According to Mathison, as she stood, Bryant also rose and requested a hug. She complied, and at that moment the married basketball star with a five-month-old daughter who lived "a clean family-oriented life" began to kiss her. Mathison kissed him back.

"[Then] he took off his pants," Mathison recalled. "And that's when I tried to back up and leave. And that's when he started to choke me."

They reported the sexual assault on the morning of July 1, roughly 12 hours after it had allegedly occurred.

Jessica Mathison was close with her mother, Lori Mathison, and after she confided in her, she insisted her daughter reach out to the Eagle County Sheriff's Office.

That's how, at approximately one o'clock in the afternoon, Deputy Marsha Rich and Detective Doug Winters found themselves turning into a nondescript suburban street and knocking on the front door of a two-story wood-frame home. Fifteen years removed, Winters couldn't recall who answered, or what words were initially stated. He and Rich had been told precious little by the chief, only that there had allegedly been a sexual assault, and the victim wanted to speak. "I didn't know who was involved or any specifics," Winters recalled. "So I explained the process to her — we'd go down to the sheriff's office and do a videotaped interview and, you know, then an exam. So we're getting ready to leave, we had everything set up, and I said, 'Okay, who is the person you're talking about?' And that's when she said the name Kobe Bryant."

Winters said his first thought was "Holy shit!" His second thought: "It doesn't matter who was involved. We need to treat this like we would any other sexual assault case."

Following a 45-minute conversation inside the Mathison living room,

Winters and Rich asked Jessica for the clothes she had worn in Bryant's presence. They then drove to the Eagle County Sheriff's Office, where — with a victim advocate named Nicole Shanor also present — an hourlong interview was conducted. It took place in a small room, with a table and some chairs. A video camera recorded everything, and Winters — "With the air conditioner going here it's kinda loud" — requested that Mathison speak clearly.

She did . . .

WINTERS: Can you kind of explain to me, um, why we're here and what happened last night?
MATHISON: Last night I was at work and I was sexually assaulted.

What followed was a meticulous ode to detailed investigative interviewing: a gathering of seemingly small slivers of information that led up to what, for Winters, was the money moment.

WINTERS: Um, so after you told him yeah, said you would come back, what happened did you get up or did you stay seated or what were you . . .
MATHISON: I stood up to leave.
WINTERS: Ok.
MATHISON: And he stood up. Um, asked me to give him a hug.
WINTERS: And you did?
MATHISON: And I did, yes.
WINTERS: And that was consensual?
MATHISON: Yes it was.
WINTERS: Um, what were you thinking at this time?
MATHISON: I was thinking that his actions were getting physical, and that I wanted to get out of room.
WINTERS: Ok. After the hug he said he kissed you?
MATHISON: Yes.
WINTERS: And that was consensual?
MATHISON: Yes.

WINTERS: And what do you mean how, do, you know, I guess this is where I want a description how, how did you mean, or how did he kiss you?

MATHISON: Um, we were still hugging and I looked up at him and he just started kissing me.

WINTERS: How long did this go on for?

MATHISON: I'd say about five minutes.

WINTERS: Where did he kiss you?

MATHISON: On my mouth, on my neck.

WINTERS: Ok. Um, what were you doing at this time?

MATHISON: I was letting him kiss me, I was kissing him back.

WINTERS: Ok. So that was purely consensual?

MATHISON: Yes it was.

WINTERS: And this lasted for about five minutes?

MATHISON: Yes.

WINTERS: About what time is this now, this stage in the game?

MATHISON: I guess it was around 11:00.

WINTERS: Ok.

MATHISON: Maybe a little bit before.

WINTERS: And when you're referring to last night you're referring to the 30th of June?

MATHISON: Yes.

WINTERS: Of 2003?

WINTERS: OK. Um, what happened after the kissing then?

MATHISON: He started um, groping me, I guess I'd say.

WINTERS: What do you mean by groping?

MATHISON: Putting his hands on me, grabbing my butt, my chest. Trying to lift up my skirt. Proceeded to take off his own pants. Trying to grab my hand and make me touch him.

WINTERS: Ok. Um, were you clothed during this whole time?

MATHISON: Yes.

WINTERS: Ok. When you say he was grabbing your butt and chest, was he, so he was actually doing that, he was grabbing you? And what were you telling him during all this?

MATHISON: That I need . . .

WINTERS: Or did you tell him anything?

MATHISON: I told him once that I needed to leave.

WINTERS: What did he, what was his response?

MATHISON: He didn't say anything.

WINTERS: Did he hear you?

MATHISON: If he did he didn't make any gestures or anything that would let me know that he did.

WINTERS: Ok. Did you ever tell him anything else?

MATHISON: No, because when he took off his pants that's when I started to kinda back up, and try to push his hands off me and that's when he started to choke me. He wasn't choking me enough, that I couldn't breathe, just choking me to the point that I was scared.

WINTERS: Ok. Um, when he was grabbing your butt and chest and groping you um, you said you were clothed?

MATHISON: Mm hmm.

WINTERS: Where was that happening? Over your clothing, under your clothing?

MATHISON: Over and he kept trying to put his hands under my skirt.

WINTERS: Did he?

MATHISON: Yes.

WINTERS: And what happened there?

MATHISON: He continued to touch me.

WINTERS: Where did he touch you?

MATHISON: Everywhere he could.

After several more minutes of questioning, Winters tried to understand the timeline of the alleged rape . . .

WINTERS: Ok so after the groping. So he, he was choking you at one time and then he let you go at some point?

MATHISON: He was groping me, I tried to leave, tried to break away, that's when he grabbed my neck.

WINTERS: Ok.

MATHISON: And at that point I was just looking at him, didn't know what to do, didn't know what to say.

WINTERS: Ok.

MATHISON: Then he held me by my neck and physically forced me over to the side of the couch or to the side of the two chairs and that's when he turned my back to him and . . .

WINTERS: When you said that he, he was choking you and had his hands around your neck, just so I understand, I may be confused. When you're trying to go from one side to the next, is he continuing on choking you at this point also?

MATHISON: I wouldn't say he was choking me, I could breathe, but he had his hands tight enough around my neck, so that I thought he would choke me.

WINTERS: Ok. So he was controlling your movements?

MATHISON: Yes.

WINTERS: Ok. So and then what happened?

MATHISON: That's when he continually had one hand around my neck and with his other hand pushed me over to the side of the two chairs then turned me around and bent me over and lifted up my skirt.

WINTERS: Ok. Um, so now you're at, you're over where the chairs are.

MATHISON: Still in the living room just over by the side of the chairs. Away from the table.

WINTERS: Are you telling him anything at this point, now?

MATHISON: At that point I was just kinda scared and I said no a few times.

WINTERS: Ok, what, you said no, were you bent over when you were saying no?

MATHISON: Yeah when he lifted up my skirt I said no when he took off my underwear.

WINTERS: How loud did you say no?

MATHISON: About as loud as I'm saying it now.

WINTERS: Did he hear you?

MATHISON: Yes. He did.

WINTERS: How do you know he heard you?

MATHISON: Because every time I said no he tightened his hold around me.

WINTERS: Ok. But he has you bent over, how is he holding your neck?

MATHISON: Like this. And then he would lean his face real close to me and ask me questions.

WINTERS: What would he ask you?

MATHISON: You're not gonna tell anybody, right?

WINTERS: What did you say?

MATHISON: I said no. And he didn't hear me or asked me to say it louder. Wanted me to turn around and look at him while I said it.

WINTERS: How many times did he ask you that?

MATHISON: Three or four.

WINTERS: What was your response every time?

MATHISON: No.

WINTERS: Why did you say no?

MATHISON: I was scared that if I told him that yes, I'm gonna tell somebody, I'm gonna get out of here now that he would become more physical with me.

WINTERS: Ok.

MATHISON: Or try harder to keep me in there.

WINTERS: And then what happened?

MATHISON: And then he lifted up my skirt, took off my underwear and, and came inside of me.

WINTERS: So he took off your underwear?

MATHISON: *[Nodding.]*

WINTERS: Ok. And then, then what happened?

MATHISON: That's when he kept coming inside me and then he leaned his face toward mine and asked me if I liked it when a guy cums in my face I said no. Then he was like what did you say. Grabbed and like tightened his hold on my neck, I said no. He said he was gonna do it anyway. And then at that point I got a little bit more aggressive with him and tried to release his hands from my neck. And he was still behind me and at that point he's still choking me. I was not trying as hard as I could of to get away, but I was still trying . . .

WINTERS: Ok. Ok. When, when you say he's coming in from behind, what do you mean?

MATHISON: He's, he's cuming inside me.
WINTERS: Ok and so I'm assuming his penis is in your vagina.
MATHISON: Yes.

By the time the interview was complete, Winters knew — with near-absolute certainty — that Jessica Mathison was telling the truth. The details. The sincerity. The lack of wavering. The conviction. Now in his fourth year as a general crime detective, he had interviewed hundreds of sexual abuse victims. "It was the majority of my job," he said years later. "Most of my cases involved that sort of thing."

Armed with Mathison's allegations, Winters understood what he and his partner, Dan Loya, needed to do next. Around the same time the detective had arrived at the Mathison household, Bryant was going under the knife of Dr. Richard Hawkins at the Steadman-Hawkins Clinic. The procedure lasted approximately an hour, and by two o'clock Bryant could be seen limping through the lobby of the Lodge & Spa at Cordillera. At 8:50 p.m., Bryant placed a room service order for $39.01. Then, roughly two hours later, another room service order of $20.66.

At 11:30 p.m., Winters and Loya arrived. They pulled up to the resort, then planned to walk through the lobby and knock on Bryant's room door. With his wealth of experience, Winters knew how this would likely unfold: *Bryant says nothing, refuses to speak without an attorney present, blah, blah, blah.*

Nope.

To the detectives' shock, when they reached the parking lot, they spotted Bryant, on crutches. "It was close to midnight, and he's there as we pull in," Winters recalled. "To me that's always been odd. Was he tipped off? Did he know? I have no idea."

Winters and Loya exited the car, made certain a tape recorder was surreptitiously running, and introduced themselves to the famous basketball player.

It was not Kobe Bryant's happiest moment.

After some obligatory chatter, the detectives explained why they were at the resort, and what they were looking for.

The dialogue was recorded . . .

WINTERS: We received a call and took a report of a possible sexual assault allegation so we just want to talk to you about it and find out, yeah, find out your side of the story and find out what's going on.

BRYANT: What's gonna happen?

WINTERS: What's gonna happen?

BRYANT: Yeah.

WINTERS: Well, right now nothing's happening at this time. We just want to get your side of the story and figure out what's going on, OK. We wanna, we wanna get our, what our policy is, is um, get every side of the story. OK. Um . . .

LOYA: So that's why we want to talk to you and get your side of the story.

WINTERS: Yeah, get your side of the story and figure out what's going on.

LOYA: But we don't want to do it in front of everybody, OK? That's why we wanted to go back to . . .

WINTERS: We don't want to make a scene for you, because we understand the situation.

BRYANT: All right, 'cause it's personal. I don't understand what's going on. What side of the story will you follow? What exactly?

LOYA: Do you want to talk about it in front of everybody else or do you wanna go into a room?

WINTERS: This is, this is your . . .

BRYANT: This is my career.

At this point, 99 out of 100 celebrities facing two detectives and a sexual assault accusation cease speaking. They call a friend, a spouse, an attorney. They break out the bodyguards. They exercise their right to say nothing. Bryant, however, was either too naive or too scared to summon logic. He also failed to recognize that Winters and Loya were pulling out every stop to get him to escort them to the scene of the alleged crime.

Still in the parking lot, the detectives asked Bryant whether he had been in the company of a woman one night earlier. He said he had been — that she gave him a tour of the resort, then returned to his room to talk and show him her tattoos.

LOYA: Um, did you guys hug or kiss?

WINTERS: Kiss or hug?

BRYANT: No.

WINTERS: Nothing like that happened?

BRYANT: No.

WINTERS: OK, um, I'll be blunt and ask you. Did you have sexual intercourse with her?

BRYANT: No.

With that single word, Kobe Bryant was in enormous trouble. Both detectives knew that he and Mathison had sex. *Bryant* knew he and Mathison had sex. It was a lie. A panicked lie. Moments later, still in the parking lot, Bryant asked, "Is there any way I can settle this, whatever it is?" then added, "If my wife, if my wife found out that anybody made any type of allegation against me she would be infuriated . . ."

LOYA: Kobe . . .

BRYANT: That's all I care about.

WINTERS: And I understand.

Winters *did* understand. No matter how this was destined to unfold, it wouldn't end well for Bryant. It was hard enough being accused of rape if one was innocent. But Bryant *wasn't* innocent. Of this Winters was certain.

LOYA: Listen listen, listen. Let me explain something to you. This is what happened, OK. And this is what's going to happen. We're going to get to the bottom of it one way or another, whether it's true or not.

BRYANT: OK. OK.

LOYA: She's consented to an exam.

BRYANT: OK.

LOYA: OK. We've received blood, pubic hair . . .

BRYANT: OK.

LOYA: Semen.

BRYANT: OK.

LOYA: All that.

WINTERS: We've got physical evidence.

Then, a few seconds later . . .

LOYA: Just be straight up. We're not gonna tell your wife or anything like that. Did you have sexual intercourse with her?

BRYANT: Uh, this is what I need to know because, uh, I did have sexual intercourse with her.

Bingo.

Over the next few minutes, Bryant offered his version of the story. Which was pretty much Mathison's version of the story. They met. They flirted. They flirted some more. They kissed. When the narrative turned specifically to the intricacies of sex, however, things became uncomfortable. Bryant admitted that he had a hand around Mathison's neck, and when Loya asked about the firmness of the grip, Bryant said, "My hands are strong. I don't know."

It turned worse.

There was this:

LOYA: Did she, did you get any blood on you or anything like that?

BRYANT: She didn't bleed, did she?

LOYA: Yeah, she had, she had a lot of bleeding.

BRYANT: What, you got to be kidding. From where?

LOYA: From her vaginal area.

BRYANT: Did she cut herself or something? There's no blood on me whatsoever, man. Matter of fact, I still have the boxers. They're all white,
they're all white, there's nothing on them.

And this:

LOYA: Did you ever ask her if you wanted, if you could cum in her face?
BRYANT: Yes. That's when she said no. That's when she said no. That's
when she said no.
LOYA: So what did, what did you say?
WINTERS: What did you say, how did that, how did that come about?
BRYANT: Um, you know, that's when I asked if I could cum in her face. She
said no.
LOYA: So you like to cum in your partner's face?
BRYANT: That's my thing. Not always. I mean, so I stopped. Jesus Christ,
man.

And this:

WINTERS: Um, did she give you oral sex or anything like that?
BRYANT: Yes, she did.
WINTERS: She did?
BRYANT: She did.
WINTERS: For how . . . when did that happen?
BRYANT: For like five seconds. I said, um, give me a blow job, um, and then
kiss it. She gave me a blow job.
LOYA: So the blowjob lasted about five seconds?
BRYANT: Yeah, it was quick.
LOYA: Then what happened?
BRYANT: Wait, not . . . I mean like she was, kept on doing, I just told her to
get up. She didn't know what she was doing.

And this:

BRYANT: She must be trying to get money or something.

LOYA: Are you willing to pay that if she is?

BRYANT: I got to. I got to. I got to. I'm in the worst fucking situation.

And this:

LOYA: So when you penetrated her, was it a simple penetration? Was there difficulty there?

BRYANT: No, it was . . . it was easy. It just slid in there.

As the interview progressed, the detectives slyly escorted Bryant toward his quarters. They couldn't drag him, but they led, guided, prodded. As they neared the door, Loya said, "Will you let your security guards know you're OK, and you don't need them?"—which can be translated into *The last thing we want is your security guards advising you to keep quiet.*

Inside the room, Bryant directed Winters and Loya to his worn underwear and T-shirt. He promised ("I swear on my life") he had not committed sexual assault, said he would willingly sit for a polygraph examination, looked at his hands and noticed that they were shaking.

Winters had something to say . . .

We appreciate your cooperation with us and allowing us in your room and, you know, being cooperative with us to let us talk to you about this issue. These are tough issues. I'm gonna tell you right now, OK. These are very tough issues. They are serious allegations and she's fully aware of the consequences behind these allegations that are being made, OK. Um, but I guess we're, you know, this is what I'm having problems with, Mr. Bryant. For one, I don't know if you're telling me the truth or not. OK. I'm gonna be flat out honest with you and let me finish, OK. I'm gonna tell you why, alright. I'm the kind of person that I'm gonna tell you . . . I'm gonna tell it like it is, OK. I'm not gonna beat around the bush.

One, you lied to us right off the bat. OK. That doesn't help. Two, then we confront this issue and you seemed a little bit skeptical in the details of exactly what happened throughout the entire incident. I'm not saying you're a person that would do something like this, OK. I agree with you. I agree with you that you got caught up in the moment. OK. No doubt about it, you know, no doubt about it whatsoever. What I think you got caught up in also, Mr. Bryant, is that, and I agree, I completely agree with you, it was consensual up to the point of the hugging and kissing issue. I agree, completely consensual. I have no problem with that whatsoever. What I, what I'm being, what I'm skeptical on is that I don't know how consensual the sexual intercourse was. OK. I don't, I don't, I guess to be honest with you I'm not sure, I'm not sure if we're getting all the facts presented to us as far as what exactly happened. See this is the way I see it. I, you know, I look at it this way. She's an attractive young lady, OK . . .

In the minutes that followed, Bryant (who, it can be said again, would have been wise to keep quiet and *call an attorney ASAP*) told Winters that (a) Mathison "wasn't that attractive"; (b) he masturbated after she left; (c) he had repeatedly cheated on his wife with a woman named Michelle; and (d) he liked grabbing Michelle by the neck from behind, and she had the neck bruises to prove it.

He consented to allowing the detectives to call in a colleague who'd collect evidence from his room in a series of plastic bags as part of a sexual assault examination kit. At approximately 2:30 a.m., Bryant was driven 52 miles in a sheriff's patrol car to Glenwood Springs and Valley View Hospital. Once there, he provided DNA samples, then checked into the nearby Hotel Colorado. He flew back to Southern California that evening, hoping the worst of it all had passed.

It was naive thinking.

"I knew he was guilty," Winters said years later. "And I still know it."

15

R.A.P.E.

On March 2, 2003, a 31-year-old British tourist named Robert Alexander Wills decided to attack the slopes at the Breckenridge Ski Resort, in Breckenridge, Colorado. While soaring down the hill, Wills somehow lost control, swerved off the chosen path, and slammed into Richard Henrichs, a salesman from Naperville, Illinois, who was cautiously working his way through the beginner course.

The impact sent Henrichs flying out of his skis and into a nearby tree. When the paramedics finally arrived after 15 minutes, he was barely breathing. Flown to a hospital in Denver, Henrichs died that evening. He was 56.

Under a unique-to-Colorado state law, skiers and snowboarders are required to avoid people below them on the slopes. Failure to do so can result in a misdemeanor for reckless skiing. That's why, when the death was announced, Mark Hurlbert, the 35-year-old Eagle County district attorney, had Wills arrested.

What followed was pure craziness.

"It all blew up," Hurlbert recalled. "You had the BBC calling, you had the *New York Times* calling. Connie Chung called, the *Today* show called. It was really wild. And I thought, *Yup, this will be the big case of my career.*"

Four months later, on the evening of July 1, Hurlbert was sitting in his office when he received a call from Doug Winters, the detective. "Mark," he said, "we've got a sexual assault case involving Kobe Bryant."

A former collegiate skier at Dartmouth with a strong knowledge of American sports, Hurlbert uttered the first thing that entered his mind: *"Who?"*

Then, after digesting the name, a more appropriate follow-up: *"Oh, crap."*

Winters sought Hurlbert's approval to proceed with an interview, and he was granted permission for what turned into the 90-minute chat between Bryant and the two detectives. A day later, however, Hurlbert was contacted yet again, this time by Joseph Hoy, the Eagle County sheriff. Armed with the rape kit results, the Bryant interview, the Jessica Mathison interview, the underwear, the visit to Room 35, the terrified basketball player, and the seemingly credible college student, Hoy asked Hurlbert for permission to make an arrest.

"You know what," Hurlbert said, "let's hold off on this."

His reasoning was sound: First, it wasn't as if Kobe Bryant would be hard to find. The Lakers' day-to-day schedule was readily available. Second, at that moment, news of the alleged sexual assault wasn't yet news. All was quiet on the Colorado front. "But as soon as we arrest him, the investigation stops, because the press is going to get involved and things are gonna go in different directions and everyone will want their 15 minutes of fame," Hurlbert said. "So I told the sheriff to wait until we had everything we needed and all our information was lined up."

To the DA's great dismay, Hoy took matters into his own hands and (using a little-known legal technicality) obtained the necessary arrest warrant from Russell Granger, a district judge. On the morning of July 4, Bryant's newly hired Colorado-based attorney, Pamela Mackey, called her client and said, bluntly, "You need to come and turn yourself in right now."

Accompanied by his wife, Vanessa, Bryant entered the Eagle County Sheriff's Detention Facility that afternoon. He was fingerprinted. He was interviewed. He was photographed (staring straight ahead, emotionless, eyes slightly sleepy). He was booked on suspicion of felony sexual assault and false imprisonment. He posted $25,000 in bail and was quickly released. Mackey, best known for having defended Colorado Avalanche goalie Patrick Roy in a 2001 domestic violence case, wasted little time in doing her job and exploiting inconvenient (to the sheriff's office) information. "It's very distressing that the sheriff's office, who is supposed to be conducting an unbiased investigation, ignores what the district attorney says and goes out and gets a warrant," she told the media. "It's outrageous."

Inside the Los Angeles Lakers' executive offices, there was disbelief (why had he scheduled a surgery without consulting the organization?), then panic. Jerry Buss, the team owner, refused to believe it. Kobe? His Kobe? "No way," he told people. "Not possible." It was similar to the way he once viewed a historically promiscuous, coach-undermining Magic Johnson, who could do no wrong even when he did wrong. Kobe Bryant wasn't a rental. He wasn't a Laker via trade. He was an original. A lifer. "My dad loved Kobe," said Jeanie Buss. "Like a son." Mitch Kupchak, the general manager, was standing at the finish line of a 10K race in Pacific Palisades, waiting for his wife, Claire, to complete the course. His cell phone rang and the number for Arn Tellem, Bryant's agent, popped up.

"You're not going to believe this," Tellem began.

Within hours, Kupchak issued a statement that read, in part, "These allegations are completely out of character of the Kobe Bryant we know." Yet when he called Phil Jackson to break the news, the coach barely flinched. He was sitting inside a motel room in Williston, North Dakota, and Kupchak's familiar first six words ("You're not going to believe this") were simply untrue. Though Jackson had never literally thought of his star guard as a rapist, he knew him to be immature, emotionally stunted, and fueled by an unhealthy rage. For Christ's sake, he was in Colorado undergoing a procedure without the organization's consent. Phil Jackson *did* believe this. "Kobe can be consumed with surprising anger," Jackson recalled, "which he's displayed toward me and toward his teammates."

On July 18, Hurlbert formally charged Bryant with a single count of felony sexual assault. If convicted, he faced four years to life behind bars or 20 years to life on probation, as well as a fine of up to $750,000. One day later, in the most awkward husband-and-wife press session since

Mike Tyson and Robin Givens sat down for a 1988 Barbara Walters interview, the Bryants appeared at a news conference inside Staples Center, holding hands and appearing on the brink of tears. "I sit here in front of you guys, furious at myself, disgusted at myself for making the mistake of adultery," Bryant said. "I have a lot at stake, and it has nothing to do with the game of basketball and it has nothing to do with endorsements. It has to do with my family and being falsely accused."

Vanessa remained silent, even as her husband turned toward her and pleaded (pathetically), "You're a blessing, you're a piece of my heart, you're the air I breathe." Shortly thereafter, he bought her a $4 million eight-carat purple diamond ring from Rafinity, prompting a jeweler to tell the *Los Angeles Times*, "He's got a lot of money and he's in a lot of trouble."

Thanks in part to the power of bling, the marriage survived. For Kobe Bryant, though, it wouldn't be nearly so easy with his teammates. Most Lakers didn't like Bryant *before* they were led to believe he had raped a woman. Were they now expected to be sympathetic?

In the months that followed the second-round playoff defeat to San Antonio, Buss and Kupchak had committed themselves to a quick rebound, not a lengthy rebuild. Basketball was their business, even with the Bryant drama. They believed that while Shaquille O'Neal — now 31, with three years remaining on his contract — was both slowing down and apathetic about physical fitness, he remained the game's most dominant inside force. Plus, in Bryant the Lakers employed an all-but-certain future scoring king. Sure, the guard had told ESPN's Jim Gray that he planned on opting out of his contract at the end of the 2003–04 season (meaning he was allowed to entertain bids from other teams, though the Lakers could offer the most money), but that had to be just talk. He was a Laker. Forever a Laker.

So, with eyes on a fourth title in five years and a somewhat thin supporting cast, Los Angeles went big-game hunting.

First, on July 9, the Lakers came to terms with free agent point guard Gary Payton, a nine-time All-Star who'd spent the initial 12 and a half seasons of his career in Seattle before playing the final 28 games of 2003 with the Milwaukee Bucks. The 34-year-old Oakland native signed a one-year, $5 million deal, largely after the nonstop recruiting efforts of O'Neal, who had devoted the past half year to all but begging him to come to Los Angeles. Payton could have made far more money elsewhere but agreed to the midlevel exception in the name of capturing a ring. "It's a good situation for me," Payton said. "All the money — I got money. The opportunity to play with Shaq and Kobe, I couldn't bypass an opportunity like that."

Second, later that day, Los Angeles added Karl Malone, the 40-year-old power forward whose entire 18-year career had been spent as a member of the Utah Jazz. The Mailman signed for a paltry $1.5 million (a $17.75 million pay cut from the previous season), shocking a league accustomed to money-obsessed participants milking every penny out of an organization. Malone's Jazz had appeared in back-to-back NBA championship series in the late 1990s, both times losing to Michael Jordan's Chicago Bulls. Like Payton, he was desperate for a crown, and if that meant leaving Utah for a hated rival, so be it. "I'm 40 years old and I'm honored someone wants me," Malone said at an introductory press conference. "I'm honored to get a chance to play with Shaq and Kobe. I understand that this is their team."

It was the weirdest time to be a Lakers fan, a dizzying period of never knowing where to look. Here, on one side, was Kobe Bryant being charged with sexual assault and facing the potential of decades behind bars. Here, on the other side, was the glitzy business of building a competitive basketball team. Malone and Payton came aboard, as did power forward Horace Grant (back after one and a half seasons in Orlando). Mark Madsen left for the Timberwolves, Samaki Walker signed with the Miami Heat. Los Angeles was — on paper — the clear favorite to rule the NBA. They were a superteam, featuring four future Hall of Famers in the starting lineup and another future Hall of Famer pacing the sidelines.

And yet . . . how could anyone get overly excited about basketball?

On August 6, Bryant returned to Eagle, Colorado, to appear in court for the first time since he had been charged. The specific event was legally unremarkable — he exited a Chevrolet Suburban resplendent in a cream summer suit, entered the courthouse, and, when asked by Eagle County judge Frederick Gannett whether he objected to setting October 9 for a preliminary hearing to determine whether the case (Case No. 03 CR 204

— The People of the State of Colorado vs. Kobe Bean Bryant) should go to trial, he said, "No, sir." The words were stated softly, sans emotion. The accompanying carnival (termed "Cirque du Kobe" by *LA Weekly*), however, was something out of *The Twilight Zone*.

In the 37-day span between Bryant's arrival in Eagle (as a patient) and his return (as an alleged rapist), the story had exploded into a modern-day O.J. Simpson–esque drama, replete with gossip, rumor, innuendo, nonsense. Leading the way was Randy Wyrick, one of two dozen writers on the staff of the *Vail Daily* and a man who took ownership of all things Kobe and Eagle. On July 24 alone, Wyrick bylined articles headlined FRIEND: INJURIES VISIBLE DAYS LATER (according to Mathison's pal, "When the jury saw the evidence their jaws would hit the floor") and SOURCE: ACCUSATION RUMORS UNTRUE (there was talk that Mathison had accused a co-worker of sexual assault). Every day was something new and exciting and bold.

Now, with Bryant back in town, an empty field across the street from the Eagle County Courthouse was transformed into a media parking lot. Two dozen mobile satellites were uplinked. One hundred and twenty phone lines were added to the courthouse. Hundreds of onlookers lined the street, parade-style. One girl, a 13-year-old named Yvette Parra, painted INNOCENT across her forehead. A 21-year-old Denver man named Ethan Sahker arrived in a Bryant jersey with a cardboard sign that read I NEED TICKETS. Twenty-five reporters and photographers (including three Pulitzer Prize winners) had staked out Eagle County Regional Airport, just in case. A few days earlier, an 18-year-old local woman named Katie Lovell had been wrongly identified as Bryant's accuser, and her picture was splashed across the Internet alongside the words WHORE ALERT. "I feel violated," she told reporters. Understandably so. It was madness. Wrote Patrick O'Driscoll of *USA Today*: "White canopies shaded the outdoor TV stages. Portable toilets and a parade of gawkers filled the streets and sidewalk. A booth at one corner peddled hot almonds, pecans and hazelnuts for $4 a bag."

When it wasn't hosting the potential trial of the century, Eagle was best known as . . . eh, a town. A small, working-class town, population 3,558, with one main street highlighted by a couple of restaurants and the presence of a business named the Nearly Everything Store (which, in all honesty, does not sell nearly everything, or even close to nearly everything). When the *Los Angeles Times* sent two writers to Eagle to find out what one does for fun, they wound up in the parking lot of a Texaco gas station, watching teenagers smoke cigarettes and "flirt, cuss, primp and preen." Roxie Deane, Eagle's mayor and a town native, greeted the onslaught of media attention as one might greet an onslaught of charging nuclear alligators. She was terrified. "When I went over to the courthouse and I saw kids wearing Kobe Bryant jerseys, and other people holding signs against Kobe Bryant . . . it didn't make me very happy," Deane recalled. "You want people in a small town to get along and be neighborly. This was unlike anything we'd ever experienced."

Kobe Bryant would not have to return to Eagle, Colorado, until October 9.

In the meantime, there was basketball.

Training camp was scheduled to begin on September 30 in Honolulu, and if Bryant was hoping to at least have his most important teammate on his side, eh, that would not be happening.

During his initial 75-minute interview with Doug Winters and Dan Loya, the Eagle County detectives, Bryant had said many things that quickly made their way into public consumption. One nugget that remained largely concealed, however, came toward the end of the talk, after Loya had switched off his recording device. Wrote Winters in a sealed file: "Bryant made a comment to us about what another teammate does in situations like these. Bryant stated he should have done what Shaq (Shaquille O'Neal) does. Bryant stated that Shaq would pay his women not to say anything. He stated Shaq has paid up to a million dollars already for situations like this. He stated he, Bryant, treats a woman with respect, therefore they shouldn't say anything."

When O'Neal learned of the comments, well, he was not pleased.

Had he treated females poorly? Yes. It was well known that O'Neal fooled around on his wife, Shaunie, whom he married in 2002, and that he had engaged in a lengthy affair with a well-known female Los Angeles sportscaster. O'Neal was hardly a loyal-to-one-woman member of the basketball world, but who among the team (besides the departed Madsen) had been? The Los Angeles Lakers were a traveling rock band, and the arenas and bars were filled with gorgeous young women anxious to lounge alongside fame. Hell, the Rick Fox sexual liaison stories could fill a chapter of a book — and nearly did when his ex-wife, Vanessa Williams, co-authored an autobiography titled *You Have No Idea*. Fox was one of the league's legendary off-the-court players, and when a tabloid ran photographs of him with a sexy blonde in a Hawaii nightclub, few were shocked. Peter Cornell, a 2001 training camp invitee, forever loved telling the story of the time he was asleep in his hotel room and the phone rang at 4:30 a.m. "Hello?" Cornell answered.

"Hello? *Hello?!*" a woman's voice said. "Stop fucking around and tell me who the fuck you're with. Motherfucker, who is in that bed with you?"

"Um," Cornell said, "who is this?"

"This is Vanessa — Rick's wife," she said. "Who is this?"

"Pete Cornell. I'm trying to make the team."

"Oh," an embarrassed Williams replied. "I've got the wrong room. I'm so sorry."

Cornell laughed at the memory. "I can't blame her," he said. "Rick was all over the young girls in Hawaii."

This, though, was not about Fox. It was the ratting out of O'Neal, and Bryant's words were a major violation. There was an unspoken code among NBA teammates, and it read (inexactly): What happens with the club stays with the club. Whether or not O'Neal had paid women up to a million dollars was beside the point. It wasn't Bryant's place to say such a thing. "That made a big division," recalled Jackson. "Divulging things about Shaq that were personal — not good for us. The irritation caused a huge rift."

"That didn't change the dynamic player-wise, but street-wise, it did," recalled O'Neal. "Street-wise it definitely did. I can't tell you how that came about, but me paying off women — no, that never happened. Never. I told him that as a story, just saying it happened to make it comfortable for him to go on and settle and just get rid of his own problem. Check all my files. I said, 'Hey, man, it's easier to just handle this shit now and get it taken care of. I don't know what happened, I don't care what happened. Just get this shit taken care of.' He's like, 'I didn't do all that, blah, blah.' So I said, 'Man, I had to pay $1 million one time.' Just being the big brother. Because sometimes being the big brother is about stories. Not actions. Stories. Pay the money and move on. 'I had to pay a million and you never heard about it.' That's not true, but it's the story I told him. Then he did what he did."

On October 2, the Lakers' private plane flew all the players and coaches from Los Angeles to Honolulu — with the exception of Bryant, whose representatives contacted Kupchak and explained that he was "sick." Jackson tried reaching out to check in on his star but was informed by a woman who answered the phone at the Bryants' Newport Beach house that he was "resting." The coach was beside himself. If he was really sick, wouldn't Bryant have gone to a doctor by now? It was all nonsense.

"I'm not privy to his condition," Jackson said when asked what was bothering Bryant. "I wasn't told that he was sick, I was told that he was under the weather. Now is that the marine layer fog that's in L.A. that's been plaguing us for two weeks? Yes, I think that's probably under the weather."

Back in 1998, while making his first All-Star Game start, Bryant had infuriated Karl Malone when he waved the Mailman out of his way in order to go one-on-one against a defender. It was a dark moment that screamed "young basketball entitlement." Yet Malone, to his credit, was not one to hold grudges. He came to Los Angeles to win a title, and if that meant embracing a mercurial star facing rape charges, so be it. Also, while Malone's wholesome reputation had persisted ever since he was drafted out of Louisiana Tech with the 13th overall pick in 1985, he — like Bryant — possessed his share of ugly secrets.

In the fall of 1983, when he was a 20-year-old college sophomore, Malone had returned to his hometown of Summerfield, Louisiana, and impregnated a 13-year-old named Gloria Bell. When, on May 3, 1984, she gave birth to a son named Demetress, Karl was nowhere to be found. The

Bell family held off on suing Malone for statutory rape because they were aware he would soon be making big money in the NBA, which could help in raising the child. Yet Malone denied paternity of the boy, and when the family took him to court to request he pay $200 per week, he (*poof!*) vanished. Ultimately, a judge ordered Malone take a paternity test, and a positive result led to the court's ordering him to surrender $125 a week — $6,500 a year — plus medical expenses. Malone, making $825,000 with the Jazz, argued that the sum was too much.

This was actually Malone's second dalliance with out-of-wedlock children. When he was 17, he impregnated a girl from his hometown, and after she gave birth to twins, Malone denied being the father until a newspaper broke the story years later.

Hence, out of understanding or a shared experience, Malone was the one Laker who seemed to have empathy for Bryant, especially when — on the same day the team flew to Hawaii — the news came out that a judge in Colorado said defense lawyers would not be allowed to interrogate the alleged rape victim in a preliminary hearing. Making matters worse, a different judge rejected a request for a press moratorium.

When asked, Malone uttered repeated support for Bryant. *The team needs its shooting guard. The kid is strong and determined. We won't win a title without him.* Yet the Mailman was largely alone in these sentiments.

The Lakers held their first workout on Friday morning, the day after their arrival, and all the media wanted to discuss was life without Kobe. O'Neal, who was seeking a contract extension and felt underappreciated by a franchise that now clearly prioritized its other superstar, set the tone for the ensuing weirdness by greeting the first Kobe-related question with (yes) a cat noise.

"Do you think the team needs Kobe to compete?"

Meow.

"Have you spoken with Kobe?"

Meow.

"Are you worried about —"

Meow. Meow.

Finally, when asked, "How does it feel to not have the full team here?" O'Neal set aside his Whiskers impression and provided a response.

"The full team," he said in his deepest of baritones, "is here."

The other Lakers loved it. O'Neal was speaking for the unit — they acknowledged Bryant's talent, but they were just fine without his presence.

On Saturday, Bryant finally arrived in Hawaii via his own chartered jet, which he expected the team to pay for. (The Lakers did not.) Tim Brown and Steve Henson of the *Los Angeles Times* wrote that "he was thin and looked tired. His skin was nearly the color of shale, as though he hadn't been outdoors in months." There was no real explanation; certainly no apology. Kobe Bryant was late because Kobe Bryant was late. Tough shit.

He entered the gym at the University of Hawaii and was met by teammates with a couple of halfhearted hugs (Malone and Payton greeted him warmly) but mainly uncomfortable stares and shrugs. Less than a month earlier, in a brief late August meeting at the Lakers' facility, Kupchak told Bryant that the team cared about his well-being and wanted to make sure he was handling things well.

Bryant wasn't feeling it. "Shaq," he said, "didn't call me this summer."

"Kobe, I gave you a message from him," the general manager replied. "He invited you to Orlando to get away from everything."

"Shaq didn't have to leave a message through you," Bryant said. "He knew how to reach me."

Later, while talking to Jackson, Bryant snapped. "I'm not gonna take any shit from Shaq this year," he said. "If he starts saying things in the press, I'll fire back. I'm not afraid to go up against him. I've had it."

Bryant's debut practice was no thing of beauty. A man who prided himself on physicality and always being in the best possible shape had been worn down by his recent trials. He worked out when he could, but the daily routine had turned largely to mush. Now, on this first day, he spent much of his time on an exercise bike off to the side of the court, sweat pouring down his temples. Unlike in past years, when Lakers training camp felt more like a tropical luau than a hardened effort to prepare for battle, the 2003 version featured Malone demanding the doors be shut and the large fans be turned off every day. As a result, the gym became a sauna, and Bryant's limited off-season conditioning revealed itself.

After the practice concluded, Bryant allowed the media to gather around and ask their questions. It had long been one of his better qualities. Certain superstars were known to hide when things went poorly. Not Bryant. Now, staring down two dozen reporters, he admitted, "Basketball to me just took a back seat," and then: "I'm terrified. Not so much for myself, but just for what my family is going through. They had nothing to do with this, but just because their names have been dragged in the mud I'm scared for them."

Toward the end of the Q&A, he was asked by Bernie Wilson of the Associated Press whether he would discuss the case with his work colleagues. It was a perfectly legitimate question that ignored Kobe Bryant's history as a Laker. He had told no teammates of his engagement, invited no teammates to his wedding, and called no teammates when the rape accusations were made. None of the Lakers had ever visited his house, and most had never even shared more than one or two meals.

Would he discuss the case with his teammates? "Why?" he said. "I could put it into words a million times, they'll never understand, they'll never get it. It doesn't matter. We'll come here, we'll work together as a team and we'll play the game. [My family] is living through this. Everybody else is just watching."

Some of the veteran Lakers presumed Bryant would spend his time in Hawaii humbly going about his task, contrite, soft-spoken, head down. But to the franchise's all-time leader in lacking awareness, such behavior was an impossibility. There were 18 men invited to camp, and Bryant — as always — felt compelled to establish his dominance. The one real battle for a roster spot featured Eric Chenowith (a 7-foot-1, 270-pound University of Kansas product) and Jamal Sampson (6-foot-11 and 235 pounds, out of Cal) grappling to be O'Neal's backup. Early on, Bryant decided he had a problem with Chenowith, or at least that he should give the rookie as much grief as humanly possible. Only Chenowith wasn't a rookie. After being tabbed by the Knicks 43rd overall in the 2001 NBA draft, then cut,

Chenowith had spent time on the payrolls of the Kings, the SuperSonics, and the Clippers, playing for the Greenville Groove, the Huntsville Flight, and the Roanoke Dazzle of the National Basketball Development League (NBDL), as well as Pau-Orthez, in France's top league, the LNB Pro A. He had been around, and the other Lakers treated him with respect. O'Neal, in particular, went out of his way, inviting Chenowith (but not Bryant) to a summer party at his house in Bel Air to celebrate Malone's and Payton's joining Los Angeles. Each guest received a personalized 12-by-16-inch engraved-in-marble invitation that read (in this case) ERIC CHENOW-ITH — SHAQUILLE O'NEAL CORDIALLY INVITES YOU TO HIS HOME TO WELCOME NEW TEAMMATES.

Chenowith was shocked, and entered the mansion knowing not what to expect. Upon being approached by O'Neal, he introduced himself and said, "It's an honor to be here."

The center — wearing a red-and-white throwback Julius Erving 76ers jersey — laughed. "Naw, man, I'm thrilled to have you," O'Neal said. "I've heard all about you, and my house is your house. Whatever you want. What do you need? You need a cigar? Come with me . . ."

The two giants walked to the rear of the backyard, where, beneath a tent, a team of Cuban immigrants in white suits were rolling stogies. "Make him the best one you can," O'Neal ordered. Then, turning to Chenowith, "Bro, make sure and take some home for a friend."

"He treated me like I was one of them," said Chenowith. "Really, he treated me like I mattered."

To Bryant, however, guys like Eric Chenowith didn't matter. They were scraps of excess fat, meant to be gnawed on by the neighborhood dog. One day, instead of practicing, Jackson and the coaches honored the training camp tradition of surprising the Lakers with a game of paintball. A bus picked the team up at 10 a.m. and drove 40 minutes to a mock battlefield in Waimānalo, on the east side of Oahu. Once there, the players filed off the vehicle to be greeted by personalized military gear with names and numbers embroidered into the vests. Over the next two hours, the four teams of five engaged in all-out war ("Karl and Shaq, they hid all day," Bryant said. "They went way back in the trees. I think they were searching for Bigfoot or something"), and when it ended, the Lakers were introduced to 21 United States military airmen from Bellows Air Force Station invited to meet the team with their families. Jackson wanted the Lakers to see what heroism really looked like, and he wasn't disappointed by the overall reaction. "This," Malone said while shaking a soldier's hand, "is what gets my dick hard. The chance to thank these men."

After a few minutes for autographs and pictures, an ice cream truck arrived, stocked with every imaginable style and flavor. Payton, a comically loud man with a cutting-edge sense of humor, cackled for all to hear, "You motherfucking rookies better be getting me my ice cream!" The team's two first-year plebes, forwards Luke Walton and Brian Cook, shuffled over to the vehicle.

From behind, Chenowith felt someone's palm pushing into the back of his head.

"Rook, you better get me my motherfucking ice cream. Get me my ice cream, rook . . ."

It was Bryant.

Chenowith rose. Kobe Bryant was a five-time All-Star. Eric Chenowith averaged 9.8 points in the Development League. What choice did he have? So he commenced with the creamsicle walk of shame, then heard Bryant bark, "You better fucking run! Don't walk, run!"

Chenowith started to jog, only to hear Jackson's familiar two-finger whistle. "Chenowith!" he yelled. "Get over here! You're *not* a rookie!" He was, however, humiliated, and felt Bryant's glare as he returned to his initial seat with the other veterans. "You're still a fucking rookie to me," Bryant said.

Out of nowhere, an enormous arm reached around Chenowith's neck. "Listen," O'Neal said, "fuck that dude. Fuck him. I've got your back. Fuck him. You're with me. You ain't a fucking rookie. It's all good. I've got your back."

That was all Chenowith needed to hear.

"Kobe was a complete prick," he said years later. "Not only is he a douchebag, he's a douchebag who's a prick. If he knows he can get something from you, he'll treat you with respect. If there's nothing in it for him, he can't give a shit."

With the exception of sharing ice cream with veterans, the entire training camp was a train wreck. Though it seemed impossible, O'Neal had arrived in the worst shape of his career — a fat blob of athletic indifference. As part of an endorsement deal with 24 Hour Fitness, that off-season he had been assigned a personal trainer named Cory Gilday, a 25-year-old Canadian who relocated from Portland, Oregon, to Orlando to work specifically with the Laker. Gilday loved O'Neal more than anyone he had ever helped — "I mean, the gym we worked at was next to a tanning salon," he recalled. "One day the woman at the front desk at the salon was crying. He asked her what was wrong. She was three months behind rent, and had her eviction papers with her. Shaq made a phone call right then and there, took care of it. That was him." Yet O'Neal was dead-dog lazy. He refused to keep to a diet. He hated weights. He abhorred running. "I tried getting two workouts a day from him," Gilday said. "That was impossible. We were near a high school, so we'd go to the field, get some guys and play flag football. That was okay. I saw an article that talked about his 'grueling' summer workouts. I laughed. He's the best guy. Maybe ever. But he didn't work hard, and it showed."

Shaq hated Kobe. Kobe hated Shaq. John Black, the team's media relations director, came up with the idea of staging an *Abbey Road*–inspired media guide cover, with the four superstars crossing a street, à la the Beatles. Everyone liked the idea — save O'Neal. "It wasn't even, 'Let me think about it,'" recalled Black. "It was, 'Fuck no. I'm not doing that.' Shaq was just in a nasty mood. There was some discomfort going on at that time."

O'Neal was fed up with the team's unwillingness to give him a three-year extension that would afford him more than $100 million, and after blocking a Mike Dunleavy shot in an October 7 exhibition against the Nuggets, he turned toward the Laker bench and Jerry Buss and shouted,

"Now you gonna pay me?" Later, after spotting reporters in the arena's hallways, he rubbed his fingers together and yelped, "Show me the money! Show me the money!"

"It was disrespectful," said Black. "We had a lot of inquiries, people wanting to know what was our comment, what was Dr. Buss' comment to him doing that. Dr. Buss said publicly it didn't bother him at all. We declined to comment as an organization and tried to downplay it as much as possible. But it did bother Dr. Buss."

That was a Tuesday. On Thursday, Bryant was back in Eagle, this time appearing for his preliminary hearing. The *Vail Daily*'s front-page headline screamed, GRAPHIC DETAILS EMERGE, and that was no lie. With hundreds of people once again gathered outside the Eagle County Justice Center, Bryant sat on a chair and listened to Winters and Gregg Crittenden, the deputy district attorney, lay out the argument for why the case should go to trial. Along with a play-by-play of the night, Winters and Crittenden presented as evidence a T-shirt found in Bryant's hotel room that was stained with Mathison's blood.

Pamela Mackey, the high-priced defense attorney, fired back with a cross-examination that was as thorough as it was controversial. In the course of noting that Mathison's vaginal injuries needed neither stitches nor topical ointment, Mackey blurted out the name "Jessica Mathison" six times in less than 10 minutes — a well-established no-no when it comes to sexual assault cases. She also asserted that Mathison's injuries might have been caused by having multiple sexual partners in a short span. "So her injuries were recent, but you couldn't say how recent?" Mackey asked Winters.

"No," Winters replied. "I couldn't."

"Are they consistent with someone who'd had sex with three men in three days?" Mackey asked.

The question was a stunner. No one claimed Mathison had three sexual partners in three days. But, in Mackey world, no one claimed she *didn't* have three sexual partners in three days, either. "The defense hopes the public will hear that," explained Denver district attorney Norm Early, who attended as an observer. "No one thought the defense would stoop *this* low."

The session ended without Fred Gannett, the Eagle County Court judge, deciding whether there was just cause to send the case to district court for trial, so all the parties were asked to return in six days.

Tim Kawakami, the *San Jose Mercury News* columnist, perfectly surmised Bryant's new existence: "Alone, with his once-charmed life in disarray, his reputation probably gone for good, his knee wobbly after surgery and his freedom over the next few decades in jeopardy. Who is Kobe Bryant now, if he isn't the phenom, the single-minded basketball puritan, the smile that sells a million Big Macs? Who is he if the image is gone, the reputation is in tatters and the game of basketball cannot save him?"

Around the same time Bryant was flying to Colorado, the rest of the Lakers were wrapping up their run in Honolulu and returning to Southern California to finish the preseason with a handful of exhibition games. As the members of the team boarded the plane at Honolulu International Airport, O'Neal yelled to a baggage handler, "Wait! Wait! That suitcase! I need that suitcase!"

A man pulled the black portmanteau from a cart and delivered it to the smiling center. Once the plane lifted off, O'Neal laid the bag across his lap, pressed a couple of buttons, and laughed as it magically unfolded into side-by-side turntables. He placed headphones over his ears and spent the next half hour quietly working on a project. When he was done, he yanked the headphone cord from the jack and called for everyone's attention.

The familiar sounds of 50 Cent's "P.I.M.P." blasted from the speakers (yes, O'Neal also traveled with speakers), only the lyrics were altered. Were one to rap along with 50 Cent, he would open with:

I don't know what you heard about me
But a bitch can't get a dollar out of me

O'Neal, however, had penned his own lyrics . . .

I don't know what you heard about me
Kobe's a bitch, everyone can see
But you ain't never gonna see me on TV
Talking about R-A-P to the E.

Chenowith was sitting alongside Luke Walton, and the two couldn't believe what they were hearing. First, because O'Neal happened to be a shockingly adept freestyle rapper. But second — sweet Jesus. It was the all-time greatest/worst filleting of a teammate. And everyone on the plane (players and coaches) was laughing.

"I turned to Luke," recalled Chenowith, who would be cut a few days later, "and I was like, 'Holy fuck. Is this happening?'

"'Is this what it's like to be a Laker?'"

16

The Last Season

Phil Jackson never wanted Gary Payton to be a Laker.

It's true, and while Los Angeles's coach greeted the veteran point guard's signing with smiles and nods and a big thumbs-up, he had been around long enough to know that even the most smoothly run operation was always one bad apple removed from rot.

In this acquisition, however, Jackson was granted no say. Shaquille O'Neal aspired to put together a superteam. Kobe Bryant aspired to put together a superteam. Karl Malone aspired to join a superteam, but not without Payton, his longtime rival/friend. So even though the triangle offense was no place for a score-first point guard with an ego and a love of the forever dribble, and even though Jackson considered Derek Fisher to be the perfect runner of the show, Jim Buss — Jerry Buss's son and the team's assistant general manager — insisted that Payton be signed. And now he was a Los Angeles Laker.

Oy.

In terms of pure accomplishments, Payton was the best point guard to wear the purple and gold since Magic Johnson's brief 1995–96 comeback. He was a nine-time All-Star and nine-time All-NBA First, Second, or Third teamer with lifetime averages of 18.2 points and 7.4 assists per game. His nickname, "the Glove," was an homage to his lightning-quick hands and ability to pickpocket other guards. In the pantheon of all-time NBA floor generals, there was Magic Johnson, there was Oscar Robertson, there was Bob Cousy, there was Isiah Thomas, there was John Stockton — and there was Gary Payton.

It was, however, complicated. The youngest of Annie and Alfred Owen Payton's five children, he grew up in East Oakland, watching one friend after another succumb to the siren call of gang life. Gary survived, in large part, because of a father who worked a morning shift as a chef at one restaurant and an evening shift as a chef at another restaurant, and put in extra hours as a laborer at a local cannery. A former shooting guard at Alcorn State, Al devoted his free time to coaching kids in the Oakland Neighborhood Basketball League. He was nicknamed "Mr. Mean," and it fit. Al Payton didn't want his players to engage in the sport for joy or for recreation or for a mere escape from the streets. No, you stepped on the court to win at all costs — and as you stomped on an opponent's skull, you told him about it.

That's how Gary rose from the streets to an All-American career at Oregon State to being selected second overall by Seattle in the 1990 NBA draft. He never backed down. He never cowered. He stomped on your skull and told you about it, just like Dad. "I taught the kid the look, the intimidation, the meanness," Al recalled. "When I played, I liked to hurt people."

Gary Payton did not like to hurt people so much as humiliate them. His trash talk history belongs in a museum of the loquaciously absurd. Or, as longtime NBA power forward Michael Cage once said of Payton's lippiness: "He makes you just want to go find a library or something. Some place totally quiet."

If you were married, Payton banged your ugly-ass wife. If you were dating, he banged your ugly-ass girlfriend. Your car was trash. Your house was on fire. Your butt smelled of rotting lizard. You sucked dick. Your teammates sucked dick. Your children sucked dick. When a journeyman forward named Jamie Feick once barked nonsense at Payton, he replied by noting, "Man, you won't even be in the league next year." Moments later, to Payton's delicious delight, an opponent asked him to hold his tongue: he had hurt Feick's feelings. When Timberwolves coach Sidney Lowe (5-foot-11) stood to say something, the 6-foot-4 Payton shouted, "Sit down, you Smurf!" When Chicago's Scottie Pippen was playing without Michael Jordan, Payton went to town. "Where's Mike at?" he bellowed. "I ain't scared of you now, Scottie. You ain't top 50 of all time. You want me to show you my list? I had you at 51, Scottie. I had you at 51!"

When Denver's Ricky Pierce went after Payton, the Glove snapped, "I'll kill your family."

Wrote Phil Taylor of *Sports Illustrated:*

It will not surprise you to learn that the first time I saw Gary Payton in person, he was talking. It was in 1990, when he was a senior at Oregon State and I was a writer for *The National*, and I had arrived in Corvallis to interview him for a feature story. A sports information staffer brought me to the gym, where I waited while Payton finished his end-of-practice shooting drills, catching passes and hoisting jumpers from the top of the key.

Every release came with accompanying commentary. "Put your hand down, you can't stop this. Too late. Take the early bus and get here quicker next time. Don't even turn around, you know it went in. Ooh, another one. How'd that feel?" All the trash talk wouldn't have seemed so unusual, since Payton's chatty reputation was already well known, except for one thing: No one was playing defense. Payton was taunting the air.

When he was finished, I asked if he always verbally abused imaginary defenders. Payton cocked his head to one side and gave me that quizzical look that would become so familiar to NBA fans, the one he would give referees who called a foul on him when his plastic wrap defense became a little too aggressive. He looked confused for a moment, as if he didn't realize he had been yapping while shooting. Then he said, "It just comes out of me. If you know me, you know I'm always gonna talk."

People laughed at Payton, because his barbs were funny and his voice was high-pitched and his enthusiasm never faded. They also laughed at

Payton because he was talented, and an NBA superstar's goofiness will receive a far more enthusiastic reception than that of, say, Lucious Harris or Calvin Booth. But there was a dark side, and Jackson rightly worried about it. Throughout his era in Seattle, Payton's heroics were matched by his selfishness. He was — in the words of Jelani McCoy, his teammate for three years with the Sonics — "the fucking worst example for any NBA player to be around."

On far too many occasions, Payton would order a Sonic forward or center to get out of the post by screaming, "Move, n — r!" or "Out of the fucking way, n — r!" It was never uttered lightheartedly, always as a threat. "He was really offensive," said Olden Polynice, the former Seattle center. "What happened is he believed his own hype, and it impacted him. I remember one day he came to practice after a night of hanging out wearing his pajamas. He laid on a table and didn't want to practice. I said, 'Motherfucker, get your ass up. You're not *the Glove*. You're just some asshole with a basketball.'"

When he hit a winning bucket, Payton was the happiest man on the planet. When a teammate hit a winning bucket, Payton could be surly and cruel. Once, during the 1999–2000 season, Sonics coach Paul Westphal called for Shammond Williams, a second-year point guard out of North Carolina, to take the game's final shot. He succeeded, and as the ball went through the net, teammates absorbed the newcomer in a swarming hug. Payton, meanwhile, found Westphal and cursed him out. "Don't ever take the ball out of my fucking hands!" he screamed. "Never!"

Like Payton, McCoy was from Oakland, and he, too, possessed a savviness and street sensibility. He laughed at the point guard's motor mouth but refused to cower when, during practices, the insults were aimed in his direction. One day, Payton took things too far and McCoy snarled. "Fuck you, man!" he screamed. "I'll beat your little ass right here. No 'Glove' or 'G.P.' shit. You wanna do this? We can do this right now."

McCoy was 6-foot-10 and weighed 250 pounds.

Payton was 6-foot-4 and 180.

"Fuck you!" Payton screamed. "I'm gonna have my boys come to town and fuck you up. You best hide, bitch."

McCoy giggled. "You mean the same guys you always talk about?" he said. "I'm friends with them, too. They're not gonna do shit."

He was right.

"Gary was a bully," McCoy said. "All that 'Glove' nonsense was image. He ruined teammates on purpose. He would fuck with guys' heads just to test them and be selfish. If you came in with, say, a new watch, he couldn't be nice. It'd have to be 'I'm gonna have 10 of those tomorrow.'"

This was the Lakers' new point guard, and as the regular season approached, Jackson and the coaching staff braced for the worst. And while Payton was a legitimately appalling match for the triangle ("It was just a bad basketball fit," said Kurt Rambis, the assistant coach. "He was not suited for our system at all"), he was — to the shock of many — the most important new face in the locker room.

No longer burdened with having to be the head of a franchise, he willingly deferred to O'Neal and Malone and Fox as team leaders. The trash talk remained, but it was less pointed and not nearly so serious. He also was sensitive to Fisher's status as a respected starter benched in favor of a new arrival, and he never uttered a derisive word to his understudy. "I always tell people Gary wasn't the best player I've ever been around, but he was by far the best leader," said Jamal Sampson, the backup center. "His confidence never wavered, no matter the circumstance. I just watched him to learn how to be a professional."

From the very beginning, the 2003–04 Lakers were a mess, as well as an ongoing test of whether talent and experience could somehow overcome a total lack of chemistry and team spirit and (oh, by the way) a superstar in the midst of a sexual assault trial that might send him to prison. "The good news has less and less staying power for the Lakers," wrote J.A. Adande in the October 21 *Los Angeles Times*. "These days the happiness seems to last for the duration of a sunset, and then the darkness comes down on the franchise all over again."

The regular season was scheduled to commence with an October 28 game against Dallas at Staples Center, and while Payton was talking up "the most talented team I've ever been on," the most talented team he'd ever been on was tearing itself apart. Still recovering from the off-season knee surgery (the one that brought him to Colorado), Bryant made his debut five days before the opener, playing 32 minutes and scoring 15 points in an exhibition loss to the Clippers in Anaheim. Happy faces filled the postgame locker room ("He needed to come back and see that the fans still love him!" Payton said), but it was a mirage. The Lakers — who went so far as to shield Bryant from the media with a black protective curtain by his locker — were furious that he'd rejected the team's four-year, $74 million contract extension in order to become a free agent at season's end. Where was the appreciation? The loyalty? The team agreed to cover a percentage of his private plane expenses to travel to and from Colorado for court hearings — *and Bryant was complaining about the plane.* ("He wanted one with higher status," noted Jackson. "He should feel fortunate he's not footing the whole bill himself.") The Lakers were doing their all to accommodate Bryant, and this was their reward? "In sports," Bryant said snidely, "everything comes to an end." At one point during the Clippers game, Bryant had the audacity to turn to Mike Dunleavy, the opposing coach, during an inbounds play and say, "Get me over here."

Equally troubling was O'Neal — pouty and standoffish over the team's refusal to extend *his* contract — taking his anger out on his head coach. For no apparent reason. When told of Jackson's innocuous and criticism-free injury update comments before a preseason game, O'Neal replied, "Who?" He then added, "I had two Phils in my life (referring to his stepfather, Phil Harrison). I only got one now."*

On October 25, Jackson was in his office watching video of the Mavericks when Bryant walked in, fuming.

"He popped off!" Bryant said.

Jackson didn't have to ask for the *He* to be identified.

"You're kidding me," Jackson replied. "What did he say?"

"Did you read the paper?" Bryant said. "It's in the paper."

Indeed it was. And O'Neal's quote was historically scandalous. He told

---

* Jackson, meanwhile, was trying to negotiate his own new contract, and the Lakers were being stubborn. Yet the coach did his all to keep the news out of the media.

the *Los Angeles Times* that Bryant (wait for it . . . wait for it) needed to rely more on teammates until he regained strength. Which was, eh, correct.

"Kobe, what's wrong with this?" Jackson asked. "Shaq is right. This is exactly what we want you to do."

"Maybe," Bryant replied. "But it's not his business to say that. He can't be talking about my game, about what I should be doing."

"You're not gonna take offense at something like that, are you?" Jackson asked. "It doesn't make any sense."

"Yeah," Bryant said. "I am."

On October 27, Jackson called a 20-minute team meeting to clear the air. Both superstars spoke, then Malone stood and begged for peace and basketball. "I didn't come here to babysit," he said. "I came here to win a ring. You're not paying me enough for this bullshit."

Within the hour, Bryant was back to talking, this time via phone with ESPN's Jim Gray. He told the veteran reporter that, were he to leave the organization, it would be because of O'Neal's "childlike selfishness and jealousy." He proceeded to elaborate on several Shaq-related subjects.

Kobe on O'Neal's leadership: "Leaders don't beg for contract extensions and negotiate some $30-million-plus deal in the media when we have two future Hall of Famers playing here basically for free. A leader would not demand the ball when you have three of us besides you, not to mention the teammates that he's gone to war with the past three years . . . By the way, you also don't threaten not to play defense and not to rebound if you don't get the ball every time down the floor."

Kobe on O'Neal playing in pain: "I don't need Shaq's advice on how to play hurt. I've played with IVs before . . . with a broken hand, a sprained ankle, a fractured tooth, a severed lip and a knee the size of a softball. I didn't miss 15 games because of a toe injury that everybody knows wasn't that serious."

Kobe on O'Neal not staying in touch: "He is not my quote-unquote big brother. A big brother would have called me up over the summer."

On the morning of October 28, as Jackson was in his car driving toward Staples Center for the evening's opener, he received a call from John Black, the team's longtime public relations director. The Lakers wanted a player to give a quick pregame thank-you address to the fans, and Derek Fisher had been chosen to do the job.

Then O'Neal's business managers, Mike Parris and Perry Rogers, asked if their client could speak instead. Black wanted to throw the idea at Jackson.

"Why not?" the coach said. "What better way to welcome in the new season than with some words from the big guy?"

Black stammered.

"I ran that idea past Kobe," he said. "And he wasn't too keen on it."

Jackson was flabbergasted. Why were they running the idea past Kobe? Why were they running *any* ideas past Kobe? He was an immature 25-year-old man-baby facing rape charges and threatening to leave the organization that loved and nurtured him. The Los Angeles coach and his assistants were befuddled by the Buss family's willingness to kneel before a child. Around the same time as he was being accused of sexual assault, Bryant started behaving in curious ways. There were the new tattoos scrolling down his right arm — a crown, his wife Vanessa's name, a halo and angel wings above Psalm XXVII.* He had his daughter's name — Natalia Diamante — scripted onto his lower left arm. There was a marble-size diamond earring that matched the $4 million *Please forgive me for cheating on you* ring he had given Vanessa. He began riding a motorcycle and hired an even-larger-than-usual fleet of bodyguards to protect him from, eh, someone. His God-related quotations increased one hundredfold. How were the Lakers taking this person even slightly seriously?

A compromise was reached. Jackson addressed the crowd, and O'Neal — fed up — commenced with a media boycott. He was done talking. Screw the press.

The game was scheduled for 7:30 p.m., and Gary Vitti, the Lakers' trainer, said Bryant could play up to 30 minutes without doing damage to his knee. But Bryant disagreed. Or, to be precise, he just didn't feel like suiting up. Which, coming on the heels of his ripping O'Neal for minimal effort, was shocking and misguided. But with Bryant in street clothes,

---

* "The Lord is my light and my salvation — whom shall I fear?"

the new Lakers were announced — O'Neal at center, Malone at power forward, Fisher at shooting guard, Payton at point guard, and Devean George at small forward. Before taking the court, the players formed a customary hype circle — arms over arms, bodies swaying. Bryant wanted nothing to do with it, and remained in the locker room for the majority of his team's 109–93 triumph. Playing against a deep and talented Mavs squad, Los Angeles looked every bit the dream team. All five starters scored in double figures, led by a slashing, driving, trash-talking Payton's 21 points and 9 assists. The ball movement was tremendous (16 assists on 22 first-half baskets), the attitudes uncommonly positive.

"I'm not giddy," Jackson said afterwards. "But we're hopeful."

Hope is a vapor.

You have it, you inhale it — you dream it doesn't vanish.

Los Angeles had three dead days before traveling to Phoenix to face the Suns, and for the first time since Payton and Malone signed their contracts, things felt somewhat upbeat. During a Halloween morning practice, Malone and O'Neal engaged in a three-point contest as Payton stood to the side, heckling and howling with each brick. It was the loquacious guard at his absolute best — funny, quirky, upbeat. "Even when things were hard, Gary made it so much fun," said George. "You couldn't take him seriously, because he was so crazy. But fun crazy. Not jerk crazy." O'Neal's silent act toward the press ended ("In marriage," he said, "if you keep talking about a problem, the problem will be there. And I didn't want to talk about 'the problem' if there is a problem"), and — at Jackson's urging — he openly declared a peace settlement with Bryant. "I don't ever take things personally," he said. "He's the yin and I'm the yang. And opposites attract. He's different, but as long as we're on the court it's a must we play team ball and do what's best for the team. Off the court he does his thing, off the court I do my thing. But we're going to continue to get it done on the basketball court."*

---

* The next morning, most of the Lakers enjoyed a chuckle over the story of Travis Taylor, a Baltimore Ravens wide receiver who on October 31 attended the Ravens

Bryant returned for the second game, a 103–99 victory against the Suns on November 1, and while a good portion of the sellout crowd at America West Arena took delight in booing the accused rapist, the Lakers looked sharp. Playing together for the first time in a regular season game, O'Neal (24), Payton (19), Bryant (15), and Malone (18) all scored in double figures, and the fifth ~~Beatle~~ starter, George, contributed 12 points, 12 rebounds, and a couple of steals. Sensitive of losing his preferred point guard, Jackson made certain to give Fisher plenty of time off the bench. His 13 points in 26 minutes were invaluable.

That same day, Jerry Buss sat down with Howard Beck of the *Daily News* for a 30-minute interview about the plight of basketball's most talented and dysfunctional franchise. Twenty-four years had passed since he purchased the team from Jack Kent Cooke, and through the various potholes and apartment fires, everything generally worked out. So, the owner promised, would this. O'Neal, Buss said, would get his contract extension. "I'm sure that when he signs," he said, "he'll be the highest-paid player in the league." Jackson, Buss said, would also be extended. "When Phil signs," he said, "he'll be the highest-paid coach in the league. What more can I say?"

And Kobe Bryant—well, Kobe Bryant was special. Buss referred to him as "my son," insisting he would never trade the lifetime Laker. "Kobe," he said, "is probably going to end up on a level that maybe only two or three players have ever achieved. And I want to be around to see him when he reaches his peak, which is still many years away."

The assurances proved soothing, and Los Angeles went on a familiarly fruitful run, winning the next three games. That stretch included an enchanting 120–117 overtime subjugation of San Antonio, in which Bryant led the way with 16-of-29 shooting for a team-best 37 points. The new-look Spurs featured Robert Horry—an off-season free agent signee—coming off the bench, and while his 12 points in 17 minutes made lit-

---

Gridiron Halloween Party with he and his wife, Rashidah, dressed as Bryant and Mathison. "It's silly, man," Taylor said. "We were out there having fun. It was for a good cause. I have nothing against Kobe. If I offended anybody, I apologize."

tle dent, his visage served as a reminder of a calmer time in Laker land. It was particularly jarring when juxtaposed against Payton, who — Tim Brown wrote in the *Los Angeles Times* — "started to rag Ginóbili, backed him straight down the court, his square jaw chopping at Ginóbili's game and psyche. Ginóbili backpedaled, grinned and flushed, but he didn't turn away, and eventually they both got technical fouls, when Payton had done most of the talking."

Many of the Laker players took the winning streak as a sign that normalcy had returned, a championship was in sight, and another ring would be added to the jewelry box. Much of the optimism, though, was a mirage. The Lakers fell hard at New Orleans, 114–95, as Bryant simultaneously shot 4 for 14 and ignored passes to wide-open teammates. Three nights later, the team again lost badly, this time a 105–95 setback to the Jake Tsakalidis–powered Grizzlies. Falling to Memphis was no longer an embarrassment (the team, pieced together by a general manager by the name of Jerry West, would finish 50-32), but everything about this game represented Bryant at his worst. Los Angeles trailed by 16 entering the fourth quarter, so the shooting guard took eight shots, missing five. Afterwards, in a dejected locker room, players walked past Bryant without saying a word. Jackson told the press that Bryant's legs seemed tired, but it was more than that. "Nothing alienates a player more than the sense that he is being ignored," Jackson later explained. "These are the best players in the whole world, and are not accustomed to being ignored by anybody. Kobe knows how to play basketball the right way. So why does he persist in playing the game his way?"

Asked if Bryant's approach was by design or self-motivated, Jackson shrugged. "I wouldn't choose either of those two options," he said. "It was not by design and I think he just felt he had to punch it up there."

As Bryant took repeated ill-advised shots, Payton and Malone stood and watched. In Utah, the Mailman was used to pick-and-rolls with John Stockton. In Seattle, the Glove was used to perfecting give-and-goes with Shawn Kemp and Vin Baker. Now they were shiny ornaments in purple-and-gold packages. "Maybe when Shaq was out [in the past] Kobe felt he needed to take over," Malone observed afterwards. "But you don't have to now."

By now, anyone well versed in the behavioral sciences of Kobe Bryant knew that the superstar guard came with all sorts of contradictions and complications. He was selfish, moody, arrogant, dismissive, brash, rude. In no particular order.

That said, he had something of an excuse.

On November 13, Bryant returned to Eagle, Colorado, for what was — by legal measures — an enormous nothingburger. He entered Courtroom One of the Eagle County Justice Center that morning, accompanied by attorney Pamela Mackey, and sat for a whopping 12 minutes. The judge, Terry Ruckriegle, had planned on advising Bryant of his rights, explaining the charge against him and reviewing the potential penalty should he be found guilty. The defense waived the process, however, and the $25,000 bail for Bryant remained unchanged. Ruckriegle scheduled a pretrial hearing for December 19, and another for January 23. Bryant would have to return to Eagle for both.

And that was that.

But not really.

Positioned on chairs in the front row of Courtroom One were Al and Lori Mathison, the victim's parents. So were her two brothers and a cousin. They were all there, appearing emotionless but filled with disgust, as Bryant, nattily dressed in a gray suit, sat feet away. He never looked in their direction; never exchanged glances with the mother and father of the woman he allegedly raped. "The family came together to show support for her," Krista Flannigan, a spokeswoman for the Eagle County District Attorney's Office, said. "They want people to recognize there is a victim."

Outside the justice center, hundreds of media outlets elbowed for space in a tent kept warm by generators and emergency heaters the county had acquired four years earlier in anticipation of the Y2K crisis. A parking lot alongside Gallegos Masonry was rented out by the county for $10,000 so that TV trucks had a place to set up. It was pure nuttiness — millions of dollars in travel and salary spent so journalists could shout unanswered questions at an NBA All-Star as he entered and exited a building. For many of the reporters, it was a reunion of those who specialized in the abhorrent ambulance media chase. They had seen one another a few weeks earlier, at the Scott Peterson murder trial preliminary hearing in Modesto, California. Or they covered the Hayman Fire, outside of Denver, in 2002. Or the Columbine shooting of 1999. Inside the tent there were hugs and laughs. A correspondent for *People* magazine saw Peggy Lowe of the *Rocky Mountain News* and yelled, "Hey, you cut your hair!" Steffan Tubbs, an ABC national radio reporter, told a *Vail Daily* reporter that it was wonderful seeing everyone again, then griped that the days were a bit long. That same morning, representatives of more than 100 press outlets fought over who would receive the 22 available courtroom seats for future proceedings. There was screaming and taunting and all sorts of vileness ("Testy," Kathy Heicher, an *Eagle Valley Enterprise* reporter, chose as a kind adjective) — with one important factor somehow forgotten.

They were all here because a woman was accusing a man of grabbing her by the neck and raping her.

The one worthwhile stance to emerge from the sideshow belonged to Don Rogers, managing editor of the *Vail Daily*, who wrote in his Quick Takes column: "The fantasyland, the bickering with teammate Shaquille O'Neal, the still mostly adoring fans — all that faded for another perp walk into court. The family, at the prosecution's invitation, watched the defendant with interest, and not in wonder at his skills at a game. It was a nice visual to ground the case, to help us all remember that this is not merely another tabloid story. These are real people here. Thanks, we needed that."

Bryant would not have to return to Eagle for another month, but that doesn't mean the story faded. Everywhere the Lakers traveled, the boos followed and the insinuations lingered. On one memorable evening against the Nuggets in Denver, two fans arrived wearing orange prison jumpsuits with No. 8 on the front. Eagle, Colorado, hung over the player, the team, the NBA, the nation.

Beginning on November 12, Los Angeles went on a tear, winning 13 of 14, but the run shared space with an unquenchable media thirst for stories. A 22-year-old University of Iowa student left a profanity-laced death threat on Jessica Mathison's answering machine, promising that he would attack her with a coat hanger and kill her. (He was later sentenced to four months in prison.) The *National Enquirer* staked out Mathison's every step and reported that she was suffering from drug addiction (two alleged overdoses in the past year) and had been checked into a treatment center. Talk radio had a field day — Bryant was a rapist! No, Mathison was a gold digger! No, Bryant wanted to use his fame and wealth to suppress the truth! No, Mathison's drug use made her unreliable! "Is it just me," Gideon Rubin wrote in a letter to the editor to the *Vail Daily*, "or has this country gone completely nuts?"

It wasn't just him.

Bryant played well, averaging 21.6 points during the Laker run and (to the dismay of sane humanity) leading the Western Conference All-Star voting. But inside the locker room, he was as distant and disliked as ever. He was also — eight years into his professional career — still uncomfortable. At the time, Jon Finkel, a writer for *Men's Fitness*, was reporting a lengthy profile of Malone. He had spent several days working on the piece, and scored a media credential for the November 26 game against Washington at Staples Center. The Lakers won, 120–99, and afterwards Finkel entered the locker room to meet with his subject. "It was a really tension-filled locker room," Finkel recalled. "Everyone was at their own lockers doing their own things. It was like a 5 p.m. Friday at work — people anxious to leave." The writer and the power forward were sitting on adjacent chairs when suddenly Malone rose, said, "Excuse me one minute," and approached Bryant.

"It was pretty amazing," Finkel recalled. "Karl walked over, gave Kobe a hug. I heard him say, 'Young fella . . .' and then he leaned in, like a dad leaning into his son. Kobe's shoulders slumped and he gave Karl a look the way a kid looks at his dad when he's given a lesson." Bryant proceeded to walk teammate to teammate, offering a mumbled, seemingly insincere "Have a good Thanksgiving" to each man. He glanced at Malone for approval, and received a nod.

"So *that* was interesting," Finkel said when Malone returned.

"That," the power forward replied, "does not appear in your story."

It did not.

In the winter of 2003–04, it was easy — almost expected — to hate Kobe Bryant.

In the minds of many, he was a rapist who used celebrity and money to get by in life. He was a bad man living a charmed existence, and there were many infuriating things about that.

And yet . . .

Even Kobe Bryant's biggest loathers had to be grudgingly impressed by how he (professionally) was handling things.

On December 13, the Lakers fell at Portland, 112–108, with a starting-to-feel-under-the-weather Bryant scoring 35 points on 10-for-18 shooting from the field. He was pacing the team with 22.1 points per game, and the 18-4 Lakers were the class of the league. The next morning, though, Bryant woke up with a clogged head and a slight fever, and two days later he called in sick and missed practice with flu-like symptoms. The question (asked by teammates and beat reporters) was whether this was merely a run-of-the-mill, shit-happens malady, or if the pressures of being Kobe were catching up with him.

Los Angeles was scheduled to host the Denver Nuggets on December 19 at Staples Center, and the day was guaranteed to test Bryant in ways that a mere drive to the hoop over Michael Doleac couldn't possibly compare to.

That morning, he woke up at 4:30 to catch the two-hour charter flight to Eagle. He arrived shortly before 8 a.m. Pacific time, with a black SUV ferrying him from the airport to Colorado District Court for a motions hearing. Sitting alongside his two attorneys, Mackey and Hal Haddon, Bryant listened as his defenders argued why they needed to tell the jury all about Mathison's sexual history, as well as her past psychiatric records (highlighted by antipsychotic drug treatment) and two suicide attempts. Mackey argued that the alleged victim had brought the charges against Bryant as a way of "creating drama in her life to get attention."

Attorneys for the prosecution, meanwhile, contended that Mathison's sexual history was irrelevant, and that her medical records had to remain confidential because of Colorado's physician–patient privilege laws. Disclosing the details, Deputy District Attorney Ingrid Bakke argued, would "have a considerable global impact" in discouraging sexual assault victims from coming forward.

Come day's end, an exasperated and overwhelmed Judge Terry Ruckriegle delayed testimony, sending nine witnesses home and scheduling the next motions hearing for January 23.

What followed was, NBA-wise, unprecedented.

Bryant departed the courthouse at 5:30 p.m. Pacific time, slid into the parked SUV, rushed to the airport, and flew back to Los Angeles, where another SUV (this one white) was waiting to dart him to Staples Center. At 7:53 p.m., the vehicle pulled into the Staples Center garage and out jumped Bryant, flanked by two security guards. The trio sprinted through the stadium bowels and into the home locker room, not altogether unlike Clark Kent dashing down a Metropolis side street seeking out a telephone booth.

The game had commenced 23 minutes earlier, with Kareem Rush starting at shooting guard. Bryant spent roughly 25 minutes in seclusion — changing from street clothes into his familiar No. 8, stretching. "Someone brought him some McDonald's," recalled Jamal Sampson. "He gobbled it down." At the start of the second quarter, with Los Angeles leading 27–19, Jackson put his star guard on the floor and the crowd of 18,997 greeted their very own accused rapist with a loud standing ovation. (Nicole Richie, the reality star, exclaimed, "I want [Kobe] to have sex with me!" during a mid-game interview.) It was the first time since 1999 that he had come in off the bench.

The game encompassed everything a basketball player could love and loathe in Kobe Bryant. Although his team had rolled along without him, Bryant — being Bryant — felt compelled to take over. That's why, over the next three quarters of play, he launched one ill-advised shot after another and drove into one double-teamed corner after another. The flow that had been established (dump it down to O'Neal in the paint, let a red-hot

Slava Medvedenko fire away from midrange turf) was quickly destroyed, and with 2.5 seconds left to play, the Carmelo Anthony–led Nuggets tied the score at 99. "[Kobe] was anxious to show the fans he could spend an entire day in one court and yet be his usual self at night in the other," Jackson recalled. "But he wasn't his usual self."

The Lakers had a final opportunity to avoid overtime. Bryant took the inbounds pass from George, sliced left, pump-faked Jon Barry, the Denver guard, and hit a 21-foot jumper for the victory. As he fell backwards to his rear end, Los Angeles's players sprinted onto the court and mobbed their comrade. The 101–99 win was thrilling, and afterwards the other Lakers were . . . furious.

Inside the locker room, any anticipated "For Kobe's a Jolly Good Fellow!" sing-along was swiftly muffled. Los Angeles should have won by 10, maybe 15. The Nuggets were a mid-level team with a rookie superstar (Anthony, the guard out of Syracuse) who, of course, Bryant *just had to* attack. It always came down to a test of manhood for the Laker, an unhealthy and unattractive need to prove might. When Los Angeles played Cleveland and its rookie phenom LeBron James that season, the other Lakers knew Bryant would be on his worst behavior. The same went for a trip to Miami to meet Dwyane Wade. Now, despite the victory, no one wanted anything to do with Bryant. Payton left without speaking to the media, as did O'Neal. Malone, usually the best talker of the bunch, also darted out quickly. When Ramona Shelburne of the *Daily News* asked why the rapid exit, Malone said, "I was just thinking about what my mother always told me . . . that sometimes it's best just not to say anything." Asked if Bryant's shot selection was an issue, he said, "Uh, yeah," while rolling his eyes. Then, "That has something to do with it, you think?"

Regardless, Bryant's mettle could not be denied. Rapist or no rapist, in the span of a day he had woken before dawn, flown to Colorado, sat in a courtroom 750 miles from home, returned from Colorado, rushed to a stadium, arrived late, changed, stretched, entered in the second quarter, scored 13 points, and hit a game-winning shot. Few even knew that, at halftime, he was connected to an IV. "You can't compare the stress [of the trial] to anything else," Bryant recalled. "One is life, real life, the other is a game. Can't compare them. Basketball, for me, was my refuge, my sanctuary."

That night, Bryant received a handful of calls from friends, telling him how inspiring it all felt. "For them, if that's what they get from that, I'm happy and I appreciate that," he said. "But for me, it's just going out there and playing."

The victory improved Los Angeles to an NBA-best 19-5, and Mitch Kupchak and Phil Jackson were lulled into believing this all might go surprisingly smoothly. NBA reality, however, can be harsh, especially when you're relying on a roster of elder statesmen to last an entire season. On December 21, in a 107–101 win against the Suns, Malone played four minutes before limping off the court. An MRI revealed a tear in his right knee, and what was expected to be three missed games turned to five missed games, then ten missed games — then a nightmarish 39 missed games. The injury had been misdiagnosed. Malone had spent 18 years in Utah as an iconic ironman, sitting out just 10 total contests. But he was 40 now, and a 40-year-old body isn't a 25-year-old body.

A day after the Mailman went down, Jackson spoke at length with — of all the people in all the places — Dennis Rodman, now 42 and the newest member of the Long Beach Jam of the minor league ABA (American Basketball Association). Following his brief span with the Lakers in 1999, Rodman caught on for 12 games with the Dallas Mavericks before vanishing. Yet for all the smoking, the drinking, the drugs, the late nights, the man could *always* rebound. Jackson told the media he and his former player had chatted via phone but that it wasn't serious. Then, a few days later, Tex Winter went to the Pyramid in Long Beach to watch Rodman play with the Jam. The experience was memorable. Winter rose from his seat at halftime to use the bathroom and somehow found himself inside the Jam locker room, where Rodman was sitting alone, head in hands, crying. He hadn't played organized basketball in nearly three years, and an underwhelming first-half performance left him irrational. Winter reassured him the talent was still there — that he just needed to get back into the groove. The words were merely to placate. Rodman was no more a viable 2003 NBA player than Wilt Chamberlain. Who was dead.

Yet the next afternoon, Rodman's handlers issued a press release that read: "Tex Winter told Dennis Rodman that he needs another week or two to be able to play at the level he is used to playing and will need a few weeks before he is ready to play in the NBA again."

The Rodman idea died a quick death. Malone's spot in the lineup was handed to the game-yet-antiquated Horace Grant. But it was never right. Never felt right. Never looked right. Never fully blended. In a January 2 loss at Seattle, O'Neal strained his calf after 14 minutes of play, and what seemed to be a minor malady resulted in the center's missing nearly a month. Though few dared admit it aloud, O'Neal was no longer the same dominant force who'd arrived in Los Angeles seven years earlier. Everything was a second or two slower. His motion. His recovery time. His enthusiasm. "When he was younger, he bounced off the floor with amazing quickness for a big man," Jackson wrote. "Now he had to bend down and load up before he jumps. I'm concerned about him." Suddenly a self-anointed superteam was down to George, Grant, Medvedenko, an in-and-out-of-court Bryant, and Payton, whose happy-to-be-here mood quickly soured.

The veteran point guard was great when everyone was healthy and performing well, but as the wheels started to fall off, his attitude worsened. Though he never called out Bryant, the backcourt was an ill-suited pairing of need-to-shoot point guard and need-to-shoot shooting guard. Wherever the ball went, it rarely returned. Communication between the players was minimal. There was no natural feel. No flow. Los Angeles dropped a third-straight game (and fifth loss in six contests) with a 106–90 setback to Minnesota on January 6, and afterwards Payton flipped. He stood by his locker, half dressed, and unloaded. "I didn't sign up for this shit," he ranted to reporters. "This is B.S. I'm not gonna even sit here and lie to you. I am frustrated. But I've got to be the one to be the older statesman and try to go through it. I'm the one that can't let it really get to me. *We* have to deal with it."

By "we," many assumed Payton meant Jackson, who — despite a calm exterior — wasn't dealing with it particularly well, either. The longtime criticism of the coach was that his charmed career had always featured superstars who made the winning nearly automatic. Suddenly the Lakers were coming apart, and Jackson was allowing the principles he had initiated and enforced to be ignored. Midway through a January 7 loss to Denver, Jackson scowled toward Bryant after a sloppy play led to a Nuggets bucket. "You can't make that pass!" he barked at the guard.

"Well," Bryant replied, "you better teach those motherfuckers how to run the offense."

The disrespect — to his coach, to his teammates — was staggering, and Jackson was fed up. This was his fifth year of Kobe Bryant babysitting duties, and enough was enough. Bryant was rude to his peers, rude to his seniors, rude to . . . everyone. The franchise had gone out of its way to support him during the sexual assault ordeal, and Bryant showed nary an ounce of gratitude. He talked a good game about winning but oftentimes seemed most concerned with taking his 30 shots and receiving the postgame glory. One January day, after Bryant refused to listen to his orders, Jackson called his agent, Todd Musburger, and told him it was time to resign as coach. "No, no, no," Musburger replied. "Let them make the move. Don't do it." Jackson listened, then walked into Kupchak's office and demanded the Lakers trade their young cornerstone. He was not kidding. "I won't coach this team next year if he is still here," Jackson said. "He won't listen to anyone. I've had it with this kid." It was similar to the words he'd shared with his assistant coaches a few days earlier, when he told them, "Kobe has become un-coachable. If he's here next year, I won't be."

The All-Star weekend was held in Los Angeles in mid-February, and what was supposed to be a celebration of all things Lakers turned to hell. Jerry Buss was informed of his coach's stance, and he hated it. Kobe Bryant was the future. Not Shaq, not Phil Jackson. A few days earlier, the team had issued a press release explaining that a contract offer to Jackson (he was seeking an increase from $6 million to $12 million annually) was being suspended. "That," said J.A. Adande, "was wild." When asked for a comment on the news, Bryant said, sans a sliver of emotion, "I don't care."

Around this same time, when the team was in Miami, Jackson invited Fox and O'Neal to visit his hotel room for a state-of-the-Lakers powwow. He first asked whether the two veterans thought Bryant should sit out the season and focus solely on the trial. Neither believed that to be a good idea. Then a second question. "I'll never forget it," Fox recalled. "He asked whether we thought we could win a championship with Kobe."

O'Neal didn't need time to think. "No," he said. "No way."

Fox agreed. "Honestly, Phil," he said, "I don't think we can win a championship with Kobe or without Kobe."

Damn.

Meanwhile, several of the team's veterans were horrified by the way the vaunted triangle offense had been turned to applesauce. Yes, by Bryant's continued selfishness. But also by Payton. The system played to all of Payton's weaknesses — it required patience, humility, a willingness to share the ball. And as the squad struggled, Payton more and more wanted to revert to his Seattle ways. To hell with the multiple passes, to hell with the designated spots on the court. Slash, cut, drive — that was the Glove's game. "Gary was asked to be disciplined when his entire career was about instinct," said Rick Fox. "I understood his anxiety about it."

"The offense was too complex for Gary," Jackson said. "He was just lost."

With Jackson watching helplessly from the sideline, the Lakers were a muddy puddle of disarray. They posted a 17-13 mark in January and February, with Bryant (who was continuing to fly to Colorado for court appearances) missing nearly 13 games, owing to two causes. First he sprained his right shoulder in a matchup against Cleveland. Then he suffered a severe cut on his right index finger while either (depending on whom one asks):

A. accidentally punching his hand through a glass pane while moving boxes at his home (the reason presented by the team).
B. [*fill in the blank with the most sinister action you can imagine*] (the reason presented across the Internet by his detractors and conspiracy theorists).

Whatever the case, little was going well, and when the Utah Jazz were fined $15,000 by the NBA for an on-court skit during which a Karl Malone impersonator pretended to beg Jazz owner Larry Miller to let him return

to Utah (featuring the quote "I guess it could be worse. I could be Ko —"),
it was clear the once mighty Lakers were now the joke of the league.

"Nothing felt right," said Fox. "That's what I remember about the season. Even when we were playing well, nothing ever felt quite right."

On April 11, 2004, the Lakers visited Sacramento for a game that —
thanks to recent history — now felt like some sort of blood war.

Over the preceding six weeks, the team had (sort of) managed to regain
its footing, at least enough so that a 54-25 record had Jackson's squad
feeling relatively good about itself.

Was everything roses and peaches? Hardly. Payton butchered the triangle. Bryant continued to fly in and out of Colorado for his hearing, and
on the afternoon of March 24 he had the pleasure of sitting for three hours
as Mathison (in a closed-door session) testified all about their encounter.
The team suspended contract talks with Jackson. O'Neal was sued by a
company that claimed he took $63,000 to promote a youth basketball
clinic and then failed to attend. Outside of Derek Fisher, the bench was
woefully thin. It had been a long, winding, uncomfortable road of raised,
lowered, then once again raised expectations. "A joyless ride," wrote Bill
Plaschke of the *Los Angeles Times*.

Now, however, there was reason for optimism. Malone and O'Neal
were back, and the postseason was in sight. Once they dispatched with
the Kings, the Lakers could focus on what they were here to do. Namely,
capture another NBA championship.

Only nothing for Los Angeles would come that easy.

The Lakers and the Kings tipped off at 3:30 p.m. inside Arco Arena,
and fans anticipating a highly competitive afternoon between bitter rivals
were broadsided with a harsh dose of reality. Sacramento jumped out to
an 8–0 lead, and by the end of the first quarter they were up 31–15. The
lopsided score was eye-opening, but what really stood out (especially to
the Los Angeles players and coaches) was the play of Bryant, who did . . .

. . . absolutely nothing.

This is no exaggeration. A man who loved to shoot the way a horse
loves to gallop let loose precisely zero shots in the first quarter. Even when

O'Neal was placed on the bench after picking up two quick fouls. Even when George, Medvedenko, and backup forward Bryon Russell combined to shoot 1 for 11 in the first quarter. Why, Bryant didn't so much as attempt a field goal until there was 6:41 remaining in the half, when his three-point try clanged off the rim. By then the Lakers were trailing 40–23, in a key game tossed into an incinerator thanks to a player who — to cite Plaschke — "didn't shoot, didn't penetrate, didn't create . . . Didn't care?"

The final score, 102–85, featured a Kobe Bryant statistical line (3-for-13 shooting, 8 points, 4 assists) that didn't read as appallingly as it truly was. But inside the Laker locker room, enough was enough. The belief among his teammates, as well as the coaching staff, was that Bryant was making a statement to the men in purple and gold who devoted their lives to criticizing his shot selection, his need to take over a game, his desire to be the alpha. Just a few days earlier, Jackson had complained to the media that "Kobe is doing too much again." Now, by refusing to shoot, Bryant would show them all. It was the ultimate "fuck off" to people he deemed unworthy of his presence, and when, in the immediate aftermath, he said the Kings had "doubled me every time I touched the ball," teammates had to laugh to keep from punching a wall.

"I can't tell you what he was thinking," Payton said afterwards — even though he knew exactly what he was thinking.

"I thought he was feeling the team out, which was good," Jackson said — even though he was merely protecting a player who warranted no such protection.

The only honest take came one day later, when Tim Brown of the *Los Angeles Times* was standing with a player after practice. Provided a guarantee of anonymity, the Laker told Brown, "I don't know how we can forgive him." A second member of the team, also assured his name wouldn't be used, said that Los Angeles could no longer be certain of Bryant's mentality. When, on the morning of April 13, Bryant saw Brown's 838-word front-of-the-sports-section piece, headlined AIR IS HEAVY FOR BRYANT, LAKERS, he lost his mind.

He stormed into the practice facility on Nash Street in El Segundo, a rolled-up *Los Angeles Times* sports section tucked beneath his arm. He walked from player to player, shoving the article into each man's face. "Did you say this?!" he screamed.

No.

"Did you say this?!"

No.

"Did you say this?!"

No.

The furor was palpable. So was the awkwardness. *Someone* had uttered the words. Later, during a team meeting, Bryant continued with the questioning. "Right here and right now!" he said. "I want to know who said this shit!"

Again, silence.

Uncomfortable.

Awkward.

Painful.

Silence.

Finally, Malone cleared his throat. "Kobe," he said, "obviously no one said it or no one wants to admit they said it. You've just got to let it go."

Bryant was not prepared to let it go. He told Malone to fuck off. Malone suggested that perhaps Bryant should fuck off. This was not a discussion, but a screaming match with the potential to turn physical. It wasn't altogether unreminiscent of the summer 2001 fight between Bryant and O'Neal—the scrappy guard blind to the fact that the man he was agitating could physically destroy him.

At long last, Jackson stepped in. His grasp on the team—once as strong as a vise—had all but vanished. The triangle was a thing of the past. Bryant (who'd recently told John Black he didn't "have long to be in the gold armor") had one foot out the door and would refuse to speak with the press for the next 11 days. O'Neal wasn't sure whether he'd be back. Malone would certainly retire at season's end. Payton was miserable. His backup, Fisher, was frustrated over limited minutes.

The Lakers would finish out the regular season with a pair of victories and — thanks to a rare dose of good fortune — enter the playoffs as the second seed.

They had won 56 games in the ugliest of manners, and by now many of the players just wanted it all to end.

One way or another.

17

Survival

On the evening of Friday, June 17, 1994, the New York Knicks and the Houston Rockets met inside Madison Square Garden for Game 5 of the NBA Finals. The series was tied, and a matchup of marquee big men — New York's Patrick Ewing vs. Houston's Hakeem Olajuwon — made this must-witness sports television.

Yet at the same time the teams were going back and forth, the United States was captivated by a far more riveting drama. In Los Angeles, O.J. Simpson, the Pro Football Hall of Famer and celebrated pitchman/actor/broadcaster, was being driven around the city in a white Ford Bronco, wanted by police for the murder of his ex-wife, Nicole, and a man named Ron Goldman.

As the car led law enforcement on a 90-minute slow-speed chase along the 405 freeway, NBC settled on a split screen. The network would show Rockets-Knicks as the main image, with the Ford Bronco cut in on the right side.

It is one of the most riveting events in television history, only the NBA hated it. The night was supposed to belong to the league, and now it was being hijacked by a competing narrative. The game's 7.8 rating was the lowest for a Finals telecast since 1981. People wanted O.J., not John Starks.

A decade later, the National Basketball Association was once again facing a split — basketball over here, legal drama over here. The date was May 11, 2004, and the Los Angeles Lakers were trailing the San Antonio Spurs two games to one in the second round of the Western Conference play-offs. As expected, Phil Jackson's club had dispatched the heavily flawed Rockets in a five-game opening-round cakewalk, but now they were in a hole against a postseason-tested squad with a coach, Gregg Popovich, accustomed to winning big games and a superstar forward, Tim Duncan, who never shied away from an important shot.

Yet instead of all the focus being on the night's game, there was a distraction. For the fourth time in 2003–04, Kobe Bryant would be spending the morning of a workday inside a faraway courtroom. Hence, after no more than three hours of sleep, he woke inside his Newport Beach home at 4:30 a.m., rushed to the airport, flew to Colorado, and arrived at the Eagle County courthouse in time for a 10 o'clock pretrial hearing. By now Bryant was accustomed to all the ritualistic annoyances that came with said ordeal, but that didn't mean he was hardened to them. As he prepared to walk through the courthouse metal detector, Bryant placed his cell phone in a basket and reached into his pocket for a small wooden crucifix. Taking a deep breath, he touched the cross to his forehead, then to his lips and his heart. It was a sliver in time — three seconds, no more — that said so much. "I'll never forget that," said Randy Wyrick, covering the trial for the *Vail Daily.* "He looked very vulnerable."

Over the course of the next six and a half hours, Bryant stood feet away from the alleged victim's parents, appearing small and feeble. Though his attorneys waived the formal reading of the charges, Terry Ruckriegle, the judge, detailed the allegation of a forceful sexual assault. He told all 200 or so spectators seated inside the building that Bryant was facing four years to life in prison. The arraignment was being televised, so hundreds of thousands more were viewing at home. Outside the courthouse, media members from around the globe watched on monitors.

"Do you understand the charges against you?" Ruckriegle asked.

"Yes, sir," Bryant replied, standing at the courtroom lectern.

"How do you plead — guilty or not guilty?" he followed.

"Not guilty," Bryant said.

Shortly thereafter, he was back on the private jet, flying to Los Angeles for Game 4 of a tight series. Unlike on past trips, which turned into last-minute will-he-or-won't-he suspense thrillers, Bryant reached Staples Center roughly two hours before tipoff. He took a 20-minute nap inside the car and joined the other Lakers for pregame shooting. Just like NFL executives 10 years earlier during the O.J.-along-the-405 intrigue, many inside the NBA offices cringed whenever announcers or media members referenced rape or sexual assault or potential life imprisonment for a star. Marv Albert, calling the game on TNT, began the network's broadcast with a few words as producers played a video of Bryant being ferried via golf cart to the locker room — "This the scene at 5:19 Pacific Coast Time this afternoon, when Kobe Bryant arrived here at Staples, making it back from his pretrial hearing in Eagle, Colorado. He is in the starting lineup."

The look — alleged rapist superstar — wasn't quite what the NBA was going for.

The drama — alleged rapist superstar — was gold.

During player introductions, Bryant received a standing ovation from the 18,997 in attendance — then led the Lakers with 18 first-half points. It was a remarkable display. Bryant was physically and mentally exhausted. One morning earlier, the *Los Angeles Times* ran a piece that quoted O'Neal's father, Phil Harrison, questioning Bryant's commitment to the team. He then spent the first part of his day saying he hadn't raped a woman in a Colorado hotel, and now he'd somehow placed it all behind in the name of a basketball game. With the exception of maybe Michael Jordan, no one could remember a professional athlete with a better ability to compartmentalize. Yet despite his efforts, Los Angeles trailed 27–21 after a quarter and 53–43 at the half. "The Spurs have to feel very good," Doug Collins, calling the game with Albert, said. "They've come in, they've maintained their poise, and they've executed very nicely here tonight."

The NBA is a league of rallies, and the Lakers rallied. They outscored the Spurs 31–16 in the third, setting up a Kobe Bryant quarter for the ages.

With O'Neal looking old and sluggish and Malone looking old and sluggish and Payton looking old and sluggish, Bryant scored from every conceivable angle, going off for 15 points in the period and totaling a game-high 42. At one point, with the Lakers up 5 and 9:04 left, Bryant dumped the ball down low to O'Neal, who was immediately surrounded by three Spurs. The center passed it back out, and Bryant — standing just beyond the three-point line — was met by Bruce Bowen, San Antonio's best on-ball defender. Bowen positioned himself no more than five inches from Bryant's face, and when the Laker faked right, faked left, Bowen shifted right and left with him. Then — one dribble to the left and (*whoosh*) Bryant fired a deep three-point attempt over his perfectly positioned shadow. Somehow, the basketball swished through the net, and a vanquished Bowen bowed his head. "It's easy to forget how deadly Kobe was," said Malik Rose, the Spurs forward. "You caught yourself worrying about Shaq, and his sidekick was unstoppable."

Afterwards, with the Lakers celebrating a 98–90 triumph that evened the series, Bryant stood alongside TNT's Craig Sager. A white towel was draped across his shoulders. Sweat coated his forehead. He looked ready to crumble. It was, he later said, the best game he had ever played, and now all he wanted was a bed.

"How emotionally drained are you?" Sager asked. "And where did you get the energy?"

"It was a big game," Bryant said. "And, um, just wanted to come out and play as hard as I possibly could. Leave it all out on the floor."

Moments later, a giddy O'Neal told the assembled reporters that his teammate — the one he hated; the one who made his life miserable and uncomfortable; the most selfish basketball entity he had ever known — was "the best player ever."

At that moment, the point was a difficult one to dispute.

Two nights later, the Lakers and the Spurs engaged in an all-time classic playoff game — a back-and-forth battle of the titans that ended when a resigned-to-the-shadows Derek Fisher came off the bench to hit a fadeaway 16-footer with 0.4 seconds left and give visiting Los Angeles a 74–73 win. It was a remarkable moment in the most trying season of the guard's eight-year career. Once upon a time, Fisher had been the obscure rookie first-rounder who lived in Bryant's shadow. Then, with Nick Van Exel running the show, he was the understudy itching for minutes. Then, with Jackson's arrival, he was the point guard of the future. Then, with Payton signing on, he was back to the pine — lightly regarded and eternally frustrated. Fisher, Jackson recalled, "made a greater sacrifice than anyone on the team," and it was about as fun as a pocketful of bees. Fisher was a better fit for the team than Payton, and he knew it. But Payton was famous and heavily hyped and had sacrificed dough to chase a title, and Jackson *had* to start him. Even if he was a poor fit. He *had to*. The shot against the Spurs, therefore, was Fisher's revenge, and afterwards he was greeted in the locker room by a giddy Bryant, who screamed, "You little motherfucker! Way to kick their ass!" Fisher played it down to the media but confided in friends that the long season had ground down his psyche. "I needed that moment," he told George. "For myself."

When the press had cleared the room, Bryant — standing alone — started to hyperventilate. Nobody paid it much mind at first. Kobe was Kobe, probably seeking attention as usual. But then, with sweat pouring down his forehead and his hands shaking, he collapsed to the floor, his brown eyes rolling to the top of his head. He was rushed to the trainer's room, a pair of IVs attached to his arm, people screaming, "Shit! Is he okay? Shit!"

He was quick to regain consciousness, but the same teammates who damned him to hell were amazed. Had anyone played through so much turmoil at this high a level? Even Jackson, who wanted Bryant banished to Siberia (or Milwaukee), couldn't contain his bewilderment. "The kid," he wrote, "is remarkable."

The series — once seemingly slipping away — was wrapped up back in California on May 15 as Bryant's 26 points led the Lakers' convincing 88–76 win.

"If they continue to play like this," Duncan said afterwards, "it's tough to see anyone going around them."

Those words were stated on a Saturday. Four days later, Los Angeles learned the team standing in the way of yet another trip to the NBA Finals would be the Minnesota Timberwolves, who had finished off Sacramento in a grueling seven-game series.

With a 58-24 regular season mark, the Wolves were the Western Conference's top seed. History, though, wasn't on their side — over the previous seven seasons, Coach Flip Saunders's group had always qualified for the playoffs, then always lost in the first round. "Disappointment," said Mike Wells, the beat writer for the *St. Paul Pioneer Press*, "was a Wolves specialty." There were reasons to believe, however, that this season was different. Minnesota's leader was 28-year-old forward Kevin Garnett, the NBA's Most Valuable Player, who averaged 24.2 points, 13.9 rebounds, and 2.2 blocks and was widely considered (along with Bryant and Duncan) one of the sport's three brightest young stars. In the past, the seven-time All-Star's supporting cast had too often been a Who's Who of Who's That? — Sam Mitchell and Dean Garrett, Tom Hammonds and Rasho Nesterović. These Wolves, for once, were loaded. Three other members of the squad averaged double-digit scoring, and in point guard Sam Cassell and small forward Latrell Sprewell, Saunders boasted a playoff-tested duo that wouldn't cower in the Lakers' presence. The team's shooting guard, Trenton Hassell, covered Bryant as well as anyone in the league. "The Wolves had the better team, and I don't think there's much doubt about it," said Steve Aschburner, the *Minneapolis Star-Tribune* beat writer. "But there were so many more factors than just talent. Flip had to overcome a bunch of obstacles."

Two, to be exact.

First, the Lakers had the Timberwolves' number. In Garnett's nine pro seasons, he toppled Los Angeles in just 13 of 41 tries. Why, just one season earlier, when the teams squared off in the first round, Los Angeles vanquished the Wolves in six dirt-off-their-shoulder games. It was simple stuff — even as Minnesota took three of four during the regular season. "Honestly, I don't think they believed they could beat the Lakers," said Aschburner. "They thought they were still playing the 2000-to-2003 Lakers. They weren't. This wasn't that good of a team. But the Wolves were intimidated."

Second, there were Cassell's balls — his *really* big balls. After hitting a particularly clutch shot against Sacramento in Game 7 of the Western Conference semis, the Minnesota point guard celebrated by commencing what would famously come to be known as the "Big Balls" dance. In short, he knee-highed down the court while extending his arms, cupping his hands, and pretending to cradle a pair of, eh, grapefruits adjacent to the front of his shorts.

The 19,944 fans filling the Target Center loved it. But inside the locker room after the win, Cassell — who was already suffering from a bad back and a strained hip flexor — experienced excruciating pain. Thanks to the Big Balls dance, Cassell had either strained his groin or torn it. Out of respect for their gritty standout, the organization never released details of the embarrassing malady. But Saunders was simultaneously devastated and outraged. He had coached players who broke legs chasing loose balls, cracked skulls sprawling across the court. He'd seen men collapse to the hardwood from exhaustion and heart disease. The idea of the mimicking of enlarged testicles costing his men a championship shot? It was too much to digest.

With a somewhat healthy Cassell, Saunders was convinced Minnesota would beat Los Angeles. Without him, it was a long shot. Even Cassell, who long denied that Big Balls did the team in, admitted years later that his injury doomed Minnesota. "It's the only way Los Angeles won," he said. "The pick-and-roll with me and Kevin? They had no answer for it."

The series opened on May 21 in Minneapolis, and a 97–88 Laker win rightly forecast the future. Cassell, who failed to practice the day before, sat out the final 13 minutes and 30 seconds when his body tightened, and home hope died. The Wolves picked up a victory two nights later, but when Los Angeles scooped up two straight triumphs at Staples Center ("this charade of a Western Conference finals," Bill Plaschke called it), it became clear that the year would end in another disappointment for Garnett and Co. Cassell was limited to 64 total minutes in the six-game series, replaced by the non-dynamic duo of Fred Hoiberg and Darrick Martin. It was unfair. "We had Fred Hoiberg at point guard in Game 6 of the Western Conference Finals," said Wally Szczerbiak, Minnesota's small forward. "*Fred Hoiberg*. Great guy. But are you winning against Kobe and Shaq? No."

By the time Los Angeles wrapped up a trip to the NBA Finals with a

96–90 Game 6 victory at home, the narrative of the season should have, once again, dramatically shifted. There was a story to be told. A festive one. Here was a team that had suffered numerous problems throughout the run but now was heading on a path toward glory. It was a story of Shaq and Kobe putting winning above animus. It was a story of Malone and Payton finding validation in the City of Angels. It was a story of Phil Jackson somehow bringing calm to chaos. The Los Angeles Lakers should have been reveling in the greatness of their basketball journey, of their basketball accomplishment.

But . . . no. Throughout the series, the two main stars continued to behave as toddlers separated in a crib. After the fifth game, a 98–96 defeat, O'Neal stalked out of the locker room while moaning that "the team" (aka Kobe Bryant) had become too selfish and wasn't getting the basketball to him down low. Bryant countered that O'Neal was big and strong enough to grab the rock whenever he felt the need. Translation: *Stop being so damn lazy.*

Earlier in the week, O'Neal had once again griped about money, insisting he needed a fat extension. "I won't be devalued," said a man making (on average) $20,678,530 per year to throw a round object through a round metal rim. "Never, ever devalued. I will never take less than what I am worth." He then took a knife to Mitch Kupchak, adding, "I've been the general manager of this team for the last two years. So I don't wanna hear about blah-blah-blah, blah-blah-blah. Because I'm the one bringing them in. I'm the one making the phone calls. Everybody wants to play with the Diesel."

It was all infuriating. But it also spoke to the Lakers' mindset entering their fourth Finals appearance in five seasons. This was a team that was conditioned to view the Western Conference Finals as the toughest test. With Jackson, O'Neal, and Bryant, they had posted a 13-1 mark in the NBA Finals. The Pacers, Sixers, and Nets were all roadkill for a franchise destined for greatness, and 2004 appeared to be no different.

"It was gonna be easy," said Devean George. "I think we all believed that."

· · ·

Throughout his reign as one of the all-time greatest coaches in NBA history, Phil Jackson didn't exactly endear himself to colleagues.

It was not a matter of peers hating Jackson, or wishing any sort of harm to his family and friends. Nothing like that. No, it was more that Jackson never aspired to be *one of them*. Coaching fraternities exist in all major professional sports leagues, born of an understanding among a small group of people that there are others who can appreciate and empathize with their plight. There are tons of stories of coaches from rival organizations surviving heated seven-game series, only to sit down over beers and steaks and laughter days later.

Jackson, though, existed on a different plateau. He seemed to think of himself as better, as elite, and it rubbed peers wrongly. Pete Babcock, the longtime NBA executive who spent 13 years as the Atlanta Hawks' general manager, used to regularly chat with Jackson during his time coaching the CBA's Albany Patroons. Babcock worked as the Denver Nuggets' director of player personnel at the time, and Jackson called every few weeks, talking up his players and seeking out slivers of wisdom. "He'd send me reports, tell me about guys he had," Babcock recalled. "I felt like we had a close friendship."

When Jackson was hired to coach the Bulls, that all changed. In particular, Babcock recalled the time the two were attending league meetings, and he was planning a program to teach basketball to youngsters on reservations. "I knew Phil was appreciative of Native American culture, so I thought it'd be right up his alley," Babcock said. "I went up to him, started telling him about the program. He was looking over my shoulder, not listening. It was insulting, but not that surprising." In the middle of the chat, Babcock stopped what he was saying, uttered, "Hey, Phil, nice talking," and walked off. It was the last time they ever spoke.

Fair or not, Jackson was known as a guy who would lobby for positions occupied by peers. He was also known as a guy who looked down on others, who convinced himself that he simply worked at a higher level of excellence.

This did not sit well with Larry Brown.

As the Lakers were (as expected) taking care of Minnesota, in the Eastern Conference, Brown's Detroit Pistons were (as was *not* expected) rolling through the playoff field. With a 54-28 record, the team didn't even win the Central Division, placing seven games behind Indiana and snagging a third seed overall. Yet after walloping Milwaukee in the opening round, Detroit toppled the No. 2 seed New Jersey Nets in seven games, then got back at the Pacers in a convincing six-game series.

Despite having coached the Danny Manning–led Kansas Jayhawks to the 1988 NCAA title, and despite having coached the Allen Iverson–led Philadelphia 76ers to the 2001 NBA Finals, the job Larry Brown was doing with the Pistons was his most remarkable work in a 32-year sideline career. Detroit's roster featured zero future Hall of Famers, and zero players one would characterize as a "superstar." The leading scorer, guard Richard (Rip) Hamilton, averaged just 17.6 points per game, and the best overall player, power forward Rasheed Wallace, picked up an NBA-high 41 technical fouls and had been deemed uncoachable in his previous career stops with Washington and Portland. The team's starting center, Ben Wallace, was a 6-foot-9, 240-pound power forward with no offensive repertoire. Heading into the 2003 NBA draft, the Pistons held the second overall pick and an opportunity to add Carmelo Anthony of Syracuse, or Chris Bosh of Georgia Tech, or Dwyane Wade of Marquette. They took 18-year-old Darko Miličić, out of Serbia — who contributed nothing. "If you looked at that matchup on paper, team against team, we're 100 times better," said Devean George. "We might have made the mistake of thinking that."

Jackson certainly seemed to. In the five days between Detroit's vanquishing Indiana and the tipoff of Game 1 in Los Angeles, the Lakers' coach appeared far more concerned with the status of his legacy than any problems Detroit might bring to the table. Many people affiliated with the Pistons (Brown included) read a June 3 Associated Press piece, headlined PHIL JACKSON CLOSING IN ON RECORD 10TH CHAMPIONSHIP, and found themselves startled by the presumptuousness and lack of humility. Here was the Lakers' coach, preparing for the biggest series of the year, calling a 10th championship ring "a real feat," as if it were already in the bag. In that same story, O'Neal said that after Los Angeles trampled over the Pistons, Jackson "will probably be either the greatest coach or one of the greatest coaches. I don't know what Red Auerbach would say about that. I'd put him right up there."

In an interview with the *Orange County Register*, meanwhile, Jackson responded to a question about Brown's nomadic career (he had previously served as the head coach for nine different collegiate and professional teams) by noting, "Eventually your voice is going to wear 'em out. When you see them develop a deaf ear and things change up, it might be time to move on."

When asked about the Laker coach by the media, Brown was polite and courteous. He praised his record and his achievements. But did he like the man? Enjoy his presence? Not particularly. Brown had actually interviewed Jackson for an assistant coach position with the New Jersey Nets 23 years earlier. He hired Mike Schuler instead. "Phil separated himself," Brown said years later. "Coaches are a community. Phil never wanted a part of that. I don't know why. You'd have to ask him."

As a roster, the Lakers reflected their leader's confidence. Man to man to man, the players oozed self-assuredness. Malone and Payton had come to Los Angeles for the ring, and they knew the jewelry was merely a week away. O'Neal and Bryant had led the team to three crowns, and they knew the jewelry was merely a week away, too. The main rookies, Luke Walton and Brian Cook, presumed the veterans knew whereof they spoke. "It felt pretty certain," said Cook. "I was sure we were gonna win in a walk."

The one player who expressed concern — genuine concern — was Rick Fox, now 34 and in the final season of a distinguished career. The small forward had been limited to 38 regular season games by a series of injuries, but even when he was out, he paid close attention to a franchise showing serious cracks. Los Angeles and Detroit had split their two games during the season, and both times the Lakers were held under 100 points. "I was alone in my thinking, but I did not feel good about our odds," Fox recalled. "Everyone was predicting we'd kill the Pistons. *Everyone*. It was gonna be a sweep, right? Easy. And one reporter asked me what I thought, and I was very honest. I said, 'We're not respecting them enough.'"

The series commenced on June 6 at Staples Center, and the ritualistic collection of sunglasses-adorned, plastic-faced celebrities entered the building to oohs and aahs and requisite appearances on the Jumbotron. They were pretty people anticipating pretty results, and the Detroit Pistons were mere obstacles between tipoff and postgame cocktails at the Rose Venice.

Only no one told the Pistons. Calling the game alongside Al Michaels for ABC, Doc Rivers countered predictions that Los Angeles might win in a sweep by noting that "the Detroit Pistons are not looking at the Lakers like everyone else is looking at the Lakers. They are looking at them as an opponent, and they believe they can beat them." In the minutes before his players jogged onto the court, Brown gathered them all and insisted they were the far-superior *team*. Like, not-even-close far superior. Yes, the Lakers had Shaq and Kobe. But Detroit's muscle was the great equalizer. They would beat the snot out of Shaq and Kobe. They would bloody and bruise them, just as the 1980s Pistons of Rick Mahorn and Bill Laimbeer had bloodied and bruised opposing clubs en route to back-to-back championships. They would slow the pace to a crawl. In the six-game Eastern Conference Finals, Detroit had limited Indiana to five games with less than 80 points. "People don't believe me, but I was far more worried about playing Sacramento than the Lakers," said Corliss Williamson, a Pistons forward. "No disrespect, but we matched the Lakers perfectly. They were predictable, not as good as they had been. A lot of confidence, but real flaws. Plus, Coach Brown convinced us we were about to win. I knew we would. Honestly, I did."

The Pistons opened the scoring when Rasheed Wallace hit a three-pointer 12 seconds into the game, and then . . . everything . . . moved . . . sort . . . of . . . like . . . this. The game was plodding and stilted, a glob of damp clay sliding off a placemat. Los Angeles wanted to run and gun and burst up the court. But Detroit did not allow it. Brown decided he would single-team O'Neal with an ever-rotating collection of tree stumps (Williamson, Ben Wallace, Rasheed Wallace, Elden Campbell, Mehmet Okur) and let the big man score his points. So he did—34 in total, coupled with 11 rebounds. The other Pistons simultaneously presented a PhD-level course in lockdown defense—a pressure-packed, intensity-fueled operation that frustrated the most potent of offenses. Malone, still battling the effects of the knee injury, was held to 4 points on 2-of-9 shooting. Payton, five years past his sell-by date, tallied 3 points on 1-of-4 shooting. The masterpiece, though, was the work Tayshaun Prince did on Bryant. A 6-foot-9, 212-pound bundle of elasticity, Prince was ordered to blanket the Lakers' leading scorer, to force him into terrible shots and even more terrible shots. Bryant scored 25 points, but it came on 10-of-27 shooting over 47 grueling minutes.

The final score, 87–75, told the story. The Pistons had spent the entirety of the 2003–04 season perfecting the art of keeping opponents in check. The Lakers had spent the entirety of the 2003–04 season seeking an identity. "You know, to hold them to 75 points, I think, is pretty incredible defense," Brown said afterwards. "I don't know if we could ever defend better. We contested shots, we did an incredible job, but I think that's what it's going to take."

The next morning's *Los Angeles Times* referred to the defeat as a "Wake-up Call" for the Lakers, as if it were merely a matter of the team taking Detroit too lightly. But the problems for Jackson's squad would require far more than merely arising from a slumber. The Lakers actually bounced back to capture Game 2, 99–91, after blowing an 11-point lead. The key moment belonged to Bryant, who hit a long three-pointer with 2.1 seconds remaining in regulation to tie the game at 89 and send it to overtime. "The greatest Laker shot of this era," opined a breathless Bill Plaschke of the *Times*. But while the 18,997 in attendance cheered and screamed and sang along with Randy Newman's "I Love L.A.," Jackson sat inside his office and assessed the 8,000 problems at hand. He had given the media all the answers they wanted, yet deep down he knew — genuinely knew — the Lakers were in a world of trouble. "If we could have coasted to a convincing double-digit victory," he recalled, "we might have been able to put some doubt in the minds of the Detroit players. They would have left town with a split, but also with a reminder that their defense is not impenetrable. But instead they left thinking they should have won both games."

The situation was dire. First there was Malone, who aggravated his knee injury and spent much of the afternoon limping up and down the court. At one point during the game, trainer Gary Vitti instructed Malone to return to the locker room to have his knee checked out. Malone refused. He would remain on the court with his teammates. "Karl," Jackson later wrote, "is a true warrior." But would that warrior be able to continue throughout the remainder of the series? No one knew.

Second, there was O'Neal — never a tremendous defensive player, but at least one who used to bring forth an effort. The Pistons ran an endless string of pick-and-rolls with point guard Chauncey Billups and cycled big men, and on nine of ten occasions O'Neal would imitate a plotted plant. The player who signed with the Lakers in 1996 had been agile and slender and powerful. This version, however, was chubby and slow and a tad laconic. Worst of all, he was apathetic. On the day after the game, Tex Winter watched tapes and couldn't contain his outrage. "When I'm all done," he yelled toward Jackson, "I'm going to expose this guy as overrated."

An hour or so later, as the players and coaches sat together to review, Winter fired a direct criticism at O'Neal. It was not taken well.

"Why don't you just mind your own business, old man?" the center screamed.

Jackson asked his assistant to elaborate. "Shaq shrugged his shoulders and threw up his hands when you said something," Winter said.

"I told you to shut the fuck up," O'Neal snapped. "We don't need to hear from you about this shit. Just mind your own business."

"This," Winter replied, "*is* my business."

The tension could be felt from wall to wall. The following afternoon, at Jackson's urging, O'Neal apologized, but nothing inside the Laker universe felt particularly joyful.

Third, there was Payton — never a good fit, but now a brutal one. Playing for his third franchise in seven seasons, Billups was on no one's list of the NBA's elite floor generals. Yet he humiliated Payton through the first two games, outscoring him 49–5 and making the Laker look slow and old. Over the course of the season, Payton failed to embrace the triangle offense, and now — when discipline and ritual were vital — he was an Edsel.

An exasperated Jackson played Fisher 46 minutes through the two games, but he was little better, shooting 3 for 15 from the field and hobbling on a bruised right knee.

Based on the win, and a history of dominance, many in the press pushed forth the narrative that the Lakers would go to Detroit and take care of business over the next three games. But as Malone walked out for the Game 3 opening tip, a thick brace covering his right leg, it was increasingly hard to picture this going Los Angeles's way. He was their toughest player and their most prideful player, but he could barely move against the faster, stronger Pistons. As the nine o'clock start time approached, Malone took a break from layup drills to confront a Detroit fan who, while heckling, had spit in his face. The man held a beer in his hand, and took several steps onto the court. "Where was the security?" Malone later asked. It was an irritating beginning to an irritating evening. The power forward played a mere 18 minutes, scoring 5 points.

Even worse, the offensive scheme was nothing short of awful. After enough exasperation, Payton made the solitary decision to completely scrap the triangle (or any remnants of the triangle) and just do what came naturally. Which meant a whole lot of dribbling as dumbfounded teammates — accustomed to spacing and gaps — watched. The Pistons jumped out to an 8–0 lead, were up 39–32 at the half, and used a 9–1 fourth-quarter run to extend the lead to 20. They won 88–68, a farcical score that included O'Neal and Bryant teaming for a paltry 25 points. "Turnovers, bad shots, bad decisions," said Jim Cleamons, the assistant coach. "Rather than doing what we'd done for all those years, we got sloppy and dumb."

When the game ended, and after the Lakers slunk back into the locker room, Fox called an unofficial meeting in the bathroom with solely Bryant, O'Neal, George, and Fisher — the five remaining members of the three championship teams. Banged up and past his prime, Fox had played no minutes in the humbling defeat. Still, he was disgusted. "Guys, we need to get back to the triangle," he said, surrounded by a couple of toilets and some sinks. "It won us a bunch of rings. Why are we abandoning it?"

"Rick was right," recalled George. "It worked, we had proof it worked. Why do it all differently?"

Fox asked Jackson to join the players in the john, and the five unburdened themselves. For all his greatness as a coach, Jackson was abandoning the principles that had made the organization great. Where was the meticulousness? Where was the sharpness? Fox liked Payton, but what the hell was he doing? Especially with Fisher, the grand triangle orchestrator, glued to the pine? "You know how much I hate this fucking offense," Bryant said. "But I'll settle in and we'll just execute the triangle and get the ball in to Shaq and beat them up on the inside."

"At least give us a shot together," Fox pleaded. "Let's try it."

Three nights later, Jackson tried it — *a bit.* He refused to start the five together but played Fox 16 minutes, Fisher 21 minutes. The optimism of an early lead (Los Angeles was up 22–21 at the end of the first quarter), though, died beneath the weight of a festering suspicion that one man's focus wasn't just winning. Through the first three games of the series, Bryant would have spurts of excellence mixed with spurts of out-of-control buffoonery. One moment he seemed engaged, the next a drunk high schooler popping threes on a dare from Potsie and Ralph. Many of his teammates believed — rightly — that he felt compelled to outduel Hamilton, the Detroit guard, who as a prep phenom at Coatesville Area High School in Chester County, Pennsylvania, was often ranked alongside Bryant as one of America's elite talents. The two were AAU teammates, competed in tournaments and camps, and Bryant deemed him a rival to be vanquished. It was the warped modus of Kobe — a never satiated desire to stomp, crush, humiliate. So, with Malone still a shell (he played 21 useless minutes before leaving the series for good with 7:30 remaining in the third quarter) and only O'Neal doing anything of note (he scored 36 points and grabbed 20 rebounds), Bryant again reverted to his worst self, missing 17 of 25 shots en route to 20 points. He was particularly tragic in the first half, when he fired off 14 attempts, hitting 3. Time after time, he ignored O'Neal in the post in favor of launching bombs. Jackson was astounded. What the hell was going on? Why couldn't anyone stick to a plan?

Billups later explained the Pistons' genius approach.

Our game plan was very calculated. We knew we were going to play Shaq straight-up. We knew there was no way we could stop Shaq straight-up. And there was also no way we could stop Kobe straight-up. But, if we're going to play Shaq straight-up, [the Lakers'] eyes are going to get big, which means they're going to keep throwing it down there. We're telling Ben the whole time, "Take fouls when you need to, but don't get yourself into foul trouble. You need to give up a layup, cool, we're going to get what we want on the other side." But what's going to happen is Mr. Bryant is going to get a little discouraged with getting no touches and now the second half comes around . . . now he's pressing. He's going to start coming down and just breaking the offense. When you do that, you're done — you're playing right into our hands. Even if you start making those shots, you're finished.

Though Bryant wasn't due back in court until June 21, Jerry Buss and Jackson both assumed (rightly) that the rigors of a trying season were finally taking their toll. On the road, Bryant existed largely free of people trying to remind him of his plight. But in Detroit, where fans weren't known to bite their tongues, the scene was ruthless. Hecklers. Beraters. On the Lakers' first night on the road, a 23-year-old Pistons fan named Dominic Piscopo entered the Townsend Hotel, spotted Bryant sitting in the lounge, and pounded on the window while screaming, "You raped my sister, Kobe! You raped my sister!"

From the bench, Kareem Rush had his own theory. Having spent two years shadowing Bryant in practices, he felt as if he understood the star. He grasped his moods, his desires, his impulses. This, to Rush, was crystal clear. "Kobe wanted to be the MVP of the series — guaranteed," Rush said. "Shaq got the first three MVPs, and Kobe wanted it. That's why he kept shooting, even when shooting that much made no sense. He always felt this need to validate himself. It was selfish, and it killed us."

Fifteen years after the fact, Rush was asked why an MVP trophy —

shiny, gold-plated tin affixed to a base — mattered so much. "Kobe wasn't just playing for a championship, he was playing for legacy," Rush said. "Michael Jordan had all those MVPs under his belt, Shaq had those MVPs under his belt. It burned Kobe. He wanted his."

At the end of the night, 22,076 Pistons loyalists giddily exited the Palace of Auburn Hills, 88–80 victors and one game away from a title. The Lakers again talked a good game about returning from the dead and the heart of a champion and winning for the people of Los Angeles. But hope was dead. Mike Wise, the *Washington Post* basketball scribe and ghostwriter of *Shaq Talks Back*, visited his collaborator after the game. As the two men walked through the stadium bowels, Wise provided an unsolicited pep talk. "Listen," he said, "you and Kobe need to work together. You can still win this thing, but the Pistons are tough. I just think —"

O'Neal held his hand up, a signal for Wise to hush. Ilana Nunn, the daughter of veteran official Ronnie Nunn, was standing a couple of feet away, her back toward the men. "I've gotta say," O'Neal cracked, "she's got a fine bubble butt."

Um . . .

"That's when I knew it was done," Wise recalled. "I'm thinking about the Lakers winning a championship, and Shaq is more focused on a woman's bubble butt. They were toast."

They were, indeed, toast.

Magic Johnson, now a minority owner and uncomfortable with his name out of the news cycle for more than 27 minutes, gathered round the media to tell them how humiliated he felt. After savagely ripping Payton for his shoddy play, he issued a broader take on the team. "I have eight rings and I want nine," he said. "My anger is that we haven't competed in this series. I don't know what's going on. I don't know what the mindset is, but this is unacceptable."

The Lakers would play Game 5 with Slava Medvedenko starting at power forward for Malone, which meant the dream team that many had predicted should win 70 games and dominate the postseason was down to a starting lineup of a selfish Bryant, an overweight O'Neal, a befuddled Payton, a mediocre Devean George, and, in Medvedenko, a 25-year-old Ukrainian who boasted an unparalleled inability to grasp anything basketball-related. Medvedenko had signed with the organization in the summer of 2000, fresh off averaging 20 points and 6.1 rebounds for BC Kiev in the North European Basketball League championships. He was the first European-born player to join Los Angeles since Vlade Divac 15 years earlier, and many within the organization thought he could develop into a Vin Baker–type talent. Only Medvedenko was dumb. Or at least seemed dumb. And played dumb. In a 2002 *Los Angeles Times* piece, Tim Brown wrote how "it is not unusual for players to come off the floor wondering why Medvedenko went right, say, instead of left."

He was a chronic screwup. But with Malone out and Horace Grant lost long ago to injury, Medvedenko was — at 6-foot-10 and 250 pounds — the best option to counter the Pistons' power and ruggedness.

It did not bode well.

During the morning shootaround at Seaholm High School, in suburban Birmingham, Michigan, with the Lakers scrambling for any solutions and O'Neal staring into the stands and Malone sitting to the side in street clothes, Bryant interrupted Jackson to say, "Let me take Billups. Let me see if I can slow him down."

The request came as a surprise — Bryant had been guarding Hamilton and doing a fairly good job; Detroit's best offensive player was averaging 21.5 in the series.

"I don't know," Jackson replied.

Moments later, in private, Bryant confessed to his coach that he'd only made the request to see if Payton would stand up for himself and demand another shot at Billups. He did not. "I think he's scared," Bryant said. "He doesn't care if I take Billups or not."

That night, Bryant arrived at the arena at 5:45, an hour before players were required to be there. Given that their backs were to the wall, he expected to enter the locker room to at least a handful of fellow Lakers. Instead, the door was locked and he needed security to let him in.

In the last pathetic gasp of a proud franchise done in by 100 cuts, Jackson's team stormed out to a 14–7 lead behind the early jump shooting of (gasp!) Medvedenko, who scored eight points in the first quarter.

Then — *whoosh!*

O'Neal picked up two quick fouls, which led to his exit and the arrival of Cook, the 6-foot-9, 234-pound rookie, who possessed all of Shaq's skills — minus strength and athleticism. The Pistons went on a 9–0 run, and by halftime they held a 55–45 advantage. As Detroit extended the lead to as much as 28, Bryant did his all to help the cause. He shot 21 times, making a mere 7. In a surprise to no one, he rarely looked to pass. Isolated to the side, O'Neal, Payton, and George were reduced to exchanging exasperated glares. Bryant's 24 points led the team. They meant nothing. "It was the most selfish I'd seen him," said Rush, who scored 5 points off the bench. "Maybe he felt like he had to carry us."

The final score, 100–87, seemed like a misprint. Those watching could have sworn Detroit won by 30. Or was it 40? Billups, who averaged 21 points and 5.2 assists during the series, earned the Finals MVP trophy Bryant had so coveted. He was also single-handedly responsible for the murder of the NBA's most talkative player. After the game, Gary Payton had, literally, nothing to say.

"That's not the way you want to end this, that's for sure," Fox said above the cramped quiet of the Laker locker room. A few minutes earlier, the faded veteran sat alone in the bathroom and sobbed. His eyes were red. His cheeks still had the residue of dried tears. This was the end of something beautiful. He just knew it. "A team always beats a group of individuals," he said. "We picked a poor time to be a group of individuals."

With that, Fox walked off to the shower to clean off the stench of humiliation.

With that, a dynasty appeared to die.

18

The End

I ain't playing with that motherfucker again."

The words were uttered, and Kareem Rush did a double take. What had Kobe Bryant just said? Who was a motherfucker?

The backup Lakers guard was sitting at a table inside the lobby restaurant of the Townsend Hotel, in Birmingham, Michigan, roughly two hours removed from the dispiriting Game 5 NBA Finals loss to the Pistons. At just 23, Rush was green and naive and blissfully unaware of many of the league's inner workings. Sure, he knew the Lakers had their problems. They were old. They were often disjointed. The organization's two biggest stars possessed their differences. But hadn't they just reached the championship series and won four out of five titles in a loaded Western Conference? *There's no way they tear this team up,* Rush thought. *That would be crazy.* In Rush's mind, the difference between glory and agony had been Karl Malone's injury. "With a healthy Mailman, we win it all," he said years later. "I'll always believe that."

As he looked toward Bryant and heard his teammate's proclamation, though, the reality hit hard. It was over.

"We were done," Rush said. "It broke my heart."

Much like the reaction to a solid 90 percent of the world's assorted office parties, few with the vanquished Lakers felt like attending the postgame soiree planned by Jerry Buss. But he was the payer of millions of dollars in salaries, and before long Rush and Bryant were no longer alone.

Malone limped in, accompanied by Gary Payton. The two rookies, Luke Walton and Brian Cook, shuffled through the door. There was Devean George. There was Derek Fisher. There was Slava Medvedenko. There was Rick Fox.

There was Shaquille O'Neal — *the motherfucker.*

He entered alongside Shaunie, his wife of one and a half years. A larger-than-life man nattily decked out in slacks and a collared shirt, O'Neal was a master of turning on the charm. So he smiled and he joked and he held court and he ordered a drink. When, a few minutes later, Jerry Buss arrived, O'Neal planned on paying proper homage to his boss, which meant thanking him for yet another season of wearing the purple and gold.

Only that's when the weirdness commenced. Buss immediately approached Bryant, who was now sitting alone at a table with his wife, Vanessa. The O'Neals were 10 feet away, but Buss paid them no mind. "I call it the *Godfather* reign," O'Neal said years later. "You have this old guy who's been the godfather for a long time. You have this young guy, he's planning and planning and planning. And at dinner one day — *Pop! Pop! Pop! Pop! Pop!* You pop him. And the moment I got popped was at that party. Jerry talked to Kobe and his wife, then left."

Hurt and dumbfounded, O'Neal turned to Shaunie and said one thing: "Uh-oh."

The couple rose and left.

"It was a clear signal that we were done," O'Neal said years later. "If we win that series, it's four rings for me and another Finals MVP. We could have won, too. But Kobe had to be the hero. It was him. He *needed* to be. I'm down low, killing Ben Wallace, and Kobe ignored me. It's not all his fault. We played like shit and the Pistons were great. But . . . it could have been different. Look, we lost. It ended. And when you have two dogs — this championship dog that's getting older and this puppy running behind the old dog — who do you love? You love the puppy."

The next morning, the Lakers players and coaches boarded the team charter and flew the four and a half hours back to Los Angeles. Two people not on the plane were Malone and Bryant, who sat alongside Buss long into the night, discussing the plight (present and future) of the Los Angeles Lakers. Both traveled to California on their boss's private jet.

The owner had taken a genuine liking to Malone. His willingness to play hurt and give his all to the team (on a discount rate) stirred something deep within the self-made multimillionaire. But Bryant? Few understood Buss's love affair with a player he referred to as "my son." Wasn't his son accused of raping someone? Hadn't his son insisted the Lakers pay for his flights to the trial — then complained about the quality of the plane? Hadn't his son been the selfish SOB who, for years, enraged coaches and teammates? Hadn't Jackson and Mitch Kupchak warned Buss about Bryant's immaturity, Bryant's me-first life outlook, time after time after time?

When the Lakers used the top overall pick in the 1979 draft to select Earvin "Magic" Johnson out of Michigan State, Buss's affections made sense. Johnson was a beacon of joy, equipped with a sunshine-infused smile and the PR savvy to reinvent a struggling franchise. He was hope and optimism in one 6-foot-9 bundle. But what, exactly, had Kobe Bryant brought the Lakers? Hadn't O'Neal been the one most responsible for the organization's on-court revival? Hadn't Jackson brought all the pieces together?

When the Laker team plane landed at Los Angeles International Airport, Jackson and Fox sat inside a Town Car parked on the tarmac. The coach wanted to have season-ending exit interviews with every player, and this would serve as the first. Jackson knew Fox had no interest in continuing his career as a player. The men had spent five years together. The kinship was real. "I think you should consider being a coach," he said. "You have an understanding of the game that's pretty unique."

"Nah," Fox said. "I need to get away from basketball for a year."

Jackson understood.

"It's a grind, isn't it?" he said. "I don't know what I'm gonna do yet, either. When I decide I'll let you know."

At this point in their careers, both O'Neal and Jackson possessed the confidence of men who believed they controlled their own destinies. When O'Neal entered the 1992 NBA draft after his junior year at LSU, it was with the knowledge that he would be the No. 1 overall pick. When he decided to leave Orlando as a free agent four years later, it was with the knowledge that he would make more money than any basketball player in league history. Jackson arrived in Los Angeles with six Chicago Bulls championship rings on his fingers. He was widely considered the answer to the franchise's prayers. The accomplishments spoke for themselves. Human beings of such accolades generally answer to no one.

But times had changed. Bryant — free agent superstar whom Buss desperately wanted to build around — was the kingpin of the Los Angeles Lakers, and his happiness was the top priority of an organization in flux. The No. 1 rumor floating around the NBA was that Bryant might/could/would leave the Lakers for the in-the-same-building Clippers, the basketball equivalent of removing Jerry Buss's heart from his chest with a rusty butter knife and handing it to Donald Sterling for dinner. Losing a 26-year-old megastar would be crushing. Losing him to a stale-bread franchise coming off a 28-54 season? Unbearable. But as soon as free agents were allowed to meet with suitors, Bryant was sitting down with Elgin Baylor, the Clippers' general manager, discussing a future of playing alongside Chris Kaman and Elton Brand. For Bryant, much of the appeal was taking the woeful franchise in town and carrying it to greatness. The Lakers were Magic and Kareem and Worthy. The Clippers were Benoit Benjamin. "We all thought he was going to them," said Bill Plaschke, the *Los Angeles Times* columnist. "It seemed absolutely certain."

The Lakers were at his mercy. Kobe no longer wanted to play for Phil Jackson, whose five-year, $30 million contract was expiring. *Okay.* Kobe certainly no longer wanted to play alongside Shaquille O'Neal, whose desire for a contract extension had been rebuffed. *Okay.* Just two days after the season came to an end, the center was sitting in his kitchen, eating Frosted Flakes, when Kupchak held a press conference to announce, in part, that the team would listen to trade offers for O'Neal.

What?

What?

O'Neal was furious. Not because he was on the block, but because, even after eight seasons in Los Angeles, no one with the Lakers had the cour-

tesy to call and offer a heads-up. He knew Bryant was behind the maneu-
vering. The organization was surrendering to the whims of a child. "I'm
a fucking man," O'Neal said years later. "You wanna make changes? Fine.
Just call me like a fucking man. Maybe I don't wanna be here with you
guys either. Maybe I'm tired of it all, too. But at least give me the respect.
At least *tell me*."

That same day, Jackson headed into the team facility in El Segundo to
meet with various players. He told his guys he was likely retiring but that
there was always a chance of a change of plans. If Kobe wanted him back
and Shaq wanted him back and Buss wanted him back — who could say
for certain? After wrapping everything up, he stopped into the office of
Jeanie Buss, the executive vice president of basketball operations, as well
as his girlfriend of five years. The relationship was arguably the most bewildering one in sports, crisscrossing all sorts of ethical barriers but also
coming across as sincere and decent. Was Jeanie tipping Phil off about
things she shouldn't have? Was his job safer because he was working for
a man who (one day soon) might be his father-in-law? Did Jeanie consult
with Phil on decisions that had nothing to do with coaching? Did Jeanie
tell her dad of dialogues that occurred beneath the sheets? No one was
entirely sure.

Now, though, she delivered a plea, followed by a warning. "Go tell
Mitch, or call up my dad and tell them that you can coach Kobe. Tell them
that you guys worked together great in the last three months, and that it's
no longer an issue. Look at how well you did at the end of last season."

"Okay, Jeanie," Jackson replied. "What happened?"

According to his girlfriend, the organization had reached the decision
to move on to a different coach. She learned the news from John Black,
the Lakers' PR director, and felt the need to share it with her love. As she
delivered the information, Jeanie began to sob. Phil Jackson didn't quite
know how to react. Was this about coaching the Lakers or dating the
daughter of the owner of the Lakers? Basketball or affection? Or both?
He hugged Jeanie for a solid 10 minutes, then left the facility. "If I lose
this job, she figures, she loses me," Jackson later noted. "I'll go back to
Montana and never be heard from again."

One day later, Phil Jackson was officially out of work. He began the morning by returning to the facility to meet with Bryant — an exit interview, but not in the traditional sense. Usually, coaches hold season-ending meetups to discuss the future with a player. This time, both men knew not what was to come. Would Bryant be a Laker for 2004–05? Maybe, maybe not. Would Jackson be coaching the Lakers for 2004–05? Maybe, maybe not. The two men sat in Jackson's office along with Rob Pelinka, Bryant's agent. After some chatter about basketball and the ongoing sexual assault trial and summer plans, Jackson turned serious. "Will my presence or absence have anything to do with your desire to play for the Lakers?" he asked.

Bryant appeared to be bewildered.

"Would my being with the Lakers or retiring have any influence on your desire to remain with the Lakers?" Jackson repeated.

Jackson wanted Bryant to tell him he was needed. That he was important. He wanted Bryant to say, "You know, we have something special here. Let's keep it going . . ."

He also wanted to believe Santa Claus was real.

Bryant told Jackson he should make up his mind on his own terms, that it should have nothing to do with his future.

"I'm going to retire," Jackson replied.

"Really?" Bryant asked.

Yes, Jackson said. He then asked whether O'Neal returning to Los Angeles would be a factor in whether he came back. Jackson insisted the Shaq-Kobe duo could persist. But Bryant was having none of it. "I've done that for eight years with him," he said, "but I'm tired of being a sidekick." This was no shock. Bryant entered the league as an 18-year-old alpha, and now he was a 25-year-old alpha. It was official — arguably the greatest on-court partnership in NBA history was about to end.

Jackson departed the facility once again, this time summoned to Jerry Buss's home. It was a 10-minute drive, and en route the (still) coach of the Los Angeles Lakers pondered every way this meeting could go. He also likely pondered a rumor that had been circulating for several days. According to O'Neal, at the same time the basketball world had concluded that Jackson was done, Pat Riley was telling the Lakers that he wanted the job. The Miami Heat president had played for Los Angeles from 1970 to 1975, then coached the team to four titles in the 1980s. Southern California had always been his place, his first geographical love. "We all knew Pat was after it," O'Neal said. "He wanted to be the Laker guy."

Jackson parked, rang the doorbell. After a couple of minutes of small talk, Buss said, "Phil, we're going in a different direction."

"I suppose so," Jackson replied. "That seems logical."

Then he left.

The following Tuesday, Jackson and O'Neal met up at the St. Regis in Los Angeles. By now the center had put his Beverly Hills home up for sale, an acknowledgment that this was all really happening. "I just wanted to get ahold of you before this all broke apart," O'Neal said over sips of iced tea. "We had a great run."

Within a month, the Lakers and the Heat completed the year's blockbuster trade. After O'Neal told Kupchak he would sign off on a swap to Miami, he was sent to South Florida for three players (Lamar Odom, Brian Grant, and Caron Butler) and a pair of draft picks. The teaming of O'Neal and Dwyane Wade, the explosive guard who had just wrapped his rookie season, was a coup from Riley, who told his new center he was no longer interested in a return to Los Angeles. "Pat knew he had gold," O'Neal recalled. "We were a lot closer to winning a ring in Miami than the Lakers were without me."

On July 14, Bryant's will-he-return/won't-he-return saga for the ages came to a conclusion when he signed a seven-year, $136.4 million maximum deal with the Lakers. The call to Elgin Baylor was as awkward as any Bryant had ever made. The Clippers' GM truly believed Bryant was coming. Nope — "At heart I'm a Laker," Bryant told him. The next day, in a press conference at the practice facility in El Segundo, Bryant sat at a table alongside Mitch Kupchak and let loose an orchestra of uttered sentiments that called to mind the Benjamin Franklin line "Half a truth is often a great lie."

"We don't have the most dominant player in the game, so things are going to drastically change for us," he said. "It's going to be a struggle.

And we know that. It's not even close. We know that. It's going to be an uphill battle."

He was asked whether he would have been willing to continue to play alongside O'Neal. The answer was no. He had said no to Jackson, no to Kupchak, no to Jerry Buss. No — he would never, ever, ever, ever, ever, ever again play with Shaquille O'Neal. Never, ever, ever.

Or . . .

"That I had something to do with Shaquille leaving, that's something I laugh at," he said. "It upsets me. It angers me. If he'd re-signed for whatever, I'd still be here today. Unfortunately, it just didn't work out that way."

Watching from his home, O'Neal couldn't believe what he was hearing. Watching from his home, Jackson couldn't believe what he was hearing. Had Jerry Buss extended O'Neal's contract, Kobe Bryant would be holding up his new Los Angeles Clippers jersey at this very moment. O'Neal knew it. Jackson knew it.

"Can I win without Shaq?" Bryant said in a continuation of the nonsense. "I don't know. We had an incredible run together, in spite of the ups and downs. But you just have to trust the track record of this organization. They've always been able to bounce back. I'm just a piece of the puzzle."

A few days after he arrived via trade from Miami, Caron Butler decided to reach out to Bryant and seek advice on the move to Los Angeles. A friend of a friend hooked him up with the superstar's cell phone number, so he called.

Ring.

Ring.

Ring.

BRYANT: Hello?

BUTLER: Yo, Kobe. It's Caron Butler. Your new teammate.

BRYANT: How'd you get my number?

BUTLER: Oh, [*fill in the name*] gave it to me.

BRYANT: Oh . . . oh . . . okay. What's up?

The two spoke for several minutes. It all seemed friendly enough. The next day, when someone tried calling Bryant's phone, he was greeted with a message from AT&T.

Bryant had changed his number.

The Los Angeles Lakers were now Kobe Bryant's team — no ifs, ands, or buts. Wrote J.A. Adande in the *Los Angeles Times:*

> OK Kobe, now that the best center and most successful coach in recent NBA history have left on your watch, now that NBA executives have zipped around the country and bowed to you at your whim, tell us exactly when the Lakers will win the championship. How many games will the NBA Finals last, when's the parade, where should the new banner go? Kobe Bryant had better have the answers — or, more accurately, the results — now that he has ended this long charade and confirmed Thursday what we've known for some time: The Lakers officially belong to him.

The happy-go-lucky, skipping-through-the-puddles joy of O'Neal was gone to South Beach. Karl Malone had decided to retire. Derek Fisher signed as a free agent with Golden State. Gary Payton was sent to Boston, a box of rusty screws disguised as a viable NBA player. Rick Fox, included in the Celtics deal for salary reasons, would never play again. After a failed effort to hire Duke's Mike Krzyzewski to replace Jackson, Buss and Kupchak settled upon Rudy Tomjanovich, the former Houston head coach, who'd guided the Rockets to back-to-back titles in the mid-1990s. Tomjanovich was a safe choice, but hardly a dynamic one. He had retired from coaching after the 2002–03 season, when he was diagnosed with bladder cancer. He underwent chemotherapy, the cancer vanished, the cancer returned, he underwent more chemotherapy. This wasn't the equivalent of having to overcome Michael Jordan. It was life-or-death terrifying. He decided to end his coaching career and focus on health, family, happiness.

"Out of nowhere the Lakers called," Tomjanovich recalled. "I wasn't looking for a job. But I had to listen."

He accepted the position, but the cupboard was bare. The new starting center would be Chris Mihm, a 2000 first-round pick out of the University of Texas whose best move was height (he was 7-foot, 265 pounds). The point guard, Chucky Atkins, was a nondescript journeyman. The bench was a collection of odd marbles. Bryant had gotten his way — O'Neal was gone. But so was most of the talent. A team that reached the NBA Finals in 2004 would, one season later, finish 34-48 and miss the playoffs for the first time in 11 years. Tomjanovich lasted 43 games before resigning for health-related reasons. Bryant's scoring average (27.6) paced the team. It was his dream come true — *shoot to your heart's content, kid. Nobody is here to stop you.*

Plus, while the basketball turmoil garnered most of the headlines, in the summer of 2004 there remained a far more pressing story to worry about. Yes, the Lakers had agreed to pay Bryant a load of money to play basketball for the next seven years. But would he be available to do so, or would he be shooting his hoops inside a prison yard for the next 20 years? Jury selection for the criminal case was scheduled to begin on August 27, a looming nightmare for the Lakers star.

Nearly 15 years later, both Mark Hurlbert, the Eagle County district attorney, and Doug Winters, the lead detective, remained convinced that Kobe Bryant had raped Jessica Mathison. They didn't think it *might* have happened, or it *perhaps* happened. There was no misunderstanding. "There's zero doubt in my mind," Winters said. "He raped her."

"I'm 100 percent certain," said the DA. "He did it."

That's why Hurlbert was so furious when, on August 10, Mathison ignored his advice, hired an outside attorney, John Clune, and filed a civil suit against Bryant, seeking unspecified damages. It was a crippling move for the criminal case, in that it allowed people to wonder whether, in fact, Mathison was all about the money. "When her attorney called me I said, 'You need to hold off on this!'" Hurlbert recalled. "'It's just giving them one more avenue of cross-examination that she's only in it for material gain.'" Around this same time, Mathison penned a letter to Gerry Sandberg, a state investigator, admitting that some of the initial details she'd provided to Winters might have been a tad off. While insisting that she was, indeed, raped, Mathison wrote: "I told Detective Winters that Mr. Bryant had made me stay in the room and wash my face. While I was held against my will in that room, I was not forced to wash my face. I did not wash my face." Nothing seemed to be going well in the case against Bryant. There were increased discussions about Mathison's alleged promiscuity and erratic behavior. There were threats of violence. The media would not leave her alone — staking out her house, following her around Eagle, desperate for any nugget of juicy information. "One day there were all these reporters positioned outside her house, and I could see it from my back porch," recalled Randy Wyrick, who covered the case for the *Vail Daily*. "There was a kid who lived next door, she was also blonde, and she walked into the street and was just accosted by dozens of reporters. Poor kid — she was going to her gymnastics class or something. This is BF Eagle, Colorado — Bum Fuck Eagle. There's nothing to do here. She became *the* story."

On a late August day, Hurlbert was in his office when he received a call from Mathison. Jury selection was under way. The trial was approaching. He was gearing up and supremely confident.

"Mark," she said, "I don't want to go forward."

What?

"It's just too much," Mathison said. "I need this to end."

He urged her to take a day to consider the ramifications. In the meantime, Hurlbert called Bill Ritter, the Denver district attorney, to ask his advice. "Mark," Ritter said, "you're very limited. You can subpoena her, drag her in, and put her on the stand. But she'll be unconvincing and the jury won't find him guilty. You can also try and go without her, but I don't know how you do a sexual assault case without a victim.

"Or you can dismiss the case."

On September 1, just a week before the trial was scheduled to begin, a dispirited Hurlbert dropped the criminal case, noting, "The victim has informed us . . . that she does not want to proceed with this trial. For this reason, and this reason only, the case is being dismissed." As part of the arrangement, Bryant agreed to issue a statement that Mackey distributed to reporters. It wasn't admitting rape, but it was admitting rape:

Although I truly believe this encounter between us was consensual, I recognize now that she did not and does not view this incident the same way I did. After months of reviewing discovery, listening to her attorney, and even her testimony in person, I now understand how she feels that she did not consent to this encounter.

Within a year, Bryant paid Mathison an undisclosed amount of money and bought her a house near Denver.

She vanished into the abyss, never to be heard from again.

When, in 2009, he led the Los Angeles Lakers back to another NBA title, not one media member mentioned the sexual assault accusations in coverage of Kobe Bryant's redemption.

He was once again the king of a city that expected championships.

He could do no wrong.

Epilogue

On the morning of December 21, 2018, at approximately 9:30, I pulled up to what I believed to be the house belonging to J.R. Rider, ran my sweaty palms along my shorts, and — with great trepidation — rang the doorbell.

Ever since playing his final NBA game 17 years earlier, the former Slam Dunk Contest champion and erratic Laker for 67 games had largely vanished from the public eye. He'd conducted one or two interviews that made their way onto YouTube, and a 2011 clip showed him dunking a basketball. Otherwise, nothing.

Having spent the previous day a stone's throw from his Chandler, Arizona, address, and after repeated failures to land a phone number, I decided to give the *"Surprise! I'm here"* thing a shot. These books, after all, are only as good as the most obscure person an author speaks with. So as I stood, waiting and waiting for someone to answer, I considered two questions:

A. What would I ask J.R. Rider?

B. What would I do if J.R. Rider tried to impale me with a steel pipe?

So I waited, and waited, and waited, and wai —

"Hello."

It was a little boy. Maybe four or five. He opened the door ever so slightly, peeking through the crack.

"Hi!" I said in my best Barney voice. "I'm looking for J.R. Rider!"

The lad vanished, and two seconds later a woman appeared. She was about my age, thin, long brown hair. "Can I help you?" she asked.

"Hello," I said — less Barney, more Magnum P.I. "My name is Jeff Pearlman. I'm a writer. I wrote this book" — I held aloft a copy of my recently published USFL chronicling — "and I'm trying to find J.R. to talk about his time with the Lakers."

She asked me to hang tight and closed the door. Again I waited and waited. Then I overheard the muffled sounds of two adults barking. The woman seemed calm. The man seemed irate. *"Who is it?"* I heard him say.

The door opened again.

There stood J.R. Rider.

Shit.

He was familiar, but different. The goatee was now speckled with gray. His physique — once herculean — was soft, with a flat Goodyear midsection. What struck me as unchanged was the scowl. He was scowling *at me.*

"Who are you?" Rider said.

"Yeah, so I'm Jeff Pearlman. I tried reaching you. I'm writing a book . . ."

The scowl remained.

"Wait," he said from behind a screen door. "Wait, wait. You come to my house! You just show up?"

"Um, yeah," I said. "But —"

"No, no, no," he said. "No. You just show up unannounced at my front door?"

"The thing is," I said. "I —"

"Not cool," Rider replied, now stepping toward me. "Not cool at all."

I was bracing for the steel pipe. He stood inches from my face, the refreshing splash of J.R. Rider spittle brushing against my cheeks.

"You don't call, you just come?" he growled. *"That's* how you operate? Are you fucking kid —"

"I mean," I said. "I tried . . ."

A pause.

"Why are you here?" Rider asked. "What are you writing?"

"A book," I told him. "About the Lakers from 1996 to 2004. The Shaq-Kobe-Phil years. I thought you'd be a good guy to talk to."

Suddenly Rider took a step back. I saw his facial expression shift, ever so slightly, from *I will fuck you up* to *Perhaps I will fuck you up.*

"Hmm," he said. "Those were some good teams, huh?"

I nodded.

"I've got some stories," he said. "Man, I have some stories . . ."

J.R. Rider and I wound up speaking for two and a half hours.

If there is a beauty to the three-ring dynasty that was the 1996–2004 Lakers, it's that (with rare exceptions) members of the organization love looking back, love recalling, love sharing memories of a blissful span. I found that with Rider. I found that with Shaquille O'Neal, who gave me a large chunk of time inside Atlanta's Turner Studios. I found that with Phil Jackson, who greeted me gruffly outside the Montana Coffee Traders, in Kalispell, Montana ("I'm talking to you because Jeanie asked," he snapped. "Not because it's you"), then invited me on an eight-hour whirlwind tour of Flathead Lake, of local eateries, of his back porch and his life as a cat-loving 73-year-old retiree. I found that with Nick Van Exel and Eddie Jones; with Glen Rice and Samaki Walker; with Jeanie Buss and Del Harris and Rick Fox and Mike Penberthy and hundreds of other people somehow associated with the run.

I also found one other thing: minimal sadness that the ride hadn't lasted longer.

"Is what it is," Jackson said to me. "Nothing lasts forever."

As soon as the Lakers lost to Detroit in the 2004 NBA Finals, it was clear that Jerry Buss deemed it impossible for the journey to continue. He saw a disinterested big man exiting at the prime of his career and a head coach who — unparalleled success be damned — no longer seemed to command the respect of his players. He also saw a shooting guard, just 26 and at the top of his game, desperate to break free and inclined to explore the idea of playing for the (sweet Jesus, *noooo*) Los Angeles Clippers.

So Buss did what he felt needed to be done by blowing things up.

And, in most regards, it worked out. O'Neal joined the Miami Heat, teamed with the up-and-coming Dwyane Wade, and helped the franchise capture the 2006 NBA title. Bryant endured an awful 2004–05 season under coaches Rudy Tomjanovich and Frank Hamblen, then welcomed Jackson's return to the sideline and — after briefly demanding a trade in 2007 — brought the Lakers two more banners to hang from the rafters. The initial post-divorce bitterness (in 2008 O'Neal famously dropped the line "Kobe, nigga, tell me how my ass tastes" in a freestyle rap) faded with time, and when Bryant played his final game, on April 13, 2016, O'Neal sat courtside at Staples Center, resplendent in a gray suit and cheering wildly as the man who refused to be Robin scored 60 points (as Batman) in a win against Utah. His enthusiastic presence was, O'Neal told me, a concession toward the passing of time. Did he like Kobe Bryant? Not particularly. Did he respect Kobe Bryant? Begrudgingly, within limits. When I mentioned how Bryant had coined his own nickname ("Black Mamba") and referred to himself as "Mamba" with odd earnestness, O'Neal grimaced. "Now," he said, "you understand what I had to deal with."

As Bryant walked off the court for the final time, the 18,997 in attendance rose to their feet — a fitting tribute to a figure who, from the day he'd arrived as a 17-year-old high schooler some two decades earlier, brought immeasurable highs and wide-ranging dramatic flourishes. He would retire as the greatest player in franchise history — its all-time leader in games, in points, in field goals, in thrills, in oohs and aahs and Jordan-esque highlights. "He never wanted to win our hearts," Bill Plaschke wrote in the next morning's *Los Angeles Times*. "He just wanted to win."

Only later — after the confetti was mopped from the court and the last spectator had left for home — would it occur to many of his former teammates and coaches that Kobe Bryant had unleashed an ungodly *50* shots against the Jazz. It was the most single-game attempts in NBA history, and it felt right.

Kobe Bryant needed one last moment in the spotlight.

Acknowledgments

I am writing these acknowledgments at a table inside the Pandor Artisan Bakery & Café, a tiny shop located in the heart of downtown Orange, California. A half-consumed niçoise salad sits before me, resting alongside a large cup of iced coffee. MC White Owl's "Chinese Dreidels" blasts through my headphones. My black basketball shorts are baggy, my Spider-Man T-shirt ratty and loose. It's sunny and warm outside. Probably 75 degrees. I'm wearing sandals.

This is the visual of my life.

This is the visual of a biographer's life.

And, truth be told, it's 83.7 percent authentically awesome. The freedom that has accompanied a career in writing is something I would never trade. I've been afforded the bliss of being there for the vast majority of my daughter's and son's activities.* I make my own schedule. I never (thank you, יונדא) attend meetings.† I am a walking directory of Orange County cafés.‡ It's great, and I am blessed.

---

* Admittedly, it probably would not have been a bad time to be an accountant at his desk the day my daughter projectile-vomited all over the bathroom of the Huguenot Children's Library.

† Best advice I can give you kiddies out there: Take a job with no meetings. None. Zero.

‡ Active Culture, in Laguna Beach. Order the coconut shake. Tell the guy with the tattoos Jeff sent you.

And yet, writing is a torturous journey through the depths of Sheol, and anyone who thinks this job is mentally relaxing has never spent 50 minutes slaving over a single word choice* or stared so long at a screen that the glass melts into maple syrup, or wondered — truly wondered — whether the skill of applying meaning to language has mysteriously vanished. I often joke that these projects take two years off my life, and it's not because — literally — they take two years *of* my life. No. If you care about writing, you want every sentence to be perfect. And, since perfection does not exist, we writers often resort to some unhealthy combination of overeating, overdrinking, oversexing,† overkicking the shit out of a garbage can, overthinking, overwondering whether that lump is a precursor to ALS, and overwatching *Diff'rent Strokes* marathons on late-night television.‡

But, inevitably, we keep going.

This is a long way of saying that the book in your hands (or on your phone) is pretty and shiny and colorful — and propping up that well-crafted mirage is two-plus years of toil, of sweat, of anxiety, of depression, of highs and lows and rocky flights and lengthy drives and shitty meals (a quick note on the Impossible Whopper: it tastes like my dog's wet hair) and missed family outings and nonstop thoughts of the 1996–2004 Los Angeles Lakers.

And it was all worth it.§

I get to do this for a living in large part because I'm supported by a home squad that offers nothing but love and encouragement. Catherine Pearlman, the world's finest one-kidney paddleboarding parenting expert/author, is my best friend, my therapist, my hero, and my purveyor of TKs. She is the person who has to not only live with this monster as deadline approaches, but also reassure him roughly 16 times per week

---

* This just happened one line above, with "Sheol." I was going to go with "hell," but that felt a bit cliché.

† Regrettably, not a problem I've had.

‡ The addition of Dixie Carter to the cast ruined everything. Her and her stinkin' son, Sam.

§ Sorta.

that the world isn't ending, that the book will be okay, that he's not dying of fibrodysplasia ossificans progressiva.*

Our children, Casey and Emmett, both know every single word to Snoop Dogg's "Gin and Juice" — which simultaneously makes them the best kids and their father the worst role model. (That said, with so much drama in the L.B.C., it is legitimately quite strenuous being Snoop D. O. Double G.) Without exaggeration, seeing them grow has been the great joy of my existence.

I was raised by Stan and Joan Pearlman, parents who always encouraged me to go after my passion. As my mom once said, "If you can survive the mean streets of Mahopac, you can survive anywhere."† I'm eternally grateful.

Although the book jacket reads JEFF PEARLMAN, these projects are team efforts. My agent, David Black, is the Chuck Ramsey of literary reps, which makes the equally excellent Lucy Stille her very own Bruce Harper. This is my third book with Houghton Mifflin Harcourt, and also my third book working with Megan Wilson, the best publicist on the planet and a woman who will be forgiven for her choice in baseball teams. It was a true pleasure teaming up with Susan Canavan, and I'm equally honored to be wrapping this with David Rosenthal and his magical pen.

Michael J. Lewis, the fine tennis writer/pendant collector/milk spiller/ Marvin Washington Fan Club president, is a tremendous friend and a huge literary asset. Casey Angle has been teaming up with me as an editor/fact-checker since the early days, and his skill and kindness and devotion to righteousness remain unmatched. Amy Balmuth and Will Palmer, meanwhile, did remarkable work with a messy canvas. Thank you.

So many random folks helped with *Three-Ring Circus*. I've been blessed to work with countless fine journalists through the years, and so many came through to assist. Big ups to L. Jon Wertheim, Vincent Bonsignore, Mike Wise, Jonathan Abrams, Mike Moodian, Mirin Fader, Alex Kennedy, J.A. Adande, Howard Beck, Russ Bengtson, Steve Aschburner, Andy

---

* This is a real thing. It's a progressive disorder that turns soft tissues into bone.
† They're not mean.

Bernstein, Rick Bonncell, Marcos Bretón, David Brofsky, Tim Brown, Ric Bucher, Cheo Hodari Coker, Bob Condotta, Wendy Cook, Scott Howard-Cooper, Roger Cossack, Sean Cunningham, George Diaz, Kevin Ding, Kerry Eggers, Steve Cannella, Robyn Furman, Adrienne Lewin, Howard Eskin, Jon Finkel, Tony Gervino, Anthony Gilbert, Jim Gray, Lisa Guerrero, Paul (Ferragamo) Gutierrez, Kevin Harlan, Mark Heisler, Jonathan Eig, Seth Davis, Giana Nguyn, Steve Henson, Fred Hickman, Rex Hoggard, Shawn Hubler, John Ireland, Melissa Isaacson, Dwight Jaynes, Elliott Kalb, Tim Kawakami, Elizabeth Kaye, Roland Lazenby, Michael C. Lewis, Arash Markazi, Bobby Marks, Jack McCallum, Geeter McGee, Joel Meyers, Ian O'Connor, Bill Plaschke, Shaun Powell, Jeff Proctor, Norma Cockapoo, Ray Richardson, Selena Roberts, Jeremy Schaap, Brian Schmitz, Suzy Shuster, Susan Slusser, John Smallwood, Shelley Smith, Marc Stein, Rick Telander, Brad Turner, Ailene Voisin, Jennifer Weiner, Dick Weiss, Mike Wells, and Ronnie Zeidel.

Jeanie Buss and Linda Rambis have been tremendous resources for nearly a decade, and their warmth, assistance, and access will not be forgotten. I had the honor of spending good chunks of time with dozens of former Lakers players and coaches and am most appreciative for the access. Phil Jackson showed me the beauty of his home state. Shaq let me hang with him in Atlanta before a broadcast. Jim Cleamons and I chatted over pancakes. Kurt Rambis and I lounged by a pool. Samaki Walker introduced me to a new café. Rick Fox explained the world of eSports outside an L.A. Starbucks. Mike Penberthy is surely sick of my constant DMs. John Salley extolled the virtues of marijuana. I peed four times during an amazing afternoon with Del Harris. Paul Shirley is a far better writer than NBA player. Eric Chenowith is blessed with an elephant's memory. J.R. Rider scared the shit out of me (but I wound up loving the guy).

Thank you, one and all.*

I'd be remiss not to cite the help of Matthew Mickelson of the Eagle Public Library; of Ryan O'Neil and Dave Robinson and Art Gruwell

---

* Well, almost one and all. The Lakers' PR team made much of this unnecessarily difficult. I'm still not entirely sure why.

and Joe Kurrasch and Lauren Abulfetuh and Hannah Harlow and Sally Nation and Ronald Roberts and Ivy Givens and Ramon Maclin. Much respect to Drew Corbo, the finest winless Blue Hen on the West Coast. Chunks of love to David Pearlman, Daniel Pearlman, Imma Doeshbahg, Norma (100) Shapiro, Laura Cole, Leah Guggenheimer, Jordan and Isaiah Williams, Jessica and Chris Berman, Richard Guggenheimer, Sandy Glaus, Rosie Widemutt, Lou Marshall, Jasmin Sani, Carolina Valencia, Dayna Li, Mitali Shukla, Luca Evans, Zach Davis, Natalie van Winden, Kate Hoover, Kali Hoffman, and Emma Reigh.

As anyone reading this book surely knows by now, Kobe Bryant and his daughter Gianna died in a helicopter crash on January 26, 2020. They were two of nine victims. The other lost souls are John, Keri, and Alyssa Altobelli; Sarah and Payton Chester; Christina Mauser; and Ara Zobayan. The tragedy will resonate for decades. RIP.

Lastly, a moment of silence for two dear men who passed on during the completion of this project. Bill Fleischman, my University of Delaware professor turned lifelong pal, remains a role model for professionalism, kindness, steadfastness. And my uncle Dr. Martin Pearlman was a great man who knew nothing of sports but could belt out one helluva Had Gadya.

He attended a fine Hebrew School.

Bibliography

A History of Eagle County. Self-published, Eagle, Colo., 1940s.

Abrams, Jonathan. *Boys Among Men*. New York: Crown Archetype, 2016.

Amaechi, John, with Chris Bull. *Man in the Middle*. New York: ESPN Books, 2007.

Babb, Kent. *Not a Game: The Incredible Rise and Unthinkable Fall of Allen Iverson*. New York: Atria, 2015.

Bender, Mark. *Trial by Basketball: The Life and Times of Tex Winter*. Lenexa, Kans.: Addax, 2000.

Blatt, Howard. *Gary Payton*. Philadelphia: Chelsea House, 1999.

Bryant, Kobe. *The Mamba Mentality*. New York: Farrar, Straus and Giroux, 2018.

Buss, Jeanie, with Steve Springer. *Laker Girl*. Chicago: Triumph Books, 2010.

Deveney, Sean, ed. *Facing Kobe Bryant: Players, Coaches, and Broadcasters Recall the Greatest Basketball Player of His Generation*. New York: Sports Publishing, 2016.

Eggers, Kerry. *Jail Blazers*. New York: Sports Publishing, 2018.

Fisher, Derek, with Gary Brozek. *Character Driven*. New York: Touchstone and Howard, 2009.

Geoffreys, Clayton. *Karl Malone: The Remarkable Story of One of Basketball's Greatest Power Forwards*. Washington, D.C.: Calvintir Books, 2016.

Grody, Carl W. *Mitch Richmond: Sports Great*. Springfield, N.J.: Enslow Publishers, 1999.

Hareas, John. *Blue Collar Champions: 2004 NBA Champion Detroit Pistons*. Solana Beach, Calif.: Canum, 2004.

Harris, Del. *On Point: Four Steps to Better Life Teams*. Charleston, S.C.: Advantage, 2012.

Heisler, Mark. *Madmen's Ball*. Chicago: Triumph Books, 2004.

Horry, Keva D. *Glamorous Sacrifice*. Amherst, Mass.: White River Press, 2013.

Jackson, Phil. *The Last Season*. New York: Penguin, 2004.

Jackson, Phil, and Hugh Delehanty. *Eleven Rings*. New York: Penguin Press, 2013.

———. *Sacred Hoops*. New York: Hachette Books, 1995.

Jackson, Phil, with Charles Rosen. *Maverick: More than a Game*. Chicago: Playboy Press, 1975.

James, Steve. *Kobe Bryant: A League of His Own*. San Bernardino, Calif.: Steve James, 2016.

Kalb, Elliott. *Who's Better, Who's Best in Basketball?* New York: McGraw-Hill, 2004.

Karl, George, with Curt Sampson. *Furious George*. New York: Harper, 2017.

Kaye, Elizabeth. *Ain't No Tomorrow*. New York: Contemporary Books, 2002.

Krugel, Mitchell. *Jordan: The Man, His Words, His Life*. New York: St. Martin's, 1994.

Layden, Joe. *Kobe: The "Air" Apparent*. New York: Harper Paperbacks, 1998.

Lazenby, Roland. *Blood on the Horns*. Lenexa, Kans.: Addax, 1998.

——. *Mad Game: The NBA Education of Kobe Bryant*. Lincolnwood, Ill.: Masters Press, 2000.

——. *Mindgames: Phil Jackson's Long Strange Journey*. Lincoln: University of Nebraska Press, 2001.

——. *Showboat*. New York: Little, Brown, 2016.

Lewis, Michael C. *To the Brink*. New York: Simon & Schuster, 1998.

O'Neal, Shaquille, with Mike Wise. *Shaq Talks Back*. New York: St. Martin's, 2001.

O'Neal, Shaquille, with Jackie MacMullan. *Shaq Uncut: My Story*. New York: Grand Central Publishing, 2011.

O'Neal, Shaquille, with Jack McCallum. *Shaq Attaq!* New York: Hyperion, 1993.

Parr, Ann. *Coach Tex Winter: Triangle Basketball*. Nashville: NDX Press, 2006.

Payton, Gary, with Greg Brown. *Confidence Counts*. Dallas: Taylor, 1999.

Pratt, Larry. *Only the Strong Survive*. New York: Regan Books, 2002.

Reynolds, Jerry, with Don Drysdale. *Reynolds Remembers*. Champaign, Ill.: Sports Publishing, 2005.

Rodman, Dennis, with Jack Isenhour. *I Should Be Dead by Now*. New York: Sports Publishing, 2005.

Rubinstein, Barry, and Lyle Spencer. *The Big Title: NBA 2000 Champion Los Angeles Lakers*. New York: Broadway Books, 2000.

Shapiro, Jeffrey Scott, and Jennifer Stevens. *Kobe Bryant: The Game of His Life*. New York: Revolution, 2004.

Shields, David. *Black Planet: Facing Race During an NBA Season*. Lincoln: University of Nebraska Press, 1999.

Smith, Sam. *The Jordan Rules*. New York: Simon & Schuster, 1992.

Thomsen, Ian. *The Soul of Basketball*. Boston: Houghton Mifflin Harcourt, 2018.

Van Buuren, Andrew. *Between Dynasties*. San Bernardino, Cal.: Fletcher Thomas, 2020.

West, Jerry, and Jonathan Coleman. *West by West*. New York: Back Bay Books, 2011.

Williams, Vanessa, and Helen Williams with Irene Zutell. *You Have No Idea*. New York: Gotham Books, 2012.

Winter, Fred (Tex). *The Triple-Post Offense*. Englewood Cliffs, N.J.: Prentice-Hall, 1962.

Notes

1. Magic

2 *"I guess we're going to watch":* Gary Nuhn, "Magic Teaches Us All a Lesson, if We'll Listen," *Dayton Daily News,* February 10, 1992.

3 *Nine days later, the Associated Press's:* Ken Peters, "Magic Johnson on Comeback: 'I Haven't Decided,'" Associated Press, January 26, 1996.

4 *"We're adding a wonderful piece":* John Nadel, "Saying 'Now or Never,' Magic Johnson Ends Retirement," Associated Press, January 29, 1996.
   "We need him": Ailene Voisin, "He's Talk of Town in Emotional Return," *Atlanta Journal and Constitution,* January 31, 1996.
   "With Magic back": Dan Garcia, "It's Showtime Again as Johnson Flashes His Old Form for Lakers," *Newark Star-Ledger,* January 31, 1996.
   Johnson commenced his heroic: Voisin, "He's Talk of Town."

5 *"It's amazing":* John Nadel, "Lakers Ecstatic About Playing with Magic," Associated Press, January 31, 1996.
   "I know I can get out there and do my thing": Wendy E. Lane, "Magic Johnson Hopes for Olympic Berth," Associated Press, January 31, 1996.
   They were props: Mark Heisler, "It's a Sorry Excuse, but He Didn't Even Say 'Sorry,'" *Los Angeles Times,* March 31, 1996.

6 *By his fourth game back:* Geno Barabino, "Johnson Takes Act on Road," *Chicago Tribune,* February 7, 1996.
   By his fifth game, opposing players were: Dan Shaughnessy, "We Need to Dig Deeper into Magic's Story," *Boston Globe,* February 11, 1996.
   Los Angeles dropped a 98–97 crusher: Scott Howard-Cooper, "Van Exel Takes a Detour," *Los Angeles Times,* March 18, 1996.
   Having averaged 21.7 points for the 1994–95 Lakers: Mark Heisler, "Lakers Drop Anchor Right on His Career," *Los Angeles Times,* January 11, 1997.

7 *Mark Heisler, the* Los Angeles Times's: Heisler, "It's a Sorry Excuse."
   "He's out water skiing, having a great time": Associated Press, "Ceballos AWOL from Lakers; Agent Says He's Water Skiing," March 23, 1996.
   "I had some very personal and family problems to deal with": Scott Howard-Cooper, "Ceballos Returns, Blames Absence on Family Crisis," *Los Angeles Times,* March 25, 1996.
   One teammate after another took a turn: Beth Harris, "Magic Johnson Questions Commitment of Runaway Ceballos," Associated Press, March 25, 1996.

8   *The most unlikely and unqualified captain:* Scott Howard-Cooper, "Ceballos Is Back, but Not All the Way," *Los Angeles Times,* March 27, 1996.

     Ira Berkow, the New York Times*'s star columnist:* Ira Berkow, "N.B.A. Lets Magic Off Much Too Easy," *New York Times,* April 16, 1996.

9   *"Is it my last game?":* W.H. Stickney Jr., "Lakers Salute 'Clutch City' Performance," *Houston Chronicle,* May 3, 1996.

2. The Chosen One

11   *As soon as the 1995–96 season came to an end:* Lazenby, *Showboat,* p. 224.

13   *The students in attendance went crazy:* Michael Bamberger, "Boy II Man," *Sports Illustrated,* May 6, 1996.

     Hell, at age five Kobe was bouncing a basketball: Nita Lelyveld, "Kobe Bryant Bound for NBA," *Philadelphia Inquirer,* April 30, 1996.

14   *On the surface, nothing about Bryant's move:* Dick Weiss, "Bryant Seeks NBA Degree," *New York Daily News,* April 30, 1996.

     "He's kidding himself": Mark Heisler, "Is Bryant, 17, Ready for This?" *Los Angeles Times,* April 30, 1996.

     "You watch Kobe Bryant and you don't see special": Raad Cawthon, "Scouts Wonder If Bryant's Ready," *Philadelphia Inquirer,* April 30, 1996.

     "I think it's a total mistake": Bamberger, "Boy II Man."

15   *His departure from the NBA was greeted:* Fred Hartman, "Rockers Release 1983–84 Slate," *Baytown Sun,* August 7, 1983.

     Kobe was just under five years old: Lazenby, *Showboat,* pp. 82–84.

     He was on the fast route to advancing from white belt to yellow belt: Lee Jenkins, "The Last Alpha Dog," *Sports Illustrated,* October 21, 2013.

16   *"From day one I was dribbling":* Layden, *Kobe: The "Air" Apparent,* p. 12.

     "I loved the feel of [the basketball] in my hands": Bryant, *The Mamba Mentality,* p. 8.

17   *When Kobe arrived for his first day of competition:* Lazenby, *Mad Game,* p. 44.

     "I'm out there looking like the Cable Guy": Jenkins, "Last Alpha Dog."

19   *"I knew right away I had something":* Deveney, *Facing Kobe Bryant,* p. 7.

     Once, during a practice, Downer barked: Lazenby, *Showboat,* pp. 106–7.

     On a school trip to Hersheypark: Martin Rogers, "Kobe Bryant: 'Lower Merion Made Me Who I Am,'" *USA Today,* March 27, 2016.

25   *He had been hired in 1993 by Speedy Morris:* Dick Jerardi, "Joe Bryant Returns to La Salle as Assistant," *Philadelphia Daily News,* June 24, 1993.

27   *He never attended Lower Merion games:* Lazenby, *Showboat,* p. 162.

30   *With Larry Drew, a Lakers assistant coach, monitoring the workout:* Abrams, *Boys Among Men,* pp. 56–57.

33   *The Nets were paying Calipari a league-high $3 million a year:* "Rebuffed by Pitino, Nets Hire Calipari as Coach," *Chicago Tribune,* June 7, 1996.

3. Kazaam!

36   *On February 11, 1995:* Blake Harris, "How Did This Get Made: Kazaam (An Oral History)," Slashfilm.com, January 12, 2016.

37   *"It was a time in my life when":* Harris, "How Did This Get Made."

38   *"mind numbingly bad":* Barry McIlheney, "Kazaam Review," *Empire,* January 1, 2000.

43   *All the team had to do was pay Shaquille O'Neal:* Joel Corry, "The Inside Story: How the Magic Let the Lakers Steal Shaquille O'Neal," CBSSports.com, July 21, 2016.

44   *When he learned of her passing:* O'Neal and Wise, *Shaq Talks Back,* p. 45.

45   *"We can't give you more than Penny":* O'Neal and Wise, *Shaq Talks Back,* p. 48.

     On May 30, 1996, O'Neal was spotted having lunch: "Shaq's Summer Break Starts with Trip to L.A.," *Charlotte Observer,* June 1, 1996.

48   *Gabriel called the newspaper:* Bob Ryan, "O'Neal: Lakers Takers," *Boston Globe,* July 19, 1996.

50 *Earlier that day he'd told an* Orlando Sentinel *reporter:* Scott Howard-Cooper, "Lakers' Price of Poker Reaches $121 Million," *Los Angeles Times*, July 18, 1996.

51 *"It's kind of devastating":* David Kolberg, "LA Lakers Lock Up Shaq with $120 Million Deal," *Chicago Sun-Times*, July 18, 1996.
    "It was a very, very tough decision": Ryan, "O'Neal: Lakers Takers."

4. Formation

53 *En route to the event:* Beth Harris, "Lakers Welcome Teen-ager Kobe Bryant," Associated Press, July 12, 1996.

57 *"You could see the swagger about his walk":* Lazenby, *Showboat*, p. 235.

60 *"Welcome to Shaq's World, Lakers":* Larry Guest, "Shaq Craqs the Whip on New Employer," *Orlando Sentinel*, October 3, 1996.
    "I was a medium-level juvenile delinquent": Mark Anthony Green, "Talking with Our Mouths Full: Shaquille O'Neal," *GQ*, April 2, 2012.

64 *"It was like hearing your grandfather talk sometimes":* O'Neal and Wise, *Shaq Talks Back*, p. 59.
    He was a 4-H Fair, a pony ride, a picnic on the church lawn: Carter Cromwell, "'Preacher' Harris Has the Rockets Believing," *Austin American-Statesman*, May 4, 1981.

65 *He spent one year at Nissalke's side:* Brian Meyer, "Del Harris Still in Love with the Game of Basketball," *The Republic* (Columbus, Ind.), January 10, 1986.

68 *"I looked up from my lunch":* Mike Downey, "No Bull, Knight a Pivotal Laker," *Los Angeles Times*, December 22, 1996.
    "We did not get to haze him quite as much": Deveney, *Facing Kobe Bryant*, p. 33.

69 *Wearing his new No. 34 purple-and-gold uniform:* Mike Fitzgerald, "Boom! Shaq a Laker," *Honolulu Star-Bulletin*, October 11, 1996.

71 *Harris viewed Bryant as a deep reserve whose minutes:* "Bryant Gets No Slack from Lakers Coach," *The Leaf-Chronicle* (Clarksville, Tenn.), October 18, 1996.

5. Nick the Quick

72 *"He snatched out their stereos and things like that":* "Nick Van Exel," *Beyond the Glory*, Fox Sports Network, April 27, 2003.
    Nick would come home from school to either: Scott Howard-Cooper, "A Look Inside at Nick Van Exel," *Los Angeles Times*, October 30, 1997.

73 *"When I got there," Nick recalled, "there was nothing":* "Nick Van Exel," *Beyond the Glory*.
    He was one of the first boys in his school to sport: Pat Stiegman, "Van Exel Glitters as All-Star," *Wisconsin State Journal*, June 24, 1989.
    He shaved two diagonal marks: Scott Howard-Cooper, "Nick Van Exel's Story: Image, Reality Overlap," *Philadelphia Inquirer*, January 16, 1994.

74 *he allegedly kicked:* Don Yaeger, "Breaking Through," *Sports Illustrated*, December 2, 1996.

75 *Nick learned that he had two half sisters:* Kevin Blackistone, "For Some of the NBA's Stars, Father's Day Means Little," *Dallas Morning News*, June 18, 1995.
    "It seemed like he had a certain motive at that point": "Nick Van Exel," *Beyond the Glory*.

76 *In Seattle, he was told to start at the baseline:* Howard-Cooper, "Nick Van Exel's Story: Image, Reality Overlap."
    "I started to read the magazines": "Nick Van Exel," *Beyond the Glory*.

77 *Upon joining the franchise, he purchased a $350,000 Ferrari:* O'Neal and MacMullan, *Shaq Uncut*, p. 117.
    The new, Shaq-fronted Lakers opened the season: Scott Howard-Cooper, "Opener a Hit, Not a Smash," *Los Angeles Times*, November 2, 1996.
    Less than three minutes into the game: Bill Plaschke, "Supporting Cast Helps Their Leading Man," *Los Angeles Times*, November 2, 1996.
    Two days later, Los Angeles won again with a 91–85 triumph: Scott Howard-Cooper, "Lakers Still Kidding Around," *Los Angeles Times*, November 4, 1996.

78   *"The way it sounded, you thought the whole room":* Scott Howard-Cooper, "Disputed Calls Cause Shaq Attack," *Los Angeles Times*, November 13, 1996.

    Five days later, at Phoenix: Duane Rankin, "Kobe Bryant Reveals How Feud with Shaq Showed Itself in 1996 Game Against Phoenix Suns," *Arizona Republic*, August 27, 2019.

79   *"Nothing surprises me with the coach we got":* Scott Howard-Cooper, "Van Exel Puzzled by Fisher Minutes," *Los Angeles Times*, November 27, 1996.

    "We were energized": Scott Howard-Cooper, "Lakers Clear Air for New Take-off," *Los Angeles Times*, November 30, 1996.

    In a private conversation with a friend from his Orlando days: Shaun Powell, "Shaq Guardedly Makes His Point," *Newsday*, January 5, 1997.

80   *During one practice, Harris felt that his point guard:* O'Neal and Wise, *Shaq Talks Back*, pp. 60–61.

82   *In early December, Bryant failed to appear:* Scott Howard-Cooper, "Bryant Learning About Patience," *Los Angeles Times*, December 8, 1996.

84   *With 7:12 remaining in the final period:* Bob Young, "Horry Accosts Ainge," *Arizona Republic*, January 6, 1997.

    "I've been in the NBA for 15 years": Bob Young, "Horry Gets 2-Game Suspension," *Arizona Republic*, January 7, 1997.

85   *"The coaches, the training staff, everybody":* Mark Heisler, "Lakers Drop Anchor Right on His Career," *Los Angeles Times*, January 11, 1997.

    Why, four years earlier Horry had earned league-wide disdain: Glenn Nelson, "Horry Adds More to LA than Temper," *Seattle Times*, January 26, 1997.

87   *On April 2, 1994, his wife, Keva:* Broderick Turner, "Daughter of Former Laker Robert Horry Dies at 17," *Los Angeles Times*, June 14, 2011.

    After winning his first NBA title, in 1994: Kay Campbell, "Keva Horry Reflects on the Special Gifts of Mothering a Special Needs Child," *Huntsville Times*, May 10, 2013.

    "As soon as one thing would go wrong, boom, we'd be there": Scott Howard-Cooper, "Through His Switch to Power Forward and Much Criticism, the Laker Has Endured the Numbing Illness of His Daughter," *Los Angeles Times*, February 18, 1998.

88   *The Lakers tried bolstering the roster:* David Steele, "Mullin Won't Turn Up Heat," *San Francisco Chronicle*, February 18, 1997.

90   *"If you want to be entertained":* Kevin Modesti, "Take Stock in Campbell," *Los Angeles Daily News*, May 10, 1997.

91   *"They had all the energy":* Marc J. Spears, "Lakers Are Happy, but Cautious," *Los Angeles Daily News*, May 9, 1997.

    "It's a challenge": Jon Wilner, "Can This Group Regroup?" *Los Angeles Daily News*, May 12, 1997.

95   *"He'd freeze up in a tight situation":* O'Neal and MacMullan, *Shaq Uncut*, p. 129.

    "Look at all these people laughing at you": O'Neal and MacMullan, *Shaq Uncut*, p. 126.

6. Fox Catcher

96   *Third, there was the departure of Byron Scott:* "Scott Takes His Game to Greece," *Los Angeles Daily News*, July 4, 1997.

97   *Back in 1976, the Rancho Cotate (California) High School:* George Lauer, "Uptight Cougars Declawed," *Daily Independent Journal* (San Rafael, Calif.), January 29, 1976.

    On December 3, 1982, the New York Knicks: Harvey Araton, "Bullets Outmuscle Knicks, 105–98," *New York Daily News*, December 4, 1982.

    "My team trusted me and I didn't come through": Kevin Modesti, "It's No Wild Shot: Kobe Can Step In," *Los Angeles Daily News*, May 14, 1997.

102   *The Bird Rights, named for Larry Bird:* Frank Urbina, "What Are Bird Rights in the NBA," Hoopshype.com, October 10, 2018.

103   *Like O'Neal, he had already dipped:* Howard Beck, "Fox Signs with Lakers," *Los Angeles Daily News*, August 27, 1997.

"I can't tell you how much we think the versatility": Howard Beck, "West Sports Fox as Missing Piece," *Los Angeles Daily News*, August 29, 1997.

104 *"I always felt like if I started my day early"*: Bryant, *The Mamba Mentality*, p. 26.
When Bryant walked off the court: Lauren Abulfetuh, "Bryant Faces Changes, Challenges," *Los Angeles Daily News*, November 2, 1997.
"Eddie spent most of his time looking over": O'Neal and MacMullan, *Shaq Uncut*, p. 124.

105 *In the early days of training camp, O'Neal*: O'Neal and Wise, *Shaq Talks Back*, p. 66.

106 *"Nobody thinks I've done anything all year"*: Karen Crouse, "On This Night, Kobe Had Captain's Class," *Los Angeles Daily News*, November 1, 1997.
"O'Neal has plugged soft drinks": Rick Bozich, "Skyrocketing NBA Salaries Should Be Linked with Victories Not Potential," *Louisville Courier-Journal*, May 29, 1997.

107 *"looking as if he'd spent his summer in a deli"*: Lewis, *To the Brink*, p. 63.

108 *"I obviously prefer a calm sea"*: Crouse, "On This Night, Kobe Had Captain's Class."
West was even more furious, positioning himself: O'Neal and MacMullan, *Shaq Uncut*, p. 127.
"I apologize to Greg": Gary Washburn, "Slapped Back: O'Neal Suspended, Fined $10,000," *Los Angeles Daily News*, November 4, 1997.

110 *On November 25, Pippen — in his 11th season with Chicago*: Howard Beck, "Pippen a Laker? Unbelievable," *Los Angeles Daily News*, November 25, 1997.

111 *The Lakers wanted to rid*: O'Neal and Wise, *Shaq Talks Back*, p. 59.
O'Neal, already out with the abdominal strain: "Bad Break for O'Neal," *Los Angeles Daily News*, December 23, 1997.
"Twenty-seven years old, and he still doesn't": Scott Howard-Cooper, "Van Exel's Knee Needs a Break," *Los Angeles Times*, January 7, 1998.

112 *At the behest of his wife, Ann*: Jeffrey Denberg, "Web Site Offers Views of Harris," *Atlanta Journal and Constitution*, May 20, 1998.
With the Lakers leading 5-0: Howard Beck, "Bulls Put Lakers in Their Place," *Los Angeles Daily News*, December 18, 1997.

113 *"In the third quarter of the blowout"*: Lazenby, *Showboat*, p. 283.

114 USA Today *took time to ask readers*: David Leon Moore, "Bryant Puts Hype Behind, Waits Turn," *USA Today*, May 6, 1998.

115 *On a flight to New York*: O'Neal and Wise, *Shaq Talks Back*, pp. 60–61.
"Players couldn't take him": O'Neal and Wise, *Shaq Talks Back*, p. 62.

116 *"I found it kind of funny"*: Scott Howard-Cooper, "Bryant Doesn't Approach Malone," *Los Angeles Times*, March 29, 1998.

117 *"We've got a lot of Rex Chapman wannabes"*: Joseph White, "Shaq: Heads Will Roll If Refs Don't Whistle," Associated Press, March 3, 1998.
One day earlier, O'Neal and six teammates: Jean Godden, "Shaq Won't Tell This Story to Kids," *Seattle Times*, May 6, 1998.

118 *"He looks like a woman coach sometimes"*: "O'Neal, Karl Engage in War of Words After Sonics' Game 1 Win," *St. Louis Post-Dispatch*, May 6, 1998.
"We need a big guy": J.A. Adande, "In Closing, Karl Keeps His Chin Up," *Los Angeles Times*, May 13, 1998.

119 *"We're real good . . . when we show up"*: Bill Plaschke, "Race Is Going the Lakers' Way," *Los Angeles Times*, May 13, 1998.
"The rest of the Lakers better hope": J.A. Adande, "No Showtime? This Was a Real No-Show," *Los Angeles Times*, May 17, 1998.
"We should be embarrassed": Eddie Sefko, "Jazz Applies Stranglehold to Lakers," *Houston Chronicle*, May 23, 1998.

120 *"If I were the coach"*: Randy Harvey, "Laker Future Rests with 1-2 Punch of Shaq, Kobe," *Los Angeles Times*, May 25, 1998.
"Everyone who was in that locker room": Tim Kawakami, "Famous Last Words," *Los Angeles Times*, February 10, 1999.
"We had a couple of players that should be embarrassed": J.A. Adande, "It Simply Wasn't the Team's Banner Day," *Los Angeles Times*, May 25, 1998.

7. Worm Food

122   *Dave Fogelson, the company's spokesperson:* Kevin Saunders, "Sponsor to Give O'Neal the Boot," *Daily Telegraph* (Sydney, Australia), July 6, 1998.
"I don't really know what they're fighting about": "Shaq: What's the Fuss?" *New York Post*, July 25, 1998.
"Right now, by NBA standards": Mark Rowland, "Prince of the City," *Los Angeles Magazine*, January 1, 1999.

123   *"Kobe's all-around splendor":* Peter Vecsey, "Worm Turns to Lakers," *New York Post*, February 23, 1999.
"He's quickly becoming one of the main": Lazenby, *Showboat*, p. 290.

124   *It hardly helped that midway through the lockout:* Mark Asher, "It's No Secret: Little Progress in NBA Talks," *Washington Post*, December 25, 1998.

126   *"You can't touch him in practice":* O'Neal and Wise, *Shaq Talks Back*, pp. 96–97.

127   *"I think we looked pretty good":* Ken Peters, "Lakers' Voluntary Workout Draws Few Volunteers," Associated Press, January 11, 1999.

128   *The Scottie Pippen talks resurfaced but died:* Mitch Lawrence, "Lakers Won't Win Scottie Lottery," *New York Daily News*, January 17, 1999.
The Associated Press was reporting: J.A. Adande, "Bryant Getting a Big Deal," *Los Angeles Times*, January 28, 1999.
O'Neal was ranting about a new: Tim Kawakami, "Lakers Break Camp with Shaq Upset Over an Early Snub," *Los Angeles Times*, January 27, 1999.

129   *"The story was Kobe coming in":* Tim Kawakami, "Getting Out of the Blocks," *Los Angeles Times*, February 6, 1999.

130   *"Dennis Rodman, the game's greatest rebounder":* Mark Heisler, "Rodman Ready to Join Lakers," *Los Angeles Times*, February 13, 1999.

132   *But two days after the* Los Angeles Times *report:* John Nadel, "Rodman Remains Out of Sight," Associated Press, February 15, 1999.
Which caused an agitated Jerry West to rant: Lacy J. Banks, "Worm's Delay of Game Is Irritating Lakers' West," *Chicago Sun-Times*, February 17, 1999.
"If he comes in with all his antics": "Van Exel: Lakers Making a Mistake," *Chicago Tribune*, February 24, 1999.

133   *"From what I'm told":* Peter Vecsey, "Lakers One Del of a Mess," *New York Post*, February 19, 1999.
"There are a lot of things that have to occur": Sam Smith, "Hard to Tell Through the Sobs, but Rodman Says He'll Be Laker," *Chicago Tribune*, February 23, 1999.

134   *"What got me over the hump":* John Nadel, "Rambling Rodman Says He's Ready to Join Lakers," Associated Press, February 23, 1999.
"I've been a team player, honey": Mark Heisler, "Lakers Going Hollyweird," *Los Angeles Times*, February 23, 1999.

135   *In one of the most bizarre:* Ken Peters, "Rodman Upstaged on First Day with Lakers," Associated Press, February 24, 1999.
"I've never been on a team that's 6-6": Brad Ziemer, "Grizzlies Chew Up Lakers," *Vancouver Sun*, February 24, 1999.

137   *"[Rodman's] intelligence for the game amazes me":* Peter Vecsey, "Rodman Wins the West," *New York Post*, February 26, 1999.
"As I am positive that you know": West and Coleman, *West by West*, pp. 182–83.

138   *One of the first players to greet him:* Michael Murphy, "Lake Show Disintegrates into Soap Opera," *Houston Chronicle*, February 28, 1999.

139   *"He finally arrived, with his people":* Tim Kawakami, "L.A. Hooked on the Worm," *Los Angeles Times*, February 27, 1999.
The Clippers were the perfect meal: Neil Greenberg, "The Worst Top-Five Draft Picks in NBA History," *Washington Post*, June 25, 2015.
Carmen Electra, wearing a midriff-baring crème outfit: "Rodman, Rambis Enjoy Opening-Night Victory," *Springfield News-Leader* (Springfield, Mo.), February 27, 1999.

A few seconds later, he tapped a loose ball: Kawakami, "L.A. Hooked on the Worm."

140   *"He's a free thinker":* "Rodman Late to First Practice," *San Jose Mercury News,* February 28, 1999.

141   *"Whatever the room":* Rodman and Isenhour, *I Should Be Dead by Now,* p. 66.
      There were rumors that Rodman had $600,000: "Dennis Rodman Stacks Up 600,000 Dollars Worth of Gambling Debt," *Agence France-Presse,* April 23, 1999.
      There were rumors that Electra was cheating on Rodman: "Rodman in Stalking Mood?" *Calgary Herald,* April 2, 1999.
      When all was said and done, Dennis Rodman: "Am I a Genius?" *Chicago Tribune,* April 5, 1999.

142   *On the one hand, he was a small-town kid:* Rick Bonnell and Leonard Laye, "Rice Is History," *Charlotte Observer,* March 11, 1999.
      A three-time All-Star and former first-round: John Nadel, "Rice Says He'll Fit In Just Fine with Lakers," Associated Press, March 11, 1999.

143   *"He's going to bring us a dimension":* Nadel, "Rice Says He'll Fit In Just Fine."
      "It was a great feeling": Tim Kawakami, "Steak Served with Big Helping of Rice," *Los Angeles Times,* March 13, 1999.

144   *"He let Kobe do whatever he wanted to do":* O'Neal and Wise, *Shaq Talks Back,* p. 96.

145   *Before a game at Sacramento in April:* O'Neal and MacMullan, *Shaq Uncut,* p. 132.

8. Phil the Void

151   *There was no television:* Jackson and Rosen, *Maverick,* p. 17.
      "I was curious about the female body": Jackson and Rosen, *Maverick,* p. 29.

152   *"having the physique of an upside-down hanger":* Sam Smith, "Jackson Spiritual, Intellectual Type," *Chicago Tribune,* July 11, 1989.
      Instead, Jackson said, he "started taking shortcuts": Jackson and Rosen, *Maverick,* p. 26.
      Every day, a different letter arrived: Jackson and Rosen, *Maverick,* pp. 33–34.
      By now Jackson was 6-foot-8: Jackson and Delehanty, *Eleven Rings,* p. 27.

153   *He had never traveled to the Big Apple:* Vic Ziegel, "What a Long, Strange Trip," *New York Daily News,* April 25, 1993.

154   *On other teams, players lived in fear of a disciplinarian coach:* Jackson and Delehanty, *Eleven Rings,* p. 32.
      "I learned that he usually had an Alka-Seltzer": DeAntae Prince, "To the Surprise of Some, Phil Jackson Became a Basketball Lifer," *Los Angeles Times,* October 18, 2010.
      Following the 1978 season: Alex Sachare, "Loughery's Nets No Longer a Laughing Matter to Foes," *Binghamton Press and Sun-Bulletin,* January 30, 1979.
      "I was a little stunned when I heard this": Jackson and Delehanty, *Eleven Rings,* p. 60.

155   *The job wound up going to Stan Albeck:* Bob Sakamoto, "Pippen Makes Early Impact on Bulls — Especially Jordan," *Chicago Tribune,* October 8, 1987.
      The news of his hiring was barely news at all: "Phil Jackson Signs as Bulls' Assistant," *Chicago Tribune,* October 11, 1987.
      The GM wanted to be deeply involved in the Bulls' day-to-day operations: Smith, *The Jordan Rules,* p. 84.
      On July 6, 1989, Collins was fired: Sam Smith, "Jackson Gets Bulls Job," *Chicago Tribune,* July 10, 1989.

156   *Under Winter's ideal:* Jackson and Delehanty, *Eleven Rings,* pp. 74–75.
      "The important thing": Jackson and Delehanty, *Eleven Rings,* p. 83.

157   *One of the passages featured Jackson:* Lazenby, *Mindgames,* p. 354.
      "[Jerry] told me in no uncertain terms that Phil was trouble": West and Coleman, *West by West,* p. 177.

158   *"Phil . . . broke the guy's nose":* Lazenby, *Mindgames,* pp. 355–56.
      "Apparently we don't do things right": Lazenby, *Mindgames,* p. 356.
      One was Chuck Daly: O'Neal and Wise, *Shaq Talks Back,* p. 71.

159   *"Are you Phil Jackson?":* Jackson and Delehanty, *Eleven Rings,* p. 202.

Bryant — who paid an unannounced visit: Heisler, *Madmen's Ball*, p. 171.

160   *"They ain't gonna win with what they've got":* "Rodman Says Lakers Still Want Him," *The Town Talk* (Alexandria, La.), August 27, 1999.

161   *It distanced itself from the shore:* O'Neal and Wise, *Shaq Talks Back*, p. 75.

162   *"We added guys," Bryant said with a laugh:* David Leon Moore, "Lakers Stars Ready to Follow Jackson," *USA Today*, October 5, 1999.

       Jackson very much wanted a sage basketball guru: Mike Freeman, "Nets Get Benjamin in Swap for Bowie," *New York Times*, June 22, 1993.

164   *"This is your team, Shaq":* O'Neal and Wise, *Shaq Talks Back*, p. 76.

165   *"The Triangle's basic setup":* Parr, *Coach Tex Winter: Triangle Basketball*, p. 61.

167   *"rhythmic enough to fit his cymbal-like skills into a triangle":* Bill Plaschke, "Bryant Wins Plaudits Without Losing Style," *Los Angeles Times*, December 2, 1999.

       While reaching for an errant rebound: Steve Wyche, "For Starters, Chalk One Up for Wizards," *Washington Post*, October 14, 1999.

       "I try to keep [my anxiousness] under control": Tim Kawakami, "Bryant Getting Antsy for Return," *Los Angeles Times*, October 30, 1999.

168   *On November 2, 1999, Jackson's Los Angeles Lakers:* Tim Korte, "The Triangle Needs Polishing Before Lakers Coach Will Be Pleased," Associated Press, November 3, 1999.

       "The energy was really weird in the first half": Tim Kawakami, "New Home Has Room for Breather," *Los Angeles Times*, November 4, 1999.

       When Bryant made his season debut on December 1 against Golden State: John Nadel, "Lakers finally have all their pieces in place," Associated Press, December 2, 1999.

169   *Rice told his agent, David Falk:* Barry Jackson, "Rice's Agent Prods Knicks, Heat for Deal," *Miami Herald*, December 30, 1999.

       Afterwards Horry told his coach: Jackson and Delehanty, *Eleven Rings*, pp. 214–15.

       "One of the problems I had with Phil was this": Ryan Rudnansky, "Jerry West's Relationship with Lakers' Phil Jackson Was Far from Perfect," Bleacher Report, October 18, 2001.

170   *In the moments following one home loss:* Brett Pollakoff, "The Time Phil Jackson Asked Then GM Jerry West to Leave the Lakers Locker Room," NBCSports.com, June 17, 2013.

171   *"[When Kobe returned], the offense wasn't flowing":* Jackson and Delehanty, *Eleven Rings*, p. 215.

       "There was a lot of hatred in [O'Neal's] heart": Lazenby, *Showboat*, p. 336.

9. Turning Around

175   *"The Laker Recession of 2000":* Tim Kawakami, "Lakers' Problems Get Bigger in Texas," *Los Angeles Times*, February 2, 2000.

176   *"We pretty much did what we had to do":* Tim Kawakami, "Lakers Blast Out of a Rut with a Rout," *Los Angeles Times*, February 5, 2000.

       "It's just one game": Ken Peters, "Lakers Hold Jazz to 21 in First Half," Associated Press, February 5, 2000.

177   *On March 6, O'Neal celebrated his 28th birthday:* Lonnie White, "Shaq's 61 Light Up Sweet 16 for Lakers," *Los Angeles Times*, March 7, 2000.

178   *"Shaq is in great condition":* Wayne Coffey, "A Higher Power," *New York Daily News*, March 19, 2000.

179   *A product of Boise State University:* Curtis Bunn, "Childs Starts Over — Sober," *New York Daily News*, January 21, 1995.

180   *When asked about the exchange:* Marc Berman, "Chris, Kobe Rage On," *New York Post*, April 3, 2000.

       "That's our little brother right there": Tim Kawakami, "A Swing Shift for Kobe," *Los Angeles Times*, April 3, 2000.

181   *"The first thing I did was call my mother":* John Nadel, "Shaq Wins MVP Award in a Runaway," Associated Press, May 9, 2000.

182   *"I heard some guy at CNN":* Ken Peters, "Shaq Thanks All Voters, Even One for Iverson," Associated Press, May 10, 2000.

"What happened? Some of Allen Iverson's boys": "Missing MVP Vote Doesn't Upset Shaq," *Miami Herald,* May 11, 2000.

183   *Bryant's personal life, though, was pure mystery:* Jennifer Weiner, "NBA Hopeful, Pop Star Put Cameras in Overdrive," *Philadelphia Inquirer,* May 26, 1996.

She was, word leaked out, a dancer: Shawn Hubler, "Kobe's Costar Vanessa Laine Was Just Another Sheltered Orange County Teen," *Los Angeles Times,* February 15, 2005.

185   *She was the daughter of a U.S. Army private:* Lazenby, *Showboat,* pp. 46–47.

"Bryant has always struck me as mature beyond his years": Dana Parsons, "Engaging Young Man Meets His Match," *Los Angeles Times,* May 21, 2000.

187   *"Anything that works, I'm fine with it":* Curtis Bunn, "Lakers Shatter Record in Win," *Atlanta Journal and Constitution,* May 21, 2000.

188   *"[He] said I wasn't being aggressive enough":* Peter May, "Lakers Rally to Reject Blazers," *Boston Globe,* May 27, 2000.

      "It's kind of funny to me": O'Neal and Wise, *Shaq Talks Back,* p. 224.

"Now the pressure's on Portland": Chuck Culpepper, "Breaking Down Some of the Key Elements of the Lakers-Portland Series," *Oregonian,* May 27, 2000.

189   *"There was a lot of bumping and shoving going on":* Landon Hall, "Lakers Blow Another Chance to Close Out Blazers," Associated Press, June 3, 2000.

191   *"The team that plays the full 48 minutes is going to win":* Eggers, *Jail Blazers,* p. 176.

192   *"Here we go again":* Jackson and Delehanty, *Eleven Rings,* pp. 224–25.

193   *"He's been a quality player in this league":* Tim Kawakami, "Brian Shaw Added for Guard Depth," *Los Angeles Times,* October 21, 1999.

Seven years earlier, while a member of the Miami Heat: Benjamin Hochman, "Nuggets Coach Brian Shaw Shows Resiliency After Family Tragedy," *Denver Post,* June 29, 2013.

194   *"Your mommy went to live with God":* Tim Brown, "Finding Peace Through Pain," *Los Angeles Times,* April 20, 2003.

196   *"We have the lead":* Eggers, *Jail Blazers,* p. 181.

"We weren't built for it the way we thought we were": Eggers, *Jail Blazers,* pp. 179–80.

197   *"The attack came from all angles":* Jackson and Delehanty, *Eleven Rings,* p. 225.

199   *"Playing the Pacers in the Finals was almost anti-climactic":* O'Neal and MacMullan, *Shaq Uncut,* p. 149.

200   *"I wouldn't," he said:* Mark Kiszla, "Can You Say 'Blowout'?" *Denver Post,* June 8, 2000.

"I'm not proud," Rose later admitted: Deveney, *Facing Kobe Bryant,* p. 65.

"A lot of people say I'm the third option": John Nadel, "Rice, Harper Step Up After Bryant Goes Out," Associated Press, June 10, 2000.

201   *"I never really got into the offensive flow":* Greg Beacham, "Rice Cools on Sidelines," Associated Press, June 11, 2000.

"I definitely think we would": Greg Beacham, "Rice Steams Over Lack of Playing Time," Associated Press, June 13, 2000.

"Jackson has never wanted Glen": Bill Plaschke, "It's Time for Rice, Jackson to Talk," *Los Angeles Times,* June 13, 2000.

202   *"This game may well be remembered":* Peter May, "Lakers Move Within Sight of Championship," *Boston Globe,* June 15, 2000.

204   *"That was disrespectful to us":* Rubinstein and Spencer, *The Big Title,* p. 98.

"I held emotion for about 11 years now": Rubinstein and Spencer, *The Big Title,* p. 106.

10. Someone Shoot J.R.

205   *"I was going to sleep and every dream":* Bill Plaschke, "West Wants off the Hook," *Los Angeles Times,* July 22, 2000.

206   *Why, after being selected fifth overall:* "Lakers Sign Bad Boy Rider," *Orlando Sentinel,* August 26, 2000.

207   *Born and raised in Oakland, young J.R.:* Paul Gackle, "Fallen Rider," *East Bay Express,* June 8, 2011.

"I saw him wearing my ring and confronted him": Eggers, *Jail Blazers,* p. 33.

208   *In the summer after his rookie year:* Gackle, "Fallen Rider."

209 *On March 5, Rider missed the team's charter:* Eggers, *Jail Blazers*, p. 57.

210 *It was all too baffling for words:* Gackle, "Fallen Rider."

212 *"They played to 10 by ones":* Horace Grant, "How We'll Remember Kobe," *The Players' Tribune,* April 11, 2016.

214 *Shortly after signing a three-year:* Tim Brown, "O'Neal Figures It's a Good Time to Share," *Los Angeles Times,* October 15, 2000.

215 *"He drove us up to Beverly Hills":* Mark Madsen, "Shaq Top Ten List of Memories," markmadsen.com, August 4, 2011.

216 *"'asking some of the girls if they were Mormon'":* Madsen, "Shaq Top Ten List of Memories."

220 *"While Kobe shot jumpers":* Kaye, *Ain't No Tomorrow,* p. 7.

"We need to play smarter": Mark Heisler, "Duo Dynamics," *Los Angeles Times,* November 12, 2000.

222 *Before every game, the Laker players:* Ric Bucher, "The One," *ESPN The Magazine,* January 22, 2001.

223 *In a December 12 home loss to Milwaukee:* Kaye, *Ain't No Tomorrow,* pp. 105–6.

In an overtime setback to Golden State: Bucher, "The One."

Against Philadelphia, Jackson berated Bryant: Peter Vecsey, "Lakers Playing Bickerball," *New York Post,* March 13, 2001.

225 *"Y'all my n ——s, y'all like brothers to me":* O'Neal and MacMullan, *Shaq Uncut,* p. 147.

226 *"This is about which one captures":* Bucher, "The One."

228 *"It was hard for Phil to rein me in":* Jackson and Delehanty, *Eleven Rings,* p. 241.

"Kobe was out of line Friday": Tim Brown, "Jackson Says Bryant Was 'Out of Line,'" *Los Angeles Times,* March 11, 2001.

229 *He made his season debut on March 13:* Tim Brown, "Fisher Makes a Winning Return," *Los Angeles Times,* March 14, 2001.

Three years earlier, he and Bryant had appeared: Fisher and Brozek, *Character Driven,* p. 59.

For one of the rare times in Bryant's life, he was battered: Jackson and Delehanty, *Eleven Rings,* p. 241.

O'Neal called Bryant's time away: O'Neal and MacMullan, *Shaq Uncut,* p. 151.

231 *"six feet of scar tissue":* Phil Taylor, "Allen Wrench," *Sports Illustrated,* June 18, 2001.

232 *He had actually been eating at a Denny's:* Kaye, *Ain't No Tomorrow,* p. 215.

Moments earlier, a clown wearing a Bryant jersey: John Smallwood, "A First-Stage Smog Alert for Lakers and Fans," *Philadelphia Daily News,* June 7, 2001.

Oddsmakers had Los Angeles as 18-to-1: Chris Sheridan, "NBA Test: Sweep or Struggle," *Dayton Daily News,* June 6, 2001.

He also loved how: Babb, *Not a Game,* p. 170.

233 *Iverson's nonstop chucking:* Diane Pucin, "76ers Put End to All the Talk," *Los Angeles Times,* June 7, 2001.

"Lue, nipping and grabbing": Babb, *Not a Game,* p. 170.

234 *"We've been in different wars, like, all season":* Bill Plaschke, "OT, Then Oh-No," *Los Angeles Times,* June 7, 2001.

"What I'm starting to feel like now": John Nadel, "Harper Provides Spark for Lakers," Associated Press, June 14, 2001.

The air was filled with a sweet scent: Phil Taylor, "Double Dip," *Sports Illustrated,* June 24, 2001.

11. The Coaching Job

239 *"He had said he was going to come in at 300 pounds":* Jonathan Abrams, "All the Kings' Men," *Grantland,* May 7, 2014.

240 *The obvious issue was O'Neal:* Tim Brown, "Little Toe Might Be Big Laker Problem," *Los Angeles Times,* September 29, 2001.

241 *Not all that long ago he had been a nobody 6-foot-2:* "It's a Better Life for George," *Inland Valley Daily Bulletin,* April 21, 2003.

He had recently seen: Marty Burns, "The Pride of Augsburg," *Sports Illustrated,* June 14, 1999.

His mother, Carol, owned a beauty salon: Burl Gilyard, "Ex-NBA Player Plans North Minneapolis Rentals," *Finance and Commerce*, November 27, 2012.

245 *"Improvising was the only way we could get through":* Jackson and Delehanty, *Eleven Rings*, p. 255.

246 *Once upon a time, in the summer of 1993:* Derrick Mahone, "JSU's Hunter Gets Attention After Desert Classic," *Clarion-Ledger* (Jackson, Miss.), May 2, 1993.
"This is fantastic": John Nogowski, "NBA Puts On Quite a Show at the Palace," *Times Herald* (Port Huron, Mich.), July 1, 1993.
He was, in the words of: Helene St. James, "Pistons Deal Hunter for Bucks' Owens," *Detroit Free Press*, August 23, 2000.

248 *"Scoop, I don't understand it":* Lazenby, *Showboat*, p. 391.

249 *"I'm not going to say he turned 180 degrees":* Lazenby, *Showboat*, p. 390.

12. Kings Without a Crown

252 *If it wasn't the awful drafting:* Greg Wissinger, "What's the Worst Trade in Kings History," *SB Nation*, May 3, 2017.
The low point (of endless low points): Reynolds and Drysdale, *Reynolds Remembers*, p. 125.
"You got this little thing right here with beef on it": Dave McKenna, "First-Round Pricks," *Washington City Paper*, April 11, 2008.
During his time in the nation's capital: "Webber Dealt for Kings' Richmond," *Boston Globe*, May 15, 1998.

254 *"Los Angeles had Jerry West, Kirk Gibson, Magic Johnson":* Geoffrey Mohan, Rone Tempest, and Laura Loh, "Sacramento Winces as L.A. Roars," *Los Angeles Times*, June 3, 2002.

255 *"As preposterous as it sounds":* John Nadel, "Two-Time Champion Lakers Say They're Underdogs," Associated Press, May 15, 2002.

256 *O'Neal, in particular, was convinced that his team:* Jackson and Delehanty, *Eleven Rings*, pp. 253–54.

257 *"We went through Chris and Vlade":* Jonathan Abrams, "All the Kings' Men," *Grantland*, May 7, 2014.

258 *measured as high as 112:* Matt Gallagher, "The NBA's Greatest, Ugliest Series," *Daily Beast*, July 13, 2017.
"That clanging heard at the Arco barn": Bill Plaschke, "Magic Moment Has Arrived, So Start Planning the Parade," *Los Angeles Times*, May 19, 2002.

259 *"I was upset and I was mad":* Abrams, "All the Kings' Men."

260 *"If we lose [Game 3]":* Sam Smith, "Kings Hold Off Lakers' Rally," *Chicago Tribune*, May 21, 2002.
"I can't explain it": Greg Beacham, "Kings Raising Game in Surprising Conference Final," Associated Press, May 25, 2002.
"They definitely handed it to us": John Nadel, "Lakers Looking Forward, Not Back," Associated Press, May 25, 2002.

261 *"Well," Bryant said, "we're not bored now":* Jackson and Delehanty, *Eleven Rings*, p. 258.

262 *"watching C-Webb figure out ways to eradicate himself":* Bill Simmons, "Question: Who Was the Undisputed Star of the 2002 Playoffs?" ESPN.com, June 6, 2002.

264 *"Thank God Robert's mother met his father":* "Divac Knocks Ball to Wrong Laker," *Edmonton Journal*, May 27, 2002.

265 *"I made a good pass":* Abrams, "All the Kings' Men."
"That was a miraculous finish": Leighton Ginn, "How? Horry!" *Desert Sun* (Palm Springs, Calif.), May 27, 2002.

266 *"I'm pretty sure I did foul him":* Abrams, "All the Kings' Men."
"You can't pull a guy's shirt off": J.A. Adande, "Series Has Become Officially Interesting," *Los Angeles Times*, May 29, 2002.
"I thought the series was over": Abrams, "All the Kings' Men."

267 *"Give me the ball":* Abrams, "All the Kings' Men."

"*Sacramento had the best team in the league*": Gallagher, "The NBA's Greatest, Ugliest Series."

268 "*You're watching Mike get absolutely plastered in the face*": Abrams, "All the Kings' Men."

"*Rumors that David Stern wanted to pull*": Simmons, "Question: Who Was the Undisputed Star of the 2002 Playoffs?"

269 "*might be the most riveting series on TV*": Chris Dufresne, "These Conference Finals Burn Cigar at Both Ends," *Los Angeles Times*, June 3, 2002.

13. Gettin' Bored with It

274 "*Few who attended [Hearn's] funeral*": Bill Plaschke, "Shaq Becomes Center of Tension," *Los Angeles Times*, August 23, 2002.

276 *upon completing the transaction, Rod Thorn:* Mike Kerwick, "Mutombo Plans to Make a Difference," *Asbury Park Press*, August 2, 2002.

"*another big man to square off*": "Kings Get Bigger, Deeper by Adding Clark," Associated Press, August 15, 2002.

Within weeks, a song titled simply "Yao Ming": Jonathan Feigen, "NBA 2002–03," *Houston Chronicle*, October 27, 2002.

277 *There was talk:* Marc J. Spears, "Counting Down 24 Stories to Follow as the NBA Opens Today," *Denver Post*, October 29, 2002.

279 *Born and raised on a farm in the small town:* Pete Holtermann, "A Gem Out of Africa," *Cincinnati Enquirer*, February 10, 2000.

280 "*He does not have a variety of moves*": Robyn Matt, "New Jersey Selects Stuff Center," *Cincinnati Enquirer*, June 29, 2000.

"*The difference between this guy and Manute Bol*": Steve Adamek, "No Parent Would Like This Dismal Report Card," *The Record* (Hackensack, N.J.), April 18, 2001.

"*He'll be OK*": "Samake Likely to Start for Shaq," *Great Falls Tribune*, October 22, 2002.

282 *So he fired away:* Peter May, "It's a Return to Glory Days for Storied Rivals," *Boston Globe*, November 8, 2002.

283 "*Jackson explained the move as being*": Lazenby, *Showboat*, pp. 396–97.

"*I look around the locker room*": Tim Brown, "It's One of Doze Games," *Los Angeles Times*, November 20, 2002.

284 *Twice he had his shots swatted away:* J.A. Adande, "By Leaps and Bounds, He's a Long Way Off Peak Form," *Los Angeles Times*, November 23, 2002.

285 "*He's not hurting any more than*": "Bryant Wants Walker to Play Hurt," *San Bernardino Sun*, November 27, 2002.

"*Talk to the fuckers*": Howard Beck, "Shaq's Complaints Puzzle Teammates," *Los Angeles Daily News*, December 11, 2002.

286 *Bryant — a man who considered few* Homo sapiens *worthy of his presence:* Bill Plaschke, "He Makes It His Kind of Mad House," *Los Angeles Times*, April 28, 2003.

Why, heading into the 2001–02 season: Tim Brown, "A Bad Mark," *Los Angeles Times*, December 4, 2001.

288 "*The league still no doubt belongs to O'Neal*": Howard Beck, "Rockets Time Is Yao," *Inland Valley Daily Bulletin* (Rancho Cucamonga, Calif.), January 17, 2003.

"*I never played a game sober*": "In Hearing, Ex-NBA Player Clark Says He 'Never Played a Game Sober,'" ESPN.com, December 15, 2007.

That's why he laughed as Mutombo: Ohm Youngmisuk, "Dikembe Won't Be Tricked," *New York Daily News*, October 1, 2003.

289 "*Everything went through the monster*": Tim Brown, "Lakers Earn Their Spurs," *Los Angeles Times*, May 2, 2003.

After the game ended: Howard Beck, "The Number Is Twelve," *San Bernardino Sun*, May 2, 2003.

292 *The coach was immediately scheduled:* Paul Wilborn, "Lakers Coach Phil Jackson Sidelined Following Angioplasty," Associated Press, May 11, 2003.

His shot flew through the air: Tim Brown, "Out on a Rim," *Los Angeles Times*, May 14, 2003.

14. Room 35

294 *A few days earlier, Wong had been quoted:* R.E. Graswich, "Where Else Did Kobe Eat That Night? The Chanterelle Knows," *Sacramento Bee,* May 31, 2002.

296 *There is a long history to this:* Jessica Marie, "The Funniest Athlete Aliases Ever," *Bleacher Report,* February 22, 2013.
Michael Jackson was "Doctor Doolittle": Cailey Rizzo, "The Fake Names That Celebrities Use at Hotels," *Travel and Leisure,* August 10, 2018.

297 *In November 2002, Mathison and a friend named Lindsey McKinney:* Francie Grace, "D.A. in Kobe Case Calls Timeout," CBSnews.com, July 13, 2003.

298 *"So, do you have a boyfriend?":* Shapiro and Stevens, *Kobe Bryant: The Game of His Life,* pp. 4–5.

299 *Jessica Mathison was close with her mother:* Jana Bommersbach, "The Kobe Case: From the Perspective of the Valley Man Who Was Hired to Help Send Him to Prison," *Phoenix Magazine,* April 2005.
Following a 45-minute conversation: Shapiro and Stevens, *Kobe Bryant: The Game of His Life,* pp. 10–11.

15. R.A.P.E.

312 *On March 2, 2003, a 31-year-old British:* Andrew Gumbel, "British Skier Held After American Is Killed in Accident," *The Independent* (London), March 5, 2003.

314 *Mackey, best known for having defended:* Jack McCallum, "The Dark Side of a Star," *Sports Illustrated,* July 28, 2003.
"It's very distressing that the sheriff's office": Tim Brown and Richard Marosi, "Bryant Facing Felony Count," *Los Angeles Times,* July 7, 2003.
"These allegations are completely": Jason Felch and Marc J. Spears, "Deputies Arrest Kobe Bryant," *Inland Valley Daily Bulletin* (Rancho Cucamonga, Calif.), July 6, 2003.
"Kobe can be consumed with surprising anger": Jackson, *The Last Season,* p. 10.
On July 18, Hurlbert formally charged: John Marshall, "Bryant Fighting for Family, Image After Sexual Assault Charge," Associated Press, July 19, 2003.

315 *"I sit here in front of you guys":* John Nadel, "Tearful Kobe Bryant Says He's Innocent of Sexual Assault Charge," Associated Press, July 19, 2003.
Shortly thereafter, he bought her a $4 million: Beth Moore, "Bryant Gives His Wife a $4-Million Ring," *Los Angeles Times,* July 26, 2003.

316 *"It's a good situation for me":* Tim Brown, "Happy to Assist," *Los Angeles Times,* July 10, 2003.
"I'm 40 years old and I'm honored": Tim Brown, "They've Got Mailman," *Los Angeles Times,* July 11, 2003.
The specific event was legally unremarkable: Tom Kenworthy and Patrick O'Driscoll, "'Very Fast Event for So Much Attention,'" *USA Today,* August 7, 2003.

317 *"When the jury saw the evidence their jaws":* Randy Wyrick, "Friend: Injuries Visible Days Later," *Vail Daily,* July 24, 2003.
Twenty-five reporters and photographers: Chuck Plunkett and George Merritt, "Spectacle Takes On Air of a Carnival," *Denver Post,* August 7, 2003.
A few days earlier, an 18-year-old local woman: Jill Lieber and Richard Willing, "Lives in Eagle, Colo., Turned Upside Down," *USA Today,* July 29, 2003.
"White canopies shaded the outdoor": Patrick O'Driscoll, "Bryant Media Circus Sets Up All 3 Rings," *USA Today,* August 7, 2003.

318 *When the* Los Angeles Times *sent two writers:* Steve Henson and Lance Pugmire, "A Drowsy Town Now Wide Awake," *Los Angeles Times,* July 21, 2003.
"Bryant made a comment to us about what another teammate does": Jeff Benedict, Tim Brown, and Steve Henson, "Bryant Told Police of O'Neal Payouts," *Los Angeles Times,* September 29, 2004.

320 *"I'm not privy to his condition":* Bernie Wilson, "Lakers: Bryant 'Under the Weather,' Not in Hawaii Yet," Associated Press, October 2, 2003.

When, on May 3, 1984, she gave birth: Charles Ross, "Karl Malone: The Scumbag," *Medium*, December 16, 2015.

321 *Ultimately, a judge ordered Malone:* Jemele Hill, "Karl Malone Falls Short, as a Father," ESPN.com, May 12, 2008.

Hence, out of understanding or a shared experience: Bill Plaschke, "Already an Ill Wind Blowing in Laker Camp," *Los Angeles Times*, October 3, 2003.

322 *"he was thin and looked tired":* Tim Brown and Steve Henson, "Court of Last Resort," *Los Angeles Times*, May 17, 2004.

Less than a month earlier, in a brief late August meeting: Jackson, *The Last Season*, pp. 16–17.

323 *"Why?" he said:* Kevin Ding, "Bryant Shows Up," *Orange County Register*, October 5, 2003.

324 *"Karl and Shaq, they hid all day":* Howard Beck, "Lakers Detour for Little R 'n' R," *San Bernardino Sun*, October 5, 2003.

326 *"It wasn't even, 'Let me think about it'":* Ric Bucher, "An Oral History of the 2003–04 Los Angeles Lakers, the 1st Super Team," ESPN.com, May 26, 2015.

327 *"Now you gonna pay me?":* Tim Brown, "Shaq's Talks Are a Scream," *Los Angeles Times*, October 9, 2003.

Later, after spotting reporters in the arena's hallways: Kevin Ding, "O'Neal Hammers Home His Desire for Extension," *Orange County Register*, October 9, 2003.

"It was disrespectful": Bucher, "An Oral History of the 2003–04 Los Angeles Lakers"

"So her injuries were recent": Randy Wyrick, "Bombshell Question Clears Courtroom," *Vail Daily*, October 10, 2003.

328 *"Alone, with his once-charmed life in disarray":* Tim Kawakami, "In Bryant, Shades of Mike Tyson," *San Jose Mercury News*, October 9, 2003.

16. The Last Season

331 *A former shooting guard at Alcorn State:* Blatt, *Gary Payton*, pp. 20–21.

"I taught the kid the look": Curry Kirkpatrick, "'Gary Talks It, Gary Walks It,'" *Sports Illustrated*, March 5, 1990.

"He makes you just want to go find a library": Karl and Sampson, *Furious George*, p. 119.

334 *"The good news has less and less staying power":* J.A. Adande, "Four on the Floor, but No Shift in Mood," *Los Angeles Times*, October 21, 2003.

335 *"He needed to come back and see":* Ken Peters, "Bryant Plays in First Exhibition Game; Lakers Lose," Associated Press, October 24, 2003.

The Lakers — who went so far as to shield Bryant from the media: Doug Krikorian, "No Tear If Kobe Leaves," *Pasadena Star-News*, October 22, 2003.

"He wanted one with higher status": Jackson, *The Last Season*, p. 32.

When told of Jackson's innocuous: Howard Beck, "O'Neal Knocks Jackson," *San Bernardino Sun*, October 17, 2003.

On October 25, Jackson was in his office: Jackson, *The Last Season*, pp. 35–36.

336 *"Leaders don't beg for contract extensions":* Tim Brown, "Bryant Is Talking It Up," *Los Angeles Times*, October 28, 2003.

337 *"I ran that idea past Kobe":* Jackson, *The Last Season*, p. 44.

There were the new tattoos scrolling down his right arm: "Bryant Persona Takes On New Look," *Denver Post*, November 6, 2003.

338 *"I'm not giddy":* Howard Beck, "From Feud-alism to Optimism," *Inland Valley Daily Bulletin* (Rancho Cucamonga, Calif.), October 29, 2003.

"In marriage": Mike Terry, "O'Neal Is Conciliatory in Ending His Silence," *Los Angeles Times*, November 1, 2003.

339 *"I'm sure that when he signs":* Howard Beck, "Buss Won't Trade 'My Son,'" *Inland Valley Daily Bulletin* (Rancho Cucamonga, Calif.), November 2, 2003.

340 *"started to rag Ginóbili":* Tim Brown, "5-0 Doesn't Come Easily for Lakers," *Los Angeles Times*, November 7, 2003.

"Nothing alienates a player more than the sense that he is being ignored": Jackson, *The Last Season*, p. 49.

"Maybe when Shaq was out [in the past] Kobe felt he needed to take over": Kevin Ding, "Bryant Must Share the Load," *Orange County Register,* November 12, 2003.

341 *On November 13, Bryant returned to Eagle:* Jon Sarche, "Kobe Bryant Makes First Appearance Before Trial Judge," *Glenwood Springs Post Independent,* November 14–15, 2003.
Positioned on chairs in the front row of Courtroom One: Veronica Whitney, "Kobe Bryant's Accuser's Family Appears in Court," *Vail Daily,* November 14, 2003.
Outside the justice center, hundreds of media outlets: Kathy Heicher, "Media Tent Up Again for Bryant," *Eagle Valley Enterprise* (Gypsum, Colo.), November 13, 2003.

342 *Inside the tent there were hugs:* Veronica Whitney, "On the Road for the Kobe Bryant Case," *Vail Daily,* November 14, 2003.
There was screaming and taunting and all sorts of vileness: Kathy Heicher, "Media Vies for Seats in Bryant Courtroom," *Eagle Valley Enterprise* (Gypsum, Colo.), November 20, 2003.
"The fantasyland, the bickering with teammate Shaquille O'Neal": Don Rogers, "Landing in Reality," *Vail Daily,* November 15, 2003.
On one memorable evening against the Nuggets in Denver: Tim Brown and Steve Henson, "Court of Last Resort," *Los Angeles Times,* May 17, 2004.

343 *A 22-year-old University of Iowa student:* Teresa Taylor-Fresco, "Man Gets Jail for Threatening Kobe's Accuser," Associated Press, July 16, 2004.
The National Enquirer *staked out Mathison's every step:* Randy Wyrick, "Bryant Accuser Checks into Center," *Vail Daily,* November 26, 2003.
"Is it just me": Gideon Rubin, letter to the editor, *Vail Daily,* November 30, 2003.

344 *The next morning, though, Bryant woke up:* Tim Brown, "Uncertainty Surrounds Bryant," *Los Angeles Times,* December 19, 2003.
Mackey argued that the alleged victim had brought the charges: T.R. Reid, "Bryant Defense to Target His Accuser," *Washington Post,* December 19, 2003.

345 *Disclosing the details, Deputy District Attorney Ingrid Bakke argued:* Marcia C. Smith, "Bryant Hearing Placed on Hold," *Orange County Register,* December 20, 2003.

346 *"[Kobe] was anxious to show the fans he could":* Jackson, *The Last Season,* p. 70.
The 101–99 win was thrilling: Beth Harris, "Lakers Defeat Nuggets," *Fort Collins Coloradoan,* December 20, 2003.
"I was just thinking about what my mother always told me": Ramona Shelburne, "Bryant's Teammates Irked by His Shot Selection," *Pasadena Star-News,* December 20, 2003.
"You can't compare the stress [of the trial] to anything else": Ric Bucher, "An Oral History of the 2003–04 Los Angeles Lakers, the 1st Super Team," ESPN.com, May 26, 2015.

347 *That night, Bryant received a handful:* Larry Stewart, "Bryant Says He Owed Team One," *Los Angeles Times,* December 21, 2003.

348 *"Tex Winter told Dennis Rodman that he needs":* Tim Brown, "Winter, Rodman Reunite," *Los Angeles Times,* January 20, 2004.
"When he was younger, he bounced off the floor": Jackson, *The Last Season,* p. 76.
"I didn't sign up for this shit": Howard Beck, "Payton Sounds Off After Defeat," *Inland Valley Daily Bulletin* (Rancho Cucamonga, Calif.), January 6, 2004.

349 *Midway through a January 7 loss to Denver:* Jackson, *The Last Season,* p. 79.

351 *"A joyless ride":* Bill Plaschke, "If Bryant Is an Empty Vessel, Their Ship Will Never Come In," *Los Angeles Times,* April 13, 2004.

352 *By then the Lakers were trailing 40–23:* Plaschke, "If Bryant Is an Empty Vessel."
It was the ultimate "fuck off": J.A. Adande, "When Bryant Doesn't Shoot First, Questions Asked Later," *Los Angeles Times,* April 12, 2004.
Provided a guarantee of anonymity: Tim Brown, "Air Is Heavy for Bryant, Lakers," *Los Angeles Times,* April 13, 2004.

353 *"Right here and right now!":* Jackson, *The Last Season,* p. 143.

17. Survival

355 *As the car led law enforcement on a 90-minute:* Jack Hatton, "The O.J. Simpson Chase, 25 Years Ago, Squeezed the Knicks-Rockets NBA Final off and on NBC," *Sports Broadcast Journal,* June 17, 2019.

356 *"Do you understand the charges against you?":* Steve Lipsher, "Bryant Enters Not-Guilty Plea to Rape Count," *Denver Post*, May 12, 2004.
Unlike on past trips, which turned into last-minute: Tim Brown, "Lakers 98, San Antonio 90," *Los Angeles Times*, May 12, 2004.

357 *With O'Neal looking old and sluggish:* John Nadel, "Lakers' Bryant Plays Best on Longest Days," Associated Press, May 13, 2004.

359 *"You little motherfucker! Way to kick their ass!":* Jackson, *The Last Season*, pp. 194–95.
"If they continue to play like this": John Nadel, "Lakers Playing Their Best Entering Conference Finals," Associated Press, May 16, 2004.

362 *Throughout the series, the two main stars:* Sam Smith, "Something's Gotta Give in L.A.," *Chicago Tribune*, May 31, 2004.

365 *"Eventually your voice is going to wear 'em out":* Kevin Ding, "Lakers Still Heed Jackson's Message," *Orange County Register*, June 3, 2004.

366 *The Pistons opened the scoring when Rasheed Wallace:* Frank Isola, "Shaq Attack Not Enough for L.A.," *New York Daily News*, June 7, 2004.

367 *"You know, to hold them to 75 points, I think, is pretty incredible":* Mark Heisler, "Meet the Team That Issued the Wake-up Call," *Los Angeles Times*, June 7, 2004.
"The greatest Laker shot of this era": Bill Plaschke, "Rising to the Moment," *Los Angeles Times*, June 9, 2004.

369 *"Where was the security?":* Jay Posner, "Police Probe Incident Involving Malone," *San Diego Union-Tribune*, June 12, 2004.

370 *"You know how much I hate this fucking offense":* Jackson, *The Last Season*, p. 239.

371 *"Our game plan was very calculated":* Ric Bucher, "An Oral History of the 2003–04 Los Angeles Lakers, the 1st Super Team," ESPN.com, May 26, 2015.
On the Lakers' first night on the road: Mark Koszla, "Let's Not Go There," *Denver Post*, June 13, 2004.

372 *"I have eight rings and I want nine":* Greg Beckham, "Jackson Sidesteps Magic's Game 3 Remarks," Associated Press, June 13, 2004.

373 *Medvedenko had signed with the organization:* Tara Tartaglia, "Lakers Sign Medvedenko," *Santa Maria Times* (Santa Maria, Calif.), August 16, 2000.
In a 2002 Los Angeles Times piece: Tim Brown, "Medvedenko Isn't Playing the Angles," *Los Angeles Times*, October 19, 2002.
That night, Bryant arrived at the arena at 5:45: T.J. Simers, "With Everything on the Line, They Just Go Through the Motions," *Los Angeles Times*, June 16, 2004.

374 *"That's not the way you want to end this, that's for sure":* Bill Plaschke, "Rout of Order," *Los Angeles Times*, June 16, 2004.

18. The End

379 *"Go tell Mitch, or call up my dad":* Jackson, *The Last Season*, pp. 255–66.

381 *"We don't have the most dominant player in the game":* Eddie Sefko, "No Shaq, No Problem for Kobe?" *Dallas Morning News*, July 16, 2004.

383 *"OK Kobe, now that the best center":* J.A. Adande, "He Loves a Charade, Not a Parade," *Los Angeles Times*, July 17, 2004.

386 *"Although I truly believe this encounter between us":* Kevin Fallon, "Kobe Bryant, Accused Rapist, Will Probably Win an Oscar," *Daily Beast*, February 20, 2018.

Index